Educational Partnerships

For Patrick, Cate, and Vance

Educational Partnerships

Connecting Schools, Families, and the Community

Amy Cox-Petersen
California State University, Fullerton

Los Angeles | London | New Delhi
Singapore | Washington DC

For information:

SAGE Publications, Inc.
2455 Teller Road
Thousand Oaks, California 91320
E-mail: order@sagepub.com

SAGE Publications Ltd.
1 Oliver's Yard
55 City Road
London EC1Y 1SP
United Kingdom

SAGE Publications India Pvt. Ltd.
B 1/I 1 Mohan Cooperative Industrial Area
Mathura Road, New Delhi 110 044
India

SAGE Publications Asia-Pacific Pte. Ltd.
33 Pekin Street #02-01
Far East Square
Singapore 048763

Printed in the United States of America

Library of Congress Cataloging-in-Publication Data

Cox-Petersen, Amy.
Educational partnerships: connecting schools, families, and the community/Amy Cox-Petersen.
    p. cm.
Includes bibliographical references and index.
ISBN 978-1-4129-5212-5 (pbk.)
  1. Home and school—United States. 2. Community and school—United States. I. Title.

LC225.3.C69 2011
371.19—dc22   2009043902

This book is printed on acid-free paper.

10 11 12 13 14 10 9 8 7 6 5 4 3 2 1

Acquisitions Editor:	Diane McDaniel
Associate Editor:	Deya Saoud
Assistant Editor	Aja Baker
Editorial Assistant:	Ashley Conlon
Production Editor:	Carla Freeman
Copy Editor:	Melinda Masson
Typesetter:	C&M Digitals (P) Ltd.
Proofreader:	Scott Oney
Indexer:	Julie Grayson
Cover Designer:	Candice Harman
Marketing Manager:	Carmel Schrire

Brief Contents

Preface   xv

Acknowledgments   xix

Part I. The Basics of Educational Partnerships

1. The Importance of Educational Partnerships   3

2. History of Educational Partnerships   29

3. Meeting the Needs of All Children in the 21st Century   53

4. The Makeup of Families Today: Culturally Relevant Strategies to Enhance Partnerships   79

Part II. Building Effective Partnerships

5. Building Family-School Partnerships   109

6. Schools and Community: Working Together and Respecting Diversity   137

7. Partnering With Community Organizations and Resources   161

8. Barriers to Partnerships   181

Part III. Planning for and Sustaining Successful Partnerships

9. Seeking and Sustaining Successful Partnerships   209

10. Planning for Partnerships   237

11. Implementing and Sustaining Successful Partnerships   263

Glossary   281

References   291

Index   305

About the Author   331

Brief Contents

Contents

Preface   xv

Acknowledgments   xix

Part I. The Basics of Educational Partnerships   1

1. **The Importance of Educational Partnerships**   3

   Overview of Educational Partnerships   5
       What Is an Educational Partnership?   5
       Why Take the Time to Establish Partnerships?   5
       Who Benefits From Educational Partnerships?   6
   Examples of Partnerships   9
       Community   9
       Family   9
       Professional   10
       Characteristics of Effective Partnerships   11
   The Value of Partnerships   11
       National Board for Professional Teaching Standards   12
       A Collaborative View of Educating Children   13
   Communities of Practice   14
       Situated Learning   14
       Components and Examples of Communities of Practice   14
   Equitable Teaching and Learning   16
       Reaching Out to Families   16
       Acculturation Versus Assimilation   16
   Types of Educational Partnership   17
   Collaborative Descriptions   17
   Home, School, and Community Influences   19
       Influences on Students' Education   19
       Shared, Sequential, and Separate Responsibilities   20
   Partnership Types, Examples, and Characteristics   22
   Chapter Summary   24
   Case Studies   24
       Case Study 1.1: Action Learning Walks   24
       Case Study 1.2: CyberSisters   26
   Reflecting on the Cases   28

Activities for Further Development   28
Additional Reading and Information   28

2. History of Educational Partnerships   29

Goals of Education   31
    Public Good Versus Private Good   31
Types of Schools   32
Students and Families as Part of a System   32
Social and Cultural Capital   33
History and Policy Related to Educational Partnerships   34
    Federal Mandates, Seminal Events, and
        Educational Partners: 1900–Present   34
Educational Policy—Whose Policy? Who's Excluded?   45
    Teacher Education About Educational Partnerships   45
    Arts Education   46
Overview of Educational Learning Theories   46
Chapter Summary   48
Case Studies   48
    Case Study 2.1: Kim's Inquiry About Children's
        Learning Styles in Her Fourth-Grade Classroom   48
    Case Study 2.2: Kari's Inquiry Into Students'
        Learning and Motivation   50
Reflecting on the Cases   51
Activities for Further Development   52
Additional Reading and Information   52

3. Meeting the Needs of All Children in the 21st Century   53

The Implementation of No Child Left Behind   55
    Enhancing Academic Achievement   55
    Links to Parent Involvement   56
Children With Special Needs   57
    The Individuals with Disabilities Education Act   57
    The Individual Education Plan   58
    Student Study Team   58
    Teaching Gifted and Talented Children   61
Children's Well-Being   63
    Abused and Neglected Children   64
    Characteristics of Abused and Neglected Children   65
Nutrition and Children's Well-Being   66
    A History of Nutrition in Schools   66
    Child Nutrition and Obesity   67
    Responsibility and Nutrition   68
    Physical Education   71
    After-School Programs   73

Chapter Summary   74
Case Studies   74
    Case Study 3.1: Harvest of the Month Program   74
    Case Study 3.2: Teacher-Family Partnership for Success   76
Reflecting on the Cases   77
Activities for Further Development   78
Additional Reading and Information   78

4. The Makeup of Families Today:
Culturally Relevant Strategies to Enhance Partnerships   **79**
Families in the 21st Century   81
    Diverse Family Structures   81
    Changes in Traditional Family Structure   81
    The Contemporary Family Tree   84
    Creating a More Inclusive Classroom   84
Family Participation Initiatives   86
A Culturally Responsive Partnership Between Home and School   86
    Cultural and Linguistic Education for Families and Teachers   87
    Open House, Back-to-School Night, and Conferences   87
    Communicating With Irate Parents   89
    Student-Led Conferences   90
    Multiple Communication Methods   92
    Home Visits   94
    Incorporating Multicultural and Culturally Relevant Materials   95
    Rethinking Homework Assignments   96
    Family-School Bonding Events   100
Tips for Families and Teachers During Parent-Teacher Conferences   101
    Tips for Families   101
    Tips for Teachers   102
Chapter Summary   102
Case Studies   102
    Case Study 4.1: Student-Led Conferences   103
    Case Study 4.2: Home Visits as a Home-School Connection   103
Reflecting on the Cases   105
Activities for Further Development   105
Additional Reading and Information   106

Part II. Building Effective Partnerships   **107**

5. Building Family-School Partnerships   **109**
Effective Partnerships With Families   111
Elements of Family-School Partnerships   111
    Providing a Positive and Inviting School Environment   111
    Getting to Know Students and Their Families   112

How Are Families Included?   114
    The Deficit View of Family Involvement   114
Six Types of Family Involvement   114
    Parenting   116
    Communicating   116
    Volunteering   121
    Learning at Home   124
    Decision Making   128
    Collaborating With the Community   128
Family Involvement in the 21st Century   129
    Redefining Family Involvement   129
    Engaging Parents in School Events   129
    Early Literacy and Family Support   130
Tips for Families and Teachers   131
Chapter Summary   131
Case Studies   131
    Case Study 5.1: Developing Writers
        One Pen at a Time   132
    Case Study 5.2: "Kamp Kino"   134
Reflecting on the Cases   136
Activities for Further Development   136
Additional Reading and Information   136

6. Schools and Community: Working Together and Respecting Diversity   **137**

Expanding Educational Partnerships   139
School, Community, and Business Partnerships   139
Community Partnerships   140
    Faith-Based Partners   140
    High-Profile Partners   141
    Online Partnerships   142
    Corporate Partnerships   143
    Innovative Collaborative Partnerships   144
Students Taking Action as Community Members   146
    Service Learning   147
    Stewardship   147
    Civic Involvement   148
    Types of Citizenship Participation   150
Tips for Building School-Community Partnerships   154
    Tips for Schools   154
    Tips for Community Members   155
Chapter Summary   155
Case Studies   155
    Case Study 6.1: Clean Air Zone Campaign   156
    Case Study 6.2: Simply the Best!   157

Reflecting on the Cases   159
Activities for Further Development   159
Additional Reading and Information   159

7. Partnering With Community Organizations and Resources   161

Partnerships Beyond the Four Walls of the Classroom   163
University-School Partnerships   164
Partnerships With Museums and Cultural Institutions   166
    Who Visits Museums and Cultural Institutions?   167
    Field Trips to Museums and Cultural Institutions   168
National/Local Parks and Outdoor Education   174
Tips for Organizing and Participating in Field Trips   175
    Tips for Teachers   175
    Tips for Families   175
Chapter Summary   176
Case Studies   176
    Case Study 7.1: School in the Park   176
    Case Study 7.2: Professional Development at the State Park   178
Reflecting on the Cases   179
Activities for Further Development   179
Additional Reading and Information   179

8. Barriers to Partnerships   181

Culturally Relevant Teaching and Learning   183
Barriers and Challenges That Partnerships Face   185
    Management   185
    Time and Commitment   185
    Culture and Language   186
    Power   190
    Trust   191
    Additional Barriers   191
Strategies to Address Barriers   192
    The Role of Schools When Collaborating With Families   193
    The Role of Families When Collaborating With Schools   193
    The Role of the School Psychologist
        When Collaborating With Families   194
Taking Action   194
    Communication   194
    Explicitly Teaching Tolerance and Acceptance   195
Tips to Help Overcome Barriers and Promote Diversity   201
    Books That Promote Partnerships and Diversity   201
    Music That Promotes Peace and Tolerance   201
Chapter Summary   202
Case Studies   202
    Case Study 8.1: Pakistani Families and Teachers   202
    Case Study 8.2: Pigeons, Parents, and Children   204

Reflecting on the Cases   204
Activities for Further Development   205
Additional Reading and Information   205

Part III. Planning for and Sustaining Successful Partnerships   207

9.   Seeking and Sustaining Successful Partnerships   209

Partnership Examples   211
Seeking and Organizing Partnerships   212
   Assessing Resources   213
   Inviting Partnerships With Families   216
   Creating Questionnaires for Families   217
Writing Grants That Support Teaching and Learning   219
   Before You Begin   220
   Writing the Proposal   220
Seeking Grants to Support and Acknowledge Teachers   221
   Grants for Instructional Purposes   221
   Grants That Support Educational Partnerships   223
   General Grant Information Sites   224
   Grants That Recognize Teachers and/or Provide Professional
      Development   225
Communicating With Families About Resources   227
Interagency Collaboration   229
Chapter Summary   231
Case Studies   232
   Case Study 9.1: Class Act and the Pacific Symphony Orchestra   232
   Case Study 9.2: Promoting a Fit Lifestyle for Children   234
Reflecting on the Cases   234
Activities for Further Development   235
Additional Reading and Information   235

10.   Planning for Partnerships   237

Creating an Action Plan   239
   Locating Potential Partners   240
Stages of the Planning Process   241
   Introduction and Rationale   242
   Determining the Type of Involvement   243
   Identifying Partners   244
   Front-End Assessment   245
   Stating Goals and Objectives   246
   Identifying Potential Barriers   248
   Timeline for Implementation   250
   Evaluation of the Partnership   252

Cite Your References   253
Appendix   254
Tips for Teachers From Teachers for Creating an Action Plan   254
Implementing Your Action Plan   254
Chapter Summary   256
Case Studies   256
Case Study 10.1: Creating a Family Art Night   257
Case Study 10.2: Promoting More Family Involvement   257
Reflecting on the Cases   260
Activities for Further Development   260
Additional Reading and Information   260

11. Implementing and Sustaining Successful Partnerships   263
Characteristics of Successful Partnerships Revisited   265
Parents, News, and Misconceptions   265
Professional Education Partnerships   267
Professional Learning Communities   267
Peer Mentoring and Coaching   268
Curriculum Mapping   269
National Board Certification and Collaboration   269
Teachers as Reflective Practitioners   270
Implementing and Sustaining Educational Partnerships   271
Creating an Action Team   271
"Selling" the Partnership   272
Empowering Participation From Multiple Partners   272
Promoting Ongoing Communication   273
Long-Running Partnership Examples   273
Junior Achievement   273
Drug Abuse Resistance Education (DARE)   274
Book It!   274
Local Libraries and Activities   275
Implementing and Sustaining Partnerships With Families   276
Tips for Implementing and Sustaining Partnerships   277
Final Comments   278
Activities for Further Development   278
Additional Reading and Information   278
Research Studies and Articles That Support
School-Community-Family Partnerships   279

Glossary   281

References   291

Index   305

About the Author   331

Preface

Schools and universities are seeking partnerships with community, families, and other professionals to enhance the learning and development of children. National organizations for university accreditations are setting standards for teacher education that include the preparation for and competence in working with parents and the community as partners. National teacher exams and national assessments for highly accomplished teachers also include parent and community involvement within their instructional practices.

Educators have determined that having partnerships extends the traditional walls of the classroom and provides ongoing education for all involved: parents, teachers, the community, and students. This text is written to assist educators in the development of partnerships with families and the broader community and to help them address and overcome barriers, develop strategies for creating partnerships, and find ways to sustain partnerships over time. It is my hope that after reading this book, you, as an educator, will embrace the added value that multiple individuals can achieve when they work together. In addition, I hope you will have the confidence to seek partnerships—small and large—in your own classroom, school, and community.

Educational Partnerships: Connecting Schools, Families, and the Community will be of interest to instructors who teach community partnership courses or integrate educational partnerships within their existing course work. In addition, curriculum directors, school administrators, and pre-K–8 teachers will be interested in purchasing this book to learn more about developing partnerships with families and the community. This book will generate new ideas for partnership building, provide a solid research base, and focus on the multicultural aspects of partnership development.

Features

Successful partnerships include the exchange of ideas, knowledge, and resources. Most partnership books available within the professional education community focus on partnerships with families. Few books devote a substantial amount of their content to partnerships with museums, libraries, businesses, or health services, or to partnerships within the education profession. This comprehensive text will blend family, community, and professional partnerships in a way that will assist you in learning about partnership possibilities and creating partnerships to enhance the education of children in grades K–8. In addition, this book has a variety of unique features, including the following.

A contemporary **culturally relevant approach** to teaching, learning, and partnership development is provided throughout the book. This differs from deficit models where parents and community are viewed as outside resources without power, substantial contributions, or the ability to make decisions. Culturally relevant strategies include communication and activities that respect and celebrate cultural, linguistic, and academic diversity.

Each chapter includes two **case studies** related to community, family, and professional partnership programs and models, demonstrating partnerships in action. An examination of these case studies will introduce you to challenges and successes typical of educational partnerships, and "voices" of various educational partners are included to provide multiple perspectives. In addition, you will be asked to reflect on the cases, analyze real-life situations, and apply chapter content to each case.

Connections to National Board Certification are featured throughout the text, outlining expectations for teachers related to collaboration in the professional community and outreach to families and the community. This will assist you in developing portfolios related to National Board Certification now or in the future.

"How to . . ." sections will assist you when inquiring about educational partnerships with families and the community, developing an action plan, and seeking outside funding from educational grants. Planning sheets are included to assist you and to provide a sequence of specific steps.

Innovative partnership strategies such as student-led conferences, community action walks, culturally relevant communication techniques, service learning, and integrated services will be included throughout each chapter. This will provide up-to-date partnership strategy examples that have been successful in many schools.

Pedagogical Strategies

A **Prior Knowledge and Beliefs Organizer** at the beginning of each chapter will help readers access their prior knowledge and beliefs related to major points within each chapter.

Organizational charts and **graphic organizers** are featured within each chapter to present information in a succinct format.

Enhancing Learning for Students With Special Needs sections include information, research, and inclusive practices and partnership examples to enhance learning for students with disabilities and special needs.

Notes From the Classroom include reflections, voices, and strategies from classroom teachers to enhance chapter content.

Activities for Further Development are included at the end of each chapter to provide an extension of chapter content.

"Tips" for families, students, teachers, and the community are included throughout the text. These tips relate to chapter content and are easy to implement.

Internet resources are included that relate to the chapter's content and provide connections to professional organizations, articles, and other partnership resources.

Partnership examples and resources are featured throughout each chapter. The community offers untapped resources, many that are not known to teachers and families.

Ancillaries

Educational Partnerships: Connecting Schools, Families, and the Community is accompanied by the following supplements, tailored to match the content of the book.

Student Study Site

The Student Study Site features a variety of resources, including self-quizzes, e-flashcards, useful Web resources, and articles from SAGE journals that illustrate topics in the text. Visit the study site at www.sagepub.com/coxpetersen.

Instructor Teaching Site

The password-protected Instructor Teaching Site includes a test bank, PowerPoint slides for each chapter, Web resources, sample syllabi, and teaching tips. Visit the instructor site at www.sagepub.com/coxpetersen.

If you are a qualified adopter and have your e-mail address and password on file with SAGE, you may log in to the site and begin accessing the instructor materials immediately. If you are not yet a qualified adopter with SAGE, you will need to register on the site.

The Author's Experiences

This book was written based on my experiences as a teacher in rural, suburban, and urban areas of North Carolina and California. During the past 24 years, I have been involved in education as a parent, teacher, museum educator, professor, and researcher. This book is who I am, professionally and personally.

I taught for 8 years in rural and suburban school districts in North Carolina before making a move out west to California. I thought that I was an expert teacher and that I knew everything there was to know about teaching when I was hired as a sixth-grade teacher at an inner-city school in South Central Los Angeles. Many of the students in my class were from non-English-language backgrounds and low-socioeconomic areas. I am a White female with light skin, light brown hair, and green eyes. I had never taught in an inner-city school. I had never taught students whose native language was one other than English. I had never taught in a place where I felt like a novice despite having 8 years of teaching experience under my belt. You have heard of the poem "Everything I Need to Know I Learned in Kindergarten." Well, I can say that much of what I needed to know about teaching I learned from these sixth graders that year. Everything that I thought I knew and that I was comfortable with in North Carolina did not necessarily apply to teaching these particular students in the inner city. They had different cultural beliefs and different life experiences, but in many ways they were children who had a lot to offer me. It was not long before I realized that I was teaching *students*, not just the content outlined by state standards. Although students in every area of the United States and throughout the world have many similarities, there are differences that must be acknowledged and respected. I was so comfortable with my students in North Carolina that I lost sight of the fact that a teacher must get to know students first and foremost before he or she can be effective. I needed to know each of my students, their families, their beliefs, their fears, and their interests if I was going to gain their trust and motivate them to want to learn in my classroom. In addition, my students needed to know me. I recall one of my students, James, asking me a question that really made me think about who I was and who the students were. James asked a question and then provided his own reply: "Ms. Cox, where do you live? I bet you live in a big white house, with a big white fence, and I bet all your neighbors are Caucasian . . ." The fact was that I lived in an ethnically diverse neighborhood in Los Angeles. The only thing that James knew was that I definitely did not live in his neighborhood! In fact, he was stereotyping me into where he thought I might live based on my ethnicity, behavior, and language. Needless to say, it was essential to make every attempt to learn more about the neighborhood in which my students lived and to learn more about their families, values, and cultural beliefs. In return, I would open up and discuss my background in the southern part of the United States, my life in Los Angeles, and my dreams as an adult and as a child. This process did not happen quickly, but over time, it was well worth my efforts. Throughout the year, I met with parents, grandparents, and guardians. I took my students outside their community on various field trips. We engaged in service learning by making flyers asking neighbors to keep trash off the streets because it would drain to the ocean and pollute the water. By the end of the year, I felt connected to my students and many of their families. The parents of my students were hardworking people who loved their children and wanted the best for them. Many parents wanted to be more involved in their children's education but were not always welcomed at school or within the classroom. My experiences helped me realize that these families could be involved with their child's education even if they never stepped a foot into the school building. In addition, I could provide a welcoming environment in my classroom and discuss shared decision making related to education *with* parents.

Acknowledgments

I am grateful for the love and support from my husband, Patrick, and my children, Cate and Vance, throughout the writing of this book. My parents, Jimmy and Eleanor; my sisters, Nancy and Lynne; my brother Jim; and my wonderful friends have inspired me and always believed in me. I would like to thank all of my students at Cal State Fullerton who have provided stories, examples, and insight to make this book possible. The Irvine and Anaheim master's degree cohorts provided invaluable expertise and feedback during the first few phases of this book. Specifically, I would like to acknowledge teachers who have contributed particular reflections and examples within this book: Cathy Aiken, Kim Allen, Kari Ambrose, Sylvia Angulo, Angelica Casas Barrios, Alejandra Becerra, Elisa Gornbein, Lani Blust Char, Andrea Brannam, Bridget Burke, Rochelle Cantu, Amy DeVore, Sarah Fick, Olivia Guerrero, Rosie Haynes, Glenda Howard, Jeanie Lee, Carrie Marquez, Star Morales, Gayle Morrison, April Morse, Caroline Ngo, Kathy Nygard, Karen Parrish, Kristine Quinn, Valerie Robbins, Kathryn Sampilo Wilson, Lynne Cox Thomas, Casey Weinkauf, and Lindsay Yee. Rohanna Ylagan has provided continued support throughout this project through her classroom experiences, partnership examples, and partnership resources.

A huge thank-you to my university colleagues for their continued support, research, and strategies related to this text: Jennifer Ponder for her service-learning expertise, Leah Melber for her contributions related to field trips and museum education, Loretta Donovan for information related to seeking grants, Terri Patchen for her culturally relevant strategies, Angela Freed for her work in university-school partnerships, and Leslie Edwards for her work with girls and community science. I would also like to thank my friend Gino Jooyan for his insights related to tolerance and cultural barriers in Chapter 8 and my friend Susan Kinsey for community partnership-building strategies and reflections in Chapter 6.

I would also like to thank the reviewers of this text:

Camille Cammack, *Saginaw Valley State University*

Sharon M. Darling, *Florida Atlantic University*

Larry L. Dlugosh, *University of Nebraska, Lincoln*

Raymond Gallagher, *California State University, Dominguez Hills*

Eva M. Horn, *University of Kansas*

Michelle Hughes, *James Madison University*

Colleen E. Klein-Ezell, *University of Central Florida*

Amy J. Malkus, East *Tennessee State University*

William F. McInerney, *University of Toledo*

Pat Ragan, *University of Wisconsin, Green Bay*

Elizabeth Jill Sandell, *Minnesota State University, Mankato*

Stephanie Serriere, *Pennsylvania State University*

Cheryl D. Walton, *Southern Illinois University Carbondale*

Janette C. Wetsel, *University of Central Oklahoma*

Tracy S. Williams, *Whitworth College*

Andrea Zarate, *Hartnell College*

Finally, I would like to thank all of my students (including those in elementary school, in middle school, and at the college level) throughout my career. They have enriched my life in exceptional ways and made this book possible.

Part I
The Basics of Educational Partnerships

Chapter 1: The Importance of Educational Partnerships

Chapter 2: History of Educational Partnerships

Chapter 3: Meeting the Needs of All Children in the 21st Century

Chapter 4: The Makeup of Families Today:
Culturally Relevant Strategies to Enhance Partnerships

1

The Importance of Educational Partnerships

After reading this chapter, you should have a better understanding of:

- what partnerships are and reasons for promoting them within schools and classrooms;
- the myriad benefits to creating partnerships among schools, businesses, universities, families, and other community groups;
- examples of community, professional, and family partnerships to enhance the education of students;
- how home, school, and community all influence the educational potential and access for students and families;
- the role of *situated learning* (Lave & Wenger, 1991) and *communities of practice* (Wenger, 1998) in enhancing and sustaining partnerships;
- the difference between acculturation and assimilation when working with children from diverse cultural backgrounds;
- collaboration models and examples; and
- shared, sequential, and separate responsibilities related to education of children and youth.

Table 1.1 Prior Knowledge and Beliefs Organizer

Describe your experiences with educational partnerships as a child and as an adult.	Describe your feelings related to the partnership, the partners, the learning, and any specific activities that you remember (positive and negative).

Use the information you enter in Table 1.1 to provide a background as you read about the reasons for educational partnerships and examples of different types of partnerships.

Overview of Educational Partnerships

What Is an Educational Partnership?

There are many definitions and ideas that surface when describing a partnership. Formally, a **partnership** is an agreement where two or more people or groups work together toward mutual goals. Partnerships can be formal, informal, or even unspoken as long as they include people or groups working together. Most experts agree that a partnership must benefit both sides for it to be truly effective.

When two parties come together for the common good of a school or to enhance student learning, we call this an **educational partnership**. Partners can include anyone who is interested in or committed to enriching educational experiences for students, families, schools, and the community. Most important, partnerships do not include one individual or one group dictating what should be done and why it should be done. Decisions are made collaboratively within a partnership. Although educational partnerships can be formed between teachers and students, the collaborations discussed in this book will relate mostly to those outside the teacher-student relationships to include entire families, professionals, and the broader educational community. These partnerships always include students but are integrated within larger groups, and organizations can supplement school learning and encourage lifelong learning among children and families. Joyce Epstein (1999) created a Center on School, Family, and Community Partnerships at Johns Hopkins University in Maryland in an effort to inform and promote community partnerships to enhance education for students and families. The center has three goals: (a) creating, assessing, and sharing effective partnership strategies; (b) enhancing the education of teachers and teacher education programs to encourage more community involvement; and (c) conducting research on community partnerships and best practices. This book is organized with similar goals in mind. Throughout each chapter, steps for creating and assessing partnerships will be featured in addition to step-by-step examples to help teachers plan, implement, and assess current and future educational partnerships.

Why Take the Time to Establish Partnerships?

The answer to the question above is quite simple: We should establish partnerships to provide the best education possible for all children. In reality, partnerships are created for a variety of reasons that include enhancing public relations, seeking additional funding, and working toward a particular cause or issue. Some partnerships are developed within a formal structure, and others are developed based on an unwritten understanding or handshake. Many school districts include partnerships with students' home and community within their mission statements or educational goals. However, the more difficult challenge is for schools and districts to actually enact those partnerships during the busy school year.

A principal once told me that her teachers were "maxed out" and that they had done everything instructionally to increase students' educational achievement including extra instructional minutes for reading and math. However, their students did not show significant improvements in learning in these areas. She told me that her school had decided to change its strategies and focus from additional drill and practice time to working with families and the broader community to increase academic achievement. Interestingly enough, after multiple parent sessions and the development of partnership programs, she and her teachers started to observe better academic progress for all students, a higher motivation for learning, and a more positive school atmosphere. The United States has increased spending for elementary and secondary schools, but this extra monetary support has not resulted in significantly higher academic achievement, according to U.S. Department of Education statistics. In addition, spending to assist disadvantaged children grew by 45% between 2001 and 2006, resulting in an achievement gap that continues to exist among various groups of students. When schools choose to enhance partnerships with families, this has unlimited possibilities for improving educational progress for all students. Research studies during the past 25 years all support family and community involvement as a strategy that supports student learning.

One of the reasons for continued inequities and achievement gaps could be based on the fact that there is often a disconnection between parents and teachers. Family-teacher partnerships have been strained at times due to the stress related to standardized testing and negative information highlighted within media sources. *Time* magazine published a series of articles related to teachers and parents at odds with each other (Gibbs, 2005). As a teacher and a parent, I was shocked by the cover headline, "What Teachers Hate About Parents." I believe that parents do not even realize that teachers may actually "hate" them. Couple that view with parents who feel that they are intruding if they question or impede formal schooling and with teachers who think that parents should be doing more, and you definitely have miscommunication between families and schools. And though there are many teachers who work collaboratively with families, there are just as many teachers who do not have the experience, education, or strategies to develop positive reciprocal relationships outside the four walls of the classroom.

Many positive teacher-family relationships do exist; however, many do not exist for a number of reasons. The most common reason includes the diverse cultural beliefs of teachers, students, and families; the lack of time in busy daily schedules; and work obligations. In addition, most families are doing all they can each day to take care of their children and pay bills. Allotting time and effort for creating partnerships with schools is not usually a priority. However, if families and teachers knew of the ultimate benefits that an educational partnership could have on the academic development of children, they would make it more of a priority. Educational partnerships take time and effort to develop, but once they are developed and sustained, the benefits are endless for all groups and individuals.

Who Benefits From Educational Partnerships?

Having partners in education helps provide a more even playing field for all families and children. Society benefits when students, families, the community, schools, and teachers work together to educate children. Lueder (1998) describes specific outcomes and benefits to the school, families, students, teachers, administrators, and the community when they work together as partners. These outcomes areoutlined below.

Parents and teachers worked together to create an "Island-Themed Day." Students danced to a steel drum band and sampled traditional island dishes.

The school benefits by gaining:

1. better communication among all parties;

2. improved student discipline;

3. reduced school violence;

4. better working conditions for faculty and staff;

5. better acceptance and understanding of diverse students and their families;

6. enhanced interpersonal relationships among students;

7. enhanced attitudes, communication, and relationships among teachers, students, and families; and

8. more family participation in school events.

The families benefit by gaining:

1. increased power and understanding of education;

2. closer relationships with their children;

3. better community support;

4. better communication between home and school;

5. increased knowledge about how to help their children learn;

6. more information to provide positive learning activities at home;

7. better understanding of the curriculum, instruction, and events;

8. more opportunities to work with teachers;

9. better expectations about homework and home learning practices;

10. greater access to school (and community) resources; and

11. empowerment to make decisions that will enhance their children's education.

The students benefit by gaining:

1. higher achievement and motivation to learn;

2. a positive attitude toward school;

3. better-quality homework and more frequent completion of homework;

4. better attendance;

5. decreased dropout rates, suspensions, and discipline problems;

6. improved self-confidence; and

7. better family relationships.

The teachers benefit by gaining:

1. improved morale;

2. positive teaching experiences;

3. more support and appreciation from families;

4. fewer discipline problems;

5. responsive students;

6. less stress and frustration;

7. awareness of family diversity with less stereotyping;

8. closer relationships with students; and

9. higher expectations for all students.

Administrators benefit by gaining:

1. better relationships with students, families, and teachers;

2. fewer complaints from families;

3. better use of resources;

4. increased communication with families; and

5. greater family and community support.

The community benefits by gaining:

1. students who are prepared to work collaboratively as contributing members of society;

2. families who assist in the educational development of their children; and

3. schools that work within a broader community.

Examples of Partnerships

Schools can consider different types of partnerships and how they will meet students' needs. It is common to include families and educational professionals as primary partners. However, schools can also form partnerships with the broader educational community including local corporations, media agencies, sports teams, organizations, and ordinary citizens. Teachers and schools should work closely with partners to determine overall goals; the time needed to develop, implement, and sustain a partnership; and which area or areas of the curriculum would benefit most from a partnership. Three different types of partnership are described below: community, family, and professional. It should be noted, however, that many collaborations include more than one partner.

Community

Sisters in Science (n.d.) recruits retired and currently working women in science, engineering, and mathematics and female university students pursuing careers in science. This is an example of a **community partnership**. These individuals partner with teachers and serve as mentors for girls in elementary schools. This program is organized to improve girls' attitudes toward, interest in, and achievement in science and mathematics. In addition, the mentoring activities are developed to provide a positive learning environment for females and their families and to increase their knowledge base to promote girls' interest in science. This is a community partnership because members of the broader community participate in educational activities with students.

Family

In one **family-school partnership**, for example, three kindergarten teachers and students and their families work together to implement a program called *Literacy Mornings*. Students are encouraged to bring an older family member, a sibling, or a close family friend to the classroom for the first 40 minutes of school each Wednesday. During this time teachers, students, and family members read together and engage in activities related to concepts of print, early literacy skills, and phonemic awareness. The kindergarten teachers arrange for coffee, juice, and breakfast items and provide a welcoming and nonthreatening environment. A local bagel shop donates the baked goods, and the school provides the beverages. The families attend the event, enjoy reading with their child, learn more about encouraging literacy at home, and contribute breakfast treats on some of the days. The students decorate invitations and encourage their parents, older siblings, and other family members to attend at least once each month. Teachers in *Literacy Mornings* formed a professional partnership as they welcomed students and their families as their partners in the project.

Professional

The next example describes a **professional education partnership** called *Team Time* (Haynes, 2007). Four fifth-grade teachers collaborated and created a plan to help lower-performing math students. During *Team Time,* students are taught by one of the teachers in a small group. About 30 extra minutes of math practice are provided as teachers rotate the responsibility. The teachers meet weekly to discuss, collaborate about, and exchange ideas on how to provide extra help in teaching mathematics concepts and skills. They also discuss how to include more families to help these students at home. Together, they identified a need, determined how to collaborate to meet that need, and then worked together to execute the plan.

As you can see from the three different examples, educational partnerships can be small or large in scope and can be initiated by an organization, a group of professionals, or an individual teacher. As you read the rest of the book you will notice that partnerships vary in size and can include one teacher with a few families or a community organization, parents, and an entire K–8 school. In the following "Notes From the Classroom" section, Glenda, a third-grade teacher, describes her rationale for creating a partnership with the broader community.

Notes From the Classroom:
Glenda's Reasons for Creating a Community Partnership

Voice of Glenda, Third-Grade Teacher

From my earliest days as a teacher, students at risk for reading failure have been a source of both fascination and frustration to me. I felt fascinated when I was able to somehow find a key to help a student succeed. More often, I felt frustration when my efforts seemed in vain. I quickly discovered the role [community] volunteers could play in my classroom in unlocking the potential for more of these children. By enlisting the help of volunteers to read individually with struggling students, I was able to provide those who needed it most with more individual time, without neglecting the 30 other students in my classroom. I wondered, though, whether those well-intentioned paraprofessionals had the skills they needed to be as effective as they possibly could be. When I was given an opportunity to work with a committee to develop a school-wide volunteer tutoring program, I felt an even greater sense of responsibility for preparing well-trained volunteers.

The volunteer program itself was a bit of an unusual partnership. Volunteers were from a large, local church. Church members had been active in the community for years but usually in terms of inviting the community to participate in their own faith-based programs. This project, while an expression of their faith, would be a totally secular endeavor. They would participate in an after-school program for one hour each week for a period of 10 weeks.

SOURCE: Used with permission of Glenda Howard.

Characteristics of Effective Partnerships

Take a moment to consider schools you know of that have a strong ongoing relationship with families and the community. What are the characteristics of these partnerships? Usually, there are common goals that are communicated amicably. In addition, there is some form of collegiality, mutual support, and shared responsibility for educating children. Now, consider the families who participate in school activities—whether at home or through a visible presence at school. Which families are left out? What are some of the reasons that *all* families are not part of the larger school community? Are the school activities and weekly communication partial to one ethnic group over another? Do all families know that greater parental involvement in education results in higher student achievement? Think about these questions and your answers as you read about characteristics of effective partnerships.

Myriad characteristics related to **effective educational partnerships** exist. However, the most notable ones include respect, understanding, appreciation of cultural and linguistic differences, shared common goals, accountability, high returns, meaningful goals to all parties, commitment, leadership, partner feedback, and "buy-in." Partnerships are not one-sided (i.e., "I know best; you do not"), judgmental, forced, or dictated. They must be mutually created and involve a bond of trust, communication, and respect from all parties. In addition, all groups and individuals within an educational partnership must feel that they benefit in some way. This is a high order to fill when many families do not feel that they have the time, education, power, or confidence to assist their child in educational endeavors that will enhance academic achievement and learning. Therefore, educational partnerships must be culturally relevant and appropriate if the purpose is to encourage lifelong learning for students and their families. All families want the best for their children. However, many families do not feel that they have the experience or knowledge to be partners in education. The fact is, however, that prior educational background is not required to support children in their learning. There have been numerous stories of families who make education a priority, regardless of their formal education experiences, academic skill base, or native language. These families have children who succeed in K–12 schools, at notable universities, and beyond. Teachers are educators beyond the classroom and can work with families to ensure academic excellence for all students.

The Value of Partnerships

Education is not an isolated experience but an interactive endeavor that takes place over the course of a person's life. When the community, schools, and families work together, they can provide the best possible resources and expertise to enhance the education of all children. Therefore, it is a collective responsibility of many groups to educate children. Consider the experiences and feelings related to educational partnerships that you recorded in Table 1.1 at the beginning of the chapter. Keep these ideas in mind as you read the content and examples provided in this chapter and in the rest of the book.

National Board for Professional Teaching Standards

Because partnerships among all groups enhance the learning and development of children, national organizations for university accreditations are setting standards for teacher education that include the preparation and competence needed for working with parents and the community as partners (e.g., National Council for Accreditation of Teacher Education [NCATE], 2007). National teacher exams and national assessments for highly accomplished teachers also include parent and community involvement as a mandatory standard (National Board for Professional Teaching Standards [NBPTS], 2007). The NBPTS outlines five core propositions related to what effective teachers should know and be able to do and the beliefs that characterize educators who apply for **National Board Certification**:

- Teachers are committed to students and learning.
- Teachers know the subjects they teach and how to teach those subjects to children.
- Teachers are responsible for managing and monitoring student learning.
- Teachers think systematically about their practice and learn from experience.
- Teachers are members of learning communities.

The information in this book will incorporate all five propositions but focus more intently on the fifth proposition related to teachers as members of learning communities. Within this proposition, teachers are charged with taking the initiative to collaborate and build partnerships with the larger community to enhance learning for all students, regardless of linguistic, cultural, or socioeconomic background. Teachers are also encouraged to work with other professionals to initiate and assess instructional policy, implement an effective curriculum in their classroom, and plan for their professional development needs. Most important, teachers should make it a priority to work with families to encourage collaborative participation in their child's education. If you are interested in becoming a National Board Certified Teacher, this book can assist you in planning for educational partnerships and delineating your beliefs, goals, and practices as a member of a learning community. In the following installment of "Notes From the Classroom," Sylvia, a third-grade teacher, reflects on becoming a National Board Certified Teacher.

Notes From the Classroom: Sylvia's Reflection on Becoming a National Board Certified Teacher

Voice of Sylvia, Third-Grade Teacher

Applying for and receiving National Board Certification (NBC) has been one of the most rewarding experiences of my life. The same year, I earned my master's, but it did not hold the same meaning as receiving NBC. The NBC process truly made me a better teacher because I had to inspect my practice with a fine-tooth comb and really reflect on what I was doing in the classroom, why, and what was the outcome. It is a process that I still use in my practice today.

The fifth proposition, partnerships, was my weakest area. Because I had only taught for 3 years prior to applying for NBC, I hadn't developed this area yet. However, the NBC process made me realize the importance of partnerships and their benefit for students. I am still working on this area, but I admit it is still a weakness due to my lack of time to pursue it.

A Collaborative View of Educating Children

One evening, I was listening to a segment on the radio related to inequitable schools within the United States. The program started out with well-known statistics related to the achievement gap between students from higher and lower socioeconomic backgrounds in addition to that between students from different ethnic groups. The achievement gap has decreased through the years but only by a small percentage (see Education Commission of the States, 2006, for additional information). The fact remains that children of color and those from lower socioeconomic backgrounds consistently score lower on achievement tests than White and Asian children from middle-class backgrounds. The National Assessment of Educational Progress (2004) reported that Black 17-year-olds scored at about the same level as White 13-year-olds in both reading and mathematics. While I was listening to the radio that evening, the commentator pondered why students in lower socioeconomic areas have difficulty attaining the same academic achievement levels as other groups of students. There were no definitive answers, but voices of teachers and principals from different schools were featured to address academic challenges. Teachers from a high-achieving school stated that they had an active parent-teacher organization that engaged in fundraising and a gift-giving drive totaling hundreds of thousands of dollars each year. This money is used to purchase musical equipment and to support a variety of special programs. The teachers and principals from a lower-achieving school indicated that their scores on achievement tests were so low that they provide copies of their weekly lesson plans to ensure academic standards are being met.

After listening to this discussion, it occurred to me that one reason for the achievement gap is that we are trying more of the *same* thing rather than trying to do things *differently*. This is one of the main reasons for this book. I hope that I can provide ways for educators to think outside of the box and consider community, family, and professional partnerships as one way of doing things differently to enhance the education and academic achievement of all children. More drilling, more practice, more planning, more meetings, more lesson plans, and more of everything are not necessarily the best ways to tap into the full academic potential of every child. However, bringing a network of community members, families, and schools together toward the same goal can be a fruitful place to start.

Educators can begin the journey of creating partnerships by learning more about the culture and beliefs of the families and children who attend their school. In addition, families should find out more about the teachers' background, philosophy, and goals for their children. This is an initial but extremely important step to building partnerships between schools and families. I love the story that one of my graduate students told me about how a middle school principal chartered a bus and took all of the teachers around the community to show them the neighborhoods where their students lived. The students in this school lived in federally supported housing projects, middle-class ranch-style homes, and multimillion-dollar mansions on the hillside. The principal took to the microphone and provided information about each neighborhood as the tour progressed. Teachers were asked to make careful observations about their surroundings such as the amount of open space, yards, pets, activities, and vehicles during the tour. This information was collected and used to learn more about the students they taught, where they lived, and what after-school activities and hobbies they participated in. In addition, teachers gained knowledge about the resources around family homes that they could take into account when assigning interactive homework projects. The principal indicated that some of the teachers had taught at the school for more than 20 years and had never inquired into where their students actually lived.

Communities of Practice

Situated Learning

One of the reasons that some families do not choose to become involved with formal education is that they do not feel they are a part of the school community. They may feel uncomfortable talking to the teacher or even walking into the classroom. Jean Lave and Etienne Wenger (1991) are known for their work on **situated learning (legitimate peripheral participation)** where they view learning and community as a social activity that develops from multiple experiences and different types of participation. We all partake in activities based on our home, community, and school. However, we have varying roles within each of these areas. At times we are at the core of the activity, and at other times we are on the periphery. Many times, the families of our students are on the periphery and stay there throughout their child's schooling because they never feel a sense of belonging within the walls of a school or classroom. This peripheral learning happens not just with families but also with many children who attend school as part of a classroom community for many years. These children and their families may always remain part of the periphery instead of actively engaging within the center of events. This is why educators should be aware of creating communities within the classroom that are based on culturally relevant pedagogy and a welcoming environment that includes all students and families.

Components and Examples of Communities of Practice

Collectively, learning results from the practices within these groups created over time and continued during shared social enterprises. Wenger (1998) refers to these groups as **communities of practice**, which can be formal or informal. The position of participating individuals may or may not change over time, but communities of practice always contain these three components: joint enterprise, mutual engagement, and a shared repertoire. Together, these components contribute to participation in a group or community and should be acknowledged by educators when building partnerships.

A **joint enterprise** pertains to the overall purpose of a community that is continuously negotiated and renegotiated by the members. **Mutual engagement** is what brings everyone together for a common goal. Members work together to create a functioning and ongoing partnership. **Shared repertoire** involves the type of resources such as routines, artifacts, and style that members develop over time. The repertoire is not verbally established but established through behaviors and expectations. Partnerships can be developed to include diverse groups of students and families so that they too can comfortably partake in activities related to educational events at school.

Rogoff (1994) also advocates the creation of a "community of learners" model in schools. She based her ideas on a comparison of Mayan families in Guatemala and middle-class American Anglo families within the United States. She concluded that children and adults have more success in learning situations, regardless of culture, when learning is coupled with participatory activities within their communities. Therefore, if students and families do not feel that they are part of the community at school, then learning cannot be optimized.

Another example of a school that seeks educational partnerships with the community is a K–8 public charter school where families, teachers, and outside community organizations work together to meet high academic achievement standards and promote rich cultural experiences. About 90% of the students in the school qualify for free or reduced-price lunch, and 60% of the students are from non-English language backgrounds. The school works collaboratively with a variety of community partners to supplement the arts, health, and physical education curriculum and to provide health and social services for students and their families. A community-based arts organization provides visual arts for students in grades K–8 and drama for students in grades 4–8. A community dance group provides dance classes for all K–8 students, and a music group provides flute and violin lessons to students in fourth and fifth grade. These partnerships allow the students to gain visual and performing arts skills from multiple role models and diverse perspectives. In addition to the three community partners that focus on the arts, the school works in partnership with a local medical group and the County Department of Health to provide wider access to social and medical services for families. The former principal of this school, Kendra Kecker (personal communication, June 11, 2007), discussed the following benefits of building educational partnerships:

Educational partnerships benefit the school, the teachers, the students, and their families, as well the broader community and society.

> At CNCA School, we strive to build partnerships that will help us create the comprehensive educational program we want for our students and also help to alleviate some of the barriers our children face that make it difficult for them to reach academic success. Through these partnerships we are able to incorporate arts education and provide a variety of resources to our students and families including mental and physical health services. By meeting the various needs of our students and providing resources to support the work of our teachers we believe we can truly prepare each of our students for success and put them on the path to college.

These partnerships benefit not only the school, the teachers, the students, and their families but also the broader community and society.

Equitable Teaching and Learning

Reaching Out to Families

Partnerships are necessary to obtain high educational achievement for all students—regardless of gender, socioeconomic status, family makeup, or ethnic group. Berliner and Biddle (1995) claim that schools could potentially overcome the effects of poverty and inequities among students by developing connections to community, their teachers, and their peers. Despite more intensive teacher education, standards-based education, and high-stakes accountability and testing, inequality and inequity continue to exist within many education systems. Currently, there are a growing number of students from non-English backgrounds who attend schools in the United States. This poses an additional challenge for schools and families to communicate with each other and to discuss common goals and beliefs about education. Some school districts sponsor family events to provide better links between learning at home and learning at school. Buses and child care are usually provided as families learn about volunteer opportunities at school and at home with their children. The perception of most educators and families is that one must physically be at a school site to participate in children's education. Involvement or engagement in a child's education can happen at home, a local park, a church, or another place outside of school. These activities are most successful when teachers and district personnel refrain from *telling* parents what they should and should not be doing. Instead, they provide opportunities for parents to interact with each other, share experiences, and consider ways that they could be more involved such as reading at home, playing math games, and writing for different purposes. Some school districts are reaching out in an even broader way by inviting individuals and organizations to share with families what they offer in the form of after-school clubs, free museum visitor days, public library computers and resources, low-cost sports teams, and other community activities.

Acculturation Versus Assimilation

The type of partnership described above with diverse families and the school district aligns with the idea of acculturation rather than that of assimilation. **Acculturation** celebrates the backgrounds and cultural beliefs of students and their families. It encourages individuals to integrate their beliefs with formal instruction and content, rather than abandon their beliefs altogether. **Assimilation**, on the other hand, focuses on the idea that students and families should abandon their ethnic backgrounds and beliefs and adopt a different culture, usually one that is more mainstream. The assimilation view usually results in the loss of ethnic identification and self-worth. Therefore, educators should embrace acculturation as a more culturally relevant strategy when working with students and families because it enhances power, authority, and self-confidence.

Types of Educational Partnerships

A partnership is essentially an agreement entered upon by two or more groups or individuals. This agreement can be explicit or implicit. It can be spoken or unspoken. In schools, many of the partnerships with families and communities are implicit, where tradition sets the standard partnership practices. If we apply Elliot Eisner's (1985) three types of curricula to partnership models, this would result in explicit partnerships, implicit partnerships, and null partnerships:

- In an **explicit partnership**, schools, families, and communities explicitly outline written goals, strategies, and outcomes related to enhancing the education of children. They publicize these goals for all to know.

- In an **implicit partnership**, schools, families, and communities "talk" about common goals and ideals, but there is no specific goal, strategy, or outcome in place.

- In a **null partnership**, individuals or groups occupy the same space, but there is no communication related to specific goals, strategies, or outcomes for a partnership.

Each of these types of partnerships leads to a specific type of collaboration. Collaborative descriptions will be discussed in the next section.

Collaborative Descriptions

Veigel (2000) provides a model of research-practice collaboration that is derived from a modern management perspective. Given that good management is also critical to all types of collaborations, the following descriptions might be used to identify different levels of partnerships in education:

- *The No-Collaboration Collaboration.* Collaboration here might be an agreement between two parties who want to meet some externally imposed need or to satisfy some individual want. It is a partnership of convenience that is seldom consummated or annulled. For example, students visit a local museum on a field trip. However, there is no real prior or post communication or interaction between the school and the museum.

- *The One-Time Collaboration.* This type of collaboration is actually better described as a service offered for a service rendered. For example, a pizza restaurant sponsors a school family night where teachers, students, and families buy pizza on one specific evening. The pizza restaurant then donates a portion of the purchases to the school.

- *The Arms-Length Collaboration.* As in the exchange-of-services collaboration above, each party in this type of limited collaboration has a need to be met and a contribution to offer. However, in contrast, the essence of a true collaboration is first seen here: creating shared values together. For example, health professionals and teachers may work together for the purpose of designing a health services program that will become part of the school, yet the collaboration may be restricted to a limited time period. Health professionals may come to the school for 3 days during the school year to test the speech and hearing of children. A local community group may test children's vision in grades K–6.

- *The Arm-in-Arm Collaboration.* In this collaboration, the parties bring complementary resources for ongoing work that creates new value. Despite their complementary skills and interests, these groups come to the collaboration precisely because they recognize that working outside the collaboration would make it unlikely or impossible for them to produce the results that entice them to work together. Building on the previous example related to health services, this type of collaboration includes an ongoing commitment founded on a common goal in which all groups acknowledge that working together to meet their mutual needs outweighs self-interest. Therefore, multiple health professionals, the school, and families will meet on a regular basis to discuss the goals of the partnership and how to provide ongoing health services for students and families.

- *The Hand-in-Hand Collaboration.* Here, self-interest of each party is genuinely replaced by a primary focus on the shared values and products. The health services example can achieve the hand-in-hand collaboration when a program is mutually agreed upon, accepted, enacted, and continued with shared goals for students.

Table 1.2 provides different types of partnerships, examples, and characteristics.

Table 1.2 Partnership Types, Examples, and Characteristics

Partnership	Examples	Characteristics
No Collaboration	• A company provides backpacks to students • Free coupons/offers	• Shared and separate goals • Limited communication
One-Time Partnership	• Field trip to a museum • Outdoor science camp	• Shared and separate goals • Short-lived • Limited communication
Hand-in-Hand Partnership	• DARE programs • Parent-teacher organizations • Weekly volunteers	• Shared and separate goals • Ongoing over time • Trust, respect, etc.
Arm-in-Arm Partnership	• School site council when all parties have decision-making power	• No one group has "power" over the other • Shared goals (separate goals vanish) • Trust, respect, etc.

Home, School, and Community Influences

Influences on Students' Education

What factors influence a child's education? The answer is not a simple one; nor is there one person or one group who is responsible for this. In fact, a variety of factors influence students' learning and their education over time: family, friends, media, the community, and even personality types. Judith Rich Harris (1999) suggests in her book, *The Nurture Assumption,* that too much emphasis has been placed on students' families and home environment when they succeed at school or have difficulties. Instead, she discusses the power of the teacher and how he or she can influence students' overall achievement because teachers can influence the attitudes and behaviors of an entire group of children and youth. She advocates that the world outside the student's home (i.e., interactions within the community, with peers, and at school) has as much impact on a child's development and achievement as the world within the home.

Barbour, Barbour, and Scully (2005) suggest that educators identify and examine more closely the strengths of the multiple influences on children's knowledge and experiences. They created a chart that shows home, child care, school, and community and media influences (see Figure 1.1). The graph indicates percentages

Figure 1.1	Home, Child Care, School, and Community/Media Influences on Children's Knowledge and Experiences

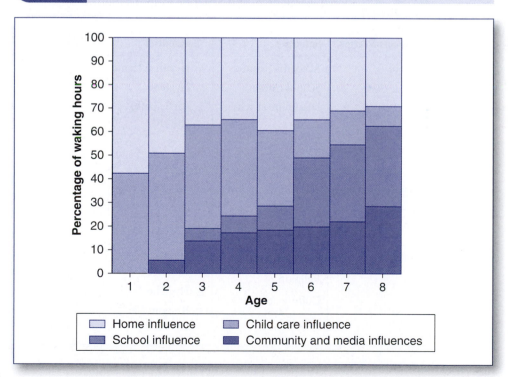

SOURCE: Adapted from Barbour, Barbour, and Scully (2005).

of waking hours of American children and what influences learning and decision making. All children are born with home and child care influences, but by age 3 school and community begin to play a part. By age 8, children are affected as much by school/peers and community/media as they are by their own family. Media include music, television programs, toys, games, computers, and print. The community includes the neighborhood and experiences that surround the home.

Shared, Sequential, and Separate Responsibilities

Think about schools you have attended or schools where you have worked. What educational responsibilities are shared among the school, students' families, and the community? Are other responsibilities separate? Take a look at Table 1.3, which outlines shared, sequential, and separate responsibilities. Joyce Epstein (2001) distinguishes between these three areas, noting that the clarity of the distinction depends on who is defining them. In the table, make a list of what you believe are the shared, sequential, and separate responsibilities of schools, families, and communities. I have provided a few ideas from former students to help you begin. As you examine the table, determine whether or not you agree with the placement of the various responsibilities listed.

Table 1.3 Shared, Sequential, and Separate Responsibilities

Responsibilities	Separate	*Sequential	Shared
School	Academic content School rules Discipline at school	1. Health screening 2. Hygiene 3. Participatory citizen	Beginning in Preschool: Social skills Communication work ethics Nutrition Safety Drug awareness Sex education Physical education Character education
Family	Media, TV, games Religion Culture Values	1. Health and vaccines 2. Hygiene 3. Responsible citizenship	Beginning at Birth: Social skills Communication work ethics Nutrition

Responsibilities	Separate	*Sequential	Shared
	Discipline Home Rules		Safety Drug awareness Sexual education Physical education Character education
Community and Society	Maintenance and funding for parks, beaches, libraries Laws	1. Health care 2. Citizens of a democratic society (i.e., voting) 3. Justice-oriented community	Beginning at birth: Social skills Communication work ethics Nutrition Safety Drug awareness Sexual education Physical education Character education

SOURCE: Adapted from Epstein (2001).

*These are numbered because they follow a specific order.

After you have examined the table and added some of your own ideas, what do you notice? You should see that it takes the school, students' families, and the entire community to educate children. Therefore, for optimum educational experiences and participation, all of these people and organizations must be involved. Take a look at the Partnership Tree in Figure 1.2. Notice that schools, families, and the community are blossoming together to support children's growth, knowledge, and development. Some responsibilities are shared, and some are separate. In addition, a firm "root system" must support the entire relationship in order for a partnership to "blossom."

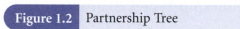

Figure 1.2   Partnership Tree

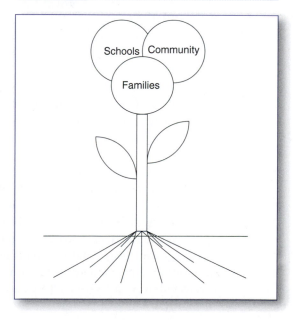

Enhancing Learning for Students With Special Needs: Positive Partnership Strategies

Partnerships are essential when working with students with special needs and their families. Teachers, service providers, and families work together to support the child's home and school environment and create an individual education plan that outlines instructional and behavioral strategies to promote optimum learning and achievement. This is a positive supportive plan that delineates separate, shared, and sequential responsibilities. Specific positive strategies include the following:

1. Include a translator for children non-English language backgrounds.

2. Determine the availability of assistive technology devices that may assist students and their families.

3. Consider positive interventions that will encourage self-confidence and responsibility in children.

4. Discuss and create strategies for connecting the students' home environment and experiences with the school environment, curriculum, and instructional strategies.

5. Create measurable, attainable goals that all parties endorse and agree with.

Partnership Types, Examples, and Characteristics

The information below provides a variety of terms that you will encounter within the book. This will help you distinguish between the multiple meanings of many of the terms used when discussing educational partnerships.

Community is a broad term used to describe a place such as a city, a neighborhood, or a classroom. A community can also be used to describe interactions and relationships among people or groups.

Culturally relevant teaching includes characteristics outlined by Ladson-Billings (1995) that include (a) assisting all students to achieve academic success, (b) focusing on cultural competence to help students maintain their own cultural integrity through classroom activities, and (c) ensuring critical consciousness activities address cultural norms, values, and social inequities.

Culture refers to behaviors exhibited by people or groups of people. These behaviors can include (but are not limited to) communication, language, gender roles, dwelling, clothing, art, music, food, and ethics.

English language learners are students who are learning English as their second language and whose native language is not English. English language learners are also described as students from non-English language backgrounds. These terms are preferred over terms used in the past such as *limited English proficiency* and *language deficient*.

Ethnic groups refer to people who may be of the same race but who share common cultural views and customs.

Ethnicity is used to describe someone's social identification and/or common cultural views and customs.

Family is a term used to describe a group of people who usually, but not always, live together at the same location. Family can include parents and guardians in addition to extended family members who play a significant role in children's lives such as grandparents, aunts, uncles, and close friends.

Individual education plans, commonly referred to by educators and parents as IEPs, are required to comply with the Individuals with Disabilities Education Act. An IEP team usually consists of teachers, service providers, and families who meet and create a mutually determined plan to assist a student with special needs educationally, emotionally, and/or physically.

Multiracial refers to people who describe themselves as belonging to two or more racial groups.

Parent is a term to describe primary caregivers of children. Anyone taking the role of raising a child is considered a parent. This includes legal guardians or grandparents who are responsible for a child or children. This also includes individuals who have shared custody of children.

A **partnership** is a written, spoken, or informal agreement where two or more people or groups work together toward mutual goals.

Professional is a term used to describe people who possess expertise and knowledge in a particular area. Their job usually requires some type of licensure or specific degree. In this text, professionals (for the most part) will refer to professional educators including teachers, university faculty, and administrators.

Race traditionally refers to a group of people sharing similar hereditary features or those who are united by nationality. Today, this term is used broadly to describe historical ancestry because there is little evidence of a "pure" human race in the world today. Many people are a combination of multiple races and therefore would have difficulty defining their exact race when asked. Many questionnaires are now asking families to specify multiple races to describe themselves. In the year 2000, the U.S. Census Bureau printed 15 different racial categories and "other race" that encouraged responders to choose multiple races. Some of the races on the census form included White, Black, African American, Asian Indian, American Indian, Alaska Native, Chinese, Japanese, Filipino, and Native Hawaiian.

Racism involves the subordination of members of a specific racial group who have little power socially, culturally, or ethnically.

Stereotypes can be positive or negative. They include mental views, comments, or beliefs related to preconceived ideas about particular groups of people. Stereotypes and examples are described more fully in Chapter 8.

Transracial is a term used most often in cases where parents and children of different races live together. Transracial adoptions are common where a family in the United States adopts a child from another country or adopts a child of a different race within the United States. Many racial issues must be negotiated within the family during the child's life.

Chapter Summary

Educational partnerships are endeavors where one or more people or groups come together to enhance the education of children. When this happens, the effect is greater than the sum of the two parts. These partnerships do not happen instantly, and many times teachers and families face challenges because of time, different priorities, language, and cultural barriers. By enacting culturally relevant communication strategies, partnerships can be enhanced. It is suggested that teachers acknowledge student differences and value the concept of acculturation when working with students and their families. The process of acculturation celebrates the students' culturally and linguistically diverse background and encourages them to integrate their ideas, experiences, and beliefs into formal instructional practices and content.

Different types of educational partnerships exist, including community, professional, and family partnerships. These partnerships can be formal or informal, spoken or unspoken. Families, schools, and the community share many responsibilities in educating the whole child. When all of these groups work together, children can become more self-confident and achieve their full potential during school and throughout their lives.

CASE STUDIES

The two case studies in this chapter include a school-family partnership (Action Learning Walk) and a school-community partnership (CyberSisters). Action Learning Walks involve families by inviting parents to school to observe, reflect, and discuss literacy activities in the classroom and home. CyberSisters is an online program that pairs girls with community mentors to encourage better math and science achievement.

❖ Case Study 1.1: Action Learning Walks

This case study is adapted from Guerrero (2006) and Barrios (2006) and will feature a description and information related to an Action Learning Walk at an elementary school in Southern California. Parents of students at the school are invited to participate in a one-day Action Learning Walk with their child, the teachers, and other parents.

An Action Learning Walk begins by parents gathering in a school meeting area to discuss what will take place. Often, refreshments are served, and families are encouraged to interact informally. During this initial meeting, a teacher-facilitator discusses the agenda that will be followed and offers information in English and Spanish because many of the parents speak Spanish as their primary language. The information is connected to state content standards related to reading and outlines what the parents will be observing and what they should look for as they are interacting with their children in the classroom during the 30 to 45 minutes. Parents are given an observation checklist that includes questions such as "Does my child participate?" "Does my child pay attention?" "Can my child summarize the story?" "Does my child talk with his or her partner during think-pair-share time and stay on topic?" and "Does my child need more practice?" Finally, parents are asked to join their child in the classroom and participate in all activities with him or her.

Afterward, the classroom teacher will respond to questions and debrief what went on during the lesson and provide tips for helping each child at home. The parents have another opportunity to participate in an activity with their child before meeting together again as a group. The teacher-facilitator will ask the parents as a group to discuss their experiences, voice concerns, and ask questions. Particularly, parents are asked to describe what they observed during class and to suggest ways of helping their child at home. Next, the teacher-facilitator will work along with the parents to create a take-home learning activity related to literacy based on their ideas and ideas from other educational sources. At the end of the session, the parents complete a voluntary anonymous survey related to their experiences with the Action Learning Walk. To close the session, parents' names are drawn, and prizes are given out in the form of flashcards, books, and other educational materials. Parents are encouraged to hang around, enjoy refreshments, and talk with each other as long as they like.

Voice of Olivia Guerrero, Third-Grade Teacher

The involvement and learning experience within an Action Learning Walk benefits students, parents, and the teacher because they work collaboratively to enhance achievement. These strategies will also help parents and family members become more aware of useful activities at home that support and encourage academic success at school. The Action Learning Walk is also aimed at building a community of learners that involves parents and teachers as learners and partners. (Guerrero, p. 4)

Parent involvement remains a vital dimension to students' academic success. Efforts designed to improve both the quantity and quality of parent involvement will continue to be an important component of school improvement programs and of strategies designed to reduce the achievement gap between economically disadvantaged students and their more advantaged counterparts. (Guerrero, p. 59)

Voice of Angelica Casas Barrios, Third-Grade Teacher

Being a Hispanic myself, I feel that it is my responsibility to take an active role in creating meaningful partnerships with parents and hence increasing parent involvement. Many teachers at my school would argue that we have already done all we can, including offering babysitting services, providing translators, and offering evening meetings. However, I know that there is much more that can be done; it is just a matter of having a positive attitude, having the true desire to involve parents, and developing common goals related to their child's education. (Barrios, p. 3)

Parents' Views

Angelica Casas Barrios surveyed 33 of the parents in her school who participated in the Action Learning Walk. The survey consisted of 10 questions related to their experiences. She found that the top three reasons that parents participated in the Action Learning Walk included (a) helping their child learn at home, (b) wanting to observe their child's learning style, and (c) wanting to become more involved in their child's education. Most parents would like to participate in more Action Learning Walks, particularly those focusing on a different subject area. Cumulatively, parents reported that they felt more informed about their child's performance at school and learned ways to help their child at home.

Teachers' Views

Olivia Guerrero surveyed teachers to determine their views related to the Action Learning Walk. One first-grade teacher, six second-grade teachers, and one third-grade teacher participated in the survey. Their experience varied from being a first-year teacher to having 10 years of teaching experience. The teachers indicated the most valuable aspects of the Action Learning Walk for them:

- Teachers had the opportunity to observe parents working with their children.
- Teachers observed parents' priorities and behavior management skills.
- Teachers met parents and connected better with them on a personal level.
- Teachers observed parents while their child was succeeding or struggling with literacy skills.
- Teachers felt that parents were on the same page as they were.
- Teachers could create more home-school connections.
- Teachers learned about parents and if they wanted additional support.

The teachers also indicated the most valuable aspects of the Action Learning Walk for students:

- Students were motivated to perform well with their parents present.
- Students were excited to have their parents at school.
- Students were able to demonstrate hands-on learning of concepts.
- Students noticed that their parents were interested and active participants in education.
- Students learned with their parents.
- Students could share information and content that they were learning in school.

Finally, the teachers indicated the most valuable aspects of the Action Learning Walk for parents:

- Parents gained a better understanding about content standards related to literacy.
- Parents obtained tools, strategies, and resources to reinforce literacy skills at home.
- Parents were introduced to concepts that were essential to academic development.
- Parents observed what and how their children were being taught.
- Parents experienced hands-on activities that can be replicated at home.

Teachers also lamented, however, that they were disappointed that not all parents were able to participate due to work schedules and other obligations. They indicated that they wanted to find a way to include more parents and increase their level of participation. Teachers also suggested that a translator be available in classrooms during the Action Learning Walk to answer questions that parents had. Moreover, the teachers wanted to have a substitute teacher in the classroom so that the classroom teacher could participate in the Action Learning Walk debriefings with the teacher-facilitator after he or she observed his or her children. The teachers indicated that the biggest barrier to the planning and implementation of Action Learning Walks was related to the time needed to collaborate with other teachers to plan the activities. In addition, they indicated that more communication was necessary between the resource teachers at the school and the classroom teachers so that they could work together to plan the activities. All eight teachers indicated that they wanted to continue offering Action Learning Walks for parents during upcoming years.

SOURCE: Used with permission of Angelica Casas Barrios and Olivia Guerrero.

❖ Case Study 1.2: CyberSisters

This case study is adapted from Roth-Vinson (2000). It includes a partnership where university women work with middle school girls to enhance their achievement in math and science. Roth-Vinson stated that when it comes to math, science, and technology, all girls are "at risk" because they are excluded from many of these careers. The CyberSisters program is a telementoring program to improve gender equity in science, math, and technology. College women serve as mentors and are paired with middle school girls. The initial funding for the project came from the Willamette Science and Technology Center in Oregon and the American Association of University Women in partnership with local universities, foundations, businesses, and school districts. CyberSisters is an online mentoring program that aims to achieve the following goals: (a) increase the number of middle schools girls who have positive experiences in science, math, and technology; (b) supplement middle school girls' knowledge and interest in math, science, and technology; (c) develop leadership skills and opportunities for middle school girls; (d) expand the number of academic-based women role models in science, math, and engineering; (e) expand the involvement of college women mentors in K–12 settings; (f) promote middle school girls' experiences with university life; (g) foster greater community awareness about gender equity; and (h) bring together appropriate organizations at the national level to begin strategizing about solutions to gender equity issues.

Voice of "Annie," Eighth-Grade Student

Working on a science project that I got to choose with my mentor and presenting it in front of an audience has made it easier for me to answer questions in my science and math classes. I feel more motivated to work harder in those areas. (Roth-Vinson p. 24)

Voice of "Caroline," Seventh-Grade Student

Through meeting other women in the science field, I have decided that science is definitely a field I will explore when I'm older. (p. 24)

Voice of "Ms. O'Connor," Middle School Science Teacher

CyberSisters has been an effective way for me to provide opportunities for girls in my classroom to learn with individual guidance. With the time and attention of an interested adult mentor, my students are much more aware of how to use local museums and computer technology to find information about science and math topics that interest them. (p. 26)

Voice of "Ms. Smithson," Middle School Math Teacher

I started a girls' club called Geogirls because I have experienced a very real gender gap in the fields of math and technology. . . . Geogirls is partnering with CyberSisters to provide the girls with one-on-one college mentors in science, math, and technology. Geogirls started as a team for girls in geometry who wanted to work together to learn how to create their own Web site. The first year, six enthusiastic girls spent one to two hours each week before or after school learning HTML coding, drawing or creating computer graphics, researching information, writing, and putting it all together in an award-winning Web site called Geogirls. (p. 26)

SOURCE: Roth-Vinson (2000). Used with permission.

❖ Reflecting on the Cases

1. How does collaboration enhance student learning within the two case studies *Action Learning Walks* and *CyberSisters?*

2. Describe the partners in each case study and discuss examples of shared power and decision making.

3. Describe the roles of each partner in the Action Learning Walks. List revisions to the current Action Learning Walk program that would make the partnership more collaborative and/or more culturally relevant.

Activities for Further Development

1. Create a list of resources in your community that would be helpful in enhancing the education of children. Next, discuss partnership possibilities related to each of the resources.

2. Think about an educational partnership that you know about or one that you have been involved with. Identify the partners. Would you consider it to be a community partnership, a professional partnership, a family partnership, or a combination of two or more? Explain why.

3. Conduct an online search to locate resources and educational activities that can be integrated into the school curriculum that will assist students with understanding and appreciating race, culture, and economic diversity within their lives and their community.

4. When a teacher invites parents to come into the classroom to showcase student work and other activities, this is not necessarily a partnership. How can you organize a student showcase evening to be more interactive and include characteristics of true partnerships?

Additional Reading and Information

Kozol, J. (1991). *Savage inequalities: Children in America's schools.* New York: Harper Perennial. This book is already considered a classic. Kozol reports of his experiences in multiple urban schools. He reports the good, the bad, and the ugly related to inequalities and challenges that these schools face daily.

Sanders, M. G. (1999). Improving school, family, and community partnerships in urban middle schools. *Middle School Journal, 31*(2), 35–41. This article includes research and recommendations related to enhancing family and community involvement in the middle grades.

The Family Involvement Network of Educators (FINE) is a monthly news Web site that is sponsored by the Harvard Family Research Project to provide resources for families and educators and to promote collegial networks within the field of education: http://www.hfrp.org/family-involvement/fine-family-involvement-network-of-educators

The Institute for Responsive Education outlines information about a parent leadership exchange project. The project is sponsored by the Cambridge College School of Education and focuses on research, policy, and advocacy activities to enhance the shared responsibility of schools, families, and the community to educate children and improve education: http://www.friendsnrc.org/download/teleconference/aug15files/ire.pdf

The National Network of Partnership Schools at Johns Hopkins University promotes the involvement of schools, families, and communities in the education of children and youth. Its Web site highlights research, evaluation, and partnership project examples: http://www.csos.jhu.edu/p2000

The U.S. Department of Education offers research, statistics, current government-sponsored educational programs, and publications: www.ed.gov

2

History of Educational Partnerships

After reading this chapter, you should have a better understanding of:

- the goals of U.S. education related to public benefits and private goods;
- types of schools and educational partnership examples;
- students and families as part of a larger system: macrosystem, exosystem, and microsystem;
- the role of social and cultural capital in helping students succeed in school;
- the history of educational partnerships and policies from 1900 to the present;
- the history, policies, and notable events that shaped education and educational partnerships during the 21st century;
- policies and nonpolicies related to teacher education, subject areas, and educational partnerships; and
- diverse theories of learning: conditioning theories, social cognitive theories, cognitive information processing, and constructivism.

Table 2.1	Prior Knowledge and Beliefs Organizer

Describe what you know about educational policies, laws, and initiatives from the past 100 years.	Explain the challenges and successes that you have faced with current educational policies.

Use the information you enter in Table 2.1 to provide a context and frame of reference for the historical events and policies that will be discussed in this chapter.

Goals of Education

Goals of education have influenced decisions and policy throughout the history of education in the United States. Therefore, **policy** is a direct result of priorities and goals in education. The term *policy* varies in meaning, but in this chapter we will use it to refer to a set of decisions or mandates that are created and implemented. Policies are usually created by local, state, or federal governments or within school districts with long-term implementation in mind, not a short-term event or action.

Public Good Versus Private Good

When looking at why policies are made, it is important to look at the different goals or purposes of education. According to Labaree (1997), goals related to education in the United States can be seen as having three different purposes: (a) **democratic equality**, (b) **social efficiency**, and (c) **social mobility**. When the goal of education is democratic equality, policies and decisions are created to ensure that all students have equal access to the curriculum and learning to become contributing members of society. If social efficiency is the goal, then students are trained in skills that will benefit the workforce. Labaree states that both of these goals are a public good. Social mobility, on the other hand, is a private good where students are taught to compete for social positions within the workforce. Therefore, a struggle often ensues when decision makers must choose between educational policies that relate to democratic views and political equality (public rights) and those that relate to the capitalist marketplace and individual liberties (private rights).

Democratic equality goals are organized so that all students, regardless of economic, language, or ethnic background, have the same equal rights and responsibilities in order to become contributing members of the community. It is the responsibility of schools and teachers to promote equality and citizenship within the curriculum. This goal is the most idealistic and has strong-held roots in democratic education. Labaree (1997) states that the three areas most addressed within this goal are citizenship training, equal access, and equal treatment. Citizenship training is set up to teach and preserve democracy. Subjects such as social studies, history, government, and civics are designed to inform students of their "duties" and obligations toward the American political system. Equal access ensures that all students have access to being successful in schools. Equal treatment stems from the belief that all students should experience a shared common culture that will benefit society. This results in universal enrollment for all students, a specific curriculum, and similar educational experiences for all students.

Social efficiency is a public good. Every student, therefore, will be educated to take a different role in society that will benefit the community. Therefore, schools and teachers train students to fulfill certain roles that society needs. Labaree (1997) explains that society benefits from an active economy that will ensure the productivity of every worker. Therefore, it is the responsibility of society to appropriate educational dollars to fund productivity and training within the entire workforce.

Social mobility provides students with competitive opportunities to distinguish themselves from others. Therefore, the educational system becomes stratified according to ability and academic achievement. Students compete for university acceptance, jobs, and other opportunities. The purpose of school based on the social mobility view is to provide opportunities for students to demonstrate their competence in order to achieve specific social and career positions. Education is considered a private good because it focuses on the individual rather than the broader good of society.

Types of Schools

Schools can be classified as public, private, magnet, or charter or as nonpublic special education schools. Homes can also be places where schooling takes place.

- A **public school** is supported by tax dollars. Public schools throughout the United States are organized in districts. District sizes vary as do the grade levels and location.
- **Private schools** can be religious or nonreligious and are not supported by tax dollars. Therefore, they generally charge tuition for each child who attends.
- A **magnet school** is a public school that operates within a school district that is open to all qualifying students. Magnet schools are organized around a specific theme or subject area such as the performing arts, professional development, or science. Magnet schools were created to promote equity for all students and enhance learning.
- A **charter school** is part of the public school system as well. It differs from a public school because its purpose is to encourage the use of innovative teaching methods and provide families, students, teachers, and administrators with expanded decision-making abilities.
- A **nonpublic special education school** provides services for students with severe learning disabilities, multiple disabilities, or mental retardation. A nonpublic school is a more restrictive environment because special needs students are not mainstreamed with their peers.
- **Home schooling** takes place in homes where families or other members of the community teach students and provide for all their educational needs.

Cumulatively, each type of school functions best with collaboration from other parties. Children who are schooled at home benefit from multiple field trips to museums, libraries, and other places within their community. Magnet schools that focus on science and math benefit from interactions with science museums, zoos, and aquariums. Charter schools, public schools, and private schools benefit from multiple community partners such as local artists who volunteer their time to teach fourth graders different painting techniques or a grocery store that interacts with students via monthly field trips to promote healthy classroom snacks. Nonpublic schools, although many times more separate than the other types, should take advantage of community resources, particularly those that provide access and opportunities for special needs students.

Students and Families as Part of a System

A core culture exists in schools, in neighborhoods, and within the child's family structure. Students and families provide a wealth of strengths from their own culture, but their culture, beliefs, and values are sometimes influenced by outside sources. Bronfenbrenner (2005) provides a description of different systems known as the macrosystem, exosystem, and microsystem.

The **macrosystem** is the largest of the three systems and includes society and the larger subculture to which children and families belong (i.e., lifestyles, social patterns, beliefs). It also includes outside influences such as the national government, political views, social trends, and larger cultural values and practices.

The **exosystem** is smaller than the macrosystem, and children do not actively participate in it. This includes such places as parents' work environment, city council meetings, and community service agencies. Although children are not active participants, the exosystem may affect their microsystem and daily experiences.

The smaller **microsystem** includes children's greatest influence and frame of reference including their peers, neighborhood, school, and family. This microsystem is often a child's most important system because of the relationships that develop. It is important for educators to have knowledge of these systems because they are inevitably part of every child's life.

Social and Cultural Capital

According to French sociologist Pierre Bourdieu (1977), capital includes human, social, and material resources activated for a desired purpose. Bourdieu makes the distinction between material wealth and cultural assets, reasoning that culture adds to the wealth of a particular class. Parents provide children with cultural capital, the attitudes and knowledge that make the educational system a more familiar place in which they can succeed. **Social capital** within a community includes the diversity of interactions and relationships including participating in community activities, service, and volunteering.

Lane and Dorfman (1997) define collaboration between schools and communities as having two main goals: (a) to strengthen and increase social capital by forming strong social networks, developing active participation, and fostering a sense of trust and community and (b) to increase the ability and capacity of the community to utilize social capital to produce meaningful and sustainable community renewal. The role of collaboration, therefore, is process oriented (building social capital) and task oriented (using social capital to achieve outcomes that benefit people). Coleman (1988) outlines three components of social capital that include the obligations and expectations of social relationships, the norms related to the social group, and access to information and resources. Coleman states that social capital as it relates to education can be increased only when and if parents contribute the time necessary to support their children at home.

Cultural capital, therefore, is the advantage gained by the majority group from understanding and living the lifestyle congruent with the dominant culture in schools (Lee & Bowen, 2006). This advantage includes enacting the types of involvement most valued by a school or by teachers. Families who do not understand the cultural nuances of involvement at school and who do not participate in ways that are traditionally expected remain at a disadvantage. Lee and Bowen state that working-class or low-income families are usually less likely to visit and participate in school activities because of their work schedules, child care issues, lack of transportation, or lack of teachers who speak their native language. Unfortunately, differences in the cultural capital of families may reduce their ability to obtain social capital from the school even though they attend school regularly. Therefore, teachers and schools can and should collaborate with students and their families to embrace the cultural capital of all who learn and work together.

History and Policy Related to Educational Partnerships

You have read about reasons for educational partnerships, types of partnerships, characteristics of partnerships, and partnership examples. In this next section, we will take a look at how these issues relate to the history and policy of education and educational partnerships. It is important to look at partnerships from a historical perspective because it allows us to view changes in families, schools, and policies as critical components when inquiring into current and future trends.

When inquiring into the history of educational partnerships and policies from the past 100 years, it is interesting to note how the potential for social capital and cultural capital has been addressed over time. Many of the events and mandates that have taken place have been developed to increase social capital within the community by forming partnerships and initiatives. Organizations help build social capital by strengthening certain areas related to literacy, inclusive practices, nutrition, physical health, and various forms of knowledge. Although this is only a partial list related to seminal events, they are events that helped define our current educational system and the potential for educational partnerships today.

Federal Mandates, Seminal Events, and Educational Partners: 1900–Present

A timeline is provided that outlines programs and events that have taken place over the past 100 years and have made an impact on education and set much of the groundwork for educational partnerships. As you read through the timeline, consider how the different events impact our current educational system and the potential for educational partnerships. Notable events related to various eras are featured including authors and books that shaped education today. As you read about each event, consider which areas contributed to educational partnerships and the building of social and cultural capital. Although this timeline only covers the past 100 years, I encourage you to inquire into earlier educational events and policies from the United States and other countries.

1900–1920: Families Determine the School Curriculum

Just before the turn of the century, Dewey's (1897) manuscript, "My Pedagogic Creed," provided a look into learning as an interactive dynamic process. This manuscript and Dewey's philosophy were the focus of many debates throughout the 20th century and helped lay the groundwork for experiential education. At this point in time, families usually determined the curriculum, appointed teachers, and influenced instructional strategies. In most communities, home, school, and church shared many goals and integrated these goals within the local school or schools. Only about 50% of U.S. children attended school during this time, and most students received an average of 5 years of schooling total (University of Minnesota, 2008).

1897:   *National Congress of Mothers* was founded by Alice McLellan Birney and Phoebe Apperson Hearst in Washington, DC. This organization is currently known as the National Parent Teacher Association (PTA).

1897: "My Pedagogic Creed" by John Dewey was published in *School Journal.* In the article, Dewey outlines his views related to education. This manuscript remains a seminal document today.

1918: The *Cardinal Principles of Secondary Education* were established by the Commission on the Reorganization of Secondary Education, which determined that subjects should be separated and schools should work under the concept of democracy. The seven cardinal principles that all schools should follow include health, fundamental subjects such as math and reading, worthy home membership, vocation/career development, civic education, worthy use of leisure time that combines the mind and spirit, and building ethical character/responsibility.

1920–1940: Change in Responsibility

Up until this point, families and communities made many educational decisions related to curriculum, methods, and teachers. Between 1920 and 1940, however, teachers' colleges became more popular as teachers began to take on roles as experts. John Dewey, Maria Montessori, Jean Piaget, and Eleanor Roosevelt published many notable books during this time period.

John Dewey

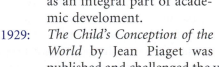

SOURCE: © Bettmann/CORBIS.

1920s: *Teachers' colleges* became more prominent, and teachers were viewed as experts in their field and began to make decisions about curriculum and instructional methods. Many teachers' colleges were integrated within state colleges between 1940 and 1960.

1920: *The School and Society* by John Dewey was published. In the book, he advocates a philosophy of teaching grounded in students' experiences, known as experiential learning. In 1938, he wrote *Experience and Education,* where he looks at the child's world outside the classroom as an integral part of academic develoment.

1929: *The Child's Conception of the World* by Jean Piaget was published and challenged the view of children's reality and conceptual understanding. As children actively engage in the world and interact with people and objects, they begin to form mental constructs of the world around them.

1930:   "Good Citizenship: The Purpose of Education" was published by Eleanor Roosevelt. In the article, she discusses the privilege of democracy and citizenship and advocates a variety of experiences that add to the notion of education. She advocates the role of women in education and their involvement and/or lack of involvement in political issues.

1935:   *The Secret of Childhood* was published by Maria Montessori. In the book, she describes an inquiry-based method of teaching young children based on years of observing children explore the world around them. Her view of teaching, the Montessori method, encourages children to be independent and self-disciplined while learning through meaningful experiences.

1940–1960: Desegregation of Schools and National Defense

Following World War II, the process of desegregating schools was at the forefront of policy based on the notable *Brown v. Board of Education* case (see U.S. National Archives and Records Administration, n.d.). More emphasis was placed on social issues within schools, particularly nutrition.

1946:   *The National School Lunch Act* was signed into law by President Harry Truman. This program was patterned after many European programs that provided free or reduced-price lunches to children in need.

1949:   Ralph Tyler's *Basic Principles of Curriculum and Instruction* was published. In the book, Tyler introduces objectives, learning experiences, the organization of the learning experiences, and evaluation as being the foundation for planning and implementing instruction.

1954:   The *Brown v. Board of Education* decision by the U.S. Supreme Court declared that separate schools for Black and White students were unconstitutional. The Supreme Court cited that this violated the 14th Amendment of the U.S. Constitution, which guarantees equal protection under the laws to all citizens. This decision led the way toward desegregation of schools and the Civil Rights Movement.

1954:   The *School Milk Program* was created and ultimately extended as part of the Child Nutrition Act. Nonprofit schools and child care centers and camps that educate children can obtain supplemental funding for their milk programs today.

1957:   The *Sputnik* spacecraft was successfully launched by the Soviet Union. This led to more funding and changes within the science and math curriculum.

1960–1970: Change in Educational Programs

The former Soviet Union was the first nation to launch the spacecraft *Sputnik* that resulted in the "race to space" in 1957. This set much of the groundwork related to curricular reform, particularly in science and mathematics education. The United States' lack of space preparedness was attributed to schools and universities, and therefore federal money was appropriated for many new math and science programs. These programs were created to provide more authentic science experiences for students and for the development of "little scientists" and "little mathematicians" to keep up with the growing technological world.

More mothers entered the workforce. The National Organization for Women was created to promote equality among women, particularly while employed. The health and nutritional needs of children and the relationship between health and learning continued to be acknowledged. Civil rights, environmental issues, and support for students with special needs also helped define this time period.

1962: *Silent Spring* by Rachel Carson was published. This book launched the environmental movement and greater public interest in environmental education. It resulted in public concerns related to pesticides, pollution, and the health of the environment.

1963: The *Learning Disabilities Association of America* was established to offer support for families, teachers, and other professionals. The organization advocates success for all people with learning disabilities and provides information and a network of resources to support teaching, learning, and other opportunities.

1964: The *Civil Rights Act* provided support for school districts and higher-education institutions to develop and implement professional development programs for teachers and staff to address instructional issues related to desegregation of schools.

1964: The *Economic Opportunity Act* was established to promote economic and social potential for all individuals and families within the United States. President Lyndon Johnson indicated that this act would launch a "war on poverty" for the purpose of eliminating poverty and promoting more opportunities for education and training.

1964: *Pedagogy of the Oppressed,* published by Paulo Freire and translated into English in 1970, is one of the most quoted educational texts in the United States, Latin America, Africa, and Asia. Freire's writings exposed the economically and intellectually disadvantaged people in Brazil and promoted social and educational justice.

1964: *Martin Luther King Jr.* delivered his famous "I Have a Dream" speech on August 28, 1963, on the steps of the Lincoln Memorial in Washington, DC, during the March on Washington for Jobs and Freedom. He spoke of everyone, regardless of skin color, living together with equal treatment and opportunities. His speech is known as one of the most important and notable of the past 100 years.

1965: The *Elementary and Secondary Education Act* provided funding for elementary and secondary schools in low socioeconomic areas to obtain textbooks and other instructional materials. This act also included funding for educational research. In 1968, amendments were added to this act that included regional educational centers for students with special needs (e.g., handicapped, deaf, blind), assistance for schools in rural areas, dropout prevention, and bilingual education programs.

1966: The *National Organization for Women* was founded to promote equality and justice for women in the workplace and in society in general.

1966: The *Child Nutrition Act* was established to retain school lunch and milk programs in schools. A pilot breakfast program was also established. Cumulatively, these programs were developed based on the link between good nutrition and students' capacity to learn.

SOURCE: © Bob Adelman/Corbis.

Martin Luther King Jr. delivering his "I Have a Dream" speech.

1966:   *Head Start legislation* led the way toward federally funded preschool programs as a result of an amendment to the Economic Opportunity Act. The program was developed to offer economically disadvantaged children and their families a variety of parent and health services, including voluntary enrollment in Head Start preschool programs.

1966:   *The Coleman Report* was a result of the Civil Rights Act of 1964. This report noted academic differences among students from different socioeconomic backgrounds and concluded that children's activities outside the home were factors in their academic achievement. This led to programs focusing on the importance of parental involvement in formal education.

1966:   *Toward a Theory of Instruction* by Jerome Bruner was published. In his book, Bruner describes how learners construct an understanding of the world by making connections between their current or past experiences and new knowledge. His work encouraged educators to encourage active learning of students through a curriculum that became more complex throughout different grade levels.

1968:   *Sesame Street* was created with funds from Head Start legislation. The show was based on years of research that included very short, entertaining segments, music, and the use of colorful Muppets to educate young children.

1968:   The *Comer School Development Program* was founded by James P. Comer of Yale University to promote collaboration of families, educators, and the community to improve the cognitive, social, and emotional needs of children. This teamwork approach to education was one of the first of its kind.

1970–1980: Shared Responsibilities and Opportunities

This decade included a variety of funding that targeted equity for girls and women, students with special needs, and families who wanted more educational choice. Federal funding was initiated for curriculum development and the implementation of drug abuse education, environmental education, bilingual Head Start programs, and alternative schools. Parent-teacher organizations gained momentum and led to more community involvement. A free breakfast program was established based on the success of the pilot program in the 1960s.

1970s: *Parent-teacher organizations and associations (PTO/PTA)* became more popular. For the most part, these groups were created and led by parents with some teacher and administrative input. Today, about 6 million parents and adults are members of a PTA. PTO is a general acronym for any group that is independent of the national PTA. PTOs are also called home school associations (HAS) or parent communication councils (PCC) and can write their own bylaws and determine dues.

1970s: *Magnet schools, open schools, and free schools* were implemented. These types of schools were developed to provide alternative educational opportunities for children and families. Families could choose to attend these schools. Free schools provide an open format where students can direct their own education with the help of teachers. Open schools include informal classroom structures without traditional walls to separate classes of students and other activities. Magnet schools focus on specialized programs related to the arts, the environment, or basic skills.

1970:   The *Drug Abuse Education Act* provided information on the development of curriculum and methods related to drug abuse in schools. Two years later, the Drug Abuse Office and Treatment Act included the integration of schools and community members to establish an office that would oversee policy and programs related to drug prevention education. The National Institute on Drug Abuse was developed in 1974 as a result of society's need for more drug abuse research and development of prevention programs.

1970:   The *Environmental Education Act* gained momentum in the 1960s and took center stage to help schools and universities develop curriculum materials and maintain environmental education in elementary and secondary schools. This act provided education for teachers, students, community groups, the general public, and industry leaders. This was one of the first attempts to integrate the whole community in an education issue.

1971:   *Skyline High School in Dallas, Texas,* was established as a school known for never closing its doors. This was due to the fact that multiple programs were established for students and their families during the day, in the afternoons, and into the night. The school included a diverse population of students from different ethnicities and socioeconomic backgrounds.

1972:   Title IX and the regulations that were outlined in 1975 provide rights for women in sports and education. This policy resulted in increased opportunities for girls and women through more gender-inclusive athletic programs.

1972: The *Economic Opportunity Act* was amended to include Head Start programs for students with special needs.

1974: The *Family Educational Rights and Privacy Act* (FERPA) was established to protect the privacy of students and their education records in public schools in the United States. The Family Policy Compliance Office was organized to ensure family and student rights related to FERPA and other educational issues. FERPA provides rights for parents to access and review their child's records, ask for revisions, and write counter-statements to be maintained as part of their child's academic file. Families must ask for permission in writing to obtain information within a student's education file.

1975: *Free breakfast programs* were established due to the fact that many students, particularly those from lower socioeconomic backgrounds, arrived at school hungry. Therefore, breakfast programs were established to provide nutrition at the beginning of the day as well as during lunch. The initiative provided states with funding to implement the program in public and nonprofit private schools as well as some child care centers. The Childhood Hunger Relief Act requires all public schools with at least 40% of students who are eligible for free or reduced-price lunch to offer breakfast.

1975: The *Education for All Handicapped Children Act* (now the Individuals with Disabilities Education Act or IDEA; see U.S. Department of Education, n.d.) was established to provide free appropriate education to meet the needs of all children. Referred to as Public Law 94-142 (see U.S. Department of Education, n.d.), this act was created to ensure the educational rights of individuals with disabilities and to provide Free Appropriate Public Education (FAPE) for all children. The law also provided provisions for parents to play a critical role in the educational decisions of their children.

1977: *Bilingual and bicultural Head Start* programs were developed in 21 different states.

Enhancing Learning for Students With Special Needs: The Individuals with Disabilities Education Act

The Individuals with Disabilities Education Act (IDEA) ensures services to children with disabilities in the United States. Specific policies and procedures are provided to assist states and public agencies with early intervention strategies for infants and toddlers with disabilities and their families (birth–age 2) under Part C. Children and youth (ages 3–21) receive special education services under IDEA Part B. Many families are not familiar with IDEA and the benefits for their children with special needs. Therefore, teachers should:

1. communicate with families about their rights and services available;

2. obtain a list of services within the community to assist families and students;

3. work with their schools and districts to obtain adequate supplementary instructional materials and services;

4. educate all students and families about the benefits of special education services;

5. educate all students and families about how having students with special needs in regular classrooms benefits students with and without disabilities; and

6. seek professional development workshops and courses to enhance instruction and communication with families and students with disabilities.

1980–1990: Back to Basics

This decade has been described by some historians and educators as the "Back to Basics" movement partially because of the seminal report *A Nation at Risk* (1983). This report advocated more federal support for education because the United States was at risk of having a substandard education system. The Coalition of Essential Schools, cultural literacy, and Even Start literacy programs were developed in part as a result of the needs expressed in *A Nation at Risk*. Although the Job Training Partnership Act was created in 1982, the focus on school-to-work issues was downsized due to the growing concern for basic education in the United States.

1982: The *Job Training Partnership Act* was established to provide funding related to school-to-work transitions. Job training was provided for youth, mostly from low socioeconomic backgrounds. Summer youth employment programs and Native American employment programs were included in this policy.

1983: *A Nation at Risk* was published by the National Commission on Excellence in Education. The report stated that the continuation of mediocrity in education would result in the demise of the United States' ability to compete within the world technologically, educationally, and scientifically. This report called for higher expectations of students and influenced the standards-based curriculum reforms in the 1990s.

1984: The National Education Association adopted nine principles for effective schools (see http://www.nea.org/tools/18940.htm). These principles were included in an open letter to America titled *Schools, Students, and Tomorrow* as a plan to restructure education. The principles indicate that students should (a) master subject matter, (b) become active participants in their own learning, (c) be provided multiple learning options, and (d) learn over time. Faculty should (a) be involved in key decision making, (b) be compensated appropriately, (c) be educated to high standards during preparation and practice, (d) be connected with school/community resources and work collaboratively to enhance students' welfare and learning, and (e) be supported financially by combining resources from the federal, state, and local governments.

1984:   The *Coalition of Essential Schools* was popularized. Headed by Theodore Sizer, the author of *Horace's Compromise,* the coalition includes a collaborative network of teachers and schools who work together under common principles in order to improve pedagogy in high schools. This program involves a set of principles instead of a specific model that schools are supposed to follow.

1986:   *Public Law 99-457* (see U.S. Department of Education, n.d.) requires that all states in the United States develop interdisciplinary services and early interventions for infants, toddlers, and preschool children with disabilities. States therefore offer free preschool programs for 3- to 5-year-old children with disabilities. In addition, families and educators must work together to develop an individualized family service plan for children.

1988:   *Cultural Literacy: What Every American Needs to Know* was published by author E. D. Hirsch. In the book, Hirsch advocates the need for Americans to obtain specific knowledge in a variety of subject areas and refers to this knowledge as cultural literacy.

1987:   The *National Board for Professional Teaching Standards* was created to enhance teaching by outlining five core propositions: a commitment to student learning, subject area expertise, management of student learning, reflective practice, and participating as part of a larger learning community (these propositions are outlined in Chapter 1). Teachers can obtain national certification by demonstrating their teaching ability and expertise within the core propositions. As part of a larger learning community, teachers are required to document how they create positive relationships with families, within the teaching profession, and within the broader educational community.

1988:   *Even Start* literacy programs were established for low-income families to improve academic achievement and give their children an even start in literacy and education. The program involves early childhood education, adult literacy, parenting skills, and family literacy activities. Goals of the program include encouraging parents to become partners in education and helping families improve their literacy and educational skills.

1988:   The *Javits Act* was established to provide grants for schools serving gifted and talented children from low-income families. All children who demonstrate high performance in the areas of intellectual, creative, artistic, or leadership skills can receive services to help them develop their talents more fully.

1990–2000: Academic Standards and Shared Decisions

A Nation at Risk continued to define much of the educational movement throughout the 1990s. Multiple organizations developed sets of standards that defined what students at every grade level should be able to do. Charter schools became popular as did the need for quality after-school programs and the inclusion of families in school-based decisions.

1990s: The national education standards movement was led by the National Council of Teachers of Mathematics' (NCTM) standards for students in 1989. The National Research Council followed NCTM's lead by publishing the National Science Education Standards to define specific science expectations for children in grades K–12. Other organizations also created standards during this time in the areas of reading, language arts, and social studies.

1990s: *After-school programs* gained popularity based on the need for students to have more supervision before and after school. The National Association of Elementary School Principals published *Standards for Quality School-Age Child Care* in 1993 and published a second edition in 1999. The guide provides research-based steps and procedures to establish effective child care programs and to encourage teachers, families, and the broader community to work together to aid in the healthy development of children.

1990s: *School-based management* is a general term that describes more decision making for families, teachers, students, staff, and administrators. Authority moves away from centralized offices or school districts as schools are given more power to create their own structure. This effort is also referred to as site-based management, school-based decision making, and school empowerment.

1990:   The *National and Community Service Act* provides authorization to promote citizenship and community service in schools. This initiative was developed to provide job skills, combat poverty, and address environmental needs. In 1993, the Corporation for National and Community Service was founded to encourage children, youth, and adults to give back to their communities. The corporation created the Senior Corps, AmeriCorps, and Learn and Serve America.

1992:   The *first official charter school* was established in Minnesota to provide teachers with "charters" to explore new approaches to teaching and to provide families, students, and teachers with innovative educational opportunities within the public school system. The U.S. Department of Education provides grants for schools that want to become charter schools. A charter school can be started by families, teachers, or community members and must be approved and operate under the auspices of a local school board.

1994:   The *Improving America's Schools Act* includes local initiatives to help disadvantaged children meet challenging standards. It requires schools to provide policy statements that promote family activism and decision making. In addition, the act mandated that family involvement be integrated into Head Start, Even Start, and other state-supported preschool programs.

1996:   *Goals 2000: Educate America Act* was signed into law by President Bill Clinton to promote excellence by encouraging more educational partnerships between the federal government and local communities. In addition, specific standards and goals were outlined and were to be accomplished by the year 2000. Included in these goals was the Safe Schools Act to ensure that all schools were free from drugs and violence. States in the United States were encouraged to apply for funds to achieve Goals 2000 initiatives.

1996:   The *National Network of Partnership Schools at Johns Hopkins University* was established under the leadership of Joyce L. Epstein. Researchers work with members of an extended network to study and develop new concepts and strategies related to family and community partnerships.

1996:   The *Personal Responsibility and Work Opportunity Reconciliation Act* changed social policies that affect children and families. It increased state decision-making services for low-income families and emphasized parental responsibility and stronger child support requirements. However, the act also restricted services and benefits for immigrant populations and stated specifications for unmarried teen parents who seek welfare.

1997:   The *Individuals with Disabilities Education Act* expanded the *Education for All Handicapped Children Act* that includes the individual education plan (IEP) and joins parents and the community as partners in providing appropriate education for all children. Parents were provided five fundamental rights with the revision of Public Law 94-142 of 1975: (a) free appropriate public education for their children, (b) parental consent related to academic assessment and placement, (c) their children being educated within the least restrictive environment and with their peers, (d) full participation in their children's IEP, and (e) participation in all decision making regarding their children's education.

2000–Present: Educational Accountability

No Child Left Behind, empowerment for families, and the expansion of health, nutrition, and exercise initiatives defined education during the first part of the 21st century. These initiatives continue to have an impact on curriculum, instruction, and partnership programs today.

2000s: The *digital divide* is a term describing the "haves and have-nots" in response to the growing use of technology during the 21st century. Families from low socioeconomic backgrounds, from diverse ethnic backgrounds, and who live in urban and rural areas do not always have the access and resources to use technology to promote their educational and employment endeavors. Social gaps and economic opportunities are divided based on access to technological resources.

2000s: *Community, family, and school partnership initiatives* continue to gain momentum. Most government-sponsored grant programs require educational partnerships for those writing proposals for funding. The U.S. government and various states provide Web links to promote educational partnerships for families, communities, and schools.

2001:   *No Child Left Behind* (NCLB, Public Law 107-110) is a revision of the Elementary and Secondary Education Act from 1965. Each state is required to provide a plan of action to demonstrate how students will meet high standards of learning. These plans lead to more accountability for states, districts, schools, and teachers. According to NCLB guidelines, schools must adopt policies and practices that actively engage families in partnerships with schools.

2001: The *National Parent Teacher Association* adopted the motto "Every child. One voice." The organization advocates links among families, educators, government, and the legal system. Important issues include the interpretation of NCLB, the digital divide, and children's health, safety, and welfare.

2002: *Charter schools* continued to expand. $200 million was appropriated for charter school development in the United States. These schools continue to focus on teacher, community, and family empowerment through shared decision making.

2007: *Health and nutrition issues* were addressed. The National Conference of State Legislatures addressed health-related issues related to childhood obesity, physical education and nutrition in schools, and school wellness policies.

Educational Policy—Whose Policy? Who's Excluded?

When you consider the role of the U.S. government and other organizations in educational activities and events described in this chapter, you will note the tremendous impact particularly policies have had on education, equity, and the promotion of educational partnerships. However, you might ask, "Who developed these policies?" or "For whom were these policies developed?" These are interesting questions that cannot be answered with one simple statement. Events, publications, legislation, and other mandates were created by multiple individuals and for multiple purposes. They continue to define the culture of education in the United States and throughout much of the broader world. The history of these events helps inform the future of education and educational partnership potential.

Teacher Education About Educational Partnerships

What is excluded in the history of partnerships can be even more interesting because it shows a lack of importance in particular areas, or holes in partnership development and implementation. One growing area—but still one that has not experienced mandates or specific policies in many states—relates to family involvement research and practices in teacher education programs. Without education, experiences, and knowledge, new teachers enter classrooms that are linguistically and culturally diverse, but they may not have the confidence or the skills necessary to create bridges among the school curriculum, students, and their families. Katz and Bauch (1999) noted positive outcomes when new teachers received education related to skills and knowledge of family involvement in their college courses. These teachers felt prepared to implement diverse parent involvement practices because of their education prior to entering the classroom as teachers. In addition, Sara Lawrence-Lightfoot (2004), the author of *The Essential Conversation: What Parents and Teachers Can Learn From Each Other,* indicates that most teachers have no preparation for working with families and that they often make up their policies and strategies as they go along. She suggests that teachers be educated as ethnographers to hone their listening, observing, and documentation skills. Engaging in this type of practice would help teachers appreciate parents' perspectives and empathize with them in relation to the challenges of parenting, working, and supporting education at home.

Harris, Jacobson, and Hemmer (2004) of the North Texas Partnership for Parent Engagement reported on the development and field-testing of six online, case-based modules for preservice teachers. These modules are aligned with the National Parent Teacher Association's goals and Epstein's (2001) six types of involvement: parenting, communicating, learning at home, volunteering, decision making, and collaborating with the community (these are discussed more fully in Chapter 5: Building Family-School Partnerships). The findings from the pre- and postassessments indicate that teachers' knowledge was greatly enhanced by their participation in at least one of the modules. For example, 66 preservice teachers field-tested the communication module in three different classes. The preservice teachers showed a 76% increase in their knowledge in this area. For the parenting module, preservice teachers showed a 62% increase in knowledge. This study demonstrates possibilities for stronger partnerships when family and community partnership content is integrated throughout teacher education programs.

Trumbull, Rothstein-Fisch, Greenfield, and Quiroz (2001) recommend that parent involvement content in teacher education programs be coupled with the benefits of cultural and social capital and the strengths that build relationships across cultures. In one of the cases described above by Harris et al. (2004), there is a module titled "Over the Weekend" that is related to Epstein's "learning at home" involvement area. The case includes the story of an elementary bilingual teacher who assigns homework regularly and has strict expectations for its completion. This teacher is frustrated because one student does not complete the work assigned over the weekend. The teacher asks for a face-to-face meeting with the student's mother and learns that the child's entire family travels across the border to Mexico each weekend to see their father. Gaining information such as this provides a teacher with empathy and a culturally relevant understanding of students, their families, their priorities, and their lives outside of school.

Arts Education

Arts education is also noticeably missing from the number of events and legislative mandates of the past 100 years. However, the Arts Education Partnership (1999, 2009) worked with the U.S. Department of Education and the National Endowment for the Arts to create a document, *Improving Learning in Schools With Arts Partners in the Community.* This publication discusses the benefits of educational partnerships and seeks to promote arts partnerships in different communities. The guide is organized around three topics: the impact of arts education partnerships to improve education for all students, the factors needed to create effective partnerships, and questions that partners should ask before and during the partnership project. The overall purpose of the guide is to encourage leaders within the arts community, education, businesses, and civic and government groups to combine talents and resources to encourage more partnerships that will enhance arts education for children and youth.

Overview of Educational Learning Theories

There are a variety of learning theories that during the past century influenced teaching, educational policies, and therefore educational partnerships. Learning is most often defined as a change in behavior. In schools, this means a change in thinking about content or demonstrating a particular skill. Schunk (2008) distinguishes between four different types of learning theories that are most prevalent in U.S. schools and the curriculum: conditioning theories, social cognitive theories, cognitive information processing views, and constructivist theories of learning. These learning theories address how students learn.

Conditioning theories have roots in behaviorism where learning is viewed as a change in behavior that is reinforced by outside stimuli in the students' environment (i.e., external factors). The work of Ivan Pavlov (classical conditioning with dogs) and B. F. Skinner (operant conditioning) has been instrumental in shaping these views. Over time, the practice of reinforcement increases the probability that a behavior will be repeated. Learning is considered passive but is influenced by positive and negative reinforcement or a stimulus and response.

Social cognitive theories of learning claim that students learn by actively engaging in particular tasks and by observing others. Teachers provide feedback and positive reinforcement of behavior to motivate students to learn, to facilitate self-efficacy, and to develop goals and values. Cognitive learning was popularized in the 1960s and includes ways that students engage in solving problems and learning concepts.

Cognitive information processing theories of learning involve brain-based educational ideas where students form networks within their memory. Students determine whether knowledge and skills will be placed in their short-term memory, working memory, or long-term memory. Organizing information, elaborating, and rehearsing on a regular basis determine where knowledge is placed within the memory areas of their brains.

Like cognitive information processing and social cognitive theory, **constructivist theories** place emphasis on the students' internal memory structure. However, the students' prior knowledge and experiences are crucial to the entire learning process. Based on the work of Vygotsky (1978), knowledge is constructed within the context of social and language processes—with the teacher, other students, and the community. In general, constructivism recognizes the learner as the center of knowing and advocates roles for teachers as facilitators of knowledge construction, rather than as transmitters of information (Hofer & Pintrich, 1997).

Although John Dewey was not an advocate of a specific learning theory, he was an advocate of active learning, interaction within multiple environments, and democratic processes. In his noted book *Democracy and Education* (1916/1997), he describes two elements related to democratic education. The first element involves a shared common interest among individuals. The second element relates to free interaction between social groups and changes in social habits. He holds firm to the assumption that learning is social and should be democratic.

Reflecting on the different learning theories—conditioning, social cognitive, cognitive information processing, and constructivist views—it should be noted that none of these views are superior. In fact, having knowledge of a variety of learning theories allows a teacher to understand the basis of his or her teaching and learning activities more fully. Having knowledge of a variety of theories allows a teacher to communicate his or her planning, instruction, and assessment strategies more appropriately to families, administrators, and the broader community.

Chapter Summary

There are various types of schools in the United States, including private, public, magnet, and charter schools. Students attend these schools but are also part of a larger system that includes the macrosystem, exosystem, and microsystem. Together, these systems influence the knowledge, skills, and beliefs that they bring to class. Many educational partnerships are influenced by the goals and values of the partner. In addition, many of these goals are influenced by beliefs in the purpose of school such as democratic equality, social efficiency, or social mobility (Labaree, 1997). Sometimes the purpose, goals, and values are influenced by educational policies and mandates. Having an understanding of various past events and legislative policies can inform teaching, learning, and partnership development in the future.

Partnerships can result in a surplus of social and cultural capital within the classroom and school. Parents provide children with cultural capital, the attitudes and knowledge that make the educational system a more familiar place in which they can succeed. Social capital takes place within a community and includes diverse interactions and relationships. Educators should consider aspects of social and cultural capital when engaging in partnership activities within the community and with families.

CASE STUDIES

The two case studies featured in this chapter involve different teachers who assessed the learning styles and learning motivation of specific students in their classroom. These case studies relate to students' preferred modes of learning and provide insight into their values, beliefs, and thought processes within a larger sphere of influence that includes their families, communities, and life at school. They will serve as "Notes From the Classroom" in this chapter.

❖ ## Case Study 2.1: Kim's Inquiry About Children's Learning Styles in Her Fourth-Grade Classroom

Voice of Kim, Fourth-Grade Teacher

The purpose of my case study was to find out what motivated students to learn. Additionally, I wanted to find out how the attitudes and educational beliefs of the family might support students in staying motivated to learn. To collect data, I interviewed the students about their interests, beliefs, and attitudes toward school. I asked them about what motivates them to want to stay on task, finish work, and seek out further learning opportunities. I also asked them to describe how they would feel in certain hypothetical situations; for example, what if they lost their homework? What if the work is too difficult? How do they deal with distractions? I hoped such a line of questioning would provide insight into their perceived positive and negative consequences for their behavior. Additionally, I surveyed the families about their philosophies of education, behavioral expectations, thoughts on homework, and routines and organization of the home. I asked about the frequency of arguments about school-related issues and how they work to resolve the arguments, if any. I also wanted to know how students are being rewarded for their hard work and what the intended consequences are for low achievement.

I conducted a case study on several fourth-grade students from diverse backgrounds, Sally, Wendy, Yumiko, and Brad. I chose these students because of their displayed range of academic behaviors that support their achievement and further their acquisition of the English language. I will discuss what I found out about one of these students, Yumiko (pseudonym). Yumiko is a male Japanese-speaking student who is acquiring English. He is highly motivated yet still scores low on tests in the content areas. The purpose of this case study was not only to discover what motivates these students to self-regulate their academic behavior but also to explore ways in which I may use their interests to further enhance their learning experiences.

Findings and Analysis

I found Yumiko to be somewhat intrinsically motivated to do well in school. He said that he works and studies hard because he "feels good [and] to be a great adult." That's good to hear! When I asked him to elaborate on this during our follow-up interview, he stated that he feels good because it makes his parents happy. He also believes that if he doesn't get good grades, he won't get into high school. When I asked him about how to use teacher feedback to enhance his overall achievement, he did not give an appropriate response. In classroom observations, when I am working one-on-one with Yumiko, I notice that he does not understand much of what I am saying to him during writing conferences. For example, when I asked him to indent the first line of the first paragraph with a two-finger space, he indented every line he wrote. In the content areas, when acquiring new words, he knows of a strategy that is successful for him.

Yumiko's family reported that, overall, Yumiko finds school extremely enjoyable and is very eager to come to school. What struck me is that despite his willingness to come to school, he is not confident academically according to his parents. Yes, interesting. What does that tell you as a teacher? I have observed this characteristic in the classroom, as he is timid and rarely responds in front of the whole class. However, in small-group rotations, he is much more vocal. The family reports that they reward him through both sums of money and other extrinsic rewards for "good grades," which they feel are As and Bs. Yumiko has serious consequences for misbehaving at home, which his mother attributes to his ability to self-monitor his behavior at home. Additionally, he wants to impress his friends, teachers, and family members.

Discussion

This case study produced recommendations for action. First of all, according to my findings and my review of literature, teacher feedback is a vital part in the self-regulation process for students. Teacher feedback, then, needs to be accessible to all students. The intermediate English learners in my classroom, whom Yumiko represents, would benefit from a simplified writing rubric that is based on the English language development standards. Assigning icons to the various traits would provide visual cuing and facilitate better communication with this population of students. Concurrently, self-advocacy on behalf of the student is also important. Students should be encouraged to ask questions and be allowed the freedom of asking for the support that they need from the teacher, whether it be more time to complete a task or a quieter place to work and concentrate. Allowing children to cultivate their strengths and present findings on a topic they enjoy and know a lot about, even if it is the ability of each *Pokémon* character, is another way to encourage self-esteem and self-advocacy.

SOURCE: Used with permission of Kim Allen.

❖ Case Study 2.2: Kari's Inquiry Into Students' Learning and Motivation

Voice of Kari, First-Grade Teacher

"Student learning" is such a broad issue that, upon considering my own thoughts on the topic, I find there are more questions than answers. I cherish the moments when I can tell a student has acquired new knowledge, but it is challenging to distinguish exactly how the learning occurred. I currently teach first grade at a Title I school with 96% English language learners. This is my third year at the site; however, for the previous 2 years I taught full-day kindergarten. Working with this population is a joy because the students are learning a plethora of language, academic, and social skills daily. However, the challenges abound, as most children come to school with little phonemic awareness, concept of print, or number sense. Despite this lack of an academic foundation, I am perpetually impressed by how much the kindergarten and first-grade students are able to learn so quickly.

I have come to realize that there are numerous factors influencing student learning, and it is impossible to fully understand how a student learns without a comprehensive understanding of these factors. I wonder: *How is student learning of phonemic awareness and phonics influenced by personal characteristics, social interactions, and environmental influences?* To answer this question, I created a research file for each student that I used to collect a variety of data at multiple times. I attached all research files to the same clipboard that was used for data collection over the 6-week observation period. The files were used to keep my data organized and to ensure that I was using multiple collection strategies throughout the observation timeline. Each file included a designated space to record and date the data related to several areas.

In order to effectively analyze the data, I constructed data tables to display the various types of data. I drew conclusions about how specific students were learning in response to phonemic awareness and phonics instruction at school and in their home environment. I will report my findings for one particular student, Lisa. Lisa's native language is Spanish, and she has difficulty with beginning literacy skills at school.

Findings: Motivation and Engagement

Reviewing the data collected during observations of Lisa's motivation and engagement in phonics and phonemic awareness learning activities during whole-group, small-group, and independent work situations reveals that she is not easily engaged in the learning and is motivated by external factors, such as teacher attention. Lisa's academic skills are significantly below grade level, and though she tries to engage in whole-group instruction, such as choral reading, blending games, and language play activities, it is difficult for her to be successful. She looks excited to be participating and mimics her peers' correct responses.

During small-group instruction in the regular classroom, Lisa is motivated to learn when the other students are at her same instructional level; however, when she is in a group with peers whose abilities surpass her own, she shuts down and completely disengages from the group by scooting back her chair, tearing up, and refusing to try.

Findings: Self-Efficacy

Lisa refuses to try challenging tasks and withdraws from activities she considers threatening. She exhibits a lack of self-efficacy and a sense of learned helplessness. Though Lisa is not performing at grade level, she possesses the requisite skills to engage in many of the activities she deems "too hard." During an informal discussion during one of her periods of upset, Lisa revealed, through sobs and sniffles, that "it is too hard and they are bothering me." It is not uncommon for her to attribute her own upset and inability to engage in a learning activity to other factors such as a stomach/headache or a troubling peer.

Findings: Home Environment

Lisa and her mother were anxiously awaiting our arrival when we visited her home. Their three-bedroom, two-bath home was neat, tidy, and adorned with family photos, figurines, and ornamentations. Lisa's mother speaks only Spanish, and using my best Spanish, we spent the first few minutes discussing the family and how Lisa interacts with those around her. Lisa lives with her mother and father, as well as her three older brothers and an older female family friend. As the youngest member of the family, Lisa receives much attention; however, her mom did point out that everyone is very busy and Lisa spends a large amount of time occupying herself with various activities around the house.

As we discussed the types of books Lisa likes to read at home, she went to the media cabinet and got her bag of Open Court decodables that I had sent home thus far this year. Ironically, the decodables are too difficult for Lisa to read independently, and her mom does not speak or read English well enough to practice them with her. She did tell me that every day she practices her letters and numbers with her mom and that sometimes they read books in Spanish together.

Discussion

The multiple sources of data reveal that Lisa enjoys learning to read; however, because she is experiencing difficulty with reading tasks and performing below most other students, her self-efficacy is low, which in turn inhibits the application of the knowledge and skills she does possess. Her observations and assessments reveal that without direct teacher assistance or peer support, it is extremely difficult for Lisa to engage in learning tasks. Nevertheless, Lisa is motivated to learn and happily contributes what she can to whole-group and small-group lessons. Continued positive reinforcement and scaffolding in the regular classroom and at home can provide Lisa the opportunity to enhance her learning and to become more confident in her reading abilities.

SOURCE: Used with permission of Kari Ambrose.

❖ **Reflecting on the Cases**

1. Describe how interviews or home visits with students' parents helped Kim and Kari understand more about the students, their background, and their motivation to learn.

2. Discuss how laws and policies influenced Kim and Kari's case studies related to their students.

3. Teachers sometimes take roles as ethnographers as in the two case studies featured above. Kim and Kari noted students' interactions with others, their learning styles, and their home environment. Discuss three reasons why collecting multiple types of data is important when trying to inquire about students, their learning styles, and their motivation to learn.

Activities for Further Development

1. Think about the three goals of American education described by Labaree (1997) at the beginning of the chapter. Which of these goals do you believe should be the focus of education and educational policy? Explain three reasons why.

2. Thinking about microsystems, how might parenting styles affect a child's success in school, interaction with peers, or other behaviors?

3. Take a look at the timeline and sequence of notable educational events described in this chapter. Describe two areas that you have direct or indirect experience with and how they have influenced your educational views.

4. Take another look at the timeline and sequence of notable educational events. Create a list of the policies that were created and implemented to make the curriculum more inclusive to all children and families regardless of their academic, language, ethnic, or socioeconomic background. Which initiative do you think had the greatest impact on our schools and policies today?

Additional Reading and Information

Turnbull, A., Turnbull, H., & Wehmeyer, M. L. (2010). *Exceptional lives: Special education in today's schools* (6th ed.). Upper Saddle River, NJ: Merrill/Prentice Hall. This book provides information on school-family collaborations. Voices of families from diverse cultures, languages, and backgrounds are featured.

The emTech Web site provides a variety of learning theories and examples: http://www.emtech.net/learning_theories.htm

National Center for Education Statistics outlines a history of federal education legislation in "Federal Programs for Education and Related Activities": http://nces.ed.gov/pubs2003/2003060d.pdf

Parent Teacher Education Connection/North Texas Partnership Program Modules for preservice teachers provide information and case studies related to learning more about partnerships with families and communities: www.tcet.unt.edu/fipse

The University of Minnesota College of Education and Human Development features a timeline of historical events in education: http://education.umn.edu/History/TimeLine/default.html

3

Meeting the Needs of All Children in the 21st Century

After reading this chapter, you should have a better understanding of:

- No Child Left Behind legislation and implications for children, families, and educators;
- enhancing education for students with special needs;
- strategies to promote children's well-being and health;
- recognizing abuse and neglect in children;
- obesity, nutrition, and exercise issues and initiatives;
- after-school programs and benefits; and
- sample partnership programs that target children's well-being and promote better health.

Table 3.1 Prior Knowledge and Beliefs Organizer

Describe what you believe are the most critical components to meet the educational needs of all students.	Discuss groups or types of students who are in the greatest need of educational interventions and/or partnerships.

Meeting the needs of educationally diverse students with special needs and those who are abused or neglected provides additional challenges for teachers and families. This chapter will focus on federal legislation, health education initiatives, teaching students with special needs, and the benefits of after-school programs. Use the information you enter in Table 3.1 to guide you as you read the information in this chapter.

The Implementation of No Child Left Behind

Enhancing Academic Achievement

No Child Left Behind (NCLB), a federal law in the United States, was signed by President George W. Bush in January 2002 to increase educational standards. It was enacted to provide more choices for families, to provide accountability standards for schools and districts, and to promote higher academic achievement in language arts, reading, and mathematics. NCLB provides specific performance goals that schools are required to implement. These goals are designed for all students regardless of their native language or socioeconomic background. The two most notable goals are (a) all students must attain high academic standards in reading, language arts, and mathematics and (b) all students must have access to highly qualified teachers. In addition, schools must ensure safety, a drug-free environment, and high school graduation for all students. Once NCLB was mandated in early 2002, colleges of education, state boards of education, and local school districts rushed to communicate these goals to faculty, administrators, teachers, students, parents, and the broader educational community. Proponents of NCLB state that teachers are more qualified and accountable. Those who are dissatisfied with NCLB state that standardized tests are biased and there is an inequitable distribution of resources.

In response to the five NCLB goals, states and the District of Columbia are required to produce a report card that publicizes students' academic progress at the school, district, and state levels. NCLB report cards are considered public information for communities, schools, and families. Therefore, children's education has changed at all levels, including the preschool and early childhood grades, to accommodate the mandated testing that begins in third grade.

The conditions cited within NCLB require that all states and the District of Columbia develop assessments in basic skills to be given to students at specified grade levels in order to receive federal funding. Each state must create grade-level standards and determine a way to assess those standards. Consequently, many of the "learn through play" curriculums in early childhood programs have been revised to include more academically focused skills and content. Table 3.2 outlines NCLB initiatives and implications for teachers, students, and families.

Table 3.2   No Child Left Behind Broad Initiatives and Implications

Initiative	Implications
Accountability for student achievement	Schools are rewarded for increased academic achievement and penalized for decreased achievement based on standardized test scores. This has resulted in a more competitive educational environment for schools, teachers, students, and families.

(Continued)

Table 3.2	(Continued)
Initiative	**Implications**
Highly qualified teachers	Teachers must fulfill all the state's credential requirements, obtain a bachelor's degree, and demonstrate subject matter expertise (that usually requires passing a standardized test related to their subject area). Many colleges of education have changed their credential requirements and prerequisite courses and procedures.
More choice for families	Parents are encouraged to play a role in educational decision making at all levels. They receive "report cards" related to the quality of their child's school. They may choose a different school if they are unhappy with their current school. Parents compare schools according to academic report card scores and other factors.

Links to Parent Involvement

Academic achievement is at the core of the NCLB initiatives to ensure children's overall well-being. Meeting this goal requires forming partnerships outside the school building, most notably partnerships with parents. It is important that teachers communicate with parents about their rights and about strategies that can enhance the educational potential of their children. This chapter will provide additional ways that schools and families can work together as partners. Strategies suggested by the U.S. Department of Education's Office of Communications and Outreach (2005) include the following:

1. *Read with children daily.* Daily reading instills a love for the activity and helps parents and children connect as they sit close together and share a story.

2. *Communicate with children.* Verbal communication and real interactions are important in building vocabulary and communication skills during the child's life. Communicating at home helps the child become more comfortable interacting at school.

3. *Decrease the viewing of media such as television and video games.* Studies have shown that children who watch too much television or spend too much time playing video games are more apt to be overweight, view violent events, and witness traditional stereotypes and gender roles. Most pediatricians recommend that parents limit their children's television and video games to no more than one hour each day.

4. *Create a successful environment to complete homework.* Parents can support children in their homework each day but should be careful not to give answers. A special place should be set up to complete homework with a variety of supplies that might be needed.

5. *Obtain a library card and check out books.* Public libraries are wonderful resources and help build a sense of community when families participate in special library programs or check out materials frequently. Children learn that literacy and literature are an integral part of their life.

6. *Use the computer to gain knowledge and skills in different subject areas.* Public libraries and community centers usually have computers available for public use. Learning how to use the computer appropriately will help children become more successful at school and complete many school projects.

7. *Encourage independence and responsibility.* Parents can be instrumental in providing opportunities for students to take initiative for daily tasks such as putting on their own clothes, pouring a bowl of cereal, and setting the dinner table each evening. These simple tasks instill confidence and pride.

8. *Listen to children.* Look at children when they are speaking and respond to them. This seems simple, but often adults do not actually listen and respond to children appropriately. When children talk, many adults will say "Yes" or "OK" without even knowing what the child said because they are too busy with daily obligations. Taking time to listen and look into a child's eyes will show respect and consideration for his or her thoughts and ideas.

Children With Special Needs

The Individuals with Disabilities Education Act

The **Individuals with Disabilities Education Act**, known as **IDEA**, was enacted in 1997 to ensure the education of all children from birth to age 21. It was created to provide a pathway for students who are academically diverse or in need of special education to get the best education possible. IDEA notes that special education includes specific instruction designed to meet the needs of students with disabilities. The act was revised in 2004 to create alignment between IDEA and NCLB. Table 3.3 shows an outline of the results of this legislation. Students can qualify for special education if they are identified as having one of the following special needs:

- Learning disability or disabilities
- Deafness or hearing impairments
- Blindness or visual impairments
- Speech and/or language impairments
- Orthopedic impairments
- Multiple handicaps
- Mental challenges
- Emotional impairments
- Autism
- Traumatic brain injury
- Other health impairments

Inclusion is a positive educational strategy where students with disabilities are educated with their nondisabled peers.

Table 3.3   IDEA Support and Instructional Plans

Type of Support	Age	Instructional Plans
Early intervention	Birth–age 3	An individualized family service plan (IFSP) is developed to meet the needs of the student and his or her family.
Early childhood and middle childhood special education	Ages 3–9 and 6–12	An individual education plan (IEP) is developed to meet the specialized learning needs of the student with assistance from family members, teachers, and other services.
Transition programs	Ages 14–21	An individualized transition plan is for students who are in need of transition services such as interagency interventions and counseling.

The Individual Education Plan

The individual education plan (IEP) was developed as the primary tool for educating students with special needs in general education classrooms with their peers. Vaughn, Bos, and Schumm (2007) describe **inclusion** as a positive educational strategy where students with disabilities are educated with their nondisabled peers but with special services available when necessary. Special education teachers and general education teachers work together to create the most appropriate instructional plan to ensure that these students are supported throughout their educational experiences. **Mainstreaming** involves placing special education students primarily in a special education classroom but having them interact with their peers in the general education classroom for a specific period of the day. Research (e.g., Fuchs & Fuchs, 1994; Zigmond, 2003) supports inclusion and mainstreaming as effective strategies, but not the only strategies, for both special education students and general education students. Vaughn et al. (2007) suggest that teachers and families should determine students' specific educational needs before determining the specific placement or services needed.

Student Study Team

Before an IEP is developed, most states require a student study team (SST), which is the first step in meeting the needs of students with disabilities or who need special education. The team usually involves parents, teachers, and a special education teacher who will meet and "study" each child in relation to his or her strengths and weaknesses. Special education services are determined based on the SST and IEP team. The IEP team must find that the child needs special education services, that the child meets the age requirements, and that the child meets at least one of the conditions such as autism, hearing impairment, health impairments, or learning disability.

It is important that preservice teachers experience SST and IEP meetings during their student teaching and fieldwork placements in order to meet the needs of special education students once they become classroom teachers. In the following two "Notes From the Classroom" sections, two preservice teachers, Sarah and Rochelle, discuss their experiences observing an SST meeting and an IEP meeting as part of their student teaching assignments.

Notes From the Classroom: Sarah's Report of a Student Study Team Meeting

Voice of Sarah, Sixth-Grade Teacher

I attended a student study team (SST) meeting in March. The meeting was held for a student who has had trouble with learning since kindergarten. It was interesting to see how many people become involved in an SST meeting and how the meetings are run. After the meeting was held, the SST leader informed me that this was not the first time this student has had an SST meeting and that it was more of a follow-up on how this student is now doing in the classroom.

Many people attended the SST meeting. Besides myself, the student's father, the student's teacher, the resource specialist and her assistant, the SST leader, and the school psychologist participated. The beginning of the meeting consisted of reviewing the student's file and what had happened at the last meeting. His current teacher did mention that the student has been improving in his math skills, but the teacher was concerned about how the pace of the math curriculum would be picking up quickly. Both the teacher and the father also voiced concerns about a lack of communication between school and home. The father said that his son tries to avoid doing homework and would rather be outside playing, which leads to many arguments between them. Other concerns that were addressed include that the student is just not motivated to learn, he needs to repeatedly be told what needs to be accomplished, he's not retaining his reading, and he tends to have low self-esteem. There were some positive aspects mentioned about the student as well, though. It is clear that the teacher does genuinely care about the student and would like to see him succeed. The father and teacher discussed things that he is interested in such as mechanics and road trips to try to provide a motivation for learning.

The team members then decided that they would develop an assessment plan for the student to track him and see how he is doing across all subjects. The team would also like to see the student get some help from a tutor to maybe help motivate him to do his homework. The team concluded by arranging a meeting with the father for a later date.

I thought that this meeting was extremely important for me to be a part of so I know how one of these meetings is run during a school year. I now understand how many people can get involved in one student's life just to help him or her succeed in school. It is amazing how much time and effort the teachers and other staff members put in to help students with special needs.

SOURCE: Used with permission of Sarah Fick.

Notes From the Classroom:
Rochelle's Report of an Individual Education Plan Meeting

Voice of Rochelle, Fifth-Grade Teacher

It is a true statement that every child has specific educational needs that must be met. For example, some children are auditory learners, and some are visual learners. Some children require extra assistance with language acquisition, while some need help with just overall comprehension. However, some students' needs are such that outside intervention is essential for them to receive an equitable education. When this occurs, the teacher should initiate an individual education plan (IEP). An IEP is a program specifically formatted to set goals for a student who has already qualified for special education services. This plan is designed by the teacher and supported by a team of specialists. It is also a collaborative effort with the student's parents.

The IEP meeting that I observed was for a 10-year-old boy in fifth grade. He is of Hispanic descent with Spanish as his primary language and has been receiving special education services since second grade. The people who attended were his parents, the student, the special education teacher, the principal, and a translator. If the student for whom an IEP is being initiated is mainstreamed or if the parent prefers, a general education teacher of the same grade level as the student may also attend. Depending on the other services provided to the student, additional people might need to attend as well. These people might include a speech pathologist, an adapted physical education teacher, a physical or occupational therapist, a representative from the regional center, and/or a social worker. In the following month, this student will have a triennial IEP, which is held every 3 years. Before this meeting, the school psychologist will administer a series of tests to make sure the student still qualifies for special education and to determine if his or her qualifying disability has not changed. Such testing also provides comprehensive data about the student's ability level as well as his or her strengths and weaknesses. If it is a triennial IEP meeting, the psychologist must also attend to discuss his or her data.

At this IEP meeting, the first order of business was to discuss the child's disability at the moment, along with any strengths and interests. Like a student study team (SST), this requires some observation. However, an SST is the beginning of establishing a need for intervention. For an IEP, the teacher must look at the past reporting to determine where a student is now. This child's disability is such that he benefits more from small-group instruction than from whole-class instruction. During whole-class instruction he disrupts other students and has a difficult time maintaining focus. He can handle only one- or two-step instructions and retain only content that is given in very small doses. His motor skills are fine and he is able to print legibly within the lines of the paper, but he cannot write in cursive. He is very outgoing and seems happy. Although he does well in small groups, he prefers to play by himself or in the company of a teacher.

The next topic was his academic performance. He is at the beginning stages of English language fluency. He can decode most one-syllable words, most short vowel words, and some familiar sight words. He can read independently at a beginning first-grade level and comprehends well. He knows basic addition and subtraction facts and some multiplication facts. He is currently working on solving multidigit addition and subtraction problems.

After assessing where he is, both behaviorally and academically, the meeting turned into a goal-setting session. This student's goals were determined based on his areas of need. Next baseline goals were established in addition to measurable annual goals and three short-term objectives. Also determined were proposed assistive technology and supplementary aids needed to obtain the goals. This student now has six goals to work on including reading (word analysis and literary response), communications (English language development), math, writing, and staying on task.

At the conclusion of the meeting, all participants signed the plan, and the parents signed a consent form allowing the instructional goals and changes to take place. The education of this child, along with that of every child, is not the sole responsibility of the teacher. It is a collaborative effort that requires a commitment from a team of people committed to one overarching goal: to help a child succeed!

SOURCE: Used with permission of Rochelle Cantu Wolf.

Teaching Gifted and Talented Children

Children who are gifted or talented are also considered for special education services and programs. However, there are no specific legislative guidelines that require states or school districts to offer services to **gifted and talented students** like there are for students with disabilities (e.g., IDEA provisions). Giftedness has traditionally been measured by assessing children's scores on intelligence tests (i.e., IQ tests) only. IQ tests usually measure language and mathematics achievement and intelligence but not necessarily areas such as art, music, or science. Therefore, many school districts consider a variety of factors, including IQ tests, annual standardized test scores, and teacher input. Children who are classified as gifted demonstrate diverse behavior patterns and learning preferences but cannot be placed within a specific "mold." In addition, many states classify some students as gifted and other students as talented. Lewis and Doorlag (1995) found that students who are classified as gifted demonstrate above-average intellectual ability and are usually high academic achievers. On the other hand, talented students demonstrate exceptional ability in areas such as drama, art, music, or leadership. The National Association for Gifted Children (NAGC) states on its Web site that a gifted child shows or has the potential to show exceptional levels of performance in one or more areas. This can include creative thinking or leadership abilities or specific talents related to subject areas (e.g., science, math, music). About 5% of the U.S. population is classified as gifted and/or talented. The following "Notes From the Classroom" section comes from a fourth- and fifth-grade teacher, Lynne, who worked with a parent to communicate her assessment strategies related to a gifted and talented student.

Notes From the Classroom:
Lynne's Reflections on Teaching Gifted Students

Voice of Lynne, Fourth- and Fifth-Grade Teacher

Every year my gifted and talented students read *The Green Book* by Jill Paton Walsh (1986). This book is wonderful because my students and I can integrate many concepts and skills related to reading, writing, science, social studies, and art. After we read the book and participate in a variety of activities related to developing a new colony, government, and jobs portrayed in the book, I have my students design a planet of their own. As part of the task of creating their own planet, my students elaborate on the details that describe the people who live there, the organization of the government, community activities, and other components. Collaboratively, the students work together to create a rubric to use as an assessment tool in which to evaluate this product. The final product will be teacher-, peer-, and self-evaluated using the class-created rubric. In addition, the students are encouraged to create the planet with materials from their homes, from their neighborhood, or within the classroom. They are asked not to purchase items at a store to complete their project. Therefore, the project is based on creative thinking and performance rather than the amount of resources.

During one particular year, after the projects were completed and graded, a father of one of my students asked why his son received a grade of C on the assignment when he had worked on the project for 8 hours! His question was a valid one as he had witnessed his son spending so much time on this project. He assumed that since his son was placed in the gifted and talented program at our school, it was a "given" that all projects/work would be met with outstanding success. I invited the father to visit my classroom and take a look at the other projects that my students had completed. I explained to this child's parent that assessing a child's work is the most difficult aspect of my job. It is a task that every teacher struggles with on a daily basis and does not take lightly. I took this opportunity to give out another copy of our rubric assessment so that he could use it as he viewed the other children's planets. By doing this, he could see how they demonstrated exceptional performance in creating and describing their planets. The father took a look at the projects, discussed the components with his son, and was satisfied that although his son did spend a great deal of time on his project, he demonstrated not exceptional performance but average performance. The father thanked me for everything that I was doing to instill excellence within his child and told me that he would never question my assessment strategies and that he deeply appreciated my taking the time to explain how I evaluated his child's achievement.

SOURCE: Used with permission of Lynne Thomas.

> ### Enhancing Learning for Students With Special Needs: Gifted Students
>
> - Communicate regularly with parents to discuss the meaning of "giftedness" where students demonstrate high performance in one or more areas such as intelligence, creativity, leadership abilities, or performing or visual arts.
> - Remind parents that being gifted does not always translate to "straight As" on a report card.
> - Provide differentiated instruction for gifted students that will enhance their strengths, meet their needs, and challenge them.
> - Work with students and their families to design differentiated instruction activities when applicable.

Differentiated instruction involves providing equitable opportunities for all students. This includes modifying the time allotted for instructional activities such as writing or test taking, altering the activities themselves, or finding other ways to meet the needs of students. Providing differentiated instruction for all students—those who are gifted and talented, those with special learning needs, and those with disabilities, as well as those classified as "average" or "on grade level"—will provide a more inclusive instructional program and enhance learning for all.

Children's Well-Being

The next section will focus on the overall health of children, strategies to improve it, and ways to meet the needs of educationally diverse children. These factors are considered crucial to enhancing academic achievement of all children.

The United Nations Children's Fund (2007) evaluated the quality of children's lives in 21 economically advanced countries. The evaluation data were based on 40 indicators that included the quality of family life, time spent with parents, the number of children living in poverty, vaccination rates, obesity, alcohol abuse, teenage pregnancy, and children's self-concept. Surprisingly, the United States and the United Kingdom ranked last (20th and 21st overall, respectively). The Netherlands and Sweden ranked highest. The most interesting finding in this study is that wealth did not correlate to children's happiness.

It is estimated that about 25% of children in the United States live in poverty and about 19% of children do not have health insurance (Northwest Education Collaboration, 2007). These numbers are even higher in areas of Mississippi and Louisiana where Hurricane Katrina adversely affected families in 2005. The Northwest Education Collaboration in Alaska has outlined specific ways to develop partnerships that provide better education and access to health and family services. The group recommends that a partnership be developed that takes into account (a) the needs of the community, (b) the number and diversity of children and families, and (c) the scope of the services available in the area. Communities and schools must therefore learn more about the families within communities before school-family-community partnerships can be developed effectively.

Abused and Neglected Children

Child abuse is a broad term used to describe acts of power or control over children that result in some form of maltreatment. The Child Abuse Prevention and Treatment Act defines abuse as an act or a failure to act by a parent or caregiver that results in any physical or emotional harm, sexual abuse, exploitation, or death. In addition, the act includes *any* act that presents a risk of serious harm as one that is classified as abusive or neglectful. Abuse is usually categorized as sexual, physical, or emotional, according to Tower (1999). **Neglect** includes failing to meet a child's needs in a way that leads to harm or emotional instability. It is the teacher's responsibility to report any suspected child abuse or neglect to his or her school administrators. Many times teachers feel uncomfortable reporting such cases because they do not feel they have enough evidence that such abuse or neglect is taking place. I remember the first year that I taught second graders in a small rural school in North Carolina. One morning, a girl came to school very happy but with the imprint of a flyswatter on her face. As a first-year teacher, I did not know what to do but decided it was best that my principal be given the information related to the girl's injury. This resulted in a social services worker talking with her parents about the marks on her face. It turned out that her mother had lost her temper and hit her out of anger (she happened to be holding a flyswatter at the time). Therefore, the social services worker helped the family locate counseling services. This child's parents were very appreciative and cooperative. However, all parents may not accept social services help in the same manner. In addition, it is difficult for any teacher to report abuse within families because teachers respect the families of all students. It should be noted, therefore, that neglect and abuse take place in all schools within the United States and with all types of students, regardless of their ethnicity, culture, language, or socioeconomic background.

The **Child Abuse Prevention and Treatment Act** (CAPTA) was enacted in 1974 and amended in 2003 as the Keeping Children and Families Safe Act. It provides federal money for initiatives aimed at preventing, assessing, prosecuting, and treating individuals in need. Public agencies can apply for grants and receive funding to enhance their programs related to these areas. CAPTA provides a definition of sexual abuse and other special cases when parents are neglectful or fail to provide medical treatment. However, it falls short of defining other types of neglect, physical abuse, or emotional abuse. CAPTA recommends that each state within the United States provide its own specific definitions of abuse and neglect in addition to civil and criminal implications.

Childhelp is a nonprofit organization founded by two women, Sara O'Meara and Yvonne Fedderson, for the purpose of aiding victims of child abuse and neglect, preventing child abuse, and providing intervention and treatment. The organization hosts a National Child Abuse Hotline that operates 24 hours a day, 7 days a week. The number is 1-800-4-A-CHILD and can be called by anyone within the United States, Canada, the U.S. Virgin Islands, Puerto Rico, or Guam. The *New York Times* publishes a Web site called "About.com" that features a variety of information and statistics related to child abuse and neglect. Table 3.4 outlines facts and statistics featured on this site.

Table 3.4	National Child Abuse Statistics

- In 2002, 2.6 million reports were filed on behalf of 4.5 million children.
- Each week, states receive about 50,000 reports of child abuse.
- About 67% of the cases that were reported resulted in an investigation of child abuse.
- About 896,000 children are abused each year, which is 2,450 children each day!
- Of the cases reported, about 60% involved neglect, 20% related to physical abuse, 10% related to sexual abuse, and 7% involved emotional abuse.
- About 14 children die each day as a result of abuse or neglect.
- Boys and girls are equally susceptible to being abused or neglected.
- All ethnicities are equally susceptible to being abused or neglected. In 2002, 54% of abused children were White, 26% were African American, 11% were Hispanic, 2% were Alaska Native, and 1% were Asian or Pacific Islander.
- Children of all ages are susceptible to abuse and neglect, although the youngest children are most vulnerable to abuse-related deaths.

SOURCE: Adapted from Iannelli (2008).

Characteristics of Abused and Neglected Children

Children display multiple characteristics related to their personality each day they enter the classroom. However, some characteristics that are portrayed over time may provide information about whether or not a child is being neglected or abused. In addition, abuse and neglect happen in many different families regardless of religion, socioeconomic background, or ethnicity. Physical abuse usually involves burning, kicking, hitting, or punching. Emotional abuse is more difficult to detect because it involves verbal, psychological, or other mental mistreatment. Emotional abuse usually occurs when a parent or a caregiver blames the child for something, belittles him or her, or creates fear in him or her. Sexual abuse happens when an adult caretaker or family member takes advantage of the child in a sexual way in the form of sexual stimulation, penetration, or another violation. Common characteristics of neglect involve depriving a child of his or her basic needs such as food, clothing, shelter, care, or supervision. With so many descriptions and so much information, it is difficult for a teacher to determine what should be done and when. Table 3.5 provides information for teachers about what to do and what not to do when investigating and reporting suspected child abuse or neglect.

Table 3.5	The Do's and Don'ts of Dealing With Child Abuse and Neglect

What to do:

- Know your district and school policies related to reporting child abuse and neglect.
- Be observant of the children in your classroom.
- Report suspected abuse or neglect to your administrator.
- Report as many facts as possible and ask the child to explain what happened in his or her own words (if appropriate and if the abuse is visible).
- Be knowledgeable about the various types of abuse and neglect.
- Contact your local child welfare agency to obtain more information about abuse and neglect.

What not to do:

- Contact the parent directly.
- Accuse the parent or another family member.
- Specify that the child has been abused or neglected. Instead, state that you *suspect* abuse or neglect based on specific facts.
- Wait to support the situation. Teachers are required by law to report suspected abuse as soon as possible.

Nutrition and Children's Well-Being

Another area that relates to a child's well-being involves healthy nutrition at home, at school, and in the community. Nutrition is a science that studies eating habits, health, and the relationship between the two. One of the biggest challenges that schools, families, and communities face is the growing number of children who demonstrate unhealthy eating habits—because of limited access to healthy foods, economics, culture, or lifestyle. As indicated on the historical timeline in Chapter 2, nutrition has been at the forefront of educational issues over the past century.

A History of Nutrition in Schools

The school lunch program that we know today in the United States was in full swing by the 1970s and has a history of more than 100 years. School meal programs are enacted to provide low-cost or free lunches for children in public and nonprofit private schools and in residential child care organizations. Any child who cannot afford to pay for lunch may receive a lunch at no cost or a reduced cost. The free and reduced-price lunch programs were patterned after many European programs when President Harry Truman signed the National School Lunch Act in 1946. The Child Nutrition Act was created 22 years later and specified that states should meet the nutritional needs of children more effectively. Unfortunately, most children from low-income communities and urban areas did not attend schools that had the facilities to provide free lunch or free breakfast for them.

The federal government in the United States has worked with schools and communities to develop nutritious meals for children who may otherwise come to school hungry (see U.S. Department of Agriculture, 2009). Free lunch and breakfast programs were developed so that children would be alert and have energy while learning in school. Researchers (e.g., Meyers, Sampson, Weitzman, Rogers, & Kayne, 1989) have found that participation in a school breakfast program contributes to higher achievement test scores, higher attendance, and fewer children marked tardy. A nutritional study in the late 1960s included 50 malnourished children during a 1- to 3-year period. These children, ages 2 to 9, were found to have increased their IQ by an average of 18 points after being provided nutritional meals. Nourished children who were part of a control group did not show changes. Nevertheless, schools are continually challenged to determine wide-scale culturally relevant food choices for students based on beliefs and cultural preferences. And although some latitude has been given to school districts to plan menus that are aligned culturally with the population of students that they serve, better policies are needed in this area.

Childhood Nutrition and Obesity

Childhood obesity and diabetes are on the rise, and the federal government, state governments, community groups, and local schools are taking notice. Most adult eating habits are established early, and that means any health behavior interventions should take place before students enter sixth grade (Kelder, Perry, Klepp, & Lytle, 1994). According to Sears, Sears, Sears, and Sears (2006), children are consuming an inordinate amount of junk food, with the following/results:

1. Diabetes is increasing in children. Diabetes leads to heart disease, stroke, blindness, kidney failure, and other complications.

2. American children are getting sick more often. Doctors are reporting increasingly more cases of high blood sugar and high cholesterol levels in young children. This can lead to cardiovascular disease and fatty deposits in the coronary arteries.

3. About 10% of school-aged children are labeled with having attention deficit disorder (ADD) or other types of learning challenges.

4. American children are becoming more obese. Excess weight and obesity are the most pressing public-health concerns, according to the surgeon general in the United States. Being overweight carries similar risks as smoking cigarettes. Overweight children have difficulty playing sports, fitting in their chairs at school, and getting through a school day without being bullied or ostracized by their peers.

The National Center for Health Statistics reported that 19% of children were categorized as overweight in 2003–2004. About 16% of children were obese in 2002. The Centers for Disease Control and Prevention in the United States defines obese children as those with a body-mass index (BMI) in the 95th percentile or higher. Children are overweight if their BMI falls between the 85th and 94th percentile, and children who are overweight are usually at risk for obesity. Obesity and overweight issues have been addressed in other countries as well. About 20% to 25% of children and youth in Australia are overweight or obese (Ward, 2003). In Japan, about 8% of children were obese (or at risk for obesity) in 2004 compared with 6% in 1980 (Mainichi Daily News, 2006). Even more alarming is the fact that the highest rates of obesity occur in groups from lower socioeconomic backgrounds (Drewnowski & Darmon, 2005). In the United States, foods that are processed and higher in saturated fats are more convenient and less expensive for most families.

Responsibility and Nutrition

When looking at the history of nutrition, educators and families often wonder whose responsibility it is to enhance nutrition and health for children. Is it the responsibility of the parents? Is it the responsibility of the community? Is it the responsibility of the school? Or is it a shared responsibility among families, schools, and the community? Nutrition seems to be a community issue as well as one that schools and families should participate in and take action to support. In addition, if families, schools, and communities work together to address nutrition and exercise, the net result will be greater than if each group works separately. The next section includes the current status of nutrition and physical education activities in schools within the United States.

The new *MyPyramid* (see Figure 3.1). was unveiled in 2005 to provide families and educators with information and guidelines related to healthy eating. (see Figure 3.1). It includes six different colors. The widest band is orange and represents grains. Children and adults should eat three servings of whole grains each day. Green is the next widest band and includes all the vegetables. Families should eat about 2.5 cups of vegetables each day with most servings taken from green and yellow vegetables. The blue band includes dairy products, about 3 daily cups of which help build strong bones and teeth. The red band represents fruits, about 2 cups of which are advisable each day. The purple band represents meat, poultry, fish, beans, nuts, and seeds. These foods are protein-rich for cell maintenance, and one's diet should include about 5 to 6 ounces of purple band foods each day. The very thin yellow band includes oils and fats. Oils such as olive oil and canola oil are beneficial when consumed in small amounts. Other fatty oils such as butter and lard have been linked to heart disease. It is important for schools, the community, and families to work together to ensure healthy eating for all children and adults.

The Alliance for a Healthier Generation is a collaborative partnership among the Coca-Cola Company, Pepsi, and Cadbury Schweppes along with the American Heart Association and the William J. Clinton Foundation. This alliance has been instrumental in developing new school beverage guidelines in the United States. Students in elementary and middle schools now have a broader range of nutritious beverage choices such as low-fat milk, bottled water, and 100% fruit juice. Diet sodas, sports drinks, and low-calorie teas are available at high schools in addition to the beverages offered at elementary and middle schools. The alliance is a partnership aimed at bringing parents, teachers, government, health professionals, corporations, and private foundations together to educate healthy children. This should help reduce the number of overweight children and encourage healthier eating. This alliance and the possibility of more culturally relevant food choices are

Figure 3.1 MyPyramid

SOURCE: Public domain. Reprinted from U.S. Department of Agriculture, Center for Nutrition Policy and Promotion (2006).

two promising initiatives to improve nutrition in schools. School districts should consider that many children are obese and at risk for diabetes when planning a variety of nutritional, kid-friendly, and culturally relevant foods. The Child Nutrition and WIC Reauthorization Act of 2004 provides funding and extends the availability of meals for low-income children in the United States.

In addition to school nutritional partnership programs, some organizations work together to encourage healthier eating at home. This can be challenging because fruits and vegetables are more expensive than processed foods and therefore families from lower socioeconomic backgrounds have more difficulties obtaining these. Project GLEAN (Gaining Leverage and Empowerment through Adequate Nutrition) delivers surplus produce and bread to school cafeterias where it is distributed to students and their families (Moya & Hampl, 2003). Volunteers and students work together each week to organize the food according to the number of students at the school. Many other programs seek to empower the educational community to make better decisions through professional development for teachers and staff, parent education events, community contributions, and collaborative activities to bring multiple partners together.

The California Department of Health Services (2007b) created a program, *Champions for Change.* One of its campaigns involves real moms from different ethnic groups who discuss how they have incorporated more fruits, vegetables, and physical exercise into their children's busy schedules. Because mothers play a key role in the nutritional habits of their children, they provide tips and suggestions for incorporating healthier eating and lifestyles. The California Department of Health Services created a Network for a Healthy California that includes more than 200 organizations within the state to promote more active lifestyles and more fruits and vegetables with meals and snacks, with the overall goal of preventing obesity. The moms in the advertisements represent various communities and ethnic groups. One mother describes her experience as a part of the healthy eating project.

The Value of Family Meals

Partnerships among family, school, and the community can enhance the nutritional choices of children and youth. Neumark-Sztainer (2006) found that adolescents have higher risks of poor nutritional intake and unhealthy weight control behaviors than younger children. Families play an important role in assisting adolescents with healthy food choices. Sitting down together for dinner and eating a healthy meal is a very simple step to promote healthier living.

Teachers and schools can communicate with families and children about the importance of family meals on school Web sites, in newsletters, or in homework assignments. Family meals can be at breakfast, dinner, or even snack time if there is no other time for meals.

Voice of a Mother

Being a Champion for Change is a big honor for my family and me. I know how hard it can be to make health a priority. However, by being a role model for my children, I am able to show them how eating fruit and vegetables and participating in physical activity are so important. I want other moms to know that moms like me are making healthy changes, and they can too. (For more information, visit the network Web site at www.cachampionsforchange.net)

Physical Education

There is a natural link between physical education and mental and emotional health. In fact, organized physical activity results in positive effects on academic achievement, concentration, and disruptive behavior. However, the National Association for Sport and Physical Education and the American Heart Association (2006) found that only 8% of elementary schools in the United States offer physical education programs. In high schools, only 5.8% of schools offer daily physical education. Compare this information to the country of China, whose schools provide between 30 and 60 minutes of physical education each day. Many schools have eliminated physical education programs based on budget cuts and other challenges. This issue is magnified because many teachers in the United States are under stress to increase reading and mathematics achievement scores and do not have time to add organized physical education activities to their instructional planning.

Experts have found that physical education at home is not much better than that at school. Richard Louv (2005), in his book *Last Child in the Woods,* argues that children are suffering from "nature-deficit disorder." He states that our culture is becoming more technological and does not include nature and other outdoor activities. He found that many communities make basketball hoops and sidewalk chalk drawings illegal because they do not appeal to some people in the community. In addition, many families work long hours and do not allow children to play outside alone.

It is therefore necessary for teachers, schools, and school districts to work together to bridge partnerships with families and the local community to encourage more physical activity for the overall health of children. This issue is a shared responsibility because there are community groups, senior citizens, and parent volunteers who would be interested in lending a hand to provide more physical education. In addition to traditional kickball and jump rope activities, students can enjoy dance, yoga, and the martial arts as part of a balanced physical education program. Teachers can work with community businesses to provide pedometers for students to clip on their clothing so that families can count the number of steps taken each day. The ultimate goal for all healthy individuals is to walk 10,000 steps. Keeping track of steps can be integrated into the health, physical education, math, and science curriculum at school.

Community members and families can be valuable resources and partners in promoting physical fitness and health education. A local acting group in Richmond, Virginia, formed a partnership with an elementary school to provide traditional and modern dance for its students. In another school, parents volunteered their time at the beginning of the school day, during school, or after school to lead yoga classes, dance classes, volleyball clubs, and other activities. Some communities encourage families to walk or ride bikes to school safely and have even created walking and biking trails. Given these examples, teachers, families, and communities can be true partners in promoting healthy lifestyles and activities. Richard Simmons, the famous fitness expert, is leading a campaign in Washington, DC, to make physical education a core subject. On Simmons's Web site, he quotes the third president of the United States, Thomas Jefferson, who said,

"A child not physically fit cannot learn" (Simmons, 2007). This is still true today as we are looking at healthy nutrition and physical activity as key factors that promote learning and the overall well-being of children.

In addition to the lack of structured physical education activities, about 40% of elementary schools have cut out recess (O'Shea, 2005). Pellegrini (2005) has studied students' interaction on the playground for more than 25 years and found that recess can improve children's ability to pay attention in class and can promote physically active children who interact socially with their peers. He states that recess is an obvious curriculum area to delete because students do not usually have a voice or the power to advocate their preferences. He recommends that families and students communicate with schools and express their needs and opinions if recess is decreased or cut out of the curriculum. One U.S.-led effort, *Rescuing Recess,* aims at increasing the number of minutes that children are physically active during school. This is a program sponsored by the National Parent Teacher Association, the Centers for Disease Control and Prevention, the Cartoon Network, and other expert groups to encourage schools to value recess as an important part of children's learning and development.

Children have multiple opportunities for play and development. Teachers can benefit by inquiring into children's interests and activities outside of school with their friends and families.

SOURCE: Used with permission of Lisa Renee Baker.

Children engaging in physical activity at the beach.

After-School Programs

After-school programs are one way to build social capital as groups of students of multiple ages work interactively with adults who care for them after school. These programs often enhance and enrich physical education as well as the arts and other subject areas. Many after-school programs are held at the school site or at a community center where tutoring is provided to meet the demands of the formal school curriculum. These programs are becoming widespread due to the number of parents working outside the home. Lumsden (2003) reports that many children still do not partake in after-school programs and that there are 7 million to 15 million children who leave school and enter an empty home without adult supervision and guidance. After-school programs are becoming more popular because they provide a safe environment for children and they can address emotional security issues. In addition, after-school programs can increase learning opportunities for children (McComb & Scott-Little, 2003). McComb and Scott-Little found that students who attend after-school programs score higher on standardized tests in both mathematics and reading. In addition, many students in after-school programs demonstrate more positive attitudes toward school. Lumsden (2003) reports that these children also have better grades, stronger work habits, positive emotional adjustments, and good peer relations.

The David and Lucile Packard Foundation (2002) published a newsletter, *The Future of Children,* and indicated that helping families access quality child care and after-school programs was one of the three most important strategies that would benefit children. (The other two strategies included helping families achieve an adequate standard of living and helping families provide stable and supportive homes.) Providing quality after-school environments and child care programs enables students' parents to work outside the home while enhancing their children's development and overall well-being. The Packard Foundation reported that low-income children in particular can benefit from positive experiences in after-school programs and advocated the creation of more high-quality child care options in low socioeconomic areas. Providing more quality child care opportunities would certainly increase the social capacity and would be ideal for schools, families, and the community to work together to extend educational opportunities outside the walls of the traditional classroom. These high-quality interactive after-school programs will be most successful when they are developed with collaborative goals and activities in mind.

> ### The Value of Partnerships to Make Healthy Choices
>
> Stelzer (2005) suggests that promoting a sense of healthy living through good nutrition and physical activity is a responsibility of multiple partners including the family, school, and community. Children's attitudes and actions toward a healthy lifestyle can still be modified, and it is with the help of such partnerships among the family, school, and community that it can be accomplished.

Vadeboncoeur (2006) conducted an extensive literature review related to learning out-of-school contexts. She indicated that increased funding for after-school programs was motivated by the desire to improve student achievement, to keep students safe after school, and to offer opportunities to expand students' knowledge of subject areas often neglected in school such as the arts and sciences. Therefore, learning in most out-of-school programs is, in fact, connected to both the formal school curriculum and the students' home life. Successful after-school programs provide children opportunities to try out activities related to physical education, science, history, and service learning (Alexander, 2000). Working together, families can provide information to schools about their children's strengths and interests, the community can offer services and resources, and educators can provide quality after-school care and programs.

Chapter Summary

The No Child Left Behind legislation has resulted in changes in practices for many children, families, and educators. NCLB provides specific information about enhancing the achievement of students, links to parent involvement, and meeting the needs of special education students. The individual education plan was developed as the primary tool for educating students with special needs in general education classrooms with their peers. Inclusion is a positive educational strategy where students with disabilities are educated with their nondisabled peers, while making special services available when necessary. Children's overall well-being and health are influenced by a variety of factors including proper nutrition, exercise, and positive programs provided by schools. Their well-being can be negatively affected by abuse, neglect, obesity, and other factors. It is important for teachers and families to form partnerships with families and the community to assess factors that may promote or inhibit learning and to be proactive in finding solutions.

CASE STUDIES

This chapter's first case study demonstrates how communities, schools, and families work together to promote children's overall well-being. This partnership example relates to a nutritional education program called *Harvest of the Month.* The second case study relates to a teacher who formed a partnership with a child with special needs and his family to enhance his education and well-being. Both of these case studies will help provide multiple perspectives related to healthy food choices, communication, and overall well-being.

❖ Case Study 3.1: Harvest of the Month Program

This case study is adapted from information from the California Department of Health Services (2007a) and a study by Yee (2007). The purpose of the Harvest of the Month program is to empower students to want to eat a variety of fruits and vegetables and engage in physical activities. The program is present in many schools throughout California where the greatest impact can be integrated into classrooms, school cafeterias, and students' homes and the community.

The program is set up to deliver one fruit or vegetable of a different color to participating schools each month. For example, in October, pears, winter squash, or pumpkins are offered. A newsletter for teachers is available each month and provides information about the benefits of each vegetable or fruit, connections to content standards, classroom cooking suggestions, and various activities that will motivate children to try the foods. There is a newsletter for families written in English and Spanish that promotes healthy eating at home. The program builds excitement and anticipation each month. Some schools choose to expand the program by growing their own food in a school garden. The program is set up to provide access for all families by featuring California-grown vegetables that are in season and therefore less expensive to acquire.

Voice of Lindsay Yee, Fourth-Grade Teacher

Our school participates in the "Harvest of the Month" program sponsored by the Nutrition Network [part of the Network for a Healthy California]. Each month students are given a fruit or vegetable to try. A bilingual newsletter is sent home with information about the featured produce and suggested recipes to try at home. Sometimes the fruit or vegetable can be served raw at school and others have to be prepared and cooked at home. Students look forward to the harvest each month . . . they have never heard of or seen [many of the fruits and vegetables] before. Participating in this program has opened their mind to trying new fruits and vegetables.

There are several benefits that I have seen as a result of implementing this program in my classroom. First, my students are making better choices when it comes to eating. I encourage them to bring a healthy snack at recess and many of them are taking two fruits or vegetables that they are allowed to take as part of their free lunch. As a class, we have transferred this healthy eating into our holiday festivities. Students are encouraged to bring anything healthy that is related to the colors of the particular holiday. For example, students brought in strawberries, watermelon, and sugar-free cherry Jell-O for Valentine's Day. For our St. Patrick's Day celebration, we enjoyed cucumbers, pickles, green grapes, and milk with green food coloring. Furthermore, in combination of inquiry on medicine and disease in our Language Arts Program and the importance and benefits of healthy eating with Harvest of the Month, my students came up with the idea of making other students at our school aware of how important it is to eat fruits and vegetables. As a result, they came up with the idea of starting a school garden. They wrote a grant and were awarded second prize. They started planting their garden in starter planters before school let out and will continue their project when school resumes in the fall. Another benefit to the program is that it gave a few parents an opportunity to get involved by preparing the fruit or vegetable of the month for the class.

To encourage parents to get more involved next year, I am going to ask for more of them to help in the preparation of the food rather than doing most of it myself. In addition, I am going to set a time aside each month and make it a family event at the end of the school day. Parents will be able to come in and participate in the nutrition lesson with their child and have the opportunity to try the featured fruit or vegetable too. Health education is important for the parents as well. They are the ones that are usually preparing the meals, so teaching them ways to incorporate fruits and vegetables into their diet will empower them. (Yee, 2007, pp. 1–2)

Voices of Students

"Jorge"

Harvest of the Month is fun because it's always a surprise. We never know which fruit or vegetable we are going to get. . . . After I tried bok choy in class, I asked my mom to buy it at the store, and now she cooks it at home. (p. 6)

"Vanessa"

The fruits and vegetables are tasty. Some taste good and some don't, but at least I got to try them. Before I didn't eat as many fruits and vegetables, but now I do. (p. 6)

Voices of Parents

"Mrs. Ponder"

My daughter is more willing to try new fruits and vegetables at home since she tries them at school. (p. 7)

"Mrs. Gonzalez"

I think Harvest of the Month is great. Students get to try new and different types of fruits and vegetables. The kids are willing to try fruits and vegetables that they never ever wanted to try before because it is a classroom activity. It is making them more open-minded. I volunteered to take the spaghetti squash home and cook it. I had never tried it myself either, but I just followed the recipe the school gave me and it was super easy. Little kindergarteners who were hesitant at first asked for seconds. (p. 8)

SOURCE: Used with permission of Lindsay Yee.

❖ Case Study 3.2: Teacher-Family Partnership for Success

This case study is adapted from Valerie Robbins's (2007) study about a partnership among a parent, teacher, and child. She believes that this type of partnership is one that is needed from the beginning of the school year to ensure a positive educational experience for all involved.

Voice of Valerie Robbins, Second-Grade Teacher

I have a student who suffers from selective mutism. According to the *Diagnostic and Statistical Manual of Mental Disorders* (American Psychiatric Association, 2000), selective mutism is a disorder of childhood that is characterized by the persistent lack of speech in at least one social situation, despite the ability to speak in other situations. The onset usually occurs before a child is 5 years old but is usually first noticed when the child enters school. The student in my class is 7 years old and was born in the United States, but his parents are from India. Hindi is the language that is spoken at home.

This child was diagnosed with selective mutism in kindergarten at his first school. According to his files, he was under the care of a psychiatrist. He was in the speech program but was "exited" in first grade at yet another school because supposedly the selective mutism does not interfere with his educational development (his ability to function in the classroom environment). I disagree with this statement. He is not performing in my class at grade level. I think he is capable, but he displays anxious behaviors. Because of this barrier, I decided to make home visits to this child to hopefully curb his anxiety and help him feel more comfortable with me so that maybe he would be able to talk to me at school. My intent during the home visits was not only to build a rapport with the child but also to gain the trust of his parents. During each home visit I made observations and tried to answer the following questions:

- Will a home visit help a child suffering from selective mutism feel comfortable enough with the teacher to speak to her in the home environment?

- If the child speaks to the teacher in the home environment, will he be able to talk to the teacher in the school environment (stimulus fading)?

While at the home I did not take notes in order for the visit to seem informal and casual. When I arrived the whole family was there. The mother greeted me at the door holding her 2-year-old daughter. The father was upstairs working, and the two sons, my student who is 7 and his 5-year-old brother who is in kindergarten at our school, greeted me. The mother told my student, "Come and sit by Mrs. Robbins." He sat at the other end of the couch and proceeded to turn his back to me, cover his ears, and bury his face in the arm of the couch. This was not a good start! I spoke to him and told him what a beautiful house he had. I then praised the work he had done in class earlier that day. My student then went upstairs during this time and returned with a toy. I was hopeful that this was a sign that he wanted to show it to me. He went and sat down. I asked him about it but got no response.

Later in the visit, the mother suggested we go upstairs to see his room. We went upstairs. He went into the room with me, and I asked him questions. He nodded a little (it is usually very hard to even get him to nod in class, so I was happy to be getting any response). After that I had some tea and snacks that the family had brought back from their trip to India. I asked about several items around the house including a temple that was near the kitchen. The mother explained the family's customs and how they worship every day by lighting candles and worshiping their temple.

After my home visits, the following themes became apparent as I reviewed my notes:

- My student seemed more responsive and alert at school the day following the home visit.
- The parents demonstrated more of a concern about their child's illness after my home visit.
- My knowledge of my student's home life and disorder is much broader. I feel like I can be a better teacher for him and shed light on this disorder to others at my school.

I gained an appreciation for the dedication of the parents. I understand that they care, and I can see why they are having difficulty with his challenges. My student is now more alert and more responsive. After visiting my student's home three times, I was able to have a better relationship with him at school. He is responding more to my questions with a nod. I have been able to get him to say one word a day! We worked on saying, "Good morning" every day when he comes to school. Visiting my student was the best thing I have done for him this whole year. I hope his teacher next year will continue these visits.

SOURCE: Used with permission of Valerie Robbins.

❖ Reflecting on the Cases

1. Identify the partners in each case study and how each partner benefits from collaboration with community organizations and families.

2. Describe the culturally relevant characteristics of each case study and suggestions for making it more effective.

3. Discuss how these partnership examples contribute to the overall well-being of children as it relates to nutrition, health, and communication.

Activities for Further Development

1. Consider the information related to nutrition and physical fitness of children. Discuss whether or not the issue is shared, sequential, or the sole responsibility of the community, family, or schools. Are there some issues with this area that should be the sole responsibility of the community, family, or schools?

2. Create a list of 10 tips for families in your school related to healthy eating and exercise. How can you incorporate these tips with grade-level standards and homework/learning at home?

3. Conduct a community and Internet search. Create a list of resources and agencies available to families who need counseling or assistance related to child abuse or neglect.

4. If you have never taken part in an IEP or SST meeting at your school or at a school where you are student teaching, ask to observe one. Note the interactions among multiple teachers, parents, and the student. How can these meetings be more culturally relevant and more effective?

Additional Reading and Information

Franklin, C., Harris, M. B., & Allen-Meares, P. (2006). *The school services sourcebook: A guide for school-based professionals.* New York: Oxford University Press. This book offers best practices for students and families with emotional, mental, and behavioral needs.

Schwendiman, J., & Fager, J. (1999). *After-school programs: Good for kids, good for communities.* Portland, OR: Northwest Regional Educational Laboratory. This publication provides information, research, and activities related to effective after-school programs.

Taras, H. (2005). Nutrition and student performance at school. *Journal of School Health, 75,* 199–213. This article reports on research related to the importance of child nutrition as it relates to academic achievement.

Childhelp is a nonprofit organization that provides information about preventing, reporting, and treating child abuse, in addition to statistics and other information: http://www.childhelp.org/about

The National Association for Sport and Physical Education (NASPE) provides several *Appropriate Practices* documents for preschool, elementary school, middle school, and high school students and teachers. It also provides information related to curriculum development, fitness activities and assessment, participation levels, group dynamics, competition, and other physical education activities at various grade levels. You can access the documents at http://www.aahperd.org/naspe/.

The *Rescuing Recess* Web site provides information, strategies, and resources to support unstructured break times for students during school: http://www.cartoonnetwork.com/promos/getanimated/index.html

4

The Makeup
of Families Today

Culturally Relevant Strategies
to Enhance Partnerships

After reading this chapter, you should have a better understanding of:

- traditional and contemporary family structures;

- implications for family and school partnerships based on federal legislation initiatives;

- activities that promote culturally relevant family activities and communication;

- cultural and linguistic education for families (and teachers);

- strategies that assist teachers in knowing their students and their families better;

- developing and implementing parent-teacher conferences that empower students and families;

- diverse communication strategies for teachers and families; and

- alternative parent-teacher communication and homework assignments.

Table 4.1	Prior Knowledge and Beliefs Organizer

Think about your views about the traditional family structure. Who is included in this family? Describe your ideas below.	Think about families in the 21st century. Describe different types of families and your views about what makes up a family.

As you read this chapter, think about your responses in Table 4.1 when considering diverse family structures, diverse needs, and the array of strengths and attributes within different family units.

Families in the 21st Century

Diverse Family Structures

As teachers consider the nature of children's lives outside of school, they notice that the **structure of the traditional family** has changed over time. This traditional structure consists of two parents and two children. Today, children live in homes with one parent, with two parents, with grandparents, with stepparents, with two mommies or two daddies, with adopted parents, and/or with foster parents. Family structures are diverse and vary within every community. Did you know that only about 4% of children come from traditional families where a biological mother, a biological father, and two children live together in the same home? Consider the students in your class or classes that you have observed. What is the family structure of each student? Is there a student with two mommies or two daddies? Is there a student who lives with his or her grandmother instead of a parent? Is there a student who comes from a single-parent home? Is there a student who lives with parents, grandparents, cousins, aunts, and uncles? Is there a student who is adopted? Is there a student who lives in a foster group home? The children's television show *Sesame Street* discusses the term *family* with even the youngest viewers and states that a family involves "people living together and loving each other." Therefore, a family goes beyond a mother, a father, and two children.

When discussing families with your students, remember that families are diverse and encourage a celebration of who your students are and who they live with. Not

The structure of the traditional family has changed over time. Children today live in homes with one parent, with two parents, with grandparents, with two mommies or two daddies, with adopted parents, and/or with foster care parents.

all children live with their biological mother or father, not all children look like their parents, and not all children have traditional family structures like those portrayed in the 1960s television show *Leave It to Beaver*. Students should be taught at an early age that there are many different kinds of families and that families are formed in different ways. Families are groups of people who "live" together and love each other regardless of their biological parentage. I state "live" in quotation marks because not all fathers and mothers live in the same home with their children. In addition, some fathers or mothers may be incarcerated in another area of the state or country. Some children live in shelters, in hotels, in family cars, and even under bridges. A family is considered **homeless** if its members do not have a permanent residence or if they are residing in a place not intended for home use. Homeless children often have inadequate academic records and immunizations and experience academic challenges (Nunez & Collignon, 1997). Providing the broadest view of the meaning of family and "home" will create a sense of community within the classroom and allow all students to feel self-confident about who they are and where they live.

Changes in Traditional Family Structure

Number of Working Mothers

One contemporary change in the family structure is that most family members work outside the home. Working mothers make up 68% of women in the workforce in the United States (Bureau of Labor Statistics, 2004). Table 4.2 shows how the number

SOURCE: Used with permission of Sherri Hedrick.

A family goes beyond a mother, a father, and two children. When discussing families with your students, remember that families are diverse and encourage a celebration of who your students are and who they live with.

Table 4.2	Number of Working Mothers	
Year	**Number of Working Mothers**	**Percentage of Working Mothers**
1964	7.3 million	32%
1974	10.5 million	43%
1984	13.6 million	59%
1994	16.8 million	69%
1997 (peak)	17.5 million	71%
2004	17.2 million	68%

SOURCE: *Bureau of Labor Statistics Population Survey (March 1960–2004).*

of working mothers has increased during the past 40 years. Given this increase, teachers should acknowledge, understand, and accept the external responsibilities that many families have outside of school.

Same-Sex Parents

Other major changes in family structure involve an increase in parents of the same sex. Several studies over the past decade have inquired into the impact of parents' sexuality and their children's success in school. For the most part, the studies are organized to compare children with gay and lesbian parents to those with heterosexual parents. Results of these studies indicate that a parent's sexuality has no bearing on a child's sexual orientation, mental health, socioemotional adjustments, academic performance, or engagement in high-risk activities (e.g., MacCallum & Golombok, 2004; Wainright, Russell, & Patterson, 2004). Nevertheless, teachers are not always prepared, though not necessarily unwilling, to work with children and their gay or lesbian parents (Kissen, 2002; Maney & Cain, 1997). More concerning, however, is the fact that gay and lesbian families report fears of bullying, feelings of isolation, and concerns that current curricular materials do not include gay and lesbian families.

Bower (2007) inquired into three different lesbian families in Nevada. She described their views as those of "normal" parents because all three families indicated that they participate in their children's education, enforce strict guidelines, provide for their children's physical and emotional needs, spend family time together, and take pride in their family. Lauren, one of the mothers in the study, expressed the following:

> We are no different than the heterosexual world. We make sure [our daughter] gets good rest. She's fed well; she does her homework. She gets to school on time. We're involved; we're both involved. You know, I guess the biggest thing is that there's normalcy in our relationship. (Bower, 2007, p. 12)

Bower and other educators have lamented that "normal" is usually an exclusionary concept. Therefore, teachers must broaden the definition of the normal family and redefine normal when making decisions about curriculum materials, class activities, and family communication.

The Contemporary Family Tree

When teachers assign the task of creating a **family tree**—a chart, a graph, or another representation that shows current family members and family members over time—the structure and content should be inclusive of all students. One of the moms in Bower's (2007) study gave this example: Her son "came home with the paper and it was two moms on the family tree. And he's [the teacher] like, 'Who's that?' At the school they totally tripped." Family trees look different in other families as well. In my own family, we adopted our two children, and they know that they grew in the "tummies" of two different women. Therefore, when my children are asked to draw a family tree, they may choose to draw two family trees, one with their birth mom and birth dad and one with their parents and extended family. Children in foster care experience multiple families if they are moved around from house to house. Children who have stepparents also need additional space on their trees to name each and every family member.

Creating a More Inclusive Classroom

Multiple activities, discussions, and resources are necessary throughout the school year to provide opportunities for students and their families to express who they are. Here are some ideas to provide a more **inclusive classroom** that respects diversity and includes all families:

1. Allow time for families and children to define themselves through individual conferences, a family history assignment, or even home visits.

2. Reconsider the family tree assignment and ask students to draw pictures or cut images from magazines and create a collage to show off their families.

3. If you must hold on to the traditional family tree assignment, provide a template with many blank lines for important people in children's families such as two moms, two dads, foster moms, foster dads, stepmoms, stepdads, birth moms, and birth dads.

4. Provide a variety of multicultural materials such as books, photographs, software, puzzles, and games that include a variety of different families such as those who are multiracial, have adopted children, have two moms, or include stepparents.

5. Provide a variety of materials that show children living in different structures: group homes, single-family detached homes, apartments, and mobile homes.

6. Be sensitive to the fact that some children do not have newborn baby pictures to contribute to a class bulletin board if they were adopted after the age of 2 or if they live with foster families who do not have access to these photos. Instead, make families more visible to others by celebrating the makeup of families and posting these on the bulletin board. You can have children draw pictures of themselves as babies, as toddlers, or at other stages of their lives.

7. Rethink projects such as "Adopt-a-Beach" or "Adopt-a-Whale." Consider other terms instead such as "Care for Our Beach" or "Save the Whales." These are more specific terms because young children already have a difficult time understanding the concept of adoption, particularly if they are adopted. These projects when termed with "Adopt-a . . ." could devalue the concept of adopted parenthood.

8. Listen and discuss issues among different children in the class as they arise. Do not ignore them! Even the youngest children observe skin color, family makeup, and ways that people form families.

9. Educate families within the class about diversity and contemporary views of families. Invite families to come together for pizza or coffee so that they can get to know each other. Establish community within the classroom and among families.

10. Obtain a variety of books that tell stories of children who live in multiracial families, are adopted, live with foster families, have two moms or dads, or live with a mom and a dad. Books have a way of helping children understand the different ways families are formed.

11. Obtain paper, markers, and crayons of all different skin colors so that students can represent themselves and their families during assignments.

12. Believe it or not, children do not wish to be different or special. Therefore, make a point to show similarities in children and families as you are celebrating differences.

Enhancing Learning for Students With Special Needs: Overcoming Negative Attitudes Toward Students With Disabilities

Negative cultural attitudes toward students with disabilities can inhibit opportunities for all students and families to participate fully in formal school activities. Hehir (2007) labels this as **ableism**, where the world is less welcoming and accessible for students with disabilities. An ableism perspective asserts that children with disabilities should use tools and act in the same way as their nondisabled peers. However, evidence shows that ableist assumptions can be harmful to students with disabilities and contribute to an uneven playing field. Therefore, it is important for families and teachers to work together to ensure that students with special needs are provided with tools, strategies, and assistance to promote equity in learning.

Here are some strategies to help negate ableism:

- Communicate with families, teachers, and students about ableism and how this strategy is not effective in promoting the best learning opportunities for students with special needs.

(Continued)

> (Continued)
>
> - Provide alternative assignments and assessment strategies for students with disabilities. For example, allow them to discuss a subject orally, draw pictures, or create a project to show their knowledge.
> - Work with schools or districts to acquire augmentative and alternative communication (AAC) devices to assist students who have difficulty communicating via speech or writing.

Family Participation Initiatives

No Child Left Behind (NCLB) requires that districts and schools develop and implement policies to connect with families. Section 1118 of NCLB (see U.S. Department of Education, n.d.) addresses the following initiatives: (a) multilevel leadership that includes parents; (b) parents as an integral component of the school and classrooms; (c) parents and teachers sharing the responsibility of teaching and learning; and (d) steps and procedures including all families, particularly those who are not usually involved. In addition, NCLB requires that schools communicate with families of school-age children on a regular basis. This act includes "right to know" provisions where parents have the right to know their child's achievement, teacher qualifications, and options for getting services such as those designed for English language learners and to be notified if schools are not making appropriate progress. All information communicated to families must be in an understandable format and must be presented in a language that the parents of the children can understand (McLure, 2002). Therefore, schools can take the initiative to communicate to parents their rights and encourage their involvement in their child's education. NCLB also offers provisions for supplementary or tutoring programs for children who attend Title I schools that receive federal funding. As a teacher, you can create a positive atmosphere and communicate with parents about the myriad community resources and options.

A Culturally Responsive Partnership Between Home and School

Every family, regardless of income level, language, culture, or home, offers tremendous resources from which teachers can draw. These resources include cultural heritage and other kinds of knowledge and experiences. Send home a written **survey** (that students can help create, if applicable) and ask families to provide information related to their favorite events, foods, customs, hobbies, movies, books, and music. Students can interview their families and report the information back to school to provide more comfort for families when divulging the information. The use of reflective journals is another way to find out more about students, their families, their fears, their concerns, and their interests. When teachers allow students time to write or draw about what is on their mind, this provides insight into the students' world.

I remember one of my second-grade students when I was a teacher in North Carolina. His name was "Leo." He was the stereotypical outcast child due to the fact that other students did not want to play with him because of his erratic behavior. Journal writing for him was a way to express his feelings. One week, Leo wrote the same thing over and over again, "I love Gerry and Gerry loves me." Gerry was the classroom gerbil. Leo was able to find positive experiences and interactions with the class pet even though many of the children in the class did not want to talk to him or play with him. This little piece of information from his journal allowed me to capitalize on his area of strength (i.e., feeling comfortable with Gerry) and promote interactive activities with other children based around Gerry the gerbil. It also sparked an idea to have Leo take Gerry home each weekend and take care of him with his family. On Monday, he was able to report what Gerry did over the weekend. After that, he was in charge of creating a class chart with specific dates and names indicating other students who would take Gerry home.

Therefore, *listening* to students and families provides much information about what they have to offer. Also, *communicating* with families and students on a regular basis will provide more of a shared understanding of classroom events. Many teachers find it advantageous to greet every child (and parent) at the door each morning with a handshake, hug, or high-five. This helps build community within the classroom and a sense of respect for all children.

Delgado-Gaitan (2004) recommends three important conditions that lead to more family participation: sharing information with families, connecting to the different families, and supporting their continued involvement. Specific strategies to promote these conditions are outlined in the next section to help teachers share more information, connect with each other, and support involvement. As you read the examples, keep in mind that a partnership is defined not by the number of hours that a parent physically spends at the school site but by the quality of cumulative experiences and activities that support formal school learning.

Cultural and Linguistic Education for Families and Teachers

Many schools and districts provide various education experiences for teachers and families. A **contemporary view of education** includes more opportunities for teachers and families to learn different languages and about different cultures. Parenting and teacher education seminars can be formal or informal. The best seminars occur when parents and teachers are learning together. Allen (2007) recommends that families provide education for teachers and students by telling stories and creating cultural memoirs. These projects can be accomplished in native languages to enhance the multicultural and multilingual benefits. Inviting parents to school to discuss their hobbies, jobs, and other areas of expertise provides a sense of community, education, and respect for all families and students.

Open House, Back-to-School Night, and Conferences

At least one or two times each year, most schools have an open house that allows families to visit the school. This is usually an informal meeting that takes place in the late afternoon or evening where teachers and students showcase their work, projects, and other activities. Since many families may have prior commitments or work obligations, many schools prefer organizing two back-to-school events at different times of the day so that more families have the opportunity to attend.

For many families, an open house, a parent-teacher conference, or a back-to-school night is the only chance to get a glimpse inside the formal classroom. Although this should not be the only interaction between teachers and parents, it may be the only time that families and teachers talk face-to-face during the school year. One of the ways that teachers can plan ahead for conferences and encourage more participation is to have parents complete an advance organizer related to their child's strengths, challenges, and questions. This organizer can be completed collaboratively with the child if appropriate. These surveys should be translated, when applicable, to provide access for all families to participate. A sample organizer is featured in Table 4.3.

When the parents arrive at the conference, let them talk first! Listen to them and encourage them to share strengths about their child. Teachers can also encourage parents to discuss their educational ideals and any struggles that their children have encountered. Teachers should consider providing information about the child's strengths and progress instead of placing so much focus on the assigned grades. Teachers can discuss academic standards and expectations as part of the process, but the conference should be focused on the child and what he or she can do; then it can

Table 4.3 Advance Organizer for Parents to Complete Before Conferences

Question	Response
What does your child like to do at home?	
What is your child good at?	
What does your child struggle with at school and/or at home?	
What concerns do you have about your child?	
What questions do you have for me?	

move toward challenges that the child may face and strategies to help meet the curriculum standards. Some other ways to provide a more interactive conference is to feature examples of student work, student-selected portfolio artifacts, anecdotal notes, and pictures of students "in action" during classroom activities. Some classroom teachers create a PowerPoint presentation and play it continuously outside the classroom while other parents wait to enter. If computer access is a challenge, students and teachers can create a collage highlighting classroom events. In addition, audiotapes or videotapes of children interacting during class activities can greatly enhance the positive and interactive nature of a parent-teacher conference or open house. Many schools provide transportation, snacks, child care, and translators to encourage greater family participation.

Although yearly or biyearly parent-teacher conferences are planned in advance, we know that there are other times that teachers or parents request conferences that are not so positive. Usually, conferences take place because of a recurring problem or other issue. These problems usually relate to students' academic progress, their social skills, or their self-discipline skills. Sometimes the issue is very specific and somewhat easy to address, such as a second grader who will not use the bathroom at school because the toilets are dirty. But sometimes the issue is much larger and will take collaboration among the teacher, the student, and the student's family with multiple interventions to address an issue, such as a sixth grader who feels that he is being bullied every day at recess.

If a parent contacts the teacher and asks for a conference, the teacher should do everything possible to schedule the conference as soon as possible. The same is true for families who are asked to attend a special conference set up by the teacher. All parties should reschedule other tasks and responsibilities in order to deal with the problem in a relatively quick manner. Make sure that the conference begins in a positive manner before delving into specific problems. The child should be present at the conference if appropriate so that he or she can be empowered to address the problem or issue. Ensure time for true interaction throughout the conference where all parties are given an opportunity to provide their views. The teacher should make every effort to listen as much as possible rather than monopolizing the conversation. After problems are discussed, a plan of action should be developed before the conference concludes. This plan of action should be documented in some way. A contract among the parent, child, and teacher usually works best to monitor the issues in upcoming weeks. Figure 4.1 shows one type of parent-child-teacher contract.

Communicating With Irate Parents

When an irate parent confronts a teacher unannounced, the most important reaction from the teacher is to remain calm. Next, the teacher can take a deep breath and listen to the parent while trying not to get hung up on the tone of the parent's voice. After listening (for as long as it takes), teachers should repeat the words back to the parent to make sure that they understand the issue or problem. For example, "If I understand you correctly, you are concerned that Angelica is not eating her lunch because other children in the class continually harass her, call her names, and make fun of her food" or "I understand your concern, and I understand how you and Sarah must have felt when the bus

| Figure 4.1 | Parent-Child-Teacher Contract |

Weekly Contract

_____
(name/date)

	MON.		TUES.		WED.		THURS.		FRI.	
	YES	NO	YES	NO	YES	NO	YES	NO	YES	NO
Objective(s)										
On-task behavior										
Complete class work										
Complete homework										

Daily Points: _____ _____ _____ _____ _____ _____
(Mon.)   (Tues.)   (Wed.)   (Thurs.)   (Fri.)

Teacher signature:	
Parent signature:	
Student signature:	

left without her on the field trip." Although I hope that you never have to face these same issues as a teacher, foresight and prevention are always best. A variety of issues will arise throughout your teaching career, and you should be prepared to deal with them in a positive manner and with parents as your partners instead of your adversaries.

Student-Led Conferences

Students and teachers can organize **student-led conferences** or student-centered conferences together as a team. These types of conferences differ from the traditional teacher-led conferences that most parents experience. With student-led conferences, students take a major role in informing their parents about their achievements, interests, and assignments. Students take the initiative to showcase their work and progress during this time. The entire preparation for the conference empowers the students to take an integral role in their own learning and to inform their families about their performance in a nontraditional conference format. During traditional parent-teacher conferences, teachers do most of the talking, and students are not involved in the process. With student-led conferences, however, the students' role is to help plan the conference, make decisions about the work they would like to show their families, and make statements about their own learning and challenges they have encountered. The teacher's role during this conference is to listen, encourage, support, and answer questions. It is imperative that teachers and students notify families in advance about the conference structure and how their children will be involved. The parent's role is to listen, ask questions, and participate in activities.

Tuinstra and Hiatt-Michael (2003) studied 524 middle school students and their parents from schools in the states of California, Oregon, Texas, and Washington who participated in student-led conferences. They found that 43% of the students who participated in student-led conferences set their own personal work goals at school. Parents of these students indicated that their children were more successful academically as a result of taking a lead in the conference. Teachers reported that they perceived their students to be more academically successful as a result of the new conference structure.

Student-led conferences can be organized in a variety of formats in an effort to include the student, the teacher, and the student's family members. A popular student-led conference model includes a total of 40 minutes of participation for each family. The entire conference is led by the students and facilitated by the teacher and parents. It should be noted that schools and teachers do not have to appropriate extra funding for these conferences because the cost of each conference remains the same. Table 4.4 outlines sample activities and time frames associated with the task. A student-led conference example that is featured as a case study at the end of this chapter will provide more information about the interactions that take place among the teacher, parents, and students.

Table 4.4 Student-Led Conference Activities

Sample Activity	Time
Interactive family activity such as making careful observations and recording information in the science center.	10 minutes
Interactive family activity such as participating in a reader's theater with puppets or playing board games related to grade-level standards.	10 minutes
Students showcasing their work in the form of portfolios, a PowerPoint presentation, or another delivery method.	10 minutes
Face-to-face conversation among the teacher, the student, and the student's family to analyze activities and student performance at school.	10 minutes

Multiple Communication Methods

At a minimum, teachers should write an introduction letter to families, in different languages if applicable, at the beginning of each school year. Better yet, hold an open house the day or week before school starts to invite families to visit your classroom. Teachers who utilize multiple communication methods such as weekly or monthly newsletters, e-mails, face-to-face meetings, and activities will improve communication and student success throughout the school year. One way to take the responsibility off of the teachers is to have students create materials informing their families of classroom events, what they are learning, and important dates to remember. Have all materials translated when necessary. The following installment of "Notes From the Classroom" shows a newsletter sent home to parents highlighting science content at school, suggested activities at home, and community resources.

Notes From the Classroom: A Sample Science Newsletter Sent to Families by Third-Grade Teacher

This month's investigation will be into how and why organisms interact. Here are some vocabulary words that your child will be learning. Please ask your child to share what they mean during dinner, in the car, or while taking a walk outside.

- population
- food chain
- producer
- community
- decomposer
- consumer
- ecosystem
- food web
- organism
- habitat
- competition
- niche

California State Life Science Standards Covered by This Unit

2. (a–c) All organisms need energy and matter to live and grow.
3. (a–d) Living organisms depend on one another and on their environment for survival.

In the classroom, we will be conducting an experiment about decomposing. We will be forming hypotheses and predictions while gathering data over 3 weeks. For this, each student should bring a slice of bread in a bag by next Monday. Please place the following information on the bag: your child's name, the date that the bread was placed in the bag, and the type of bread.

School-Home Connections

If you are interested in extending your child's learning experience at home or outside of school, here are some activities and adventures that you can embark on. Have fun!

The Yuckiest Site on the Internet

Learn about earthworms, roaches, and other decomposers at http://yucky.kids.discovery .com/flash/index.html.

An Icky Experiment: A Fungus Among Us

This Web site will help you create your own experiment at home: http://yucky.discovery .com/flash/fun_n_games/activities/experiments/experiment_fungus.html.

The Food Chain

Extend your learning and find out how the food chain works on land and water at http://www.kidport.com/Reflib/science/foodchain/foodchain.htm.

SOURCE: Used with permission of Casey Weinkauf.

Another effective and simple way to communicate weekly is to send out a newsletter that features a few key items that are being covered in class with additional notes and reminders. Keeping newsletters concise and organizing them with bullet points or short statements can maximize comprehensibility. The following installment of "Notes From the Classroom" was created by a kindergarten teacher, Alejandra, whose template allows her to insert important information for families each week.

Notes From the Classroom: Weekly News Brief

WEEK OF: November 10, 2009
TEACHER: Sra. Becerra

Look What We've Learned:

- Phonics: "e" for *Ellie, elephant;* "g" for *gordo, gorilla;* "f" for *fancy, fish*
- Math: graphing using tallies, sorting, estimating, measuring

Special Notes and Reminders:

- Thank you to all of the families who donated items for International Day.
- We will be making Stone Soup on November 24. Families are invited to share in stories, writing, and soup at 1:00 p.m.
- Parent-teacher conferences will take place on the afternoons of November 18, 19, and 20. If you cannot meet on those days, please contact me so that I can schedule another time to meet.

Home Visits

Home visits have made a comeback in many school districts. Many years ago, teachers lived in the communities where they worked, and they knew the families of every child. Today, teachers and students often live in different communities, and teachers rarely know the families of the students they teach. Home visits bring greater awareness, understanding, and respect for students and their families. For almost 20 years, Luis Moll and his colleagues have been advocating the need for teachers to conduct what they call field studies, particularly as related to students from non-English-language backgrounds (e.g., Moll & Gonzalez, 1997; Moll, Vélez-Ibáñez, Greenberg, & Rivera, 1990). During home visits, teachers are learners. They learn about their students, their students' families, and the lives that students live outside of school. In return, families learn more about their children's teachers. Once a teacher learns more about a student's family and culture, communication between the family and the school can be more meaningful, and connections between learning and school can be optimized. Moll and Gonzalez (1997) claim that teachers who visit students' homes can identify these students' knowledge and strengths. By looking for funds of knowledge, the educational potential of students' households shifts from a deficit model to one that holds possibility, meaning, and educational understanding. Teachers should inquire into the cultural backgrounds from which their students function to ensure positive and real connections between their students and their families (Eberly, Joshi, & Konzal, 2005). Home visits enable more personal contact between teachers and students' families outside the school, create improved conditions in the process of educating children, and support parents' engagement in their children's education.

Lave and Wenger (1991) view learning and community as a social activity that develops from experiences and participation. We all partake in activities based on our homes, communities, and schools and have varying roles; at times we are at the core of activity, and at other times we are on the periphery as described previously. Some children and their families may always stay on the periphery instead of actively engaging within the center. Home visits can undercut some families' hesitation to get more involved in their children's schooling, because the visits show that teachers care, are interested in their students, and are willing to take the time and energy needed to get to know their students' families. In addition, culturally relevant pedagogy and inclusive practices can be enhanced when teachers visit students' homes and interact with the entire family in informal ways.

Vadeboncoeur (2006) identified five features that influence contexts of learning outside formal classrooms: location (where the learning takes place), relationships (who interacts and how they react in relation to one another), content (what occurs), pedagogy (how learning occurs), and assessment (how informal learning is measured). Using these elements when planning home visits allows a teacher to focus on one or more of these areas to determine how learning is constructed in a particular time and space such as students' homes, neighborhoods, and communities. During home visits, students' homes serve as the location for informal learning, the relationship between the teacher and the family is a learning tool, and content and pedagogy are open entities. Assessment takes place informally based on teacher, student, and family interactions during the home visit and beyond.

Patchen, Cox-Petersen, Ambrose, DeVore, and Koenings (2008) found common themes across six different case studies of teachers who conducted home visits. They are listed in Table 4.5.

Multiple contexts including students' homes can contribute to informal learning experiences, particularly for teachers. Home visits with students and families have not been thoroughly examined as a learning tool or a context within most teacher education programs. Home visits can provide an important step to building partnerships with families and maximizing academic achievement for all students. Chapter 9 provides more details and information about a kindergarten teacher who conducted home visits with her students and their families.

Incorporating Multicultural and Culturally Relevant Materials

When choosing curriculum materials in the form of textbooks, DVDs, computer games, literature, and magazines, teachers should seek resources that highlight different races, cultures, and family structures. Look for kids who look different from their parents, kids who have one parent, or kids who have two dads. Better yet, have children provide their own drawings, writings, and interpretations and acknowledge them.

Table 4.5 Common Themes of Teachers Who Conducted Home Visits
• Teachers expressed professional growth in the area of cultural awareness and appreciation for diverse family beliefs and structures.
• Teachers gained confidence in their ability to connect with families outside the school.
• Teachers reported that families were open and expressed their appreciation of the visit.
• Teachers reported that the parents they visited communicated more frequently after the home visits.
• Teachers faced barriers initially from the school district and their administrators when they discussed visiting students' homes.
• Teachers reported that their districts and schools have few policies and experiences related to home visits.
• Multiple families from different cultural backgrounds demonstrated a willingness to open their homes and meet with teachers.
• Families demonstrated a strong work ethic and wanted to assist in their children's educational endeavors.

SOURCE: Patchen et al. (2008).

In addition, recruit family members to serve on curriculum materials committees throughout the school year.

Rethinking Homework Assignments

The results of a large study of 709 students in elementary, middle, and high schools indicate that teachers view homework more positively than students and parents (Cooper, Lindsay, Nye, & Greathouse, 1998). Nevertheless, Cooper et al. found that completed homework does correlate with higher achievement in school but does not correlate with achievement on standardized test scores. Paschal, Weinstein, and Walberg (1984) analyzed multiple studies related to homework and found mixed positive and negative results. They concluded that homework does enhance student learning if it is graded and if the teacher provides constructive comments related to the assignment. Jianzhong (2005) also found that consistent completion of homework results in approval from teachers, peers, and families and good discipline behaviors in middle school and high school students.

Although homework can instill responsibility and supplement formal school learning, sometimes homework assignments are too long, are too repetitive, and can cause undo strain on families and students. Homework should be doable and feasible. Assignments should be done in a specific amount of time and should not last for multiple hours in the elementary grades. It is helpful if the teacher writes a note to the families indicating the amount of time that children should spend on homework. If children are spending too many hours on homework after they have spent 7 hours in school, then they are usually missing out on important interactions with their families and friends, physical exercise, and other extracurricular activities after school. Assigning more homework than is necessary may cause unwanted "burnout" with children and families. Many homework assignments are nothing more than busywork, according to Bennett and Kalish (2006) and Kohn (2006). Moreover, too much homework can result in less academic achievement, according to a *Time* magazine article by Wallis (2006) describing the myths about homework. Teachers in countries such as Japan and Denmark assign less homework than teachers in the United States but have students who score higher on academic tests.

Many researchers, such as Cooper (1994), recommend that teachers and families consider the 10-minute rule when assigning homework. Children in first grade should have no more than 10 minutes of homework. In second grade, they should have 20 minutes, and in third grade, 30 minutes. However, Cooper reports that children who spend more than 2 hours each night completing homework tasks actually perform lower than their peers. In addition, homework does not seem to correlate with higher academic achievement for children in grades K–3. This view is supported by the work of Desimone (1999), who found that homework help is negatively associated with student achievement across all groups. Therefore, it is important for teachers to make an effort to provide students with meaningful learning experiences when they are completing homework at home. Also, continuous repetition of the same skill practiced at school does not necessarily aid in higher achievement. Kilman (2006) investigated alternative approaches for parents to help their children learn about math at home. One way includes distributing research findings to families and having parents and children choose specific assignments and games to complete together. Kilman found that math-related games that involve positive family experiences enhance children's attitudes toward and interest in math over time. In addition, these games provide a shared educational experience for the entire family.

Helping students build background knowledge and connect learning at school to learning at home will provide motivation for self-initiated learning and more interest in school subjects. Many homework concerns that parents have voiced include the cost of materials and time needed to complete some projects. Teachers should be aware of the fact that some students do not have outside support systems and resources to complete many of the projects that are required. Therefore, teachers and schools can be proactive and provide a variety of interactive homework assignments that come in ready-to-learn packages, such as backpack projects. Backpack activities are popular ongoing activities enjoyed by many teachers and families. Teachers can acquire backpacks and use them as learning activity "centers" that students can take home and use with their families over a weekend or during the week. Companies or retail stores will donate backpacks to schools or teachers if they indicate that there is a need for them. Backpack Science has been a popular science-based activity in which students take home a backpack full of science-related literature and activities focusing on a particular science topic. The activities are usually set up so that the whole family can participate. Teachers can take this opportunity to communicate science content standards within the backpack materials. It is usually a good idea to send a letter home to families explaining the backpacks, the activities, and the expectations. Take a look at the sample letter in the following "Notes From the Classroom" section. Note that the letter is concise and explains things in very basic terms. Remember that many family members do not have a degree in education and do not understand a lot of the education "lingo." All letters should be translated into other languages when possible.

Notes From the Classroom: Backpack Homework Assignment

Dear Families,

This month we will begin a new science unit! We will be learning about different animals and where they live, with a focus on science processes such as observations, measuring, and communicating.

I will be sending home science backpacks during the next month that will help you and your child extend this learning at home. There are several books that go along with the science activities. Enjoy reading them together. This should be a fun learning experience for the whole family.

Please contact me if you would like more information.
Mr. Wang
555–333–2222
mrwang@anyschool.k12.mt.edu

Interactive homework such as backpack activities can be created for any subject area—math, art, music, social studies, science, or physical education. For physical education, for example, have more family interaction. The point of such assignments is for families to interact and talk about school and learning. The following installment of "Notes From the Classroom" shows an example of a home backpack activity that a kindergarten teacher and a first-grade teacher provide for students and their families.

Notes From the Classroom: Backpack Activity for Students and Families

- Read the story *Jump, Frog, Jump!* by Robert Kalan.
- Discuss what happened in the story and tell about your favorite part.
- Get some exercise! Go outside and practice jumping with the jump ropes provided. Take other family members with you. Jump for as long as you can and have someone use the stopwatch to time you.
- Next, put on the calorie counter provided and see how many calories you burn while jump roping.
- Use the Jump Rope Journal provided to keep track of your times each day.

SOURCE: DeVore and Ambrose (2007).

Encourage families to engage in activities together and write about their experiences to share with classmates. This can be done via a PowerPoint presentation, poster, or video.

Some additional alternative homework assignments are included in Table 4.6 to encourage more family interaction and participation. However, it is recommended that teachers give families advance notice of these assignments because they will usually take longer to complete than one evening. In addition, be respectful of families' time. Asking parents to accompany their child to a local park when the assignment is due the next day may not fit into their already packed schedule. Better yet, teachers can offer a list of homework projects that families can choose from on a weekly basis. Teachers should remember to send home any materials such as construction paper, blank calendars, or markers that students might need to complete each project if families do not typically have these resources at home. Teachers should also be careful when requiring students to obtain information from magazines, the newspaper, or a television show because some students may not have access to these resources.

Table 4.6	Sample Interactive Homework Assignments

Grade Level	Sample Homework Assignments
Grades K–2	• Have students decorate a square piece of fabric for a class quilt. They can create a work of art that represents their hobbies, family, or culture. • Ask students to observe the moon on a daily basis, to record the moon phase and what time they saw it on a blank calendar, and to look for patterns over the course of a month. • Supply students with 80 books in the classroom related to different countries. Have them take a different book home and read it to/with their families. When they return to school, they can place their name on a world map next to the country that the book was written about. • Send home a class animal or another object. Have students write a story about their experiences at home with the animal or object and create a song to sing to it. • Ask students to count the number of shapes within the home and create a bar graph. • Have students plant a seed, water it, observe it each day, and record its growth and changes.
Grades 3–5	• Have students take a walk to a local park, in the backyard, or in a vacant lot; observe what lives there such as ants, spiders, pill bugs, slugs, worms, birds, or squirrels; and draw and write about what they see including animal structures, habitat, and behaviors. • Ask students to record at least 10 foods at home and categorize them according to the food pyramid. Then have them write about which foods are most healthy and why. • Have students locate a family recipe, preferably one that has been passed down for many generations. Next have them double the recipe and then triple it for a larger crowd. Ask them to write a story about whom they will make the recipe for and where/how the food will be served. • Ask students to take a walk around their neighborhood and count the number of steps they and other family members take. Have them draw a map of their route, record each person's steps in a graph, and then compute the average number of steps taken by all. • Have students create a collection of rocks, leaves, or other objects outside or within the home; classify these objects into different groups; and write about why they classified them in that way.

(Continued)

Table 4.6	(Continued)

Grade Level	Sample Homework Assignments
Grades 6–8	• Have students choose a type of food with a label at their home. Then ask them to calculate the percentage of fats, protein, and other nutrients and create a pie chart showing this information with an explanation of whether or not it is a food that should be eaten for breakfast, lunch, or dinner. • Have students visit the library, obtain a library card, check out a book, and write about the book they chose and why. • Ask students to play a board game with their family (teachers may have to rotate different board games and send them home with children). • Have students create a report that includes interviews with community members of different ethnicities and write about what they learned.

Family-School Bonding Events

Great value and added benefits result from promoting school-family-community events. The most successful bonding events are ones that occur each year, that families are familiar with, and that they anticipate. One notable event at my daughter's school is called the United Nations Day Celebration. Every year, students, families, and teachers in each grade level choose a country that they will celebrate. For one month, the students interact with people from this country via e-mail or within the community; work in cooperative groups to produce research reports about the country; and learn traditional and contemporary dances, sing songs, and cook traditional food. Families are asked to participate by sharing their ideas, customs, experiences, and resources. On the day of the big event, families, teachers, students, and the community come together to eat various types of food from other countries and watch students perform a dance related to their country. One year, one family filmed the event and offered DVDs to each family. This DVD is the most requested DVD at my home! My daughter and son love to watch it over and over again and sing and dance to the music of different countries.

Other family bonding events can include Literacy Mornings where parents read with their children in the classroom before school begins, pizza nights coupled with family math games, and musical concerts performed at the school by students and families.

Promoting Literacy at Home

Teachers and families can work together to support children's reading development during vacation periods and other holidays. By providing specific guidelines and resources related to leisure reading, teachers can enhance students' overall literacy development and love for reading (Mraz & Rasinski, 2007).

Early home literacy practices enhance students' reading achievement. Home literacy practices should be promoted before children attend school and once formal instruction begins (Lau & McBride-Chang, 2005).

SOURCE: Used with permission of Denise Remick.

Students in this sixth-grade class learned about ancient Egypt, sampled Egyptian food, and learned traditional Egyptian dances to celebrate United Nations Day at their school.

Tips for Families and Teachers During Parent-Teacher Conferences

The "tips" in this chapter relate to enhanced communication for parents and teachers during conferences. They are outlined below and summarize much of the information about conferences that is included in this chapter.

Tips for Families

1. Share information about your child's preferred learning style and activities that he or she enjoys. Also share relevant family issues.

2. Address specific concerns as they arise. Do not save them for formal conferences. Parent conferences are usually scheduled back-to-back; therefore, you will not have enough time to address specific problem areas.

3. Address your educational goals and collaborate with the teacher on achieving them.

4. Ask teachers about their expectations and sample class activities.

5. Scan the room. This will provide lots of information about what is going on in the classroom on a daily basis. Look for information on bulletin boards, student work, learning centers, and books on the shelf.

6. What other tips can you add?

Tips for Teachers

1. Listen! Allow parents to talk first.

2. Ask families to fill out a questionnaire before coming to the conference. This will give you more information about children's strengths and interests before you meet with families. Send multilingual questionnaires if necessary.

3. Some parents do not feel comfortable asking questions. Send home a list of questions (with space for additional questions) that families may want to ask during the conference. Have them bring the list to the conference.

4. Share actual pieces of children's work. This provides more information than letter grades on specific assignments.

5. Allow parents to participate in the conference with their children.

6. Provide an inviting and culturally relevant atmosphere. Make parents feel welcome during the conference and encourage them to visit the classroom regularly. Provide snacks as your budget allows or ask a local market to donate snacks.

7. Visit students and their families in their homes if possible, particularly if the parents are unable to schedule a conference at school.

8. What other tips can you add?

Chapter Summary

A 21st-century view of families is inclusive and celebrates diverse family structures such as families who adopt children, single-parent families, and families that have two moms or two dads. Activities at school and home can promote more inclusive and culturally relevant activities for all students. No Child Left Behind legislation and implications for family and school partnerships encourage more involvement among all educational partners. Delgado-Gaitan (2004) recommends three important conditions that lead to more family participation: sharing information with families, connecting to the different families, and supporting their continued involvement. A variety of educational strategies can be provided to empower families to want to participate more in their children's education. Some of these strategies include alternative communication, education for parents and teachers, student-led conferences, alternative homework assignments, and culturally diverse curriculum materials.

CASE STUDIES

Two different case studies are featured in this chapter. The first one, a student-led conference example, provides multiple views related to the nontraditional conference structure. This is adapted from a fifth-grade teacher, Carrie Marquez (Marquez, 2005). The second one involves a first-grade teacher, C. Gayle Morrison, and her experiences conducting home visits with each child in her classroom. This is adapted from a study by Morrison (2008). Each of these case studies will introduce you to teacher, student, and parent voices that describe their experiences.

❖ Case Study 4.1: Student-Led Conferences

The purpose of the student-led conference is to demonstrate to parents and to the broader school community students' academic mastery through performance or academic products. It gives parents the opportunity to see the academic progress of their students and allows students to take ownership of their academic progress. Specific activities and information were provided within this chapter. This case study will provide additional information and multiple perspectives related to the views of a teacher, a student, and a parent.

Voice of Carrie Marquez, Fifth-Grade Teacher

My school has adopted the use of student-learning conferences (SLC). Some teachers have chosen to implement SLC, and others have elected to continue with traditional parent-teacher conference formats. I started SLC for the first time last year and have decided that I will never go back to a traditional conference. I organized my SLC to include four stations with the last one ending with me. Each station lasts for 10 minutes, and I set the timer at my desk. My first station is reading where the students read an excerpt from a book of their choice. Sample questions are available in Spanish and English for parents who want to check their students' comprehension. The second station is math where the students complete a few problem-solving activities using manipulatives. The third station is writing where students share writing samples from their portfolios. Parents and students are asked to participate in "free writing" together if time permits. Activities vary from station to station for fall and spring conferences. When parents and students are discussing their achievement and things they need to work on, it takes the pressure off of me during conferences and allows parents and students to address their needs better. I am a facilitator and partner in this process.

Voice of Maurilio Alvarado, Fifth-Grade Student

I liked showing my parents my schoolwork. They really liked seeing stuff I do at school. Ms. Marquez helped us during class so that we knew what to do during the conference. I'm glad that kids can go to parent conferences now.

Voice of Ms. Alvarado, Parent of Maurilio

I liked this conference better than others. I was able to ask Maurilio, "What do you think you need to work on?" He answered, "I think I need more detail, descriptive language, and maybe my grammar." I agreed with him. Once we got to Ms. Marquez, we told her these things. I now know more about what Maurilio is doing at school and what we need to work on at home.

SOURCE: Used with permission of Carrie Marquez.

❖ Case Study 4.2: Home Visits as a Home-School Connection

Voice of Gayle Morrison, First-Grade Teacher

The partnership among the classroom teacher, parents, and students, though informal, has a huge impact on the education of each child in the classroom. In an effort to help parents feel more comfortable communicating with me and becoming active partners in their child's education, as well as to have more information to help me understand the individual needs of each student, I conducted home visitations. My interest was in learning the following information:

- What can I learn about my students and their families from a home visit that will inform and improve my teaching practices to best meet the student's needs?
- How does the student's home environment support the student and his or her family?

I am a first-grade teacher in a two-way language immersion program where students receive 80% of their instruction in Spanish and 20% in English. The class is composed of eight English language learners and 13 Spanish language learners. The students come from varied cultural backgrounds and socioeconomic situations. Parents of Spanish language learning students are concerned because the primary language of instruction is Spanish and many of them are unable to help with homework. Parents of English language learning students are concerned about their children learning English and about helping in the correct way. Also, the Spanish-speaking parents sometimes feel a bit intimidated by the English-speaking parents who tend to be more educated and feel more comfortable in the classroom.

As our communities become larger, it is less likely that teachers and students belong to the same community. In order for students to be successful, it is important for teachers to gather and share as much information as possible about them with the people who are most interested in their academic success, their families.

Although I visited the homes of all students in my class, I will discuss one particular visit with Jorge's family. Jorge is an English language learner and a recent immigrant from Mexico. He is a 6-year-old boy working well below grade level but is very motivated. He comes to school every day but does not seem to receive help with homework. Jorge's parents did not attend Back-to-School Night, so I spoke to his mom later that week when I ran into her outside. She does not come to the classroom, so I rarely see her. In an effort to reduce the anxiety for the parents, I explained that I was interested in getting to know the students a little better in order to better help them in class and that visiting them at home would provide that opportunity. I also wanted the students to view the experience as a positive one, so I explained to them that I was excited to visit them at home and that they should think about what they wanted to show me or play at their house. Jorge was very excited.

One or two days prior to each visit, I called the parents to remind them. I used Google Maps to locate the students' homes. I visited Jorge's home on a Thursday after school. I brought a bag with our classroom mascots (a teddy bear and a lion puppet), books, a Spanish bingo game, and a camera. I wanted the parents to feel comfortable talking to me, so I kept the visits very informal and casual and did not take notes during any of them. We exchanged information about our backgrounds, our families, school, and the students. After talking with the families for a little while, I offered to read a book or play a game of bingo. During the visit, I asked about homework habits and who helped the student at home.

I learned a great deal about each family as a result of home visits. Jorge's family is very loving and caring. There was quite a bit of activity happening at the house when I visited. Jorge's sister-in-law was cooking, his dad was busy looking for papers, his eldest brother and brother-in-law were gathered downstairs, another brother was playing with friends in front of the apartment, there were seven children under the age of 4 in the living room, and two teenaged girls were laughing and chatting. Jorge and his fifth-grade sister are expected to complete their homework in the midst of all the activity. He is a smart boy but is working below grade level and does not receive much help at home. Now, I understand why. His home environment is not conducive to sitting quietly. It must be very difficult for a 6-year-old to focus on homework when there is so much happening around him. It also explains why Jorge is so aware of all the people in the classroom. If other students ask a question or drop a pencil, he will help them, even if they are on the opposite side of the room. He has clearly developed an ability to keep track of what everyone is doing in his family. The number of people in his home is similar to the number of people in the classroom, and their apartment space is not much larger.

Jorge's mother became more comfortable with me as we spent more time together. Though she did not mention it, I got the sense that she feels intimidated at school and is much more comfortable at home. She really lit up when I complimented her food, and she talked about how she prepared it. I realized that it also must be difficult for her to spend the time necessary to help Jorge when, besides him, she has an 11-year-old, a 4-year-old, a 1-year-old, five young grandchildren, several teenagers, and a son- and daughter-in-law living with her. She would like to be supportive but is unsure how to help. The family's reaction to my visit was very positive. Since the visit, I have noticed that I am much more understanding of Jorge's situation and am more likely to ask his sister for help and create more open communication with his family.

SOURCE: Used with permission of Gayle Morrison.

❖ Reflecting on the Cases

1. How did Ms. Marquez and Ms. Morrison address cultural issues and family values during the student-led conference and home visits? What improvements can be made to enact these activities at your school?

2. Explain how enacting student-led conferences benefits (and challenges) students, families, teachers, and schools.

3. Explain how encouraging home visits as an integral part of teaching and learning benefits (and challenges) students, families, teachers, and schools.

Activities for Further Development

1. Describe two specific activities to encourage respect and appreciation for diverse family structures.

2. Describe at least three ways that you can include families, their cultures, and their hobbies in expanding the physical education, performing arts, and/or fine arts curriculum at your school.

3. Describe at least three ways to encourage better communication and active participation for families, students, and teachers.

4. Think about homework and alternative homework assignments for students. Create a list of three alternative homework assignments for your students or students in a specific grade level. Tell how these assignments will encourage positive attitudes about school and respect for students and their families.

Additional Reading and Information

Allen, J. (2007). *Creating welcoming schools: A practical guide to home-school partnerships with diverse families.* New York: Teachers College Press. This book provides background information and strategies to help schools provide a more welcoming environment for all families and to promote ongoing partnerships with them.

Bailey, J. M., & Guskey, T. R. (2000). *Implementing student-led conferences.* Thousand Oaks, CA: Corwin Press. This book provides an introduction to planning, implementing, and assessing student-led conferences. Information related to participant responsibilities and effective models are provided.

Benson, B. P., & Barnett, S. P. (2005). *Student-led conferencing using showcase portfolios.* Thousand Oaks, CA: Corwin. This book provides ways to engage students and parents in authentic assessment of students' academic progress. It provides strategies for creating portfolios, both paper and electronic.

Kelly, M. (1990). *School-home notes: Promoting children's classroom success.* New York: Guilford Press. This book provides an array of resources to help teachers create good news notes and other positive teacher-parent communication strategies.

Schumm, J. S. (2005). *How to help your child with homework.* Minneapolis, MN: Free Spirit. This book provides information to help parents assist their children with homework.

Winn Tutwiler, S. J. (2005). *Teachers as collaborative partners: Working with diverse families and communities.* Mahwah, NJ: Lawrence Erlbaum. This book provides additional information about family dynamics and the social, cultural, and historical roots of families.

Part II
Building Effective Partnerships

Chapter 5: Building Family-School Partnerships

Chapter 6: Schools and Community: Working Together and Respecting Diversity

Chapter 7: Partnering With Community Organizations and Resources

Chapter 8: Barriers to Partnerships

5

Building Family-School Partnerships

After reading this chapter, you should have a better understanding of:

- the purpose and value of educational partnerships with families and parents;

- strategies to promote a positive school environment for families to enhance learning;

- what research says about parent involvement and parent-teacher partnerships;

- groups of children and families who are excluded from the school community;

- deficit views of families and ways to overcome them;

- misconceptions about parents and ways to address them;

- Joyce Epstein's six types of family involvement: parenting, communicating, volunteering, learning at home, decision making, and collaborating with the community; and

- family involvement activities that promote culturally relevant family participation.

Table 5.1	Prior Knowledge and Beliefs Organizer

Recall events that you remember when your parents or other family members were involved in your education (positive or negative).	Describe the feelings you had when your parents or other family members participated in your education.

Consider your reflections and the information you provided in Table 5.1 as you read about how to build stronger family-school partnerships.

Effective Partnerships With Families

Effective partnerships between family and school have positive effects on both affective and cognitive domains (Hara & Burke, 1998). McWayne, Hampton, Fantuzzo, Cohen, and Sekino (2004) found that teachers rated children of parents who provided support at home higher in reading and mathematics than children of parents who did not provide a supportive home environment. When families, schools, and communities work together, student academic achievement increases, and parents exhibit more active involvement (Epstein, 1992; Lezotte, 1997). However, family participation as an educational partner is cultural, is personal, and varies from school to school. Recently, I read an article where the author indicated that the family's role is to educate children at home and the school's role is to educate children at school. If we follow this view completely, we could never optimize the strengths that both families and schools can build together. This chapter is written from the perspective that families (e.g., parents, siblings, and the extended family) and schools are partners in the education of children, not separate entities.

In this chapter we will also confront the issue of family-school partnerships, diverse family structures, and inequities in family involvement and provide research-based strategies that can improve relationships and practices. We will examine the possibilities for effective family-school partnerships and provide examples of teachers and schools that partner successfully (and unsuccessfully) with families. Epstein (2001) reported that it was the teachers and administrators who made the difference whether or not families improved their knowledge about school, classroom events, and helping their children learn. Parent education level or marital status made no difference in effective educational involvement with schools.

Elements of Family-School Partnerships

Providing a Positive and Inviting School Environment

In order for families to become partners with teachers and schools, they must feel safe and comfortable entering the school building and the classroom. Next, they must feel comfortable communicating with the teacher and learning more about what takes place during the school day. It is not entirely up to the families to take the initiative to come to school and participate. The school and teachers must create plans and implement them when encouraging families to take part in educational activities at school or home. Redding (2001) recommends the use of common experiences to help schools plan for partnerships with families and the community. These components include communication in relation to (a) school policy, (b) events, (c) instructional strategies, and (d) the curriculum. Communicating about school policy involves discussing the importance of homework and due dates, reading at home, codes of conduct, and family expectations. School events including service-learning projects, guest speakers, spelling bees, and read-a-thons are usually exciting for families and should be communicated in advance. Instructional strategies can be outlined on school Web sites and within monthly or weekly classroom newsletters. These newsletters can provide instructional activities at home that will help students be more successful at school. Finally, the curriculum is an important framework in which all schools operate. All families and students should be notified of the standards in all curriculum areas with suggestions for families to integrate the content and skills at home.

Getting to Know Students and Their Families

It is important for teachers to make an extra effort to learn about their students and families outside of school. One way to find out this information is to ask students and their families to complete a survey. This survey can be part of an interactive homework assignment that the entire family completes together. Students and families should be informed that the survey is not graded. In return, the teacher should complete the same survey and provide his or her answers to students and families such as (a) favorite sports or outdoor activities, (b) favorite pets or animals, (c) favorite things to collect, (d) family activities, (e) favorite music, (f) favorite books and stories, and (g) favorite movies. In addition to this information, it will be advantageous to ask about the child's (a) experiences/feelings with school in prior grades, (b) strengths and challenges, (c) favorite subject and activities at school, and (d) other information that the teacher should know about. This activity encourages family communication and provides writing practice for a specific purpose if the child is in an upper elementary grade. This is a reciprocal process where parents and students provide information for the teacher and the teacher provides information for each family.

In the United States, most families and schools work under the misconception that participation in a child's education only takes place at the school site. In fact, many supportive and participatory activities can take place in the community and in homes. For this reason, *teachers should work with families, embrace their cultural beliefs, and create the most productive and interesting educational experience possible.* By focusing on various types of activities that encourage more family educational involvement such as parenting, communication, volunteering, learning at home, decision making, and community connections (Epstein, 2001; Epstein et al., 2002), the process and outcome of teaching and learning are enhanced. This chapter will outline ways in which teachers can connect with families in culturally relevant ways and ensure that all families have opportunities to become partners in their child's education.

Hoover-Dempsey and Sandler (1995) proposed a model of parental involvement based on research related to reasons why parents decided to become involved in their child's education. The researchers created a graphic organizer with five levels to explain the factors associated with parental educational involvement. The model also distinguishes between school-based behaviors and home-based behaviors. Some of the reasons for parental involvement are psychological and are affected by the parents' motivation, culture, and belief system. For example, Level 1 includes basic invitations from their child or the school as motivating factors to participate. Level 5 includes student outcomes and self-efficacy for school success. The Hoover-Dempsey and Sandler model is included in Figure 5.1.

| Figure 5.1 | Hoover-Dempsey and Sandler Model |

The Hoover-Dempsey and Sandler Model of Parental Involvement

Level 5

Student Achievement

↑

Level 4

Student Attributes Conducive to Achievement			
Academic Self-Efficacy	Intrinsic Motivation to Learn	Self-Regulatory Strategy Use	Social Self-Efficacy Teachers

↑

Level 3

Mediated by Child Perception of Parent Mechanisms			
Encouragement	Modeling	Reinforcement	Instruction

↑

Level 2

Parent Mechanisms of Involvement			
Encouragement	Modeling	Reinforcement	Instruction

↑

Parent Involvement Forms			
Values, goals, etc.	Home Involvement	School Communication	School Involvement

↑

Level 1

Personal Motivation		Invitations			Life Context	
Parental Role Construction	Parental Efficacy	General School Invitations	Specific School Invitations	Specific Child Invitations	Knowledge and Skills	Time and Energy

SOURCE: Adapted from Hoover-Dempsey and Sandler (1995, 2005).

How Are Families Included?

As we discussed in Chapter 1, many educational responsibilities are shared. There are varying views related to who has the responsibility to educate children, but most teachers believe that education starts at home and that parents are the most important teachers in children's lives. The New Jersey Department of Education Web site features information related to the expectations of parents as educational partners. The site lists areas in which parents should be involved including attending board meetings, voting in elections, volunteering at school, serving on the school management team, and participating in the school parent-teacher association. Most of all, the site indicates that parents should be active advocates for their children. Teachers can help advertise the plethora of information available in print and on educational Web sites.

The Deficit View of Family Involvement

The **deficit view** of education relates to historical inequity among students from underrepresented groups. It is based on the notion that one group is superior while other groups are inferior when it comes to academic potential. When you relate this view to families, the deficit view tends to marginalize the potential of families who are less educated, from diverse ethnicities, or from working-class low-income backgrounds. The notion that children who come from non-English backgrounds should be placed in special classes is based on the fact that educators view the child's native language as a deficit rather than an asset.

Efforts to make children more "American" and more like the mainstream still resonate in some areas of the United States. Moll (1990) and Moll and Gonzalez (1994) claim that teachers who work with ethnically diverse students should inquire about and analyze activities in students' homes to determine their uses of knowledge and their strengths. This view, known as funds of knowledge, includes thinking about the value that all families can offer a community and school. By looking for funds or deposits of knowledge, we shift our definition of the culture and educational potential of students' households. This means looking at culture as a process that lives within the beliefs and contexts of students, their families, and their lives. This view—that students and their families have much to offer—differs from the traditional perspective that children and families from working-class underrepresented households lack knowledge and experiences. All families harbor expertise or funds of knowledge that grows within their social and cognitive experiences. Creating stronger partnerships with families and meeting with these families in their homes offer educators a more in-depth sense of the knowledge that families and students offer schools and classrooms.

Six Types of Family Involvement

It is common to have more family involvement when children first enter kindergarten and first grade than when they go to middle school or high school. Therefore, middle schools and high schools are making more attempts to include families in educational activities. Epstein (2001) and Epstein et al. (2002) identified six types of involvement that can help all schools work with families more effectively in all areas of education, beginning at preschool. Each type of involvement is important for creating a true collaborative educational environment; however, it is possible that schools begin with the first level of involvement, parenting, before engaging in other areas such as volunteering and learning at home. For example, within a school's strategic plan, the faculty and administrators may decide that there is a need to work with families on parenting. This does not mean that schools should ignore the other family involvement areas, but it means that they will focus on one area at a time rather than focusing on too many areas at once. Promoting more parent involvement in the area of parenting may include a checklist that is sent home to all families in the school. The checklist may include very basic parenting strategies such as eating a healthy breakfast at home or school, getting enough sleep each night, and reading together every day. Another school may want to focus on communicating with parents before it focuses on decision making or planning collaborative community efforts. The information below provides a rationale and specific strategies related to encouraging family involvement in the six areas defined by Epstein (2001): parenting, communicating, volunteering, learning at home, decision making, and collaborating with the community.

SOURCE: Used with permission of Serena Lin.

By creating stronger communication opportunities and partnerships with families, everyone benefits!

Parenting

Parenting involves establishing home environments that support children and youth's social, cognitive, emotional, and physical health. In an educational partnership, teachers may offer parenting information to families while parents offer information about their culture, beliefs, and educational goals for their children. Before a partnership can develop between teachers and families, all partners must come together to define the term *parenting* and describe the roles and expectations related to this area. The physical environment, family routines, modeling, nutrition, and activities at home all relate to parenting. The goal of positive parenting includes providing a healthy, safe environment so that children will become well-adjusted, contributing members of society.

Teachers, as educators, have the responsibility to support families in their roles related to parenting. However, support must include respecting cultural differences and philosophies related to child rearing practices. Having said this, educators can provide helpful suggestions and strategies to promote opportunities for parent education within the community. Schools can send home a list of positive parenting suggestions each month with a different theme such as "Turn Off the Tube and Strive for 10 Minutes of Family Time Each Day" or "Try to Eat One Fruit or Vegetable That Starts With Each Letter of the Alphabet." "One Positive Action or Thought Each Day" can encourage parents to state at least one positive thing about their child each day. "10 Minutes Each Day" campaigns can encourage parents to spend at least 10 minutes of uninterrupted time with their children each day playing, reading, cooking, or just cuddling. These fun but nonthreatening tips for families support the child's overall development. Providing information in the form of colorful inviting flyers that include various languages based on the student population or information written by students can provide extra motivation for families to participate.

Communicating

"We teach the bright . . . and the not so bright." Believe it or not, this quote was spoken by a principal of a K–5 elementary school who was welcoming new families one midsummer evening. She readily welcomed the parents who were in attendance but neglected to welcome the children who would be attending the meeting and who would be part of the school when the academic year began. Although these are just a few words that were spoken at a meeting, they demonstrate how challenging communication can be. Miscommunication or misrepresentation, as in the quote above, can cause a disconnection from the very beginning. Although the principal was trying to show that the school was inclusive and wanted to provide an education for all students, her comments were frowned upon by the parents because they thought that she was classifying children according to their abilities before school ever started. Therefore, teachers should think carefully about the words used when talking to parents.

Effective communication with families involves school-to-home and home-to-school interactions related to children's education and their overall well-being. Open communication between all parties is essential to enhancing students' learning. For this type of involvement, we will refer to communication that takes place between schools and families and expand on communicating with the community later. Communicating with additional partners within the community such as service agencies, businesses, and cultural institutions will be described within the sixth type of involvement, collaborating with communities.

Communication can be formal or informal. Both are necessary for optimum collaboration. Relationships build over time, not just in a formal back-to-school night session or a 15-minute parent-teacher conference. Some teachers begin communicating with families before the doors open on the first day of school. A second-grade teacher named Mr. Ramirez makes phone calls to every family before school starts each year. He introduces himself to family members, tells how excited he is to work with their child, tells them a little about his experience as a teacher, and describes his hobbies such as scuba diving, golf, and hiking. In return, he asks parents to tell him about their children so that he can anticipate meeting their needs, strengths, and interests during the school year. Parents are also encouraged to ask questions and explain their goals and desires for their children. He starts the phone calls about 2 weeks before school begins so that he can reach every family before the first day of school. At the end of the phone call, he invites them to the classroom and states that he looks forward to meeting them during Back-to-School Night where child care, snacks, and transportation will be provided. Although this process takes time and planning (and even cuts into some of his summer vacation), Mr. Ramirez believes that he actually saves time once the school year begins because he will know each family and know more about the children so that he can plan lessons more effectively. Communication via monthly or weekly class newsletters, school information packets, e-mail messages, and Web site postings is considered minimal, and teachers are advised to encourage two-way communication with families when possible. All information should be translated into languages that families can read and understand whenever possible.

Some teachers find it helpful to include a note for parents each week, either written on a large whiteboard, posted on a parent bulletin board, or sent home in children's backpacks. Take a look at the letter in "Notes From the Classroom"; all parents receive such a letter when they visit their child's kindergarten classroom. The information is provided in English and Spanish. It is important to be as concise as possible and phrase all information in terms that are general and that can be understood by the general public.

Notes From the Classroom:
Teacher Information for Parents Who Visit the Classroom

Parents and Visitors to Our Classes: The student work in our rooms reflects the state standards. Please take a minute to familiarize yourself with them so that you can see what students are learning at this time in kindergarten.

Thank you!

Mr. Delmar

Mrs. Phuntsog

(Continued)

(Continued)

Reading

- Know that print is spoken words written down.
- Know the difference between a letter and a word.
- Follow left-to-right progression of print.
- Name upper-/lowercase letters.
- Identify and produce rhyming words.
- Identify beginning/ending sounds.
- Start to produce sounds for consonant letters.

NOTE: Content standards and skills for reading comprehension, writing, mathematics, social studies, science, technology, and the arts are also included in this letter.

Caspe (2003) conducted a study that was published in *The School Community Journal* that included interviews with 13 teachers. She found that communication and observation were the most common strategies that teachers used to collect information about students' families. Teachers indicated that they collected information through face-to-face formal and informal conferences, casual "run-ins" outside of school, and written notes, phone calls, and interactive home-school notebooks taken home each week. Teachers made informal observations related to the general health of children that included their appearance, cleanliness, completion of homework, and other out-of-school responsibilities. They also made observations of family members in the morning before school or when they picked their children up after school. Cumulatively, teachers were able to learn more about their students, students' families, parenting practices, family structure, families' cultural beliefs, families' educational goals, family members' employment status, and even family members' work schedules by taking the time to observe and interact with families.

An open-door policy must be established among the families, students, and teachers. This open-door policy must be inclusive and be truly open to all families. Families should feel comfortable entering the school grounds and then comfortable and safe (i.e., emotionally) walking inside the classroom door when appropriate. An open-door policy creates an atmosphere that shows respect for all. Students can write invitations throughout the school year inviting their families to school, with or without a special event in place. One of the best ways to include families at school could be an informal reading day where children, their families, and their siblings come to school early and read together. Another time could be where the families play games with their children during recess or have lunch together. By students taking the initiative and having the motivation to invite their families to school, it increases the potential for families to feel more comfortable and welcome. In addition, students are honing their literacy skills and writing for a purpose. Students can draw, paint, or decorate the front of the invitation and address the envelope to the appropriate parent, grandparent, or guardian. Teachers should be sensitive to the fact that many families do have work schedules that prohibit them from visiting during school hours, so students can always think of alternative adults or older siblings to invite. Better yet, some family events can be encouraged in the early morning or during a few evenings.

The *Parent Teacher Education Connection* Web site (http://www.tcet.unt.edu/pte-connect/) outlines four essential strategies that assist families and schools with open and positive communication. These strategies, known as the four Ps, include positive comments, personalized information, proactive communication, and partnerships that are well informed. Positive comments can be provided in folders that go home each week, a special note written by the student and teacher, a quick e-mail, or a phone call. Traditionally, families only receive calls when their child exhibits discipline problems or is injured. The reporting of positive information redefines family and school communication and encourages families to *want* to talk to teachers.

When information is personalized rather than generalized, families and students feel like the teacher really knows the child and cares. Due to the number of form letters and wide-scale memos that families receive, personal information about their children does not usually make it past the classroom door. Recently, my daughter's kindergarten teacher told me a personalized story that happened during physical education (PE) class. The teacher said that many children were arguing about who was the winner of a certain event. The PE teacher asked the students how to determine a winner. According to her teacher, my daughter Cate proudly stated, "It doesn't matter if you win or lose; it's your character that counts!" By telling me this quick story, Cate's teacher encouraged positive thoughts and provided me with a glimpse of Cate's personality and confidence at school. As Cate's mother, I was so very appreciative to hear this positive and personalized information. One way for teachers to record personalized information about students is to have a clipboard and paper handy (or even a handheld BlackBerry) to record positive and personal anecdotal notes each week. These notes can be posted in a designated area for parents to read, sent home in weekly folders, or shared during parent-teacher conferences.

Being proactive keeps families up to date with school events and their child's academic progress. Teachers can set reasonable goals for how many events they should invite families to attend each year (in addition to open house evenings and parent-teacher conferences). Some teachers like to invite parents to one event each month. Other teachers invite parents to attend events each week. Parents can participate in a very small event such as eating lunch together or a large-scale event such as "Pajamas and Pancakes Reading Day." Keeping families informed on a regular basis and in advance works best because then they will know when to expect particular information (e.g., at the beginning of each month) and they can plan their work or home schedules around school events. Positive, personal, and proactive information all lead to the ultimate goal of achieving well-informed teacher-school-family partnerships.

School-to-home notebooks are also popular forms of communication (see the following "Notes From the Classroom" section). They can be written in the form of journals where students write what they are doing in school, their favorite part of the day, or their goals related to what they want to accomplish. Teachers make comments related to each student's writing, and then the notebook is sent home. The student asks his or her parent or another family member to make a comment in the journal at home before the journal is returned to school. When the student makes another entry, the process continues. This is not specific communication related to events, discipline, or other matters (although it could be set up this way as part of a student-parent-teacher contract), but it does provide open communication among the school, families, and students.

Notes From the Classroom: School-to-Home Notebook Sample

Dear Mr. and Mrs. Olson,

Callie is having some challenges learning addition and subtraction facts related to these fact families: 15, 16, 17, and 18. I have included a list of all of the facts in these families. Please use flashcards and objects to review these facts at home. I would suggest only focusing on one fact family each week. Please write back each week and let me know how she is doing and any questions you have.

Sincerely,

Your Partner in Callie's Education

Ms. Morales

Dear Ms. Morales,

Thank you so much for letting us know about Callie's challenges with some of the fact families. We have been practicing the fact families in the car using a small whiteboard and markers. She LOVES learning facts this way. She knows most of her 15 and 16 fact families. We will continue working on them in addition to the 17 and 18 fact families. Thank you for all you do.

Alejandra and Jared Olson

Carl Rogers (1967), known for almost a century of work related to interpersonal relationships and facilitating learning, recommended that teachers communicate three core conditions including genuineness, respect, and empathy. These interpersonal qualities still hold true today when teachers work closely with families as partners. First, teachers should be genuine and come across to families as real people with the same strengths and weaknesses as any other human being. They do not know everything, and they are not experts in every area of education. Second, teachers should demonstrate respect and acceptance while valuing families' opinions and views. They should make every attempt to honor reasonable requests that families make in relation to educating their child. Finally, showing empathy is important so that teachers can look at a child's situation from the family's point of view. To many families, their children are the center of their universe, and many families have raised their children since birth. Showing empathy and caring for challenges that the families and children may face will help build a positive relationship and effective communication over time.

Enhancing Learning for Students With Special Needs: Communicating With Families and Home Visits

There are a variety of strategies that teachers can share with families when working with **children with special needs**. For example, families who have children with autism or learning disabilities can work with teachers to communicate their goals for the child, as well as the child's special needs and strengths. Beatriz, a second-grade teacher, conducted home visits, created home-to-school journals, and used weekly activity logs to communicate better with a family whose child was diagnosed with **Asperger syndrome**. Children with Asperger syndrome have traits related to autism and demonstrate social and emotional challenges. Usually these children do not show delays in language or intellectual development. Beatriz stated, "As in many partnerships, time is always a major barrier. Committing to home visits and weekly activity logs is sometimes a challenge . . . but rewarding when parents and teachers become partners to help a child succeed in school" (B. Morales, personal communication, May 2009). Therefore, communication with families can take place outside the formal classroom and can include more than the basic form letters and e-mail updates. Beatriz has shown that multiple communication strategies can be beneficial to the teacher, student, and family:

- Home visits to get to know the child and family members better and to learn about their beliefs, values, and interests
- Home-to-school journals to communicate information related to the child's social and emotional needs
- Activity logs and differentiated instructional strategies used when applicable

---

Volunteering

Volunteering can take place at the school site, at home, or within the community. If a parent or guardian wants to volunteer during school hours, there are many businesses that provide leave time for this activity. It is important that schools recognize companies and organizations that permit parents to become more involved in their child's education. Some companies have been identified as "family friendly" based on flexible hours, onsite child care, shared positions, and other characteristics. However, *USA Today* (Armour, 2003) reported that many companies are downsizing their family-friendly work environment because of the unstable labor market, the need to increase productivity, and other cost-saving measures.

In California, the Family-School Partnership Act allows parents, grandparents, and guardians to take time off from work to participate in activities at their child's K–12 school or child care facility if they work for an employer with at least 25 employees. Under this law, parents and guardians can take up to 40 hours each year and up to 8 hours each calendar month to participate in their child's school. Employees can use existing vacation time, personal leave, or other compensatory time off to account for the time used for educational purposes. However, the employee should provide advance notice and documentation from the child's school or child care facility. Unfortunately, teachers and many other professionals do not have vacation or compensatory time off when school is in session, so therefore the only option for participating in their child's school activities (during school time) is to take personal leave or leave without pay.

Volunteering at school for the mainstream population has traditionally been focused on mothers who do not work outside of the home. Ideally, volunteer opportunities should be encouraged for all family members such as fathers, cousins, aunts, uncles, grandparents, and older siblings. In addition, some teachers have found it advantageous to recruit a few families within the classroom to serve as classroom liaisons to encourage involvement from other families. This is successful because many families feel more comfortable with other families in the community than with teachers, particularly if they are from diverse ethnic groups. Family liaisons can assist schools in recruiting and organizing family support systems and communicating various opportunities, events, and their own positive experiences at the school.

Project Appleseed, whose motto is to "leave no parent behind," seeks 50 million public school families to volunteer a minimum of 10 hours each year to improve schools in rural, suburban, and urban areas throughout the United States. To encourage volunteerism, Come and Fredericks (1995) reported positive outcomes when families are invited to read or tell stories to small groups of children on a regular basis. Parents who work full-time are asked to read or tell stories on tape or videotape to share with students. Even siblings of students in the class can record stories or sing songs if their parents feel uncomfortable doing so. Teachers can send a cassette recorder and tape home to assist in the activity. Families who speak different languages are encouraged to read, tell stories, or sing songs in their native language. This encourages volunteering and literacy development and instills a sense of pride in students and their families.

There are multiple levels of volunteerism in schools (Epstein, 2001). At the simplest level, families can volunteer their time at home facilitating children's homework, literacy skills, or other out-of-school educational activities. The second level includes involvement in school functions such as open houses or parent conferences, attending performances, and participation in family nights. The third level includes volunteering time at the school site as a sports activity facilitator, lunch monitor, recess monitor, or classroom helper. Finally, families can volunteer their time to join the local parent-teacher association or organization, attend parent meetings, or participate as a joint decision maker as part of the school council. Schools should encourage all families to volunteer at the first level as a minimum standard. Opportunities for volunteering should vary according to different time frames; that is, some events should take place in the morning, some in the late afternoon, and some in the evening. See the following installment of "Notes From the Classroom" for a sample questionnaire from a K–5 school to assess family availability and volunteer interests. The survey was called "Searching for Lots of Volunteers."

Notes From the Classroom: Sample Parent Questionnaire

Searching for Lots of Volunteers

As another school year begins, ask yourself this question: "What is the most important thing I can do to help my child succeed in school?" If your answer is BE INVOLVED, you are correct! There are many ways that you can become involved, even if you are a working parent.
  Please check below the areas where you would like to help.

Classroom volunteer _____

Room parent _____

Contributing materials or goods _____

Sharing or demonstrating your hobby or occupation to students _____

Helping the parent-teacher association (PTA) _____

Doing clerical work in the front office _____

Library helper, grades K–3 (reading stories) _____

Library helper, grades 4–6 (checking out books) _____

Bilingual Committee member _____

School Site Council member _____

School Advisory Committee member _____

Helping at home with activities _____

Helping at home with bulletin boards _____

Parent's Name _____ Phone Number _____
Child's Name _____ Teacher _____
Other Child's Name _____ Teacher _____
Other Child's Name _____ Teacher _____
Other Child's Name _____ Teacher _____

NOTE: Special thanks to Kathryn Sampilo Wilson.

There are growing efforts in the United States to promote more involvement and volunteering opportunities for dads. One group, the Illinois Fatherhood Initiative, seeks to connect children and dads by promoting responsible fathering and to help men become more comfortable as father figures and role models. As part of the initiative, the group focuses on getting more dads involved in education—at school and at home. Some schools have found it advantageous to assign a willing parent, grandparent, guardian, or community member to serve as volunteer coordinator. The volunteer coordinator can recruit other members to help collect information about volunteer time availability, interests, talents, and wishes. Some districts are hiring family resource directors or community liaisons to fulfill this role.

Learning at Home

Families are at the forefront to supplement the educational experiences of their children. But teachers must be proactive in sharing with families information related to learning-based home activities. These activities can be formal or informal. Teachers can communicate learning activities and homework tips through regular newsletters or e-mails in a variety of languages. Teachers can also model home learning strategies when families visit the school for conferences or a school open house night. It should be noted that the mother does not have to be the only family member supporting learning at home. Fathers, grandparents, and older siblings are also partners in a child's learning environment. One school organized a *Doughnuts for Dads* program where fathers are encouraged to attend education sessions to enhance literacy development through home activities. The program encourages reading books, writing for different purposes at home, providing school and home interactions, integrating technology, and storytelling (Katsaros, 2003). The purpose of the program is to encourage all family members, including fathers, to take an active role in their child's education.

The U.S. Department of Labor reported that children who go to college have the potential to end poverty in their family lines forever. Certain common elements at home can help prepare students for academic success in school and college although access to college is not always easy. This is not because students do not have good grades but because they are not provided with access and experiences throughout their K–12 education. In addition, the expectations and benefits of higher education are not necessarily hot topics of conversation in many families when both parents are working long hours to pay rent, buy food, and take care of their children. Although access to college is a topic beyond the scope of this book, schools can provide support and resources to communicate the value of education beyond high school years. Some common elements that have been successful in helping families prepare students for academic success include creating a literate environment at home, encouraging children to address and solve problems, and making school a priority.

Creating a Literate Environment

Project Appleseed, a collaborative effort to promote family and community involvement, recently reported that if every parent spent at least one hour reading or working on other academic subjects with his or her children ages 1–9 for 5 days each week, there would be about 8.7 billion hours contributed, and it would equal about $300 billion if teachers were to work one-on-one with students. *Project Appleseed* claims that every school needs a compact or pledge in order to create multiple responsible parties when educating children. Pledges can include commitments from families who cannot come to school but who can help at home by reading at least 15 minutes each day or by extending school content at home. Come and Fredericks (1995) offer a series of guidelines to help parents support literacy while also building self-confidence. These family guidelines include the following:

- Spending quality time together
- Encouraging reading for fun
- Listening to children's ideas
- Praising children
- Engaging in family activities and projects
- Sharing favorite books, stories, and music
- Talking to children regularly
- Establishing daily read-aloud times
- Playing games and problem solving
- Noting environmental print
- All family members modeling the act of reading

Students discuss oceanography topics such as beach erosion and a healthy beach environment with a university professor.

In some schools, particularly urban and rural, some families have difficulty acquiring literacy materials for their home. Therefore, Come and Fredericks (1995) suggest that teachers provide books for children to take home daily or weekly to read with their families and consider organizing a school-wide book exchange program. On the first day of each month, teachers can send blank calendars home for families and students to record the name of the book on the day they read it. Students can report their activities back to school and share their favorite books.

In addition to literacy activities, families should be encouraged to provide regular outdoor activities such as walking, riding bikes, climbing, and sports at home. They can visit the local library and obtain library cards and books and attend free or inexpensive plays and concerts. Schools and teachers should make an effort to communicate opportunities related to library resources, physical activities, and cultural events within the community.

Solving Problems

This is an area that children and families can address every day. Parents can involve children in solving problems that relate to their home life such as repairing a flashlight or making decisions about what to buy at the grocery store using coupons and within a $50 weekly budget. In addition, board games such as Scrabble, Checkers, Chess, and Concentration encourage problem-solving skills. Children can engage in solving problem situations when doing household chores such as loading the dishwasher to gain maximum capacity or helping repair sprinklers in the yard that are facing the wrong direction. Allowing children to offer opinions when solving problems will strengthen their judgment and build confidence over time.

It is never too early to encourage entrepreneurship. Children can set up their own neighborhood businesses such as recycling, selling lemonade, or doing specialized work for neighbors. Nick, a fourth grader, decided to create his own recycling business. First, he wrote a letter to all of his neighbors to save their glass, plastic, and aluminum for him. He provides a bucket for each neighbor who agrees to participate so that they can place the empty containers on their front porch on Fridays, Sundays, and Wednesdays. He collects the materials, takes a trip to the recycling center behind the local grocery store, and hurries home to record his earnings on a chart that he created. Although this activity may not relate directly to what his teacher is doing in the classroom, the net result is greater responsibility, creativity, and problem-solving abilities.

Making school a priority includes instilling positive habits at home that support and optimize children's learning at school. Almost every professional educational group recommends that families encourage a regular bedtime for children to make sure they have plenty of sleep. Table 5.2 shows the recommended number of hours that children should be getting at different ages. Going to bed early and at the same time each night with a specific routine helps students stay alert during school activities. It is also helpful to set a weekday morning routine such as getting dressed, brushing teeth, and eating a healthy breakfast with protein and fiber. In addition, parents and children should set up a quiet area to complete homework and talk often about school events and content, and parents should monitor their children's free time at home.

Table 5.2	Recommended Number of Hours of Sleep: Preschool, Elementary School, and Middle School

Age Range	Recommended Number of Sleep Hours
Preschool (Ages 3–5)	11–13 hours
Elementary School (Ages 5–11)	10–11 hours
Middle School (Ages 11–13)	9–10 hours

SOURCE: Public domain. Reprinted from the National Sleep Foundation: http://www.sleepforkids.org/html/uskids.html.

Healthy nutritional habits, as discussed in Chapter 3, are essential for development and educational potential. Sears, Sears, Sears, and Sears (2006) suggest that families teach their children about foods that help them grow, develop, and learn such as "grow foods." Grow foods are filled with nutrients in each bit relative to the number of calories. Such foods include eggs, fruits, nuts, lean meats, vegetables, whole grains, and yogurt. Grow foods are mostly whole foods that come straight from nature and are not manufactured. When foods are eaten in their natural state, more nutrients stay in the food. Sears et al. also recommend that families encourage children to eat a balanced diet throughout the day but indicate that some types of foods are better eaten in the morning rather than in the afternoon or evening. Young children should eat a breakfast and lunch that is high in protein, healthy carbohydrates, and healthy fats. They can eat less protein at dinner and more carbohydrates because children need protein during the day to perk up their brains and carbohydrates at night to relax them more. Some of the best snacks for young children include raw nuts, trail mix, apple slices with peanut butter, yogurt, edamame (soybeans), and hard-boiled eggs. Healthy eating should be integrated into the school curriculum, and teachers should seek families as partners to instill healthy eating habits at even the youngest ages.

Homework can be one of the most stressful areas between teachers and parents and parents and their children. Over and over again, you hear stories about families who stayed awake past midnight with their children finishing a literature project or a dad who developed a strained relationship with his son because his son grew more frustrated each day with the amount and type of homework that was being sent home. On a positive note, there are ways to create a more optimistic way to look at homework. Teachers can communicate best practices related to homework such as creating a homework area that is free from distractions and that includes a box or bag of supplies such as pencils, pens, markers, glue, scissors, paper, rulers, and other necessary items. If families do not have supplies at home to support homework activities, then the school should provide a homework box that students take home or homework should not be assigned. This is because not all families have support systems or the funds to buy extra materials for elaborate or daily projects. Families can support learning at home by encouraging students to learn more about subjects they like best. Teachers can recommend free or inexpensive resources within the community where students can check out books or videos, see exhibits, or participate in events. By parents initiating and participating in educational activities with their children, they are serving as role models demonstrating learning as a lifelong process.

Decision Making

Shared decision making, often referred to as site-based management or school-based management, has been a popular structure in many schools. It includes families, students, teachers, and members of the community for the purpose of improving curriculum and instruction. The concept was created to provide decision-making power to groups that were traditionally excluded from the process. Although this formal structure is successful at some school sites, other school sites have experienced unequal distribution of power even though multiple partners are represented. When looking at shared decision making, it does not have to happen within a formal structure such as within a school-based management committee; it can include informal processes as well.

Collaboration among students, colleagues, and families plays a key role in real decision-making opportunities. Teachers and families together can build an interactive learning community that acknowledges and respects diversity. The main role of families, teachers, and administrators is in the form of listening and learning from each other without debating or feeling that there should be one right answer. Having many diverse perspectives related to school issues or school change can only make an educational environment stronger and more successful. Nichols-Solomon (2000) recommends that schools use the "reflective-practice" model with teams of teachers who join together with families and the principal to discuss school issues, needs, and community efforts. She suggests that multiple opportunities are necessary to promote effective school-family partnerships, particularly in the area of leadership and decision making. Common areas known to include parent decision-making opportunities include the following:

- Site-based management committees
- Parent advisory committees for specific programs (e.g., school carnival, special event)
- Officer or coordinator as part of a parent-teacher organization
- Classroom parent
- Search committees for hiring new faculty or principals
- Parent liaison for special programs, such as recruiting community members to perform
- Parent to oversee the progress of a student-created yearbook

Collaborating With the Community

This area of family involvement includes ways to identify and integrate community resources and services within the school curriculum for the purpose of strengthening student achievement, student health and welfare, school programs, and family practices.

Communication in this area includes home-to-community, school-to-community, and home-to-school-to-community. Businesses, cultural institutions, health and social service agencies, and other community groups possess resources and expertise to strengthen education and promote partnerships with educators. Chapters 6 and 7 will provide in-depth information and examples related to this area.

Family Involvement in the 21st Century

Redefining Family Involvement

The challenge for educators is to redefine family involvement (considering working parents, socioeconomic status, cultural views, etc.) for the 21st century rather than work from traditional parent-teacher paradigms. Almost 40 years of research have shown that parental participation contributes to student academic achievement. This claim holds true for all socioeconomic levels and parent education (e.g., Griffith, 1996; Keith et al., 1993; Thorkildsen, Thorkildsen, & Stein, 1998). Nevertheless, we continue to see middle- and upper-middle-income parents who seek involvement with their child's teacher, while low-income, working-class families from diverse cultural groups often feel disconnected (Moles, 1993; Valdes, 1996). Barton, Drake, Perez, St. Louis, and George (2004) propose that involvement is not enough to engage parents—particularly those from non-English language backgrounds. They suggest shifting the focus from what parents do to engage in their children's schooling to the hows and whys of their engagement. Therefore, parents' experiences and actions inside and outside the school community become important factors in partnership development. Barton and her colleagues found that parents engage in personal ways with their children in relation to schools, and educators should consider this when building long-lasting relationships. Desimone (1999) examined the linkage between parent involvement and student achievement. She focused her study on whether or not there were relationships between different types of parent involvement and student achievement. Students' ethnicity and family income level were also noted. She found that effective parental involvement could differ according to students' race, ethnicity, and income level. Therefore, Desimone calls for more research in this area to help define specific types of family involvement activities that promote positive outcomes for diverse students.

Engaging Parents in School Events

Epstein (2001) points out that educators must meet the basic needs of a partnership before moving to more complex issues or activities. She states that a successful comprehensive partnership among schools, families, and communities includes a mixture of basic and advanced partnership activities. At the most basic level, families participate in school activities by making sure their child has breakfast and arrives to school on time. As they move to more complex involvement, they may participate in a school "United Nations Day" by cooking a food that relates to their ancestry and culture. An even more complex activity might be serving as the volunteer coordinator for "Physical Fitness Fun Day." Table 5.3 outlines types of family involvement (Epstein, 2001) and sample activities that encourage participation from families of diverse ethnicities and ethnic groups.

Table 5.3	Examples of Activities With Families	
Types of Family Involvement	**Sample Activity or Strategy**	**Sample Activity or Strategy**
Parenting	Provide children with a list of ideal breakfast and lunch foods that help them learn most effectively during school hours.	Have available to families who request them a variety of videos or DVDs related to such topics as literacy, nutrition, physical fitness, and other issues. Many of these videos are offered free of charge through government agencies.
Communicating	Have a conference at a student's home instead of school. If possible, visit students' homes at least one time during the school year to learn about them and connect better with their families.	Send calendars home at the beginning of each month with events, homework suggestions and assignments, and topics that students are learning in class.
Volunteering	Send a questionnaire home to all families (translated if needed) and have them indicate their skills, time, and availability at home or school.	Send parents invitations created by students to invite them to volunteer to read to the class or to share one of their hobbies.
Learning at home	Create a Fun Family List that includes activities at home such as taking a walk in the park or calling a relative and reading him or her a story.	Have students create a list of "Ideal Homework Guidelines" to take home and share with their families. Families and students can work together to implement the strategies such as keeping supplies in one place and working in a quiet area.
Decision making	Create a network, Web site, or bulletin that allows parent and school groups to connect with all families and contribute their ideas for the school.	Include diverse students, families, and community members as part of all school committees. Include at least one bilingual member if relevant to your school.
Collaborating with community	Create a family-community-school event where students work together toward a common goal such as cleaning up a riverbed area, collecting trash around neighborhoods, or creating recycling information and initiatives.	Set up a promotional area in front of the school during drop-off times each month with breakfast items and a list of resources in the community such as social human services, free educational materials, and public library events.

Early Literacy and Family Support

Research studies suggest that a home environment that supports literacy at an early age allows children to be more successful at school (e.g., Dodici, Draper, & Peterson, 2003; Senechal, 2006; Senechal & LeFevre, 2002). In fact, family literacy experiences in preschool and kindergarten predict reading comprehension, vocabulary development, phonological awareness, and reading for pleasure. Senechal and LeFevre (2002) propose a **home literacy model** that outlines two specific activities related to early literacy and phonemic awareness. These activities include reading stories and direct teaching about literacy. Reading stories enhances children's language skills and comprehension. Direct teaching about sounds and word meanings relates to their overall literacy and phonics development. Therefore, it is important that families and educators be aware of these findings as they work together to ensure that all children feel successful as they enter school.

Tips for Families and Teachers

1. Provide a variety of books and other literature in the home. Read with children daily. Allow them time to respond, add to the story, and discuss their favorite parts.

2. Build traditions within the classroom and within the home. Traditions cultivate a connection among peers, teachers, and family members. For example, have a build-your-own-pizza night each Tuesday at home. At school, teachers and students can participate in a Friday tradition where everyone does yoga and demonstrates his or her favorite yoga pose. Invite parents to class to participate.

3. Redefine traditional family involvement such as volunteering, learning at home, and communication. Encourage two-way communication through home-to-school journals, newsletters, home visits, and Web site postings. Encourage volunteering outside of school and parent work hours.

Chapter Summary

Students whose parents support learning at home are more successful at school. When families and schools work together to communicate strategies, ideas, and expectations, students demonstrate higher achievement in academic areas. Nevertheless, some families have more "access" to the curriculum, procedures, and formal school behaviors. Families and teachers face many misconceptions about each other that can only be overcome by working together for a common goal. It is important that teachers view parents as assets rather than a deficit. Joyce Epstein (2001; Epstein et al., 2002) provides six types of family involvement to help families and schools work together to enhance the education of children: parenting, communicating, volunteering, learning at home, decision making, and collaborating with the community. These types of involvement should be promoted with culturally relevant family participation and activities in mind.

CASE STUDIES

The first case study in this chapter describes a parent-teacher-administrator writing seminar that helped build community at an elementary school and is adapted from Akroyd (1995). Parents from diverse cultures participated in personal writing activities with their students at a school in Virginia. The second case study illustrates how teachers, students, families, and community members collaborated to provide a literacy sleepover and family night called "Kamp Kino" at their school (Ambrose, 2008). This case study illustrates how teachers, families, and the community came together to enhance learning.

❖ Case Study 5.1: Developing Writers One Pen at a Time

Susan Akroyd (1995), an elementary school principal, developed this program after attending a professional presentation by another principal in New York City. She wrote about her experiences from the beginning of the program and the outcomes. She advertised the class in a family newsletter two different times right after school started. Although her school consisted of families from 35 different countries, she only advertised the class in English because she lacked appropriate translating services. She described the event as an old-fashioned writing bee where parents could come together to write something for their children. Akroyd reflected on her experiences and described this motivating and successful event in *The Reading Teacher*. Her voice and those of parents and students are included below.

Voice of Susan Akroyd, Principal at "Parham Elementary School"

At 7 p.m. at the beginning of our first class, a teacher, a retired teacher, a PTA board member, and I sat around a table in the library smiling at one another. I was accepting but disappointed at the attendance although I knew many adults were uneasy with writing. I cautioned those present and I had no idea where this experience would lead. "Perhaps we should begin by writing about our recollections of ourselves as writers," I said. We began quietly.

Then a booming voice resounded. "Hola!" I looked up to see a family, Mr. and Mrs. Ortiz and their children, from the Parklawn Hispanic community. I was thrilled and, with my usual mix of Spanish and English, managed to ask these parents to write in Spanish. While their children looked at library books, they wrote fluidly.

"Annyong haseyo!" A Korean family entered the room 2 minutes later. After the usual introductions, I asked them if they would write and they nodded "yes." Their Korean writing looked like an art form.

I was quiet for another few minutes until I heard giggles and footsteps. I stood up to warmly welcome two women whose faces were hidden by veils. Although they knew only a few words of English, they managed to convey that their names were Sajila Khatoon and Rajila Bibi. They were from Pakistan and spoke and wrote in Urdu. I handed them paper and pencils and simply requested them to please write. Their children looked at books too.

Thirty minutes later, I decided that it was time to share. I wondered how this was supposed to work. How would we fully understand one another? I felt an acute sense of responsibility for making all feel comfortable in the sharing. This was the most critical moment. I knew that whatever happened next would determine this effort's success or failure—this effort that now seemed to have meaning for varied cultures in a diverse community and that might soon take on a life of its own. . . . I took a deep breath and smiled. "Who would like to share first?" Mr. Ortiz immediately volunteered. He had clearly laid out his life on paper. He spoke of his seven brothers in Bolivia and how they chided him when he was younger. He told of how he planned to outfox them with an education and how he came to the United States looking for a better life for himself and his children.

We were delighted by Mr. Ortiz's story and spontaneously applauded, both for his courage in sharing and for the story he told. The others shared their stories one by one and the applause by many hands from many lands intensified. . . . After the first hour of sharing, we bade each other farewell and agreed to meet again next week. I reminded everyone of the initial goal of writing something to their children for the purpose of sharing at a significant moment in those children's lives.

Week 2 arrived and almost everyone returned. Surprisingly, there were new members: one Cambodian father, one Hispanic mother, one Vietnamese mother who brought her own translator, one Greek mother, and five Caucasian parents. Mrs. Unseri, from Pakistan, was my one recruit. I had called her the first week to say that I'd appreciate her help in understanding the thoughts and writing of Mrs. Khatoon and Mrs. Bibi and could she please come to participate in our group. With hesitancy, she agreed. With steadfast commitment she remained. She wrote purposefully, and the group responded to her proud demeanor. . . . [One] evening, I surprised everyone with letters written by their children. (Akroyd, 1995, pp. 580–581)

Voice of Ms. Kenyon, Anglo Mom of an Elementary Student

I thought I'd know right away what to write and that I would go along in an orderly, chronological fashion. Instead, I got writer's block. I wrote a few false starts. As it turned out, when I met the other parents and we all shared our stories, I discovered I wasn't working alone and I learned a lot from everyone else. I looked forward to all our Thursday nights and I'm sorry to see them end. (p. 582)

Voice of Mrs. Khatoon, Pakistani Mom of an Elementary Student

When I first came to school to participate in the meeting, I was thinking that, like before, only one teacher will be talking. But when I came here, everyone treated us so nicely. I felt as if I am sitting amongst my brothers and sisters. I would like to say that people here treated us with great love. (p. 581)

Voice of Mrs. Unseri, Pakistani Mom of an Elementary Student

At first I thought maybe we would be just talking in a conference. But I met so many nice people here. I had never written anything in my whole life. This is my first experience. My husband is proud of my work. He used to think I could not do anything before I came here! (p. 584)

Voice of Mrs. Unseri's Son

I love you so much and I love the way you are writing about me. (p. 584)

Voice of Ms. Fargo's Daughter

Dear Mom, I think it is inspiring that you are trying new things still. It just confirms you are not afraid to show your true colors. Your writing has a certain flair and child-like appeal. You are also fairly good with words.

At first I found it distressing that you would be doing something else. When I saw how short a time you'd be there, though, I realized it was a small price to pay. Keep up succeeding at all you do (you're good at that)! Love, your daughter, Kati. (p. 583)

SOURCE: Akroyd, S. (1995). Forming a parent reading-writing class: Connecting cultures, one pen at a time. *The Reading Teacher, 48,* 580–584. Copyright © 1995 by the International Reading Association (www.reading.org).

❖ Case Study 5.2: "Kamp Kino"

Voice of Kari Ambrose, Kindergarten Teacher

When schools, families, and the community work together to support learning, children can experience more social, emotional, and academic success. I am a teacher at a Title I school. Ninety-six percent of the students at this site are learning English as their second language, and 100% of students receive free breakfast and lunch. "Kamp Kino" is an evening designed to invite families and community members to become active participants in our children's education. This dinner, literacy night, and campout combination is an initial step that will bridge the gap between home and school and foster the development of family involvement, an essential facet of our students' academic success. (Ambrose, 2008, p. 1)

We really wanted to bring hesitant families into the school community, and I think the families felt welcomed and were empowered to understand the importance of their role as their child's first and most important teacher by taking part in "Kamp Kino." They received information, in their native language, about the specific ways they can support and enhance their child's learning and development during the campout. Finally, students experienced the collaboration of their families, school, and community. All spheres of influence worked together to provide them with the social, emotional, and educational support necessary to make academic success a tangible goal worth working hard to realize. The following information will give a summary of what we did and provide teachers with ways to plan and organize their own campout. (p. 5)

Who?

- All your school's students and their families
- Teachers, administrators, and staff
- Community partners such as volunteer readers, local high school students, district representatives, and business organizations

What?

- All participants will come together for an exciting evening of learning and fun.
- A possible schedule of events is as follows:

  5:00 p.m.–6:30 p.m.: Dinner and Family Involvement Activities (K–5)

  6:30 p.m.–7:30 p.m.: Grade-Level Literacy (K–5)

  7:30 p.m.–8:00 a.m.: 3rd- to 5th-Grade Campout (Primary students and families leave)

Where?

- Your event can take place all around the school's campus.
- Literacy hour can be in designated classrooms for each grade level.
- Students can spend the night inside the school. For example, girls could sleep in the library, and boys could sleep in the multipurpose room.

When?

- Assess the needs of your school community when deciding upon the best time to hold your event. A Friday evening in spring is a great time to implement this type of event. Students and their families typically need a bit of inspiration to remain dedicated to their academics. In addition, this can be a fabulous opportunity to reach out to families who have yet to be involved in school-related activities.

Dinner, Activities, and Literacy

- Make sure that all families feel they are welcome. Send invitations home in parents' language, and consider using phone calls as well, to encourage participation. Greet families warmly upon arrival, and do what you can to draw them in.

- Make activity centers and literacy activities simple, yet valuable. Remember the goal is to help parents understand that they are their child's most important educator. Activities should encourage parent participation and involvement.

- Use your volunteers wisely. We found that high school student volunteers were an incredible asset to our event. It is essential that you have a volunteer coordinator directing them to their assigned station and that they are encouraged to join in and participate alongside the students and their families. This can be a teacher, volunteer, leader, [or another adult].

- Have a plan for paying vendors and handling money throughout the evening.

- Encourage your principal and vice principal to be highly visible as they welcome the children and their families.

Campout

- Be ready for early risers. Have a video projector showing an appropriate movie or cartoon for those students who wake before the rest.
- Be sure you have emergency contact information for all students. (p. 6)

["Kamp Kino" shows] how an elementary school can implement a dinner, learning activities, family literacy, and campout event that welcomes families into the school community and fosters the development of parent involvement that specifically intends to enhance academic achievement. With a focus on communicating, learning at home, and collaborating with the community, [this type of program] can positively influence all spheres of influence that affect our children. . . . Teachers and administrators will improve their relationship with families at their school. They can develop an increased awareness of the families' needs, as well as heightened understanding of how to effectively implement partnerships with these families. (p. 48)

SOURCE: Used with permission of Kari Ambrose.

❖ Reflecting on the Cases

1. Why do you think that so many ethnically diverse families attended the writing bee? How did the school encourage participation for a wide array of families?

2. How do events such as a writing bee and "Kamp Kino" help build community and bonding opportunities between families and the school?

3. Think about Epstein's (2001; Epstein et al., 2002) six types of involvement. Which type is represented most during the writing bee and in "Kamp Kino"? Explain why.

Activities for Further Development

1. Study a family different from your own. Inquire about family members' culture, interests, and traditions by making a home visit or inviting them into your classroom. If you are arranging a home visit, check with your principal to discuss the district policies. Many districts require that teachers visit homes in pairs.

2. Take a walk and/or drive through the neighborhood connected to your school. Tell a story based on your observations that describes the families who live there, their activities, the merchants, and religious structures.

3. Describe three benefits to involving parents in decision-making processes related to their child's education.

4. Describe an event that might take place in your community that would bring schools, families, and the community together to enhance learning, such as the writing bee or "Kamp Kino." Who would plan it? Who would be involved? How would you advertise it? How would you encourage involvement for all parties?

Additional Reading and Information

Fager, J., & Brewster, C. (1999). *Parent partners: Using parents to enhance education.* Portland, OR: Northwest Regional Educational Laboratory. This publication provides information, strategies, and examples of working with parents as educational partners.

Goodwin, A. L., & King, S. H. (2002). *Culturally responsive parental involvement: Concrete understandings and basic strategies.* Washington, DC: American Association of Colleges of Teacher Education. This publication provides strategies and resources to enhance more culturally relevant educational partnerships.

Henderson, A. T., Johnson, V., Mapp, K., & Davies, D. (2007). *Beyond the bake sale: The essential guide to family-school partnerships.* New York: The New Press. This book provides practical ways that families and teachers can work together as partners.

Lawrence-Lightfoot, S. (2003). *The essential conversation: What parents and teachers can learn from each other.* New York: Ballantine Books. This book provides strategies that families and teachers can use to communicate better to enhance learning.

Appleseed is a nonprofit national campaign that strives for increasing family involvement in U.S. public schools: http://www.projectappleseed.org/chklst.html

The Center for Parent Education and Family Support at North Texas University provides partnership information and strategies for families, schools, and community agencies. The center provides online training, a database for parent educators, and outreach to families with newborns: www.unt.edu/cpe/ptec/connection.htm

6

Schools and Community

Working Together and Respecting Diversity

After reading this chapter, you should have a better understanding of:

- strategies for building partnerships with the broader educational community;

- examples of community partnerships, including service organizations, corporations, faith-based organizations, and high-profile groups and individuals;

- online partnerships that connect students and teachers within the United States and around the world;

- innovative partnership models with schools, corporations, and foundations;

- service learning, stewardship, and civic involvement and the differences among them;

- classroom project examples where students and teachers take action via service learning, stewardship, or civic involvement;

- service activities and challenges for teachers and students; and

- tips for schools and community members when developing and implementing educational partnerships.

| Table 6.1 | Prior Knowledge and Beliefs Organizer |

List partnerships that you know of that involve school and community groups.	List partnerships that you know of that include students participating in community service projects.	List partnerships that you know of that include different teachers working together.

Use the information that you placed in Table 6.1 to guide your reading in this chapter. Consider the examples that you provided and determine ways that the partnerships you know of or have experience with can be enhanced.

Expanding Educational Partnerships

When multiple groups come together to enrich the education of children, academic achievement is enhanced along with many other benefits. This chapter will focus on partnership possibilities beyond parents and families. Models will be described such as partnerships with human services organizations, high-profile individuals, and other community groups. Service learning, stewardship, and civic involvement projects will be presented as a way to promote active community involvement among students and teachers. Successful partnerships with community members exist when all members participate in projects that bring about change. Relationships and actions among the people in these partnerships are as important as the product or outcome. This chapter will also include variations of community partnerships—those that have existed over a long period of time, those that are just beginning, those that involve individuals, and those that involve large groups.

Sanders and Harvey (2002) describe four factors that support school-community partnerships. These factors include a high commitment to learning, administrator support for the community partnership, a welcoming school climate, and two-way communication. The community partners in their study indicated that they liked being part of a school that focused on student learning and outcomes. They liked working with schools that were organized, family friendly, and demonstrated an academically challenging curriculum. They stated that having support from the administrator was critical for teacher buy-in and success. When community partners received thank-you letters and notes from students, they appreciated the extra effort and welcoming learning environment. Finally, two-way communication between the community partner and the school principal and teachers provided information and discussions about responsibilities and expectations from the beginning. Therefore, schools and community partners must be committed and work together in order to enhance the education of students and the educational environment.

School, Community, and Business Partnerships

Why would businesses and community groups be interested in collaborating with schools? Why would schools be interested in collaborating with businesses and the broader community? Why would teachers want to form partnerships if their schedules are already overbooked? The simple answer to all of these questions is to improve and enhance education for students. At a deeper level, partnerships are not easily formed, and both groups must benefit in order for a partnership to be successful over time. There are broad notions of the definition of community among educators. The *Encarta World English Dictionary* (2009) also offers multiple definitions. Two of the definitions that closely relate to community partnership possibilities are "a group of people who live in the same area" and "a group of people with a common background or with shared interests within society." Given this view, a community partnership would involve joint ownership in a project as well as any consequences that come with it. All schools operate as communities, and classrooms represent smaller communities involving the teacher, students, and their families. Society benefits when schools go beyond the campus community and seek support and collaboration from those organizations and individuals who can add value to the entire educational experience. As you have learned, educational partnerships do not happen haphazardly; they are planned endeavors that require time, commitment, respect, planning, and execution.

School-community partnerships can take place over a short or long period of time. When a school organizes a field trip to a local art museum, it is usually a one-time partnership or an event that takes place once each school year. Museum educators and teachers communicate in advance to plan the event. Sometimes there are formal planning sessions, and other times planning is done via e-mail or over the phone. On the other hand, some organizations have long-term partnerships with schools such as a corporation that encourages its employees to become reading buddies with students at a local school.

The level of commitment and the type of partnership will vary among groups and individuals. However, some type of shared decision making is essential for all parties. If one partner has the major decision-making power, then there is not equal distribution of potential contributions and outcomes. The issue of power as a barrier to partnerships will be discussed more fully in Chapter 8.

Community Partnerships

Community collaboration with noncorporations or organizations can include neighbors, individuals, or senior citizens who contribute their time to enhance the education of children. Sometimes, these individuals work directly with schools, and at other times they form informal collaborations.

Faith-Based Partners

Faith-based partners include organized religious groups and organizations such as Islamic, Christian, Jewish, Hindu, or Buddhist groups. Within the No Child Left Behind (NCLB) legislation, there are specific provisions for these types of partnerships. Under NCLB, diverse faith-based organizations can receive federal funds to offer tutoring or other academic services for low-income students. They can also apply for and receive funding as a supplemental service provider to support initiatives such as after-school programs, early literacy programs, and mentoring programs. NCLB advocates partnerships with religious groups for the purpose of strengthening public and private education systems.

The Orange County Partnership for Young Children in New York, spearheaded by the Orange County United Way, seeks the collaboration of businesses, schools, human services organizations, county government, religious institutions, community organizations, families, and county citizens (Orange-Ulster BOCES, 2009). The benefits of this collaboration include educational, community, and family systems that function more efficiently; partnerships across different communities and within different organizations; and collaborative communities where people want to live and work. Because many religious organizations operate as part of the community, they can be effective contributing partners to the education of children—regardless of the religious beliefs associated with the organization.

High-Profile Partners

High-profile partners exist in the form of sports teams, celebrities, and other notable individuals who can serve as role models and make an impact on the school and community. Many professional sports teams have an entire department devoted to creating educational and community partnership programs. Firefighters and police officers are also high-profile individuals and groups that serve as educational partners. At some elementary schools, city police officers and members of the sheriff's office visit the school on a regular basis to encourage safety, literacy, and community activism. Many times officers play games with students, read books with them, or take them on in a soccer game.

Other high-profile folks are contributing to the education of families and children in the form of public service announcements. Celebrities such as Edward James Olmos and Debbie Allen were featured in recent years on the radio, on television, and in print advertisements offering tips for families to help their children learn at home. Oprah Winfrey, one of the most well-known faces throughout the world, recently built and established a leadership academy for girls in South Africa (Harpo, Inc., 2009). The academy is organized to empower girls in South Africa to become leaders and generate opportunities for themselves, their families, and their communities. The school not only provides educational opportunities for girls in South Africa; it provides hope for girls around the world.

Many professional baseball, football, basketball, and hockey teams provide tickets for students and families from low socioeconomic backgrounds. The Anaheim Ducks hockey organization sponsored a program with donations from corporate partners where it made matching donations for every 50 tickets sponsored (Anaheim Ducks Hockey Club, LLC, and the American Hockey Association, 2009). About 3,500 children took advantage of this opportunity, and many area teachers integrated the event with their reading, writing, math, and physical education curriculum. NBA (National Basketball Association) Cares works with a variety of organizations serving children and youth such as the Boys and Girls Clubs of America, Reading Is Fundamental, Feed the Children, and Prevent Child Abuse America. The NBA also partners with the White House and the Library of Congress to promote the National Book Festival in Washington, DC, for children, youth, families, and the community. In classrooms, NBA players read to about 50 million children each year in the *Read to Achieve* program to help children develop a love for reading and to encourage family reading at home. A fourth-grade class in North Carolina made a "cold call" to a professional baseball player whom they admired. They wrote him letters and became his pen pal. During the first part of the season, students documented his batting average and team statistics. They watched him on television, used a map to find out where he played each week, and then wrote and directed a "play by play" scenario for the class.

These high-profile individuals and groups in the community offer their voice and support for initiatives that can provide tremendous motivation for children and youth. If schools are interested in partnering with high-profile partners such as actors, sports organizations, police officers, firefighters, or others, it is helpful to identify a person or group that lives within the school community or nearby. Schools and teachers can contact these groups and suggest projects that they might be interested in participating in.

Online Partnerships

Online educational partnerships are growing. These partnerships have the capacity to expand at rapid rates because of the use of technology and the exchange of information around the world in a matter of seconds. The U.K. Department for Children, Schools, and Families and the British Council have set up an educational partnership that features teachers and students from 70 countries. This project is called *Global Gateway.* The program seeks partnerships between students and teachers in the United Kingdom and students and teachers in other areas of the world. Schools and teachers in a variety of countries are asked to register and write a short paragraph about what the U.K. schools can offer them and what they can offer students and teachers in the United Kingdom. If a school wants its students to learn English, then it can select a participating U.K. school. If a school can provide information and resources related to Chinese paintings or textiles, then it would report this information when it registers. There is a similar program instituted by the U.S. government known as the GLOBE Program. The GLOBE Program is a hands-on environmental science and education project that recruits an international network of students in elementary, middle, and high schools who are studying environmental issues. Groups of students from all over the world make environmental measurements and share environmental data with the international environmental science community. The Science Controversies On-line: Partnerships in Education (SCOPE) project was developed by the University of California at Berkeley, the University of Washington, and the American Association for the Advancement of Science. The group features an online knowledge network community where scientists, educators, and students can learn more about science research and controversies related to processes, procedures, and outcomes.

The *Global SchoolNet Foundation* connects students and teachers throughout the world for the pupose of providing a global perspective related to a number of classroom issues. Students collaboratively investigate their community, their culture, and public science issues that will prepare them to be responsible and respectful world citizens. The program provides a variety of materials and resources for teachers including special offers from Global SchoolNet funders and partners. The purpose of the *Europa Penpal* Web site for families, students, and teachers is to encourage students to interact as pen pals while learning more about different cultures and practicing writing skills.

> ## Enhancing Learning for Students With Special Needs: Online Partnerships and Assistive Technology
>
> Online partnerships are ideal for students, particularly those students with special academic needs, because they can communicate in alternative ways. It is wise for schools and districts to acquire computers with adaptive or assisted technologies that help children with special needs navigate the Internet sites. Here are a few ideas and strategies to get started:
>
> - Many software programs or Web sites "speak" to students as they interact with them. This is especially helpful for students who are hearing impaired.
> - Braille tranlsation software programs are often available and should be acquired by schools and districts.
> - Be aware that many graphics are not accessible or visible to many students with visual impairment. Therefore, having additional materials may be necessary.
> - Provide opportunities for students with visual impairment to work cooperatively with their peers on projects so that photographs and other graphics can be described at a "kid-friendly" level.
> - Provide opportunities for students who are academically challenged to partner and communicate with other students and role models via typing their ideas and projects rather than writing them.

Corporate Partnerships

Businesses have partnered with schools and the broader educational community for many years. Many businesses provide services and resources related to student incentive programs, vision and hearing screening, book buddy programs, and joint community service projects. Some businesses allow students to "shadow" individual employees throughout a day to find out more about different careers. One of the most popular business-school partnerships includes employees working with schools and teachers on projects that relate to their company. For example, the Xerox Science Consultant Program (XSCP) places more than 100 Xerox scientists, engineers, and technicians into schools two times a month to conduct hands-on activities in the Rochester City School District in New York (Llewellyn & Wicks, 2001). Company employees or consultants work in teams of two to challenge and motivate students to learn more about science, engineering, and mathematics. Teachers commit to working with the Xerox consultants in partnership throughout the year. This program has been operating since 1968. Some of the reasons for its success are outlined here:

- The corporation seeks commitment from top levels of school administrators.
- It concentrates on only a few schools at a time.
- Regular meetings are held for corporate and school district coordinators.
- All partners in the program are recognized and acknowledged.

- Workshops are held to help business partners understand how young children learn.
- The activities complement and support the schools' teaching and learning goals.
- All participants in the program are committed to the partnership.

The DuPont Corporation has demonstrated a long history of working with students and teachers, with educational endeavors dating back to 1918. It has since established a DuPont Office of Education that facilitates partnerships among educators, universities, businesses, and local DuPont sites to "prepare today's children for tomorrow's world" (DuPont, 2009). One of its major partnership programs includes the facilitation of inquiry-based science programs in area schools near DuPont sites by providing national and international competitions. The corporation strives to increase participation of students from groups traditionally underrepresented in science and mathematics careers and to enhance teacher development in the areas of science, math, and technology.

Parravano (2001) determined that businesses usually seek educational partnerships because there is a need for a highly trained and educated workforce. In time, many of the students may be employed with the company. In addition, schools can learn important lessons from businesses while businesses can also learn about education from schools. Parravano states that businesses can play various roles as educational partners. These roles include being an advocate, a researcher, an anchor, a coach, and a broker. Businesses can be advocates because they have prestige and credibility. Businesses take roles as researchers because they use data to evaluate their success with school programs. They serve as an anchor due to the changes that often take place throughout schools and districts, particularly with teachers and administrators. Strategic planning is central to business, and this is an area where schools can reap the benefits of businesses as coaches to develop and implement action plans. Finally, businesses can act as brokers to link schools with additional resources at the local, national, and international level. Parravano concludes that having effective communication and adequate planning results in a win-win situation for schools, teachers, students, families, and businesses.

Innovative Collaborative Partnerships

The Edison Project is an innovative school concept that includes partnerships with corporations, local school districts, families, and communities to provide a holistic educational experience. About 285,000 public school students were served in 19 different states, the District of Columbia, and the United Kingdom during the 2006–2007 school year (Edison Schools, 2008). About half of the Edison schools are charter schools, and the other half are governed by local school boards. The Edison Project states that its partnership schools stand for the commitment to work with families, the school system, and the community to achieve educational goals. Specific benefits for families, students, teachers, and the community are listed here:

- An extended school day allows students to learn foreign languages, the arts, and physical education.
- A longer school year (206 days) allows schools to play a major role in education and integrate with family lifestyles.
- A computer in the home of each family allows teachers, families, and students to communicate regularly.

- Families cooperate through formal and informal learning contracts, learning portfolios, and multiple volunteer opportunities.
- A community center at the school brings together families in after-school and evening programs.
- Social services, such as child advocacy groups, law enforcement agencies, hospitals, and welfare agencies, are integrated.

The Edison Project states that its partnership school model is based on research and the best instructional practices to help teachers and children reach their full potential. The school model provides an integrated design that focuses on the use of technology, ongoing assessment, and a dynamic curriculum.

Another school, called Cary Academy in Cary, North Carolina, is a private middle and upper school that was created by the founders of a local business, the SAS Institute. The Cary Academy is located on the grounds of the SAS Institute and integrates technology into all curriculum areas. The SAS Institute also extends its support to other educational endeavors throughout the community, allowing employees to donate their time in educational settings. The company offers a $500 contribution to schools or other nonprofit groups if the employees agree to volunteer at least 8 hours each month over the course of a year. Hundreds of SAS employees participate in this community volunteer program each year.

Corporations are beginning to focus on more community service projects in collaboration with schools. Some corporations are creating foundations to support AIDS awareness, promote breast cancer screening, and eradicate world hunger through a variety of avenues including advertising, publicity appearances, and

SOURCE: Used with permission of Tom Baker.

Celebrating and singing together: First-grade students and teachers participate in an author's celebration by dressing up to sing songs related to the author's literary works.

other promotional activities. Students can find out more information about what corporations are doing to provide ideas for their own class projects. Some projects can be local in scope, and others can be international. Schools can also choose to collaborate with corporations related to causes that are important to them. For example, a school can contact the Kenneth Cole Foundation and ask how it can help encourage more awareness of AIDS or another issue in its community. Nike recently hosted an event to teach children with special needs how to surf. Working together, schools can target the issue locally, and corporations can focus on national or international efforts.

Students Taking Action as Community Members

Decision making, service, and action within one's community are not necessarily promoted in grades K–16. In addition, the process of action-based pedagogy and learning is not accessible if teachers and students are not educated about their responsibilities, their role as decision makers, and myriad opportunities to connect community activism with academic content standards. The purpose of this next section is to provide information and examples to encourage the integration of action-based pedagogical strategies into the K–8 classroom. These action-based strategies include service learning, civic involvement, and stewardship. Service learning and civic involvement are more common in the area of social studies education, and stewardship is more popular in science education. Nevertheless, all curriculum areas can be integrated in action-based teaching and learning.

Beyond the four walls: Students investigate beach sand with their teacher as part of their science lesson outside the four walls of the classroom.

Service Learning

Service learning is growing in K–16 settings. It involves a learning process where students contribute and provide a service to the community while the community in turn provides a service to students and schools. This type of project results in reciprocal learning and partnerships. Specifically, service-learning assignments are ones in which students provide a community service outside the four walls of the classroom and address a community need (Wade, 1997). Buchanan, Baldwin, and Rudisill (2002) describe how service learning differs from traditional community service or field experiences. First, it includes experiences where students learn content while performing community service. Second, students apply content to the community setting, reflect on their experiences, and develop relationships with participants. Third, service is provided "with, rather than for, the community partner" (p. 28) resulting in benefits for all parties. Cumulatively, service learning provides students with an opportunity to learn through active participation in service experiences that help the community in some way.

Kaye (2004), known for her expertise in service learning, outlined essential elements of service-learning projects:

- Integrated learning
- Meeting genuine needs
- Youth voice and choice
- Collaborative efforts
- Reciprocity
- Civic responsibility
- Systematic reflection

The KIDS (Kids Involved Doing Service Learning) Consortium is a nonprofit organization that partners with teachers, administrators, and the community to address community issues and involve schools and students in taking action. The KIDS Consortium works with local communities and schools to identify, research, and figure out how to meet a community's needs. Teachers match specific projects to state content standards and help develop hands-on interactive learning experiences. The KIDS Consortium has three basic components:

1. *Academic integrity:* Service-learning projects are linked to state content standards.
2. *Apprentice citizenship:* Students take roles as valuable members of the community and partner with community groups to take action and make a difference.
3. *Student ownership:* Students are encouraged to make decisions during the learning and problem-solving process. Teachers and community members facilitate the process, but the students actually guide decisions being made.

Stewardship

Stewardship is closely linked to service learning and includes the call for responsibility to ensure welfare of the world and in the world. This can include environmental conservation, human rights, economic welfare, education, health care, disaster relief, and animal welfare. Stewardship can include individuals or groups working together to obtain greater peace and sustainability throughout communities everywhere. Stewardship is closely related to place-based education that involves students and teachers with nature-based learning that connects them with their community (Sobel, 2004). With place-based education, teachers are encouraged to leave the four walls of the classroom and help students investigate the world around them. Stewardship and place-based learning include cumulative efforts of individuals or groups that result in positive outcomes for the environment. Stewardship, therefore, is the moral obligation to care for the earth and its people, animals, and resources so that they may be preserved for future generations. Although it is not necessarily connected to the formal school curriculum, teachers, families, and communities can work together to teach the value of stewardship and integrate formal content standards with stewardship activities. The Youth Stewardship Program in San Francisco provides free stewardship opportunities for teachers and students. Five field trips to a local park accompanied by lesson plans that connect to science content standards are provided for participating groups. These lesson plans focus on habitat restoration related to areas such as water and soil or plant adaptation.

Civic Involvement

Civic involvement is a part of service learning and stewardship but is organized specifically to encourage active community members. Goldstein (2006) reported in a *Washington Post* article that high school dropouts are less likely to vote, trust government, do volunteer work, or go to church than better-educated Americans. This information stems from a report that reveals a gap in "civic health" between students from higher and lower socioeconomic backgrounds based on several national surveys beginning in the 1970s. Keeter, Zukin, Andolina, and Jenkins (2002) describe civic involvement as incorporating three different areas: civic activities, electoral activities, and having a political voice. Civic activities improve the community or help local individuals. Such activities include volunteering time or a service, joining a civic organization, or supporting fund-raising efforts for a particular cause. Electoral activities include voting, persuading others to vote, and volunteering for a government initiative or candidate. Having a political voice includes writing or meeting with decision makers, creating or supporting petitions, and protesting. Keeter et al. also created a list of 19 core indicators of engagement. These areas include:

1. *Civic activities:* community problem solving, regular volunteering within the community, active membership within a group, participating in fund-raising efforts, and raising money for a cause or charity.

2. *Electoral activities:* regular voting, persuading others to vote or participate, displaying buttons or signs in support of candidates or initiatives, and volunteering for candidates or causes.

3. *Having a political voice:* contacting political officials or other decision makers, protesting, boycotting, contacting print or broadcast media, creating or participating in written petitions, and canvassing (going door-to-door to discuss concerns or causes or express views).

Decision making within one's community is not necessarily promoted in grades K–8 and is often not accessible to all individuals if children are not educated about their responsibilities, their role in civic decisions, and the myriad opportunities to participate. Although the Keeter et al. (2002) core indicators of civic engagement were created for young Americans, ages 15–25, it is important that teachers in grades K–8 integrate activities that build knowledge, background, and motivation to engage in civic activities. The *Buddies of Petersburg* (BOP) program in Virginia incorporates civic involvement with the education of children in grades 6–12. The program pairs every sixth grader in the city with an older teen mentor to teach him or her about civic values and life skills. After 9 weeks of mentoring, the teams are granted all rights of a "BOPer." Children are encouraged to obey laws in the city and rules at school and home. They also promise to be good citizens each day. The program was set up to create a positive atmosphere for a school district that has struggled with high dropout rates, poverty, and illiteracy. This same school district implemented a junior correspondent project where students report on the community, concerns at school, and negative news. They are encouraged to provide a voice for the community as middle school and high school students. They gather information from their peers as well as deliver information based on multiple perspectives. The issues within a community that can motivate student action are endless. The following is a list of sample service-learning, stewardship, and civic involvement activities.

Sample Service-Learning Projects

1. High school students serve as junior docents at a local museum or nature area. Teams of high school students lead and facilitate tours for elementary students who visit. They plan activities, discuss the content, and connect the content and activities to the elementary school students' lives and culture.

2. Sixth- and seventh-grade students work in peer teams to assist adults with special needs in preparing for different events within the Special Olympics. They create a plan of action, motivational activities, and a DVD with footage, music, narration, and testimonials related to the event.

3. Students in grades 4–8 work with personnel in the governor's office to research the most popular healthy foods among their peers. They create a slogan, brochures, a Web site, and posters to promote healthy eating.

4. First- and second-grade students partner with a local senior citizen center. Students create art projects, sing songs, attain "senior buddies" to read books with, share stories, and write in journals. Senior buddies read with students and tell stories from their lives as children growing up.

Sample Stewardship Projects

1. Students, families, and teachers participate in a painting project within their community. They paint "Do not litter, drains to ocean" on the gutters and create informational flyers to distribute to residents explaining the new signage. Students use informational books and online resources to determine the problems that ocean animals and ecosystems face when trash or other debris drains into ocean or river waters.

2. Students choose an area of the beach to keep clean, and the cleanup can include students, teachers, and families. Once trash is collected, it can be analyzed and classified during classroom activities. The different types of trash can be counted and graphed.

3. Students seek information through books and other resources to find out about endangered animals in their community. Students can write local news articles or make presentations to community members to inform them of how they can help protect the animals.

Sample Civic Involvement Projects

1. Fourth-grade students research human rights and participate in a human rights event. They research topics related to human rights and report on practices during team speeches at city hall.

2. Third-grade students invite local candidates for mayor to their school to make campaign speeches. Afterward, they create posters and literature in support of their favorite candidate.

3. Fifth-grade students host a community dialogue event to discuss wellness issues for families, students, teachers, community members, and businesses. They write letters to the city council to advocate more open space, bicycle paths, and parks.

Types of Citizenship Participation

Any type of community service involvement helps build a type of atmosphere that provides motivation, access, and a purpose for learning in every school. With service-learning, stewardship, and civic involvement projects, students are actually creating something and making an impact on the community and world in which they live. Such projects also provide full participation of the students, teachers, and others beyond the traditional four walls of the classroom. Westheimer and Kahne (2004) provide a framework that distinguishes among three different types of participatory citizenship projects. Their ideas are listed in Table 6.2. Notice that service learning and stewardship are participatory

Table 6.2 Types of Citizenship Participation

Personally Responsible	Participatory	Justice Oriented
Acts responsibly in community Works and pays taxes Obeys laws Recycles Volunteers	Active member of community organizations Organizes community efforts to care for those in need Knows how government agencies work Knows strategies for accomplishing collective tasks	Critically assesses social, political, and economic structures to see beyond surface causes Seeks out and addresses areas of injustice Knows about democratic social movements and how to effect systemic change
Contribute to a recycling bin at home, work, and school	Work with the community to create and organize recycling bins at home, work, and school; monitor the progress of the project	Gather info about why people do not recycle, create a plan to encourage recycling, make public announcement about recycling, and report on the progress of the project
Traditional classroom projects	Service-learning and stewardship projects	Civic involvement projects

SOURCE: Adapted from Westheimer and Kahne (2004).

whereas civic involvement includes justice-oriented activities. Traditional curriculums and lesson plans usually target the personally responsible citizen.

The following "Notes From the Classroom" section shows a letter that was sent to families by a sixth-grade teacher whose class was focusing on a service-learning project. As a result of the survey contained in the letter, the families and students determined that breast cancer awareness was the topic that they wanted to raise awareness for. Bridget Burke, the sixth-grade teacher, wrote the following reflection following the 4-month project:

> All of my students were actively engaged from February through May, every time we worked on this service-learning project. Everyone had an authentic role to be responsible for and a checklist of objectives to continue to focus all their efforts on. I feel the significant feature of this activity was the students took pride and had true ownership of each step, even deciding on the issue and how to help! Together they learned how to work as a team, democratically, in order to serve a more profound purpose, higher than themselves—breast cancer! I discovered since the students knew it was their project, they worked much harder to succeed! I honestly feel that my class worked extremely well as one team to put aside their own desires and whole-heartedly raise money for breast cancer research in finding a cure. At first they wanted to act on several different issues; picking one was the hardest. After the democratic vote of students and parents, they united their efforts and the experts inspired the entire class. I enjoyed watching the students keep one another accountable and on task. They constantly reminded one another that this was not for them but for everyone who has suffered! Since half of my students have experienced some form of pain from breast cancer, they were even more determined!

Notes From the Classroom:
Letter to Families About a Sixth-Grade Service-Learning Project

Dear Parents,

In addition to completing our sixth-grade standards of ancient civilizations, over the next two quarters your students will become "active citizens" in our community.

Our social studies class has worked extremely hard to research issues, causes, and organizations where we can focus on a learning service project. Please ask your child to discuss the following choices and as a family *vote on one cause below:*

- ☐ **CHOC Hospital**
- ☐ **Carol & Stacey**
- ☐ **Breast Cancer**
- ☐ **San Clemente Animal Shelter**
- ☐ **Surfrider Foundation**
- ☐ **Homeless Shelter**
- ☐ **Recycle Containers for BAMS**
- ☐ **Wyss Family**
- ☐ **Lymphoma/Leukemia**
- ☐ **Sponsor 2 Malawi Children in Africa**
- ☐ **American Cancer Society**

Please deliberate over the weekend—final choice DUE: Monday with signatures!

_____   _____
        Student Signature   Parent Signature

****

(Continued)

(Continued)

Our goal is to host a fund-raiser in the form of a silent/live auction, including a bake sale where all the proceeds will go directly to benefit one family, organization, or community issue with the most votes from above.

After the votes are counted, we will focus our efforts on only one cause/issue. Students will learn how to develop an action plan and form class committees to:

- research resources and create PowerPoint presentations;
- present solutions to the problem;
- deliberate alternatives;
- write letters to recruit partnerships within our community;
- design pamphlets/posters;
- create public service announcements;
- evaluate and reflect on positive differences;
- discover the process of fund-raising; and
- reinforce our class "life skills."

Perseverance	**Problem Solving**	**Common Sense**	**Friendship**
Sense of Humor	**Integrity**	**Flexibility**	
Organization	**Courage**	**Initiative**	
Cooperation	**Effort**	**Patience**	
Caring	**Curiosity**		
Responsibility			

- And . . . they will passionately experience that we all can make a powerful difference!

SOURCE: Used with permission from Bridget Burke

There are various ways to begin initiating service-learning, stewardship, and civic involvement projects in the class. The following "Notes From the Classroom" section outlines a step-by-step plan that can help students and teachers begin taking action within their community.

Notes From the Classroom: Take Action and Practice Active Citizenship!

Congratulations! You have been asked to participate in the Pay It Forward Challenge! This task will help you and your students practice active citizenship. Select an issue that you and your students are passionate about. Follow the five-step process to action. Use the outline below to format your plan of action.

These tips (based on steps recommended by the Center for Civic Education, 2006, and Kielburger & Kielburger, 2002) are helpful when launching an active citizenship project in your classroom:

1. *Increase awareness.* Explore current issues in your school/community, state, country, and world. Encourage students to watch the news, read the local newspaper, and search the Web to help them identify problems in their immediate environment and report back to the class. Use a four-quadrant chart and create a list of current problems in each category. Encourage students to document the issues by bringing in newspaper clippings or by taking photographs of problems around the community or school (graffiti, litter, etc.). Make a list of the top issues based on students' interests.

2. *Deliberate.* Let the students choose an issue. It will be more meaningful if it comes from their interests. Narrow down the issues that students have generated in an attempt to choose one problem the entire class can attempt to change. Follow the steps listed below to narrow down the problems:

   a. Ask students to list their top three choices on a Post-it note. Tally the results and identify the top three issues selected by the students.

   b. Send home a letter and ask for parents' support by involving them in a discussion with their child about the issues identified. Ask the parents and the child to discuss each issue at home, choose one issue that they think the students can change, come up with ideas that the students can put into action to encourage change, and complete a required form to document their discussion and selected problem.

   c. Next, teach students how to write a persuasive paragraph/essay. Ask students to write a persuasive essay about the issue they selected with their parents and support their opinions with reasons, examples, and commentary. Encourage students to talk about possible causes, consequences, and solutions to the problem in their essay.

   d. Have students get into groups based on common issues and share essays. Have each group plan a presentation to persuade the rest of the class that its issue is the most important to solve.

   e. After all the groups present their essays, use a structured decision-making chart to weigh the pros and cons associated with each issue.

   f. Take a final vote and select one issue.

(Continued)

(Continued)

3. *Become an expert.* Students must conduct extensive research on the issue before they can take action. To gain a better understanding of the selected issue, explore the root cause and examine possible solutions. Make a list of some possible solutions and identify pros and cons associated with each idea. Be sure to use a variety of resources to find out as much as you can about the issue you have chosen.

4. *Devise a plan of action.* Let the students lead the project and make decisions. Encourage students to think outside the box when brainstorming ideas that could possibly impact the selected issue. Also encourage students to build partnerships with groups in the community. Be sure to consider how you and/or your class could elicit support among individuals and groups in the community. You will also want to come up with a clear and detailed plan of action to address the selected issue. Possible action plans could include writing letters to local businesses or members of the local, state, or federal government; speaking at public forums such as a city council meeting; writing petitions; making posters or brochures; creating a Web site or blog to raise awareness for the issue; contacting the media; or creating a video documentary using software such as iMovie.

5. *Get busy.* Publicize the issue to increase awareness and build partnerships. After you and your students implement the project, review and evaluate each action. Consider the following questions:

   • What were the positive aspects of the project?

   • What were the major obstacles associated with this project (other than time)?

   • How could you improve the project?

   • How well did the class work as a team?

   • What did you learn from this project?

   • What recommendations do you have for other teachers/students who are thinking about doing a take-action project?

Tips for Building School-Community Partnerships

The following tips are provided to help schools and community members become more successful in working together to enhance education.

Tips for Schools

1. Advertise and recruit multiple groups to become involved in the community partnerships such as families, teachers, students, and support staff.

2. Provide professional development for teachers and families to create buy-in and motivation to participate in community partnership projects. Have children's paintings or other projects on display to create a friendly teaching and learning atmosphere.

3. Host "Share Day" for different schools in the district to come together to share examples of partnerships and create new professional partnerships such as teachers and students becoming pen pals between schools or a cohosted multicultural family day.

4. Take time to talk with diverse groups of people within the community. Ask questions about their careers, resources, time, and ideas. Invite them to speak with your students about their life and contributions to society.

5. Convince the school district office that a community liaison is needed to work within each school to enhance partnership development with families, among professionals, and within the community. Or write a grant to obtain funds for a liaison position.

6. Hold a school-family meeting and ask parents and teachers to share their connections to educational community resources.

Tips for Community Members

1. Start small by working with one school at a time. Expand the partnership later if necessary.

2. Set up a meeting with administrators, teachers, students, and family members to discuss partnership possibilities. Host the group at your organization or business.

3. Serve snacks or offer other services or events to motivate families and educators to attend the initial meeting.

4. Provide funding for a community liaison at a school within the district to coordinate partnership efforts.

Chapter Summary

Like partnerships with families, partnerships with the community can also enhance the education of children. Community partnerships can include service organizations, corporations, faith-based organizations, high-profile groups, and programs online that connect children around the world. Students can learn more about their community and community issues by participating in action-based strategies including service learning, stewardship, and civic involvement. These projects provide a purpose for learning and involve multiple groups when enacted. Collaborating with multiple community partners in multiple ways opens up unlimited possibilities for educating children and enhancing their overall well-being.

CASE STUDIES

The following two case studies provide insight and multiple perspectives related to two different community partnership projects. The first case study provides an example of a service-learning project that empowers university students, professors, environmental experts, and elementary and middle school students to take action in their community. The second case study, "Simply the Best!" describes an after-school program focusing on science and technology for middle school and high school girls from an inner-city neighborhood in Denver, Colorado.

❖ Case Study 6.1: Clean Air Zone Campaign

This case study is adapted from a paper presented by Angela Freed (2008) at the annual meeting of the Association for Science Teacher Education. The University of Maine at Farmington provides a "Green Campus Vision Statement" that describes the institution's commitment to environmental stewardship and graduating responsible, global, environmentally active citizens. The university has expressed that it would like to be a leader in promoting sustainable resources on Earth. In addition, teaching is considered an important factor in promoting sound environmental practices.

The *Clean Air Zone Campaign* is a large-scale service-learning partnership project that included (a) four environmental specialists from the Maine Green Schools project in the state's Department of Environmental Protection Air Quality Bureau and the Maine Environmental Energy Program, (b) a university professor, (c) 40 undergraduate preservice teachers, and (d) 250 local elementary and middle school students. The overall purpose of the project was to protect and enhance the air quality in the state of Maine. To accomplish this, the partners would work together to achieve the following outcomes:

- Reduce vehicle idling at schools and in communities
- Educate people in the community about the importance of clean air and its health benefits
- Encourage community involvement by sharing how small changes in daily tasks can produce healthier air

Each partner was assigned various roles and tasks during the project. The role of the environmental specialists included explaining the science and research related to the project and modeling activities for elementary and middle school teachers and students. The role of the undergraduate preservice teachers was to learn strategies related to data collecting and teaching about clean air concepts, collect pre- and postinterview data from vehicle idling in elementary and middle school parking lots, develop clean air activities for students, and share idling data and activities with elementary and middle school students. The role of the elementary and middle school students included developing an awareness of air quality concerns in the state of Maine and beyond; considering alternative ways to reduce idling such as carpooling, riding bicycles to school, walking, speaking to parents about why idling is detrimental to the environment, and reminding parents and other drivers not to idle; and building skills of environmental stewardship (continuing to make a difference in making Earth a healthier place). The following "voices" are featured to understand the perceptions of preservice teachers and a university professor who participated in the project.

Voices of Preservice Teachers

"Annie"

The No Idling project was a great way to get involved with the local school and community as well as participate in a worthwhile environmental cause.

"Sam"

It is important to link modern-day concerns with the curriculum in the classroom so students are aware of what is going on in the world around them.

"Veronica"

The project was a success in raising awareness of idling in the community. After teaching our lessons, the number of cars we saw idling decreased. The students were actively involved and it seemed to have an impact on them.

"Shane"

Idling my vehicle was second nature before I became involved in the No Idling project. After learning about the repercussions of idling our vehicles, I realized how important it is to educate the community about this issue.

Voice of a University Professor

The elementary and middle school students were capable of more than my preservice teachers expected. If more teachers are willing to include environmental service-learning projects in their classrooms, we can work together to increase awareness of environmental issues and ways that we, as citizens of the world, can make a difference now and for future generations.

SOURCE: Used with permission of Angela Freed.

❖ Case Study 6.2: Simply the Best!

This case study is adapted from an article by Eisenhart and Edwards (2004). Many girls from low socioeconomic backgrounds experience difficulty when it comes to connecting subjects at school with their lives in their neighborhoods and homes. *Simply the Best!* is an after-school program in science and technology for middle and high school girls from a low-income neighborhood in Denver, Colorado. The program was created to spark the girls' interests in science and technology by relating these fields to topics that already interested the girls. Margaret Eisenhart, an anthropologist, and Leslie Edwards, a biologist, designed the program at the request of a Denver community organizer.

The after-school program included girls from African American, recent Mexican immigrant, and third-generation Mexican American families. At the beginning of the program, Eisenhart and Edwards (2004) elicited the girls' interests and then tried to develop activities that aligned with both these interests and curriculum standards in the girls' school district. Based on the girls' responses to the initial activities, activities were revised or redesigned to be more appropriate for or interesting to them. The girls also were invited to suggest their own activities that became the basis for new program activities. Eventually the coordinators of the program created a list of content ideas and related activities that seemed to appeal to the girls from this neighborhood.

The girls in the program met two times each week for 2 hours after school. During one session, the students visited a local museum that highlighted the first African American woman doctor in the community, Black cowboys, and different African Americans who influenced Western history. This was an attempt to help connect these girls with their community and history. Although the museum trip was set, the girls were encouraged to ask questions related to anything that popped into their minds. Why do babies look like aliens when they come out? How do we get bones? Why do starving people's stomachs stick out? What does a midwife do? How old was Dr. Ford when she started delivering babies? The girls and teacher came back to these questions several more times during the year. On these subsequent occasions, the teacher directed the conversation to genetics, Down syndrome, growth and development, nutrition, the skeletal system, and skin, with reference back to this discussion.

Voices of Girls in the Program

Sara

I [see myself differently after a year in the program] because I'm not as quiet no more.

Elizabeth

I want to be a scientist of dogs, you know someone who everyone else will come to, to ask questions, and I know all the answers to all their questions.

Yolanda

I never did really like computers, but now I like science. So when I went to high school I took science as my elective class. I have taken all the science classes they offer.

Maria

When you first met me, I really didn't speak. . . . Now I have a lot more social skills.

Julia

I still don't like computers except for videos and playing music, but because of the program I can at least use them for school.

Voice of Margaret Eisenhart, Researcher

The research on Simply the Best! provides revealing distinctive patterns of discourse and interaction that characterize successful learning activities for these African American and Mexican American girls. Additional research on some of these girls in informal social groups and on the science classrooms in the schools attended by the girls highlights how local culture affects learning and is affected by schooling.

Voice of Leslie Edwards, After-School Teacher

I believe our success begins when we listen carefully to the girls and act upon their interests. Many times their interests come from their communities, their families, and youth culture. One of the ways we link student interests to science and technology is to have the girls cocreate class activities with us. For example, one sixth grader loved dogs and we created a group of activities that included taking a neighborhood survey of dogs, analyzing the data with a spreadsheet program, and using professional-level software to create an animation of how a dog sees colors, incorporating the electromagnetic spectrum, light, and optics.

SOURCE: Eisenhart and Edwards (2004). Used with permission.

❖ Reflecting on the Cases

1. Discuss why featuring multiple perspectives of the researcher, teachers, and girls in the second study provides insight into the partnership, Simply the Best!

2. Explain the benefits for students, families, teachers, schools, and community partners by implementing the *No Idling* service-learning project.

3. What elements make these two projects most successful? What is the role of the school? The families? The students? The teachers? Universities? The community?

Activities for Further Development

1. Make a list of two potential service-learning, stewardship, or civic involvement projects that your students could engage in. List the academic content standards that align with the project, the community partner(s), and how families can participate.

2. Consider some of the online partnership projects described in this chapter. Determine what you and your students could share with other schools around the world. Describe the types of activities that multiple schools could engage in via Internet communication and resources.

3. Consider community and high-profile partnership possibilities in your community. Make a list of potential partners and activities.

4. Create a list of businesses in your community that could be potential partners. Record ideas about how a reciprocal partnership could be developed and how each party would benefit.

Additional Reading and Information

Jasso, G. (1996). *Finding corporate resources: Maximizing school business partnerships.* Thousand Oaks, CA: Corwin. This book provides comprehensive information related to working with corporations to enhance education and to involve the community within the school's curriculum.

Tippins, D. J., Mueller, M. P., van Eijck, M. W., & Adams, J. (Eds.). (in press). *Cultural studies and environmentalism: The confluence of ecojustice, place-based (science) education, and indigenous knowledge systems.* New York: Springer. This book provides a view of science from an ecojustice perspective.

Civicyouth.org provides information and research related to civic involvement: http://www.civicyouth.org

EcoJustice Education is a growing movement to encourage educators and students to become more involved in preserving the planet Earth: http://www.ecojusticeeducation.org

The Europa pen pal program encourages pen pals around the world to connect and communicate: http://www.europa-pages.com/penpal_form.html

The Global SchoolNet Foundation provides sample online partnership projects: http://www.globalschoolnet.org/index.html

The U.K. Global Gateway Project includes sample project activities and encourages schools around the world to participate: http://www.globalgateway.org.uk

The Youth Stewardship Program for teachers and students provides free stewardship projects and resources: http://www.parks.sfgov.org/wcm_recpark/Volunteer/YouthStewardshipBrochure.pdf

7

Partnering With Community Organizations and Resources

After reading this chapter, you should have a better understanding of:

- partnerships that extend beyond the school grounds;

- professional partnerships with colleagues and teachers;

- creating partnerships beyond the four walls of the classroom with universities, museums, cultural institutions, and outdoor venues;

- strategies to enhance the museum experience for students, teachers, and families;

- pre– and post–field trip activity examples with steps to maximize the educational potential of field trips; and

- tips for teachers who are organizing field trips and for families who want to participate in them.

| Table 7.1 | Prior Knowledge and Beliefs Organizer |

Describe everything you remember about your first field trip when you were a student.	Describe how this field trip outside the classroom affected your school experience or learning (positively or negatively).

Consider the experiences you provided in Table 7.1 as you read about effective partnerships with museums and maximizing the field trip experience for students.

Partnerships Beyond the Four Walls of the Classroom

As we have learned throughout the first six chapters, students' entire educational experience is enhanced when teachers go beyond the four walls of the classroom and collaborate with others in the school and within the community. This chapter will focus on partnership possibilities related to professional partnerships among teachers, schools, and universities as well as partnerships with museums, cultural institutions, and outdoor venues. Information about field trips and strategies for including diverse families in field trip experiences will be presented as a way to promote learning outside the formal classroom.

There are myriad opportunities for students and teachers to partner with institutions such as museums, libraries, and historical landmarks and move the partnership experience beyond the school grounds. In addition, many corporations want to partner with schools in order to enhance the education of the children in the community who may one day be part of their workforce. These partnerships can be classified as a one-time partnership or can take place over time and result in an arm-in-arm partnership for families, teachers, and students. This chapter will feature information about optimizing the resources and partnership potential of museums, zoos, aquariums, and other institutions. It will describe activities beyond the one-time field trip and include information to help teachers prepare for field trips, engage in activities during the trip, and follow up with activities that connect the experience back to the classroom. In addition, it will feature a variety of partnerships including university-school partnerships and partnerships with museums, cultural institutions, local parks, and other outdoor venues.

SOURCE: Used with permission of Tom Baker.

The family of Leo Politi visited students, teachers, and families to showcase his artwork and literary accomplishments. Events like these bring the entire school and community together.

University-School Partnerships

Forming partnerships with institutions of higher education such as universities and community colleges can enrich the public and private school curriculum (Goldman & Laserna, 1998). In addition, there are many students who may never have access to colleges and universities if they are not provided with early experiences demonstrating how they can be a part of a college community. Diverse students from local universities can provide service learning within schools and can serve as role models. Some universities have organized large service-learning programs where undergraduate students are partnered with teachers and schools to interact, participate in enrichment activities, and become educational "buddies." Frequent visits to university campuses beginning at early ages can provide context and help students and their families see themselves as part of a college campus community.

The Island Explorers program is a unique partnership between the University of Southern California Sea Grant Office and five surrounding neighborhood schools. The program has been in existence since 1996 and includes teachers, students, families, university faculty, and graduate students who work together to promote science literacy, knowledge of marine science, and lifelong learning. The interdisciplinary curriculum is designed for students in elementary and middle school and incorporates technology, field trips, and interactions with marine science researchers and students at the university. Students participate in field trips to local beaches and aquaria, for example, and participate in beach cleanups. All activities are planned and implemented in collaboration with university faculty and university students serving as partners with teachers and role models for students. In addition, teachers, students, university faculty, and university students work throughout the year to prepare for a culminating experience, an overnight trip to Catalina Island and the Wrigley Institute for Environmental Studies. Families are included in the planning and preparation for the Catalina trip throughout the school year. Teachers host pizza nights where they show pictures of the institute and discuss what students will do, where they will eat, and where they will sleep. For many students, this will be their first time staying overnight away from their families, so convincing parents that their children will be safe requires consistent communication and information over time.

One of the more common university-school partnerships involves classroom teachers who serve as mentors when students are student teaching. However, there are various degrees of partnership, which extend from the one-time collaboration to arm-in-arm collaborations discussed earlier. Stevens (1999) discusses the ideal professional development partnership model as one where individuals enhance and expand their roles within the broader community. He recommends that teachers share their teaching experiences with universities by supervising student teachers and teaching in teacher preparation programs. University faculty should supervise student teachers and provide professional development opportunities for all teachers at a school site, not just those who host student teachers in their classroom. Universities learn more about the current school culture, school reforms, and other

University professors, teachers, students, and educators from local museums can work together to develop and implement activities at family science nights held at the school.

classroom practices. The schools learn more about current research and methods of instruction led by educational researchers and experts. This model shifts from expert learning at the university to collaborative learning at local school sites—creating a community of professionals and learners.

The School/University Partnership Team program at Western Michigan University includes a team of public school students, teachers, and administrators and university faculty, students, and staff. The program is designed to create a community of learners to explore research possibilities and other activities related to best practices. Each month, the university hosts a meeting to explore areas of interest, solve problems, and develop new aspects of the program.

Columbia University's Healthy School Healthy Families program targets one of the largest elementary schools in New York City. The partners include Columbia University General Pediatrics, the university's Mailman School of Public Health, and administrators and teachers at the elementary school. A liaison consultant is present at the school site to address health needs for students and families. This is an example of a university-school partnership that seeks to integrate services to assist teachers in identifying medical issues that can impede or optimize learning. The school and university work together to inform families of health services within the community and offer case management for families who have children with long-term medical challenges.

Each of the partnerships described above provides only a snapshot of the possibilities and benefits when schools and universities work together. If you would like to organize a partnership program with a local university, you should consider the following steps.

1. Talk to your administrator about an area of teaching and learning in which you feel students and families can benefit from work with a university.

2. Search online for a university near you that offers services related to your need. If you are in a rural area with a university that is far away, no worries! You can create a virtual partnership through e-mail, videoconferencing, and other technological tools.

3. Set up a meeting with interested faculty at the university and at your school or via videoconferencing.

4. Determine what you would like to accomplish and how you would like to accomplish it. Decide who will be involved and the time necessary to reach your overall goals.

5. Search online for grant opportunities that may relate to your project. Many government agencies provide money for collaborative partnership projects. See Chapter 9 for resources related to grants and other educational funding opportunities.

Partnerships With Museums and Cultural Institutions

Museums and cultural institutions are popular community resources for families, school groups, and individuals. They serve as ideal environments to supplement learning and provide myriad educational opportunities (e.g., Cox-Petersen, Marsh, Kisiel, & Melber, 2003; Griffin & Symington, 1997). They range in size from very small rooms to massive structures, and they serve multiple purposes including education, research, and community outreach activities. They offer a wealth of information, artifacts, and educational experts. The American Association of Museums (AAM) describes the purpose of museums as being institutions that make a "unique contribution to the public by collecting, preserving, and interpreting things of this world" (AAM, 2008). Museums can be developed and supported by local, state, or national governments, or they can be developed and funded by private organizations or corporations. The most notable types of museums relate to art, history, or science. However, zoos, aquariums, children's museums, planetariums, nature centers, and historical sites are also considered types of museums.

The Huntington Library, Art Collections, and Botanical Gardens in San Marino, California, is an example of a private institution that offers historical and botanical expertise and exhibits throughout its grounds. It serves as both a research and an education center with art galleries, library collections, sculptures, rare books, manuscripts, decorative arts, and a botanical garden. In addition, the Huntington features a teaching classroom onsite and a children's garden where families and school groups can enjoy hands-on explorations building on four ancient elements—earth, air, fire, and water. The four raw elements fuel the plant world and provide oxygen, food, resources, and habitats through plant growth.

The National Gallery of Art in Washington, DC, is a federally supported institution with the help of a large gift from Andrew W. Mellon in 1937. Mellon collected art and donated his collection in order to begin a gallery of art for the United States. The National Gallery of Art features a Web site that provides a variety of interactive online

Children investigate life as a farmer and growing crops at a local pumpkin patch.

activities for children and families, from building decorative objects for an online doll-house to creating a still-life painting. Teachers and students can also locate information online about the different galleries, special exhibits, and even the gift shop. In addition, the National Gallery of Art has partnered with inner-city elementary schools during the past 15 years in a program called *Art Around the Corner*. This program provides opportunities for fifth- and sixth-grade teachers and students to visit the museum seven times during the school year while museum docents also visit the school sites two times during the year. All activities are developed in alignment with the school curriculum and with the gallery content and artists.

The Mission San Juan Capistrano is a state-supported historical site in San Juan Capistrano, California. The Discovery Science Center in Santa Ana, California, is a privately funded science museum. Both provide invaluable community resources for families, schools, and the community. Together, the historic mission and science center have created a unique educational partnership where they provide activities for children and school groups that integrate the history and culture of the mission with science content. Such activities include collecting soil samples, building a catenary arch, and participating in a geological scavenger hunt. Multiple institutions working together can only enhance the educational output for teachers, families, and students.

Who Visits Museums and Cultural Institutions?

Given the plethora of artifacts, resources, and activities, museums can be daunting and become unapproachable to some groups of people. Certain cultures and groups traditionally visit museums, while others do not. Research has shown that low-income, working-class families from diverse cultural groups often feel disconnected from these educational institutions, as well as from schools themselves (Moles, 1993; Valdes, 1996). Even more interesting is that the proximity of the museum does not seem to be a factor, because museums are often located in large cities and urban centers with diverse populations. Museum educators are making it their mission within the United States and other countries to create museums that are more inclusive than in the past. Teachers and schools can take advantage of this by planning school visits, contacting the museum for artifact loans or other resources, and finding out about family visitation days that are often offered free of charge.

The earliest museums were developed and featured to serve an elite group of privileged citizens (Melber & Abraham, 2002). However, during the past 20 years the American Association of Museums (1992) has challenged museums to "become more inclusive places that welcome diverse audiences . . . and reflect our society's pluralism" (p. 3) in order to eradicate the traditional elite stereotypes and encourage more diverse visitors worldwide. Museums provide a rich environment to build background knowledge, vocabulary, and educational experiences for all students, particularly those from diverse backgrounds and who are English language learners. The next section will discuss how to provide better access for students and for their families while organizing field trips at the school site.

Field Trips to Museums and Cultural Institutions

Most museums and cultural institutions feature (a) connections to academic standards, (b) outreach programs, (c) school tours, and (d) public education programs. Finson and Enochs (1987) found that teachers increase the potential for cognitive and affective learning by planning structured activities before and after class field trips. The educational potential of a field trip can be maximized if the teacher provides these various activities that connect museum resources and experiences with content and activities back in the classroom (and also with the students' home and community). Pre– and post– field trip classroom activities and projects extend the trip past the usual one-day event because they allow the child to gain prior knowledge about the visit and to reflect on his or her experiences afterward. Researchers have found that preparing students for field trips and providing follow-up activities can influence the learning outcomes during and after visits (see Ramey-Gassert, Walberg, & Walberg, 1994, for more information). In addition, Falk and Dierking (1997) have conducted extensive research related to museums and found that field trips have a lasting impression well into adulthood. They found that many adults could recall specific events that took place during school field trips.

The next section will provide information for teachers about (a) **pre–field trip activities,** (b) interactive activities while at the museum, and (c) **post–field trip activities**. Including these three areas will help teachers, students, and families maximize the educational potential that museums offer.

Pretrip Activities

Before taking a field trip, teachers can communicate the purpose of the trip to students and their families. By doing this, students will know why they are taking the trip and what they will see and do. Most museums and cultural institutions have Web sites that students and families can visit and where they can inquire about the content, artifacts, and exhibits before taking a trip there. Preparation and pretrip activities are necessary because many students experience a "novelty effect" when entering a new environment for the first time (Martin, Falk, & Balling, 1981). To maximize learning and limit novelty, students should know what they will be seeing, what they will be doing, how they will be doing it, and whom they will be doing activities with. Teachers, students, and families can provide maps of the museum and trace the path to and from the different exhibits or artifacts they will see. Students can create an itinerary in advance that includes a schedule from the time they leave school until the time they return. Any information that can be provided in advance such as information regarding the content of the trip, the nature of the exhibits, bathroom breaks, lunch areas, and even the gift shop location helps students visualize the trip before they ever arrive. A letter could be sent home in advance of the trip explaining school activities connected to museum content, the purpose of the trip, the itinerary, and parents' role on the trip if they are participating. Teachers might ask for updated contact information from families before going on the trip in case of an emergency. The list can be brought to the museum and kept with the teacher on the day of the visit.

Enhancing Learning for Students With Special Needs: Museum Access

Teachers should locate a variety of information related to how museums and other field trip locations provide opportunities and access for students with special needs. Most museum Web sites provide this information. It is important to note this before arriving at the field trip site. Here are some things to consider:

- Determine handicapped parking and access to the building in advance.
- Map out the entire visit including exhibit areas, restrooms, water fountains, and elevators to ensure it is accessible to all students.
- Determine if there is closed captioning on some of the video presentations or if other assistive listening devices are available.
- Ask the museum if it provides sign language assistance if necessary.

During the Field Trip

When taking field trips, teachers might consider encouraging as many parents as possible to participate in the entire trip experience with their children. Providing pretrip activities as homework that involves the entire family can motivate families to participate in some way, even if it is at home. Having students write and send personal invitations asking parents to attend can also be helpful. If the school is lacking resources needed to pay for extra individuals to attend, arrange for a fundraising night at a local pizza restaurant or a school sales event (e.g., healthy snacks at recess, chocolate candy during the holidays) to help fund the trip.

It is important that teachers communicate with the museum in advance to arrange enough docents or other volunteers to facilitate a tour if needed. Students experience many things while visiting museums and other venues; therefore, teachers should be aware of the variety of opportunities available to them. Falk and Dierking (2000) outlined a contextual model of learning for educators and museum staff so that they would be more knowledgeable about what individuals experience at museums. They distinguish among three facets of learning within a museum setting: the sociocultural context, the individual's personal experiences, and the physical environment of a museum. Cumulatively, all of these areas play a role in the learner's experience at a museum or cultural institution. A personal context includes prior knowledge, interest, beliefs, and choices made at the museum. The sociocultural context involves group interaction/ mediation and interactions facilitated by others. The physical context includes the nature of the exhibit, the design, and experiences outside the museum. Putting all of the contexts together, a learner's past experiences with an artifact, the familiarity with the location of the object, and the discussion with another individual influence learning at a museum. Cox-Petersen et al. (2003) provide recommendations for educators when visiting a museum or cultural institution. Some of their recommendations are listed below.

- Integrate learning tools such as notebooks, clipboards, prompt sheets, and photographs when appropriate. Teachers can contact museum educators in advance to find out what the museum has available for student use.
- Encourage students to travel in groups during the visit. This will encourage more inter-action among students where they can discuss what they are seeing, experiencing, or questioning.
- Provide learning cues related to concepts that students should focus on most. Providing a graphic organizer or photographs can be helpful in addition to a chart for students to record their ideas.
- Provide active learning opportunities such as exploring hands-on objects and coopera-tive learning tasks. Young children can listen to docents and teachers for a few minutes during a museum visit; however, they lose interest quickly because of the stimulation going on around them. Encourage them to interact with areas of the exhibit where there are hands-on objects or materials. Let them explore without teacher direction during part of the visit.
- Look for labels and artifacts that prompt students to connect exhibit content with home and school. Teachers can visit the museum ahead of time (many museums offer this free of charge) to note areas of the exhibits where students can connect most with the cur-riculum and their home experiences.
- Draw on strengths of the diversity of students to integrate activities and content. Some museums are more culturally rich and diverse than others. However, teachers can note the areas of diverse historical individuals, contributions, and viewpoints during the visit.

These recommendations are important when taking field trips because most museum trips lack connections to the classroom curriculum (Kisiel, 2003). Although worksheets and other instructional forms can be helpful, teachers should be careful not to provide busywork during the tour and allow students to interact with their peers and gain a personal appreciation for the institution while visiting.

Posttrip Activities

As a follow-up to the trip, it is helpful to provide students with the opportunity to reflect on their personal experiences, their interactions with others, and the exhibit content. Students can write about their favorite exhibits or interesting experiences once they are back at school. Some students may choose to create a piece of art or produce a short documentary via videotape to showcase their favorite experiences. Other students may want to investigate more information about the museum's dinosaur collection online. Posttrip activities vary but should be connected to the field trip and the child's personal experiences, as well as the curriculum at school. Allow students to ask questions, seek answers from experts via e-mail, trade books, and reference books, and use online resources to extend the trip. If students were required to complete a task at the museum, then have them report their observations and findings. Continue to correspond with museum educators about additional materials that can be borrowed through a loan program or additional online resources that may be available to students and teachers.

The following "Notes From the Classroom" section is a set of sample activities written by two sixth-grade teachers to prepare their students for interactive investigations during a field trip to a local zoo. It should be noted that the trip to the zoo focused on researching a specific group of animals in depth before visiting other zoo exhibits. Before the trip to the zoo, students worked in groups to find out more about the variety of animals that the zoo featured and determined a particular order of animals that they would investigate. During research at the zoo, students chose three animals in their order and were instructed to observe them for at least 10 minutes and record physical characteristics, interactions with other animals, and other behaviors. For example, one group of students chose primates and set out to observe chimpanzees, gorillas, and howler monkeys before taking a general tour of the zoo exhibits. The teachers spent 3 days during science class to prepare their students for the trip and 3 days after their return to complete the entire posttrip activity. The science curriculum specified that sixth graders should know about the classification of different animals, particularly the way scientists classify animals into particular groups: kingdom, phylum, class, order, family, genus, and species.

The purpose of the trip was to learn more about the order of animals, how they are classified, their behaviors, and what distinguishes one group of animals from another. Specific steps related to the zoo activities are outlined below.

Notes From the Classroom: Planning a Zoo Visit

Preparation for the Zoo Trip

1. Ask for parent volunteers to join the research trip to the zoo.
2. Inform students and families about the nature of the trip. Students will be working in cooperative groups to collect observation data on a particular group of animals determined in advance.

(Continued)

(Continued)

Pretrip Preparation Activities at School (2–3 days in advance)

1. Provide groups of students with a variety of pictures of the different animals at the zoo. Ask them to group them according to characteristics. Once this is done, ask them if they can determine animals in the same order such as marsupials, cetaceans, raptors, and primates.

2. Next, ask students to determine a particular order of animals that they will research at the zoo. Organize students into collaborative groups who will investigate a particular order of animals during the zoo trip.

3. Ask students to ask questions about the order. They should attempt to answer the questions by accessing the information via the Internet, reference materials, and educational software. This will provide background information for students.

4. Have students go to the zoo's Web site and determine at least three animals in their order to observe. Then have them create a chart to record their observations of these animals during the visit.

During the Zoo Trip (3–4 hours)

1. Provide clipboards for students to record their observations.

2. Students break up into different groups with parents as chaperones. They use a map to visit the three or four exhibit areas that feature animals in their order.

3. After specific observation data are collected, students and parent chaperones explore other exhibits and animals within the zoo.

4. Students meet for lunch and shop at the gift shop.

5. Board the bus back to school.

Posttrip Activities Back at School (2–3 days after the trip)

1. Ask students to create a piece of art using various materials to demonstrate their favorite parts of the zoo visit.

2. Next, have students integrate language arts and science by engaging in the writing process to create a report on their research before the trip, their observations at the zoo, and their personal experiences up close with the animals. Steps to the writing process may include prewriting, a rough draft, editing, revisions, and a final copy. Students can work collaboratively during the writing process and edit each other's work. Once a final copy is completed, students convene back in their cooperative groups and become a panel of experts who will report on the zoo observations, research, and experiences. The other students are encouraged to ask questions of the panel.

3. Have a variety of books and other materials available in the classroom for students to read and access if they want to learn more about animals, the zoo, or careers in zoology.

Some institutions and schools have formed ongoing partnerships that go beyond the one-day field trip. Two such programs include *School in the Park* in San Diego, California, and *Urban Advantage* in New York City, where museums and museum-based programs are successfully integrated into school instruction over a period of time. The *Urban Advantage* program involves a partnership among the New York City Department of Education, teachers, middle school students, their families, and eight museums and cultural institutions including the American Museum of Natural History, the Brooklyn Botanic Garden, the New York Botanical Garden, the Staten Island Zoo, the Bronx Zoo, and the New York Aquarium. The purpose of the project is to enhance science learning by integrating the content and activities within museums and other institutions around the city. The project is funded by the New York City Council and the City of New York and includes materials and resources for schools, professional development for teachers, and field trips for families to participating institutions at no cost. For example, eighth graders investigate the work scientists do in various fields and participate in a citywide science exit project exposition at the end of the year. The *School in the Park* program includes 10 museums and institutions in the Balboa Park area of San Diego. The program is a partnership among Price Charities, San Diego State University, San Diego City Schools, and the San Diego Education Association. Children from local inner-city elementary schools leave their campus each week to attend school at various museums. The program blends formal and informal learning and allows students to interact with museum educators and content experts, utilize museum resources, and align activities with state standards. This program is featured in one of the case studies at the end of the chapter and includes voices from a researcher, parents, teachers, and museum educators.

Field trips are wonderful if there are funds available for travel beyond the school grounds. However, many schools do not have the money or time to visit a museum. If this is the case, teachers can inquire into virtual field trips online and museum outreach programs that may be available to them.

One popular outreach program called the *Ann Simpson Artmobile* provides visual arts throughout the entire state of Wyoming for K–12 schools, senior centers, libraries, and other community groups and locations. Housed in the University of Wyoming Art Museum, the mobile art van features artwork from the museum's permanent collection and by local Wyoming artists. Hands-on activities are incorporated with a discussion of the art pieces. A similar program, the *Earthmobile,* is sponsored by the Natural History Museum of Los Angeles County and travels to different schools to enhance students' understanding of the cultural history of local Native Americans. Museum instructors arrive at schools in a large 18-wheeled truck with the *Earthmobile* attached! If museum outreach educators are not available to visit the school, teachers can provide virtual field trips via the Internet (Cox-Petersen & Melber, 2001) and then develop a classroom museum based on grade-level content (Cox-Petersen & Melber, 1999). Cities around the United States often provide resources for teachers, students, and families that feature how the city gets its water. Several cities in the southwestern United States provide a virtual sewage treatment tour and related resources, classroom activities, and sample lesson plans. These types of virtual tours can be integrated within the curriculum throughout the school year. The Franklin Institute in Philadelphia and many other museums around the world feature a virtual tour of their exhibits as well. Virtual field trips allow students to "visit" an art museum or aquarium without ever leaving the classroom.

National/Local Parks and Outdoor Education

In Richard Louv's (2005) book *Last Child in the Woods,* he argues that children are suffering from "nature-deficit disorder" because they are not provided with enough outdoor experiences. National, state, and regional parks offer an array of educational opportunities for students and teachers. The U.S. National Park Service features a Web site that lists every national park from A to Z. By accessing the different parks, teachers, students, and families can learn more about environmental education resources online. In addition, teachers can make use of a local park area or the schoolyard that is within walking distance of school. Teachers and students can visit the park weekly or monthly to make observations of plants and animals. They can observe a tree through the various seasons, record their observations, and create a "Year in the Life" book about their tree.

Local arboretums and nurseries are also good resources that can become partners in education. Teachers and students can partner with local nurseries to create classroom gardens in pots or in their schoolyard. Two elementary teachers and their students in Arkansas formed a partnership with a university faculty member and preservice elementary students to create a more interactive field trip to a local arboretum. The elementary students and preservice teachers communicated via e-mail for several weeks and became "outdoor science buddies." During the students' field trip to the arboretum, the preservice teachers and their elementary buddies participated in arboretum activities together. Students benefited because they could learn alongside an adult. The preservice teachers benefited because they were able to gain important experiences and knowledge related to outdoor education, field trip preparation, and school-university partnerships.

The Forestry Institute for Teachers is a collaborative project that provides environmental education and professional development for teachers in California. The goal of the institute is to provide K–12 teachers from urban and rural settings with knowledge, skills, and tools to teach their students about forest ecology and resource management. Natural resource specialists and teachers work together during a one-week retreat in the forest to gain a deeper understanding of forestry and how environmental education can be integrated into all subject areas. The natural resource specialists and teachers share information about students, families, and public views related to the environment. In addition, resource specialists and teachers work together to create innovative instructional units that integrate environmental learning within the arts, reading, writing, science, social studies, and even physical education. Many other forestry agencies within the United States offer programs for families, students, and teachers related to forestry education and conservation.

Families should also be encouraged to seek outdoor educational resources to encourage curiosity, questions, and respect for the environment. Isidor I. Rabi, a Nobel Prize recipient in physics, stated that he wanted to be a scientist partly because of the mentoring of his mother:

My mother made me a scientist without ever intending it. Every other Jewish mother in Brooklyn would ask her child after school: "So? Did you learn anything today?" But not my mother. She always asked me a different question. "Izzy," she would say, "Did you ask a good question today?" That difference—asking good questions—made me become a scientist! (Paulu, 1992, p. 3)

Hiking through the woods or visiting a local river area or beach can provide children with out-of-school, community-based educational experiences that will last throughout their lives. Camping as an alternative to costly family vacations can also help children learn more about the natural world they live in. Teachers can provide lists of local, state, and national parks that provide low-cost camping facilities and activities to encourage family bonding experiences.

Tips for Organizing and Participating in Field Trips

The following sections provide information for teachers and families who want to participate in learning outside the school grounds. Teachers can feature some of these tips and their own when sending home newsletters or e-mails to parents.

Tips for Teachers

1. Examine the curriculum standards for your grade level. Determine the resources in your community that will provide valuable knowledge and resources to enhance one or more standards. Next determine one or more places that you and your students can visit.

2. Make contact in advance with the place you will visit. If visiting a museum, contact the tour coordinator and determine a date for your tour. Next, ask about educational resources and other materials that will help you prepare your students for the trip. Many museums offer pretrip teacher lesson plans, posttrip activities, artifact-loan programs, and maps of the institution.

3. Prepare students as much as possible before any field trip. This includes content related to academic standards and the general tour time line including when students will leave school, activities at the site, where students will eat lunch, and what time they will return.

4. Encourage parents and other family members to participate in pretrip and posttrip activities. If space or cost allows, encourage them to visit the site as well.

Tips for Families

1. Build background experiences that involve local field trips within the community to local parks, museums, and historical sites.

2. Encourage children to talk about their field trip experiences at school and relate them to family activities at home.

3. Participate in summer museum education programs or library programs in your area.

4. Explore nature areas in your neighborhood.

5. Take advantage of days where museums are open to the public free of charge.

Chapter Summary

Valuable professional partnerships between teachers and administrators can empower teachers and provide ongoing professional development. Museums, cultural institutions, and outdoor parks and other venues can enhance the professional development of teachers and the curriculum for students and families. Students learn more from field trips when they are prepared in advance and the teacher provides pretrip activities, provides appropriate activities during the trip, and follows up with posttrip investigations and discussions. Teachers can follow a variety of steps to optimize the educational resources within the community and take advantage of multiple programs.

CASE STUDIES

These two case studies will describe how forming partnerships with the community, local museums, and research scientists can enhance teaching, learning, and professional development activities.

❖ Case Study 7.1: School in the Park

This case study features an innovative partnership among a school, a university, and local museums known as *School in the Park*. The description is adapted from Ross (2006). This program shifts the location of "school" from a traditional classroom setting in an inner-city school to the resources and educational opportunities available within museums in Balboa Park in San Diego, California. Funded by Price Charities, teachers, museum educators, families, and university faculty work collaboratively to provide an innovative learning experience for students. Students spend some of their time on the school campus and some of their time at various museums within Balboa Park. The museums are diverse in content and exhibits and include the Museum of Photographic Arts, the Reuben H. Fleet Science Center, Aerospace Museum, the San Diego Museum of Art, the Museum of San Diego History, the San Diego Museum of Man, the San Diego Natural History Museum, the San Diego Zoo, the San Diego Junior Theatre, and the San Diego Hall of Champions. The program is part of the City Heights Educational Collaborative that seeks to improve educational outcomes.

The School in the Park program extends the walls of the classroom for students at Rosa Parks Elementary School in San Diego. The school has a population of about 1,600 students in grades K–5. The partnership was developed in part to ease the overcrowded classrooms. About half of the students at the school spend 20% to 25% of their time away from the school building and learn multiple subjects within the diverse museums and cultural institutions. This program provides more than the one-shot field trip and allows teaching and learning to take place in authentic settings while optimizing the multiple resources available at the museums and within the park. The following voices include partners who describe their experiences at the Fleet Science Center.

Voice of a Museum Educator and Community Teacher Developer:
Anson Lee, Reuben H. Fleet Science Center

The Reuben H. Fleet Science Center's curriculum prior to working with the School in the Park program was typically a series of demonstrative events that were intended to excite students about science and encourage investigation. This was reasonable in the beginning as the workshops only allowed 1.5 hours per group of students. There was little time for students to construct meaning from activities and little or no assessment. Through our participation with School in the Park (SITP) we have been able to facilitate more meaningful investigations where students can learn complex concepts through inquiry.

We strongly believed that if teachers were going to share 2 weeks of student time with us, we needed to make it as valuable as possible. We focused on the physical science standards for fifth grade. This was a natural choice being a physics-focused science center. . . . We try to maximize all of the benefits from the collaboration. The shared staff allows experimentation with concepts such as boiling points. We try to push the envelope of a typical classroom considering the support and resources at our disposal. There are not too many fifth-grade teachers who can demonstrate the range of boiling points using liquid nitrogen. We utilize the floor exhibits whenever possible to help students hone observation and questioning techniques.

School in the Park provides our staff with a working lab where we can continually expand our expectations for students and ourselves. It never looks the same from one class to the next, but we know it's always getting better. We only hope that we have had as much of an impact on the students at Rosa Parks as they have on us. (Ross, 2006, p. 110)

Voice of a University Faculty Member: Dr. Donna Ross, Associate Professor of Science Education, San Diego State University

As Dr. Ross was observing a group of fifth graders observing a shiny piece of steel wool and a rusty piece of steel wool, she noted their explanations and identification of physical and chemical changes that caused differences in the wool's appearance:

As a science educator, I find this exchange (related to the steel wool) very exciting. These students may not know yet what caused the change in the steel wool, but they [had] an authentic discussion of their observations. The students are listening to each other and responding to their peers, as opposed to waiting for an answer from the teacher. They are using their prior knowledge and their sense of smell, touch, and sight to synthesize evidence in order to form a conclusion. Ultimately, they recognize that they do not need to agree, but they need to be able to articulate a rationale for their answer. These inner-city, elementary school English learners have a better scientific approach to a question than many high school students. In fact, when these students reach high school and are studying oxidative reactions, they will have strong background experiences to draw on. (p. 119)

Voice of an Elementary Teacher #1

There are just so many materials so easy to access here. I know I can do a lot of it at school, but the kids really need the experiences they get in the museums. They haven't ever seen these things before. (pp. 117–118)

Voice of an Elementary Teacher #2

They [students] become so passionate about things I would have never thought about. We go back to school and research all kinds of things. (p. 118)

Voice of an Elementary Teacher #3

I try to get them [the students] to think of all the questions they can while we have the advantage of an expert. (p. 118)

SOURCE: Ross (2006).

❖ Case Study 7.2: Professional Development at the State Park

Elementary, middle school, and high school science teachers participated in a field-based professional development program at Red Rock Canyon State Park located in the Mojave Desert of California. The workshop was a weekend of camping learning experiences where the teachers supplied their own tent and sleeping bag. All meals were prepared by a camp cook. The teachers participated in a collaborative pretrip meeting that was held the week before they participated in the weekend campout. The purpose of the pretrip meeting was to prepare them for what they would see, do, and experience. In addition, a museum curator and paleontologist provided background content about the Red Rock Canyon area and research tasks that they would participate in. The description of this program is adapted from Melber and Cox-Petersen (2005).

During the campout weekend, teachers participated in fossil hunting excursions and bird study walks. Any specimens found or observations noted were discussed with museum curators. A museum educator also took part in the trip and provided instructional strategies based on field trip content that teachers could implement once back in the classroom. The classroom activities and examples included things like locating and excavating fossil mammal specimens, field identification of desert wildlife, an inquiry of the geology of Red Rock Canyon, fossil casting, and bird identification using spotting scopes.

This type of professional development experience differed from traditional professional development workshops because it (a) took place outside the formal classroom in a state park; (b) provided teachers with activities and information but did not specify exactly how teachers must use the information; (c) provided opportunities for museum educators, curators, and local teachers to interact and communicate about paleontology, science teaching, and research in the state park; and (d) encouraged ongoing partnerships beyond the scope of the weekend campout. The teachers gained valuable insights from experts, and they were empowered with a variety of knowledge and experiences.

Voice of a Teacher Participant A

I will always talk about this trip—forever. It was a high point, and my kids will love hearing and learning about all aspects of it! (Melber & Cox-Petersen, 2005, p. 116)

Voice of a Teacher Participant B

Background knowledge is very valuable for a teacher to be able to understand the whole picture. (p. 116)

SOURCE: Melber and Cox-Petersen (2005).

❖ Reflecting on the Cases

1. How do nontraditional professional development programs like the one in Red Rock Canyon provide empowerment and learning opportunities for teachers?

2. Describe the benefit of having the *School in the Park* program throughout the school year and in subsequent school years rather than as a one-day field trip to a local museum. What is the role of the school? The families? The students? The teachers? The community?

3. Describe how teachers who participated in the professional development program can continue a partnership with museum curators and educators after the conclusion of the trip to Red Rock Canyon.

Activities for Further Development

1. Visit a local museum, state park, botanical garden, or other cultural or outdoor venue. Observe who is visiting the area and how they are interacting with the resources and other people there. Locate educational resources available to teachers, students, and families.

2. Choose a museum in your area that you would like to visit. Next, create a list of pretrip activities, activities at the museum, and posttrip activities that you can use to optimize the students' visit.

3. Interview an educator at a local museum or other cultural institution and create a list of resources, partnership programs, and teacher professional development opportunities that it offers.

4. Consider a museum or other institution that your class could visit. Locate the museum or organization's Web site and determine how it provides access to students with special needs.

Additional Reading and Information

Melber, L. M. (2008). *Informal learning and field trips: Engaging students in standards-based experiences across the K–5 curriculum.* Thousand Oaks, CA: Corwin. This book provides practical information and activities related to planning and implementing field trips within the community, museums, and local parks. It also features lesson plans and activities related to multiple subject areas such as science, math, language arts, and fine arts.

The American Museum of Natural History's Urban Advantage program Web site provides information about this unique family-community-school partnership: http://www.urbanadvantagenyc.org/home.aspx

The Association of Zoos and Aquariums provides educational information, resources, and conservation efforts: http://www.aza.org

The Communities in Schools program encourages community partnerships to promote the integration of community and social services: http://www.cisnet.org

The Huntington Library, Art Collections, and Botanical Gardens Web site features information about the gardens and art collections in addition to lesson plans and resources for teachers: www.huntington.org

The Museum Educational Social Network features a Web site that encourages networking and educational partnerships. The site provides podcasts, videos, and other activities to promote interactive learning activities: http://mesn.museumpods.com

The National Gallery of Art in Washington, D.C., Web site provides information about visiting the museum, educational resources, exhibits, and special programs and events: http://www.nga.gov. The site also features educational activities for teachers and children: http://www.nga.gov/education/classroom

Taproot, a publication of the Coalition for Education in the Outdoors, is a network of organizations, businesses, institutions, centers, agencies, and associations linked to support education about the outdoors and stewardship: http://www.outdooredcoalition.org

The U.S. National Park Service provides education activities and resources online: http://www.nature.nps.gov/studentsteachers/linkstolearning/index.cfm

8

Barriers to Partnerships

After reading this chapter, you should have a better understanding of:

- promoting culturally relevant teaching strategies;
- specific barriers related to community and family partnerships with schools;
- strategies to help teachers identify, acknowledge, and overcome barriers;
- a "quiz" for teachers related to communicating with parents;
- the role of schools, families, and school psychologists when addressing and acknowledging barriers to promote partnerships;
- taking action in schools to promote diversity and tolerance;
- explicitly teaching tolerance and acceptance; and
- tips and resources to promote partnerships and diversity.

Table 8.1	Prior Knowledge and Beliefs Organizer
What are the challenges that schools, families, and communities face when developing partnerships?	**Based on your knowledge of effective partnerships, how can groups overcome these challenges?**

Consider your responses related to the challenges that partnerships face in Table 8.1 as you read this chapter. Think of ways to overcome these challenges, or barriers, to provide a more inclusive experience for all students, families, and community members.

The first seven chapters addressed characteristics of partnerships, history and policies that influence partnerships, and examples of partnerships with families and the broader community. This chapter will provide a description of barriers that challenge the development and sustainability of educational partnerships. These barriers must be acknowledged, addressed, and overcome. The last part of the chapter will include two different case studies where you will be asked to identify barriers and suggest ways of taking action to overcome them.

Culturally Relevant Teaching and Learning

Data from the Forum on Child and Family Statistics (2006) indicate that children between birth and 17 years of age in the United States are 58.9% White (non-Hispanic), 19.2% Hispanic, 15.5% Black, 3.9% Asian, and 4.1% other races. In addition, 21% of children live with at least one foreign-born parent, and 19% of children live with families who speak languages other than English at home. Given these statistics, it is important to consider culturally relevant pedagogy as a way to provide equal access to education for all families and students, particularly those from diverse backgrounds. **Culturally relevant pedagogy** addresses inequities and recognizes systematic power relationships within the curriculum, instructional practices, policies, and assessment. It depends not only on recognizing and capitalizing on students' experiences but also on teaching to and through those experiences in order to connect them to broader social contexts. This includes forming partnerships with families and the broader community where students live. Moreover, cultural relevance works to cultivate the classroom as a community within the school system, a community that is integrated but also aware of the realities in larger society. Culturally relevant pedagogy is an important foundation when developing and sustaining partnerships because the majority of elementary teachers in the United States fit the same profile—White, middle class, and usually female (National Center for Education Statistics, 2000)—while the student population and students' families are from many different ethnic backgrounds and socioeconomic levels.

Culturally relevant pedagogy and the focus on activist interaction and connections have been guided by the work of Gloria Ladson-Billings (1995). She advocates a communal approach and recognizes the individual humanity of all students. According to Ladson-Billings, relations in a culturally relevant classroom are "fluid and equitable," and teachers' efforts should be directed to ensure that this flexibility is maintained. This is achieved through (a) focusing positive attention on student skills and abilities and channeling them academically, (b) explicitly recognizing forms of power within curriculum and instruction, (c) utilizing students' cultures as vehicles for learning, (d) developing rapport with families and including them in the classroom, (e) encouraging the use of students' home languages, and (f) critically analyzing instructional materials and resources. All of these mechanisms then work to bolster the capacity of students and families to choose and seek academic excellence as well as the capacity of educators to work toward partnerships in support of it.

Encouraging cultural competence, high expectations for students, and proactive learning are also at the heart of culturally relevant pedagogy (Ladson-Billings, 1995). Cultural competence includes teaching and learning about individuals who come from cultures other than your own. It focuses on developing personal and interpersonal awareness and sensitivity, learning about cultural knowledge, and mastering skills related to cross-cultural teaching and learning (Diller & Moule, 2005). It is important for teachers, students, and families to develop empathy and an appreciation for life experiences of individuals who are culturally different. High expectations for students are promoted within the classroom and at home. Teachers must provide equitable instruction for all students regardless of their linguistic or cultural background. Proactive learning takes place when students are allowed to ask questions, seek answers, and take action related to their learning. Chapter 6 features a variety of action-based strategies related to service learning, stewardship, and civic involvement that promote activism in the classroom.

Lee (2005) also acknowledged the importance of cultivating the distribution of authority within the classroom where students take responsibility for their learning with the support of the teacher. Lee and Fradd (1998) support cultural relevance and have proposed an instructionally congruent pedagogy using science and literacy education as the focus. Lee and Fradd advocate that **instructionally congruent practices** can help build bridges between ethnic minority or lower-income home cultures and the more traditional middle-class school cultures. Moreover, educators must acknowledge the assumptions and stereotypes that they have about different cultures before culturally relevant pedagogy and instructionally congruent practices can emerge effectively.

Milner (2007) proposes a framework for educational researchers when acknowledging race and cultural diversity. Milner suggests that educators inquire more about themselves by asking questions such as "What is my racial and cultural background? What racial and cultural experiences have shaped my practices?" (p. 395). Next, educators should research themselves in relation to others such as the communities in which they live and work. These two areas of his framework can be applied to teachers in the classroom. Teachers must first know themselves and their influences, biases, and beliefs before they can teach acceptance, tolerance, and cultural diversity within their classroom.

Nichols-Solomon (2000) suggests five strategies to create a more culturally relevant culture within the school and the classroom. The first strategy is simple: Listen. For teachers, it is in our nature to do all the talking. It is important to listen to students and listen to families. Take a moment to think about what they are saying and plan teaching and learning around their strengths, goals, and cultural perspectives. Second, support teachers as leaders. A school should include teachers' perspectives in decision-making processes related to culturally relevant instruction and other issues involving the school. Third, create an inviting atmosphere for families and encourage them to work side-by-side in partnership with teachers. Fourth, focus on curriculum and instruction. When thinking about partnerships, culturally relevant instruction, and meeting the needs of all individuals and families, it is easy to get sidetracked. Consider family, student, and community views and partnership possibilities, but connect everything back to the curriculum and the education of children. Finally, acknowledge differences and conflict and address any problems that arise. Conflict and differences have been present in the world since the beginning of human interaction, so actually solving problems and taking action will provide opportunities for students, teachers, and families to empathize with, accept, and appreciate each other. This chapter will describe multiple barriers that teachers, families, and students often encounter and strategies to overcome them.

Barriers and Challenges That Partnerships Face

In 1994, one of the provisions in the Title I: Improving America's Schools Act specifically stated that schools must work together to identify barriers to encourage greater parent participation—particularly with parents from low socioeconomic backgrounds or non-English backgrounds and parents who have limited literacy skills, are disabled, or are from any racial or ethnic minority background. **Barriers** are obstacles that groups face when they try to accomplish a task or project. Schools must be familiar with these barriers and address them if they are to connect with students and their families and provide a successful, equitable education for all students.

All partners should consider barriers when developing, implementing, and sustaining partnership endeavors. Barriers change at each stage of a partnership, and they never fully go away. When planning for partnerships, barriers must be anticipated. During all phases of implementing a partnership or project, unanticipated barriers must be noted and addressed as they arise. Even partnerships that have existed over a long period of time still must address ongoing barriers and new barriers. The most prevalent barriers seem to exist in the form of management, time, commitment, culture, language, power, and trust. These are considered critical barriers because they are the most difficult to address and overcome. Furthermore, failure to take specific action related to these barriers may result in demise of a partnership. Other less critical barriers also exist and may be more specifically related to a particular project or group. Each of the critical barriers and some additional barriers will be described below.

Management

Many of the barriers related to management involve a lack of leadership to recruit the community, of families and teachers to form partnerships, of motivation given the number of constraints educators face each day, or of coordination of meeting and planning as a team. In order for a partnership to be a true partnership, groups (small or large) must set aside time to plan and communicate the goals of the partnership and determine who will be responsible for accomplishing certain tasks. The changing of administrators or teachers at a school, employees at a company, or families within a school can impact the continuation of a partnership if strong guidelines are not set forth for other individuals to appreciate it and want to sustain it. Leadership should be shared as much as possible, giving all partners equal access to make real decisions. When decisions are shared, individuals and groups feel empowered to participate more fully.

Schools can overcome many of the barriers related to management by increasing the motivation for collaboration and providing appropriate times to plan for partnerships. Therefore, meetings may take place at community centers, at the school in the evenings, or even on weekends. Partnerships can take place within one classroom, within an entire grade level, within the whole school, or within multiple schools in multiple areas.

Time and Commitment

Changes take time. Collaboration and true partnerships take time. Therefore, a commitment to make a partnership work requires different people taking the responsibility and allotting sufficient time to ensure that the partnership is fully executed. Usually, individuals do not mind spending time on issues and projects that they support and believe in. Therefore, buy-in for a project is crucial. Nevertheless, teachers continually feel overwhelmed and overextended as do the families of the students in their classrooms. In addition, many corporations and organizations have reduced their total number of employees and cannot spare the staff necessary to contribute time to an educational partnership with schools. Many teachers, parents, and community groups alike might ask, "Will creating a new partnership or enhancing an existing partnership require more work? We are already stretched in many different ways and don't have enough time as it is." The answer to the question is not simple, but time is a necessity to create partnerships and sustain them. Nevertheless, once a true partnership is developed, nurtured, and sustained, the sum of the outcome will be much greater than if all partners continued defining separate roles in the education of children. Specific areas that decrease the amount of time that families can contribute to a partnership include demanding work schedules, lack of day care, poor health, and other issues and responsibilities. Areas that decrease the amount of time that schools and teachers can contribute to a partnership include standardized test preparation, mandatory meetings after school, instructional planning, and multiple student work samples that must be graded daily. Therefore, all partners should respect the time that each commits to a particular project. Everyone is busy and has responsibilities. When meetings are arranged, partners should be assigned meaningful tasks that directly relate to a project. It is usually helpful to outline a plan of action that each group member can follow and use to define his or her specific role. The development of an action plan is one way to specify different roles. The steps and procedures for creating an action plan will be described in Chapter 10.

Sometimes schools can demonstrate their commitment to working with families by implementing some very simple procedures. One way to do this is to provide enough parking spaces so that the school is easily accessible to all families. Another way is to provide welcoming signs at the front of the school entrance. Many schools have district codes posted that make some families feel unwelcome (or even threatened) because of the way the signs are worded or because of the families' cultural or linguistic backgrounds. Therefore, administrators and teachers should take an intense look around the school grounds, the entrance, the parking lot, and the hallways to ensure that the school will provide a welcoming environment for all families and community members who enter.

Culture and Language

Diversity is known as the spice of life and can be the "spice of the school" if addressed properly. When cultural beliefs differ, however, it is difficult to create a collaborative partnership. One parent lamented to a teacher that "we did better before the Lees and Parks moved in. . . ." The parent was expressing disappointment with the increased ethnic diversity in the school and referred to *Lee* and *Park* as popular Asian surnames. This barrier exists in many schools and can be overcome by respecting and educating families, teachers, and students about the value of diverse cultures and beliefs within the school. Pollock (2007) introduces the term **colormute** as a way to describe how teachers and parents actively suppress race labels when talking about diverse families and students in their schools. Pollock's interest in the term *colormute* is related to situations when people choose not to label rather than the way the parent discussed the Lees and Parks above. She contends that many educators and families in the United States refuse to label people racially or refuse to talk racially about students. These active refusals to describe and analyze uncomfortable racial inequality and power conflicts result in difficult relationships that continue over time. Pollock contends that unless teachers, families, and communities actually talk about race and address cultural issues, it is impossible to repair racial inequalities and improve race relations.

Williams (2007) authored a book, *Beyond the Golden Rule: A Parent's Guide to Preventing and Responding to Prejudice.* The book is written for parents; however, teachers should have knowledge of the book, read it, follow some of the steps, and even recommend it to families in their schools. Published by the Teaching Tolerance group, the document is online and accessible to all. The book includes information for families regarding their children's preschool to teenage years. Williams discusses a few golden rules that all families should consider when teaching tolerance such as speaking openly about issues, modeling equity at home, and taking action when necessary. Speaking openly with children involves addressing any of their concerns or issues related to people who are different. It also includes discussing historical and current inequities related to slavery, segregation, bigotry, sexism, the Holocaust, and the events of September 11, 2001, at the World Trade Center and the Pentagon. Modeling equity can take place in schools, in homes, and within the community. Actions we take often speak louder than words. Therefore, it is critical that groups work together to model appropriate equitable behaviors.

Second-grade students perform traditional Spanish dances for families and the community at a multicultural celebration.

Taking action can be done at school or in neighborhoods. When students witness injustices, they should be encouraged to react to them such as by writing an editorial in the school newsletter or holding a rally to support more equity. Williams says that inaction is actually showing support for inequities. Teachers can explicitly address injustices and encourage students to take action in the form of civic involvement, service learning, or other action-based activities that were described in Chapter 6.

Stereotypes can be dangerous barriers and difficult to overcome. They exist when people form preconceived ideas about particular groups of people. Usually, stereotypes are assigned to particular groups and include overgeneralizations about the groups. Such common stereotypes include "All White single mothers are on welfare" or "All Black males are good dancers." Stereotypes can be positive or negative, but they are usually dangerous because they can provide a foundation for **prejudice** and discrimination among groups.

Enhancing Learning for Students With Special Needs: Addressing Stereotypes

1. Provide multiple opportunities for children to interact with students and other individuals with disabilities including those in wheelchairs, those who are hearing or vision impaired, or those who have other physical disabilities. It is best to provide face-to-face interaction when possible such as featuring individuals as guest speakers, peer tutors, or peer learners. If face-to-face opportunities are difficult, then feature movies and literature with a variety of individuals with different disabilities.

2. Model acceptance and inclusion for all students and individuals with disabilities. Provide a variety of apparatus such as wheelchairs, hearing-aid devices, Braille materials, and sign language lessons to encourage understanding and acceptance.

3. Help students understand children with disabilities with whom they are in class such as those with autism, learning challenges, and other disabilities. Allow students with disabilities the opportunity to "shine" and show their strengths and interests.

4. Explicitly teach students (and families when appropriate) about children and individuals with disabilities. Discuss real issues and encourage them to ask questions and seek answers.

Education and experiences that relate to understanding various cultures and individual differences can contribute to the reduction of stereotypes that exist within families, schools, and the community. Promoting cultural diversity by encouraging family involvement without prejudging why families participate or choose not to participate in some school activities can be one way to begin. Find out more about families and what events or factors would encourage them to come to school and participate more. Encourage them to provide their expertise by sharing a cultural dance, food, hobby, or piece of literature. A third-grade teacher explains her experiences addressing these issues in the following "Notes From the Classroom" section.

Notes From the Classroom:
Addressing and Acknowledging Racial and Cultural Differences

To inquire more about her students and their beliefs, Lani, a third-grade teacher, wanted to find out what her students thought about racial and cultural differences among people. The makeup of her class was 100% Latino, and every student lived in a Latino community close to the school. All students were born in the United States except for one student who was born in Mexico. About half of her students entered the school as speaking English only, while the other half were bilingual or spoke Spanish only. The majority of her students are second- or third-generation American. Lani describes herself as fair skinned, brunette, and half Latina/half Caucasian. The majority of the teachers and support staff at the school are Latino, and a handful of teachers are Anglo and Asian.

Lani created and distributed a written anonymous survey and asked students in two different third-grade classes to complete it. She informed the students that the survey was not a test, the survey would not be graded, they did not have to record their name, and most of all she really wanted to know about their views and ideas. Students in both classes indicated that they were unclear about the meaning of race. For the most part, students in each class reported never having met people of other races. Nevertheless, their minimal understanding of race revealed that they held many stereotypes about people of Anglo and African descent. They mentioned that White people were rich and that Black people were slaves. They did not reveal much about other races or colors.

Lani lamented that "our students don't know a lot about the world outside their neighborhood and culture because they are rarely exposed to it." She decided that it was important to organize a pen pal program with students from another school that had children of other ethnicities such as Anglo, Asian, and African American. The students exchanged pictures of each other and wrote about their families, their hobbies, their favorite food, and their favorite songs. Lani stated that "my students are already amazed at how much they and their pen pals have in common despite the fact that they aren't of the same culture. They are comforted knowing that all cultures fit into the concept of being American."

As a result of this project, Lani plans to invite as many volunteers and guests of other races and cultures as possible to visit her classroom and interact with her students. She believes that "there is no substitute for face-to-face interaction. It would be great to have people from the greater community come share their foods and teach the students songs or games from their cultures. Meeting them firsthand would humanize the people they learn about in their multicultural literature selections." Moreover, she plans to take her students on more field trips to various multicultural locations so that they can see and experience what exists outside the 1- or 2-mile radius of their school and homes. When looking at Lani's students and their views of the world outside their community, it is easy to see how community partnerships can provide a more inclusive and open view of education. In addition, she implemented specific strategies to encourage her students to learn more about other children who were from different cultural backgrounds.

SOURCE: Used with permission of Lani Blust Char.

Like cultural barriers, language is a barrier in many educational settings. Teachers may have difficulty communicating information to their students and families who come from non-English language backgrounds. Educational researchers have found that language differences along with lack of understanding of the formal school system, misinterpreting responsibilities, and work outside the home cause many ethnic and linguistic minority parents to participate less often in schools (Bermudez, 1994; Moles, 1993; Onikama, Hammond, & Koki, 1998).

Although many districts offer English classes for families, they should also offer language classes for teachers and administrators such as Spanish, Vietnamese, Korean, or other languages that are prevalent within families who are enrolled in the district or school. Sometimes parents in the community will volunteer their time to educate teachers about their culture and basic communication skills in their native language. Siblings are good resources to convey information to parents during a conference if no translator is available, but it is advantageous to provide a translator at the school site and learn to communicate using a common language, hand gestures, and positive facial expressions.

A Community of Learners

Zuniga and Alva (1996) reported on a community-of-learners program where the school celebrated the histories, talents, and other strengths of the families who attended. Parents were provided with opportunities to use their talents to participate in school functions and plan parent activities. They created an *instituto,* which is a term in Mexico used to promote education and training. Based on Mexican traditions, the first meetings were informal where parents were asked to come together to voice their needs, wants, and views about the school and community. This was considered a grassroots initiative because parents became leaders in the group and took leadership roles in planning the meetings and modules (activities). As the meetings progressed, parents began taking ownership of the project. One parent, Eusebio, had been an electronics teacher in Mexico but currently worked in a local restaurant. He provided valuable insight as the group started planning modules. He stated: *"Me parece que están haciendo esto a relámpago. Conozco a mi gente. Todos van a necesitar más tiempo para reconocer lo bueno de éste trabajo en la comunidad."* (I think you're trying to do this too fast. I know my people, and it will take some time for people to recognize the value of this work in the community.) His comments proved to be invaluable as the researchers tracked attendance and interactive participation during parent activities.

Power

Power is an interesting term when talking about education and the educational potential of partnerships. In most organizations, there is always one individual or one group that wants to have power over another. Most of the time, this type of power is unconscious and unspoken. Think about people who hold the most power in a school. Teachers have the power to assign tasks and evaluate students. Principals can suspend students and accept or deny certain school activities. The front office can also demonstrate power to consciously or unconsciously show acceptance toward some families and disrespect toward others. Teachers, administrators, and office staff have been known to speak too authoritatively or derogatorily when discussing educational issues with parents. Therefore, families do not feel welcome on a school campus and may not participate in school events—major or minor.

Power is sometimes more evenly distributed when community groups and schools work together. However, if a corporation provides funding for a school program, it may determine certain guidelines and specifications that must be adhered to. Lack of resources or disagreements about the appropriation of monies can strain partnerships and relationships between groups. The lack of power or the domination of power within some groups inhibits partnership development between educators, between educators and families, and among administrators, educators, and community members.

Trust

Trust develops from the resolution of management, power, language, culture, and time barriers, and without it, true partnerships cannot reach their full potential. Robles (2006) created a plan for teachers to become more sensitive to immigrant families' needs when assisting in their children's academic and social development. In her guide, she recommends that teachers need to gain trust and respect when working with immigrant families before enacting partnerships. She believes that teachers can be empowered through professional development and diverse experiences to acknowledge and appreciate the rich cultural strengths that immigrant families bring to the classroom.

Mattingly, Prislin, McKenzie, Rodriguez, and Kayzar (2002) identified parent and teacher attitudes toward schools and each other, parent emotions, and teacher practices as other important barriers that impact collaboration, involvement, and trust. Leuder (1998) discusses trust as a psychological barrier that prevents parents from fully engaging in school activities. He says that many parents' attitudes toward school are deeply embedded in their past experiences as children, particularly negative experiences.

Additional Barriers

The number of barriers and the types of barriers will vary according to the partners and the project itself. The barriers discussed above in relation to management issues, time, commitment, culture, language, and trust continue to be the most common and most crucial.

Teacher education, teacher attitudes, and changing demographics can also be challenging barriers, particularly when developing ongoing partnerships with families. As we have discussed in prior chapters, teachers in most states are not required to enroll in courses that focus on family or community partnerships within their teacher education programs. Because of this, they may begin their teaching career viewing parents as deficits rather than assets—which affects their overall attitude and the partnership potential. Teacher education partnership courses can include sensitivity and culturally relevant strategies as tools for teachers who will work with families from different cultural and linguistic backgrounds. Teacher attitudes can be changed when teachers participate in rewarding partnership programs at their school.

Political conditions can cause stress on any partnership because of the changes that take place and the accountability that schools have. Therefore time and commitment will suffer if political conditions take precedence over a partnership's goals and activities.

Strategies to Address Barriers

It takes time, dedication, and commitment to overcome barriers, particularly those related to language and culture. First and foremost, respect for all parties is essential when building partnerships, and this should be genuinely exhibited before addressing any of the barriers noted in this chapter. Buttery and Anderson (1999) advocate that teachers and schools make changes in attitude, communication strategies, listening skills, and networking initiatives to promote more involvement and partnerships with families. These same strategies can be applied to partnerships with community groups and other professionals. The first general step to overcoming barriers is communication and learning about the partners. The next step is collaborative planning. Finally, establishing a partnership built on trust and respect will help sustain and support involvement over time. Partners should note the following characteristics of effective partnerships when creating a new project or sustaining a current one:

- Equal empowerment of all partners
- Building trust through ongoing team-building activities and meetings
- Valuing the knowledge and values of all partners involved
- Providing ongoing communication between all partners
- Showing a real commitment from all members

Cerra and Jacoby (2005) created a list of ideas to help teachers address barriers and challenges related to parent interactions. They include many suggestions for teachers, such as addressing the parent who (a) wants to tell you how to teach, (b) wants to talk daily, and (c) never gets involved with school issues. Teachers can take a deep breath, listen, and communicate clearly to address and overcome these interactions with parents. When a parent wants to tell a teacher how to teach, Cerra and Jacoby suggest that the teacher be prepared by having teacher grade-level objectives, state standards, textbooks, record of grades, and other information readily available. When a parent takes too much time each day during school, the teacher should provide options for mutual meeting times. When a parent does not get involved, Cerra and Jacoby say that a voice-to-voice telephone call is absolutely necessary! They have outlined a 10-question quiz for teachers to determine how well they communicate with parents. The questions on the quiz are listed in Table 8.2. If you score 8 true statements, then you are an effective communicator. If you score between 4 and 7 true statements, then you are weak in some areas. If you score below 4 true statements, then you should reconsider some of your communication techniques and incorporate new ones.

The National Association of School Psychologists (2007) published a mission statement related to home-school collaboration and establishing partnerships to enhance educational outcomes. The association claims multiple benefits exist when educators engage in collaborative partnerships. These benefits include higher achievement and increased completion of homework and attendance of students. In addition, teachers report greater job satisfaction and gain higher ratings from families and administrators. Because successful collaboration can be difficult due to expectations, goals, and language, the organization outlined specific roles for schools and families when working together.

Table 8.2	Quiz for Teachers: How well do you talk to parents?

1. I am comfortable speaking with parents.

2. I listen more than I talk.

3. I value parent input.

4. I do not mind if an administrator sits in on a parent conference.

5. I do not believe that I know more than parents do. I anticipate and welcome questions.

6. I research solutions and methods when I do not know the answer to a question.

7. I respect the opinion of parents.

8. I do not feel uncomfortable when people are in my classroom.

9. I communicate frequently with parents.

SOURCE: Cerra and Jacoby (2005). From *Instructor* magazine. Copyright © 2005 by Scholastic Inc. Reprinted by permission of Scholastic Inc.

The Role of Schools When Collaborating With Families

1. Provide a positive and welcoming environment for all families at all times. This includes consistent messages in the form of formal notes, informal discussions, and facial expressions.

2. Support family-teacher collaboration by understanding diverse family perspectives, their ideals, and their expectations. Create an open dialogue between home and school. Ensure that resources support collaborative efforts and are culturally relevant.

3. Increase everyone's understanding of diversity including that of administrators, teachers, front office staff, cafeteria staff, and other support staff. Schools and families must make an effort to understand and educate each other.

4. Promote education as a shared responsibility with open communication, shared goals, and real decision making for all. When teachers and families encounter problems, they should be addressed together with all partners present (including the student) to come to a respectful compatible solution.

The Role of Families When Collaborating With Schools

1. Take an active role in volunteering, committee membership, and school decisions.

2. Participate in school events, sports, and other extracurricular activities.

3. Encourage reading at home and monitor homework.

4. Participate in adult education classes and other activities offered by the school.

5. Share resources and seek out partnerships with teachers.

6. Ask teachers questions! What do you want to know about your child's academic skills, motivation, self-discipline, and so on?

The Role of the School Psychologist
When Collaborating With Families

1. Establish school-based teams including families, teachers, and community members to assess needs, create plans, and implement joint efforts to improve the education of children.

2. Serve as a liaison to support communication in the school among families, teachers, and the community.

3. Ensure that families participate in special education processes and procedures and are offered opportunities to make decisions related to their child's assessment, intervention, and program activities.

4. Create a list of and provide direct services to families that promote academic, behavioral, and social success at home, in school, and within the community.

5. Work closely with administrators to make sure sufficient resources are available and allocated for family-school collaborative efforts.

6. Develop and promote continuing education for teachers, administrators, and families related to family interventions, multicultural education, and home-school collaboration models.

These roles outlined by the National Association of School Psychologists indicate the need for all professionals to work together to break down the barriers among schools, families, and communities in order to facilitate successful educational outcomes.

Taking Action

This next section will address ways that teachers can take action to overcome the many barriers discussed during the first part of this chapter. Teachers can take action by providing better communication and explicitly teaching tolerance and acceptance.

Communication

One of the surest ways of overcoming barriers involves education for all partners relating to trust, respect, understanding, and communication. Most of the time, educators can gain more information from learning why businesses and families do not participate in educational activities or educational partnerships than from learning why they choose to do so. Guerrero (2006) wanted to inquire into the reasons why some parents did not participate in parent Action Learning Walks that are featured as the first case study in Chapter 1. Therefore, she created a survey and asked parents to complete it. Of the 36 parent surveys that were returned, 23 of the parents stated that they could not attend the Action Learning Walk because of conflicts with work schedules. Two parents indicated that they did not have transportation, 4 parents had prior

Families share many experiences. Teachers can work to help students and families cross the sometimes difficult borders between home and school by inquiring into their hobbies, cultural activities, and values.

commitments, and 1 parent felt uncomfortable at school. Other parents indicated that they were sick or they did not have enough information about what the Action Learning Walk was. At least 23 of the parents indicated that they would have preferred for the Action Learning Walk to take place after 5:00 p.m. The information that Guerrero collected overwhelmingly indicates that work schedules and the time of day that the Action Learning Walks were scheduled made it difficult for some families to participate. Therefore, schools can consider this information when they plan events. One alternative is to organize multiple events that take place on various days and at various times. The best way to learn more about the families and their schedules is to send home a survey (in multiple languages if applicable) with students. This survey can be interactive where parents and children complete it together. In this way, everyone in the family is informed and accountable. The survey can include questions such as (a) what families would like to know more about, (b) when they are available to meet at school, and (c) how the teachers and school staff can make changes. This type of proactive communication can prevent many barriers before they are ever created.

Explicitly Teaching Tolerance and Acceptance

Explicitly teaching tolerance and acceptance is the only way to overcome prejudice and stereotypes and to eliminate hate. **Hate** is a powerful feeling and can only be overcome by education, reflection, and explicit conversations. **Tolerance education** is needed when addressing issues such as sexual orientation, race, ethnic background, religion, socioeconomic level, special education needs, and even physical appearance.

Mr. Jooyan's Experiences as a Child

This voice is from a father of two girls—one who is in kindergarten and another who is in third grade. Mr. Jooyan discusses the social and academic challenges that he experienced as a child. He moved to the United States from Iran and France when he was 11 years old. His experiences demonstrate that as an adult, many events that happened in school have stayed with him throughout life.

As a young boy, I spent my life bouncing back and forth between two cultures, torn between two poles in my family history (American and Persian), always finding myself an outsider in both cultures, always missing one culture's traditions and ideals when living in the other. It all started when I was 11 years old, after anti-Iranian sentiments blossomed in America in the wake of the hostage-takings in 1979. Like other 11-year-olds, I wanted to play sports with my peers, attend social gatherings, and simply "fit in"; instead, I was exposed to a more adult adventure about negotiating the difficult transition from one culture to another. This was about the great challenge of taking on a new identity without losing the old one. The unkindness of many classmates, teachers, and neighbors to an immigrant from a place about which most of them knew little was probably a defining moment in my life.

The popular belief back at that time was that all Iranians are against the Americans; they are backward and have harems. I was hoping that teachers and administrators would correct this erroneous information when confronted with it and help students understand that all Iranian Americans should not be held personally accountable for events in the Middle East and such judgments are inaccurate and hurtful. Educators at my school were not prepared to respond to harassment of foreign students with multi-cultural backgrounds. Why should they? Some of the faculty members were part of this prejudice and discrimination. For example, my algebra teacher told the class on my third day of attending his class, "You don't need to take the exam; after all, what do camel jockeys know about algebra?" Even though the class enjoyed the humor, I insisted on taking the exam and was the first to hand in my test with a smile of a victor. The teacher's response to that was "You have solved all the problems correctly, but since you did not show your work on your test, you will receive an F on this exam. You should not be in my class; perhaps elementary mathematics is better suited for you."

I recall lunch times in the cafeteria; I would be isolated from other children but never from their stares and name-callings. Having a U.S. passport since birth and an American mother was irrelevant. To them, I was different and weird because my father was from Iran. Students would walk by my table, and with faculty present, they would flip my lunch tray on my lap and say things like "Iranian, go home" and "We don't want your kind here."

After-school bullying was becoming a common way of life for me. Most people are familiar with physical bullying: a black eye, a bloody nose, and a punch in the stomach. However, I was one of the lucky few to be verbally and emotionally bullied. Verbal bullying included name-calling, put-downs, insults, and racial or sexual comments. Emotional bullying included being excluded from groups, being belittled and humiliated, and others joining in. Walking to class was always an adventure too. I had to be aware of my surroundings at all times. If they could not intentionally bump into me, my tormenters would find a way to spit at me. I will never forget the awful smell of their spit!

It's not often that experiences at such a young age affect the way we see life, but this chapter of my life has done just that. It has changed the way I perceive certain things. We need to ensure that the social and cultural tolerance that has so characterized this country continues to be a part of our community. My father used to tell me, "Life is a series of mistakes made and lessons learned." But Harry Truman said it best when he stated, "The thing we learn most in history is that we don't learn from history." Yet through this experience, I have come to see things in our society and culture that made me question the past, as well as the status quo. I have learned the dangers of ignorance.

SOURCE: Used with permission of Gino Jooyan.

Stereotypes relate to overgeneralizing characteristics and associating them with a particular group. Provide students with a variety of experiences and interactions with others to address and overcome stereotypes.

One way to help negate stereotypes involves reading a variety of books to students and discussing the characters and specific injustices that take place. *The Widow's Broom,* by Chris Van Allsburg (1992), is an interesting book to read with students because it addresses stereotypes and prejudices related to a witch and her broom—not to a particular person, race, or ethnic group. It is an appropriate book to use to begin talking about prejudice and stereotypes because the content does not target a particular group of people. Teachers can provide an advance organizer for students like the one featured in Table 8.3 to help them focus on the stereotypes within the book as they read or listen to the story.

Human Rights Watch (2008) reported that most schools in the United States do not provide a safe educational environment for gay students. In fact, only five states have laws that prohibit discrimination against gay students. It is recommended that teachers consistently teach tolerance during the good times as well as the

| Table 8.3 | Advance Organizer to Provide to Students Before Reading *The Widow's Broom* |

While reading or listening to *The Widow's Broom* by Chris Van Allsburg, think about stereotypes and prejudices that we have talked about in class. Remember that *stereotypes* relate to overgeneralizing characteristics and associating them with a particular group. *Prejudices* usually relate to prejudgments of a person or group of people.

Character	Evidence of Stereotypes	Evidence of Prejudices

challenging times. The Teaching Tolerance group recommends that educators and families implement the following strategies to promote tolerance in the classroom and at home:

- Modeling tolerance at school and home
- Acknowledging differences and celebrating these differences
- Challenging intolerance that groups face
- Taking advantage of teachable moments when they occur at home and school
- Consistently emphasizing the positive aspects of diversity

Modeling tolerance at home and in the classroom is one of the most important things that families and teachers can do because actions often speak louder than words. Parents might model their appreciation for all individuals when they walk by a homeless man and choose to acknowledge him as an individual by simply saying, "Good morning." Teachers might model their respect for a child's culture by allowing him or her to share his or her East Indian customs while truly listening and showing an interest in artifacts from his or her home. Embracing differences and showing respect are ways that actions can lead to change. Read stories and post photographs throughout the classroom that celebrate diverse family structures and ethnicities. Have students share their family traditions and photographs—making reference to the fact that all families have traditions, that all traditions are equally important, and that different traditions create a more interesting world to live in. Invite families to share their traditions in the form of music, food, language, or cultural objects during the school year. If groups have been mistreated in the past, then address these issues and the fact that everyone is a person with a different history but everyone has multiple strengths. More than anything else, teachers should make every effort to help children realize their strengths and the value of their own languages and cultures. This will help students develop confidence in school and throughout their lives.

Teachers and families should challenge comments that relate to bias, prejudice, or stereotypes immediately. When parents and teachers do not comment or remain silent, it communicates to children that they are accepting the view. In addition, there must be a discussion that follows dealing with the prejudice or stereotype so that the child understands the complete issue. Telling children that they "should not say that" is not enough to overcome stereotypes and biases. Teaching tolerance and minimizing biases and stereotypes will only come through consistent communication, experiences, and examples within the community and multimedia. When stories are read and discussed that deal with injustices, these issues should be addressed. When one child calls another child a derogatory name on the playground, this should be discussed with the child but possibly the entire class if appropriate. Parents can address these issues during television shows, movies, and interactions with individuals and groups within the community.

Cooperative group activities empower students to work together to investigate and report on specific issues of intolerance and bias that take place in their schools, in their community, and within the world. Offering praise and appreciation for children who show positive actions such as empathy and respect toward others leads to a more accepting classroom and community. Teachers can encourage these types of behaviors by instituting a system such as "Caught you being kind" or "Caught you being respectful" that rewards students in the form of stickers, small tokens, or special privileges.

An online partnership called *Peace Diaries* (Knowledge iTrust, 2002) provides a forum where students of diverse racial, ethnic, gender, and religious backgrounds can learn more about each other. Topics related to human rights, community involvement, family, culture, democracy, conflict, and peace are highlighted. It is estimated that children from about 13 countries have taken advantage of the online interactive global forum.

Table 8.4 outlines information addressed in this chapter and some suggested ways to overcome the barriers.

Table 8.4   Suggestions for Overcoming Barriers

Barrier	Ways to Overcome the Barrier
Management	All parties have decision-making power with one person as leader or coleader
Time	Use of technology Offering child care during parent-teacher events Organizing meetings to fit the schedules of multiple partners
Culture	Education for families and educators Planning and implementing informal experiences and events with diverse families Providing time for teachers to conduct home visits with students and families
Language	Providing translators during family events and parent-teacher conferences Recruiting community liaisons to interact with families in the community Providing language classes for teachers and parents
Trust	Engaging in frequent communication Scheduling informal meetings as well as standard formal conferences and events
State additional barriers that you have experienced.	**Describe how you might overcome them.**

Tips to Help Overcome Barriers and Promote Diversity

The following is a list of resources in the form of children's books and music that educators and families can access to help build a more trusting, inclusive, and tolerant educational community.

Books That Promote Partnerships and Diversity

- *Tomasito's Mother Comes to School/La mamá de Tomasito visita la escuela* is an online storybook by Ellen Mayer. Tomasito does not like it when his mother visits his classroom. He soon realizes that his mother and teacher want to know each other so that he can learn better. The book can be retrieved online at http://www.gse.harvard.edu/hfrp/projects/fine/resources/storybook/tomasito.html.
- *One Dad, Two Dads, Brown Dad, Blue Dads* by Johnny Valentine and Melody Sarecky highlights different kinds of dads, as well as children who have two dads. Children learn that dads look different and act different but they are all dads after all.
- *Good Luck Gold and Other Poems* by Janet Wong describes a girl growing up in Los Angeles who experiences different stereotypes related to her Asian background. The poems are humorous and interesting for children and adults of all ages.
- *Nettie's Trip South* by Ann Warren Turner is a story told by Nettie, who takes a trip to Richmond, Virginia, with her family during the antebellum South. She notices that Black slaves are treated poorly as they live in small shacks and are sold off auction blocks. Her perspective as a White child from the North provides a humanistic view of slavery in the South.
- *William's Doll* by Charlotte Zolotow tells the story of William, who wants a doll. His father tries everything that he can to encourage him to want "boy" things like trains and balls. When William's grandmother comes to visit, she convinces William's father that William needs a doll so that he can practice loving and caring for a baby for when he has his own.
- *The Patchwork Quilt* by Valerie Flournoy tells the story of a young African American girl, Tanya, who helps her grandmother make a quilt that tells the story of her family one year.
- *Heather Has Two Mommies* by Lesléa Newman tells the story of Heather, who has a favorite number: 2. She has two of everything—including two mommies. She goes to preschool and learns that families come in all shapes, in all sizes, and with different types of parents.
- *The House on Mango Street* by Sandra Cisneros describes the life of Esperanza, a young girl growing up in a Latino neighborhood in Chicago. She does not like her neighborhood and does not want to be a part of it. Eventually she comes to terms with her identity and gains an appreciation for her culture and community.

Music That Promotes Peace and Tolerance

- The New Songs for Peace Web site features a variety of music to promote a world culture of peace and nonviolence. The various artists, songs, and lyrics can be retrieved from http://www.newsongsforpeace.org.

- The Songs for World Peace Web site features music to promote world peace. Lists of songs that celebrate peace are provided. The songs can be retrieved from http://www .planetpatriot.net/peace_songs.html.
- The Songs of Tolerance Web site offers a variety of songs and teaching activities. The information can be retrieved from http://www.communitycelebration.org/ teach.
- Multicultural music and songs that build an appreciation for diversity are featured on a Web site sponsored by Songs for Teaching. The songs, artists, and information can be retrieved from http://www.songsforteaching.com/diversitymulticulturalism .htm.

Chapter Summary

Schools, families, and communities often encounter a number of barriers when engaging in collaborative educational partnerships. Barriers are obstacles that can impede the progress of a partnership or partnership program. There are different types of barriers, including those that are more critical and need to be addressed before a partnership is developed. The most prevalent barriers exist in the form of management, time, commitment, culture, language, power, and trust. However, once partners acknowledge these barriers and accept them, many strategies can be implemented to overcome them. There are a variety of strategies that teachers can implement to encourage more culturally relevant instruction, including activities that promote tolerance and acceptance for all students and families.

CASE STUDIES

The two case studies below describe different partnerships. The first case study relates to the barriers that Pakistani families and teachers face in a school in the United Kingdom. The second case study features a community museum project where families and museum educators form a partnership to help scientists collect data.

❖ Case Study 8.1: Pakistani Families and Teachers

This case study is adapted from the work of Huss-Keeler (1997). In a yearlong study at a British primary school, Huss-Keeler found that teacher and parent perceptions differed. She particularly inquired into the parents of Pakistani children who were learning to speak English. Her study consisted of 400 working-class and low-income children between the ages of 3 and 12 and their families. About 80% of the school population was Punjabi speaking Pakistani Muslim. Many of the teachers at the school were White British middle-class women. As an ethnographer, Huss-Keeler collected data that included structured interviews and informal interviews with students, teachers, and parents. Teacher perceptions of ethnically and linguistically diverse parents and parent perceptions of their involvement and communication with teachers will be highlighted as voices within this case study.

Voice of the Assistant Principal

The policy of the school is to have parents in school as much as possible. A lot of women don't speak English and school is frightening. When Pakistani parents come into school, they think it is for a bad reason. They think the teachers should get on with the job. I'll get on at home. (Huss-Keeler, 1997, p. 175)

Voice of the English Language Learning Coordinator

The availability of translators makes a big difference in parents' attendance at conferences. A lot of them have the attitude that the education of their children is not their responsibility. It's the responsibility of the school and the school should get on with it. I actually tried to convince parents that they have a role to play in their child's education and the school wants them to play a role. (p. 175)

Voice of a Third-Grade Teacher

Parents were not allowed in school in Bangladesh and Pakistan. School is very different; therefore parents are reluctant to come in. (p. 175)

Voice of the Main Classroom Teacher

We certainly don't do a lot of that here [telling parents about the literacy program]. We do it with the parents who come and talk to you. Again, it's parents like David's or Alan's [who are White and middle class] and those sorts of people, not really the people with the problem. A lot of them don't want to know . . . I think it's the culture and language barrier. A lot of it is the language barrier. They can't understand what we are saying, but I also think they don't think it's their place to know what we're saying and what we're doing. They don't think it's for them to do. School is for school to do and home is for home to do. It's very, very sharply divided, whereas in lots of different type schools, what's going on at school is the same at home. It's language and all the sort of moral education as well. (p. 175)

Voice of a Parent

It's too many children in one class [in Pakistan]. One teacher. Sometimes the teacher hits you. Here when you play, you learn. In Pakistan, it's not like that. (p. 179)

Voice of a Pakistani Educator

This educator confirmed the Pakistani mother's comments about the differences in schools in Pakistan and Britain. The schools in Pakistan do not encourage parents to talk with teachers. There is limited schooling for women, and there is a 12% literacy rate for women in Pakistan. The women in Pakistan have low status in the community and home. Therefore, the mothers are reluctant to visit schools, ask questions, or voice their concerns.

Voice of the Ethnographer, Huss-Keeler

What all these events had in common was that they were culturally relevant and were non-threatening. They did not involve the parents having to speak English to an authority figure such as the teacher. Parents could be with their children at the school and show their interest in their children. This type of participation and display of interest did not seem to count in the teachers' eyes as showing the parents' interest in their children. What was more important to the teachers were the parents coming in to ask about their children's school work at Parents' Evening. (p. 176)

SOURCE: Huss-Keeler (1997).

❖ Case Study 8.2: Pigeons, Parents, and Children

This case study is adapted from Melber and Abraham (2000). The PIPE Pigeon project was designed to promote parent-child interactions in science and to build better community relations between an inner-city museum and the families who live in the inner city. The project was funded by the National Science Foundation and introduces families to scientific methods of collecting information related to different color phases of pigeons. Families spend time with their children observing neighborhood pigeons, recording data like a field ornithologist, and finally sending the data to the Cornell Laboratory of Ornithology to enhance the ongoing research about pigeons and their behaviors.

The purpose of the project was to encourage more family and community involvement within the museum education programs. The community surrounding the museum is predominately Latino and African American families who do not usually visit the museum or attend museum events. The program was designed to reach out to these families and involve them in an interesting and fun program with their children. The museum educators recruited families who attended museum summer camps on scholarship, who were identified by teachers in a nearby school, and who were employed at the museum as staff. Altogether the group included seven families, six of which were Latino and one of which was Anglo. Of the six Latino families, all spoke Spanish as their native language. A translator was available at all stages of the program.

Voice of the Museum Educator

Participants' comfort level was raised through participation in the program. It can be inferred by the comments that this is in part due to increased familiarity—something that can be worked toward with other members of the community. . . . Working with a group that was perhaps more reflective of the cultural richness and ethnically diverse community that surrounds the [museum] would provide further insight into working successfully with this community.

Voice of Mother #1

After the project my family and I want to learn more.

Voice of Mother #2

Exposure breeds familiarity. . . . the kids are learning more about the museum. . . . they like to come back and visit their favorite parts.

Voice of Mother #3

Workshops with the kids can teach us, their parents. It is very empowering for the kids to teach their parents about something that they don't know about.

SOURCE: Used with permission of Leah Melber and Linda Abraham.

❖ Reflecting on the Cases

1. Identify the different barriers in each case study and ways to overcome them.

2. Identify the difference in perceptions of the assistant principal, teachers, and parents in the first case study and how these differences created barriers for Pakistani families.

3. Describe how the museum educators in the second case study attempted to break down the barriers in a diverse inner-city community. Next, describe additional measures that could be taken by the museum educators to encourage diverse families within the community to utilize museum resources.

Activities for Further Development

1. Create a list of potential barriers to partnerships with families in your school.

2. Next, list ways to overcome these barriers and how you can encourage inclusion for all students and families.

3. Describe who holds the power in a partnership when an organization is supplying funds and personnel to assist schools. Describe how shared power can be promoted and respected.

4. Create a list of potential individuals or groups with which your school could collaborate to address and acknowledge stereotypes related to disabilities, cultural diversity, linguistic diversity, and other areas. Discuss specific strategies and activities to overcome stereotypes.

Additional Reading and Information

Allen, J. (2007). *Creating welcoming schools: A practical guide to home-school partnerships with diverse families.* New York: Teachers College Press. This book provides a series of strategies that teachers and schools can use to create a more welcoming and supportive school environment.

Delgado-Gaitan, C. (2001). *The power of community and involving Latino families in the schools.* Thousand Oaks, CA: Sage. This book provides research and information to help schools provide more opportunities and decision making for Latino families.

Delgado-Gaitan, C. (2004). *Involving Latino families in schools: Raising student achievement through home-school partnerships.* Thousand Oaks, CA: Corwin Press. This book provides additional information about involving Latino families in school activities.

Delpit, L. (1996). *Other people's children: Cultural conflict in the classroom.* New York: The New Press. This book is a classic. Delpit argues and provides examples to demonstrate how many ethnic minority children are labeled early as "underachievers" due to miscommunication and a lack of shared cultural experiences between teachers and students.

Teaching Tolerance is a Web site that provides information and resources and ways to fight hate in schools: http://www.tolerance.org/index.jsp

Peace Diaries provides information online to connect children together to discuss issues of tolerance, acceptance, and peace. Students from around the world can communicate and learn about each other: http://www.peacediaries.org

Reflecting on the Cases

Part III

Planning for and Sustaining Successful Partnerships

Chapter 9: Seeking and Sustaining Successful Partnerships

Chapter 10: Planning for Partnerships

Chapter 11: Implementing and Sustaining Successful Partnerships

9

Seeking and Sustaining Successful Partnerships

After reading this chapter, you should have a better understanding of:

- examples of successful partnerships;
- seeking community resources and partnerships;
- an examination of long-standing partnerships;
- graphic organizers to help you plan partnership activities and strategies;
- guidelines for writing and seeking grants to support partnership projects;
- grant resources related to instruction, partnerships, and teacher recognition;
- communicating with families about resources; and
- promoting interagency collaboration.

| Table 9.1 | Prior Knowledge and Beliefs Organizer |

Qualities of an Effective Partnership	Ways to Sustain Effective Partnerships

Consider the qualities of effective partnerships and ways to sustain them from Table 9.1 as you read about seeking and sustaining partnerships in this chapter.

Partnership Examples

One principal of an inner-city school in Tennessee created a "neighborhood watch" program to promote accountability and safety as his students walked to and from school each day. He met with the neighbors in the community and asked them to stand in their yards or on their porches from 7:45 to 8:15 each morning and from 2:45 to 3:15 each afternoon to greet kids and make sure they arrived to school and back home safely. This proved to be a very successful collaboration that contributed to the welfare of children and the community. The program helped form bonds among the neighbors, the school, and families. It also helped enhance safety and deter students from getting into mischief on their way to and from school.

Lunch Mentors is an example of a community partnership program where senior citizens visit a local elementary school each week and partner with teachers and students. The senior citizens become mentors with students who are chosen by classroom teachers as having low self-esteem or self-confidence, having limited social skills, or struggling with one or more academic areas. Seniors from a local assisted-living center meet with students in various grade levels once a week, have lunch with their buddies, and engage in reading a book or another fun learning activity. This type of partnership has the potential to enhance the education of children who are struggling with some area of formal schooling and offers one-on-one adult interactions.

Stevenson Elementary School in Long Beach, California, has found success partnering with the local YMCA. The YMCA operates inside the school, and the YMCA staff work with teachers and administrators to organize the after-school program and link the program's content and activities with the school curriculum. In addition, YMCA staff members educate parents in literacy skills and send them out into the community to teach other families in their homes.

In the book *The Freedom Writers Diary* (1999), teacher Erin Gruwell discusses how she taught her high school English students how to take action, fight stereotypes, and reach their fullest academic potential as writers. After a racial caricature of one of the students with huge exaggerated lips was passed around in class, Gruwell decided to throw out her lesson plans and make tolerance the core of the curriculum that year. She brought history to life by accessing books, taking field trips, and inviting a variety of guest speakers to the classroom. She made a personal commitment to learn more about her students, their lives, their hobbies, their strengths, and their fears. She encouraged and motivated them to express their ideas, thoughts, and vexations through writing. Her students were invited to meet Steven Spielberg at Universal Studios to discuss the movie *Schindler's List.* They corresponded and met with a Holocaust survivor and hosted Zlata Filipovic, a child author from Bosnia. These types of experiences are at the core of culturally relevant teaching and provide students with the power, the insight, and the motivation to extend education beyond the four walls of the classroom. Gruwell's experiences are highlighted in the movie *Freedom Writers,* starring Hilary Swank. It should be noted that Gruwell formed a partnership with her students first; then, empowered, they reached out together to form partnerships with the broader community.

Community resources are only resources if accessed by schools, family, and community members. Teachers in an educational partnerships class arranged for a former major league baseball player to visit their university class to discuss his job responsibilities and partnerships with local schools. Because the teachers contacted him and *asked* him to provide information about his role as an educational community leader, he made an appearance and made a huge impact on teachers as they pursued partnership possibilities. He discussed his organization's commitment to the community and schools and the importance of seeking role models in the community. He also discussed the untapped partnership opportunities that exist. The teachers were very surprised that this sports organization had a community outreach program about 10 miles away and that they had never heard about it or prepared activities to collaborate with it.

The next part of this chapter includes steps needed to seek out partnerships and educational resources. In addition, the chapter will offer ways to inform families of community resources available to them. Finally, it will provide important steps and procedures for sustaining educational partnerships for many years to come.

Seeking and Organizing Partnerships

An examination of educational partnerships programs over time has revealed a variety of factors that affect the success, challenges, or failure of such programs. This is what we know for sure (well, almost for sure):

1. Partnerships should be as inclusive as possible for all partners. For schools that develop partnerships with families, it will take coordination, education, and commitment from the office staff, classroom teachers, the administrators, teachers, and students.

2. Funding from outside groups such as the state or federal government, corporations, museums, or community groups helps motivate partnership development and implementation. Sustaining partnerships over time is more challenging when funding is diminished or cut out.

3. Educators can form professional partnerships and become valuable resources for each other. Teachers can engage in peer coaching, participate in professional reading clubs, and attend meetings together to enhance the education of their students.

4. Communities can be valuable resources for families and schools. However, families and schools must be familiar with the community and what it offers.

5. Families can be valuable resources for schools and the community.

6. Schools can be valuable resources for families and the community.

7. Universities can be valuable resources as educational partners through undergraduate and graduate students working with children and youth via university service-learning projects or other activities. Many university campuses are embracing service-learning activities as an integral part of learning.

8. Museums, zoos, aquariums, and other cultural institutions can extend the walls of the classroom to provide an array of experiences and resources for students, teachers, families, and the community.

9. Collaboration and buy-in among all partners are important in developing, implementing, and sustaining partnerships over time. However, families, community members, and/or educators must take leadership roles to create a viable program.

10. Common goals should be developed and used to guide and support the partnership. These goals can be revised throughout the implementation of the project.

11. Expectations of each partner should be specifically outlined and revisited frequently. In addition, roles and responsibilities should be validated through purposeful activities.

12. All partnership projects require some type of action plan that includes a rationale, goals, objectives, a timeline of events and activities, and an assessment and evaluation plan.

13. Case studies are helpful when determining a need, finding out what works and what does not, and learning about various partner perspectives, as well as other useful partnership information.

14. Communication and mutual understanding are a key component related to successful partnerships between families and schools, particularly with families from diverse cultural, linguistic, and socioeconomic backgrounds.

15. All successful partnerships take time to develop. Schools and teachers should seek feedback from families and community groups on a regular basis to determine if changes need to be made.

16. When working with families, teachers should accommodate them when possible and show respect for parents' work schedules, language, and cultural diversity.

17. Barriers exist when forming any partnership. It is important for all parties to acknowledge barriers and to consider ways to overcome them in order to maximize the partnership potential.

18. An effective partnership involves commitment from multiple individuals or groups. A commitment can take place up front, but it must be sustained during the life of the partnership.

19. Students can be empowered to initiate community and family partnerships and participate in action-based projects such as service-learning, stewardship, and civic involvement activities.

20. You as a teacher can make a difference!

Assessing Resources

Knowing the resources available to teachers, families, and the community is one of the easiest ways to create connections among the three groups. A comprehensive approach to partnerships involves a variety of partners that suit a variety of needs. However, it is important that schools do not take on too many different partnership projects at once. Developing trust, respect, and appreciation for all who work together toward shared goals takes time—to plan, implement, and sustain. One school in North Carolina consistently partners with individuals and businesses in the community. These partners are within the local proximity of the school and are included within the school curriculum and activities for a variety of purposes. For example, a local textiles company provides school shirts for students, and two local banks and a variety of other businesses in the area provide reading tutors and lunch buddies for students who need extra support. A local parks and recreation department works with the school to organize exercise classes and sports activities in addition to participating in community festivals together. The school's parent-teacher association facilitates the organization of classroom volunteers, school fundraisers, and a cultural arts program. These partnerships are specifically organized in different areas of the curriculum, with different groups, and for different purposes. Although the school has a variety of partners, it has been collaborating with the community for many years. It has built these multiple partnerships over time for the purpose of benefiting students, teachers, and families.

The U.S. Department of Education has an array of family resources that teachers should be aware of and recommend to parents when applicable. One notable resource is the *Helping Your Child* series. The books provide families with tools and information to help their children at home in the areas of preschool, early adolescence, becoming a good citizen, homework, reading, math, history, and science. The books offer a practical and fun approach to learning at home. Parents do not need to have a strong background in any of these areas because the books provide easy step-by-step content and activities. The books are written in English and Spanish and are available online at http://www.ed .gov/parents/academic/help/hyc.html. However, many families may not have access to the Internet or printers, so schools can print these documents for families or seek assistance from companies within the community that can help offset the printing costs.

Enhancing Learning for Students With Special Needs: NICHCY

The National Dissemination Center for Children with Disabilities, known as NICHCY, is an organization that serves as a resource for educators and families of children with disabilities. NICHCY provides curriculum ideas to enact the Individuals with Disabilities Education Act (IDEA), an array of research-based information and strategies related to effective special education practices, and grant opportunities. Information is provided in English and Spanish. You can access this information at http://www.nichcy.org.

The Office of Special Education Programs (OSEP), part of the U.S. Department of Education, provides a variety of grants to support and assist schools and districts to work more effectively with students who have disabilities.

Sanders (2006) outlined four specific steps that schools should follow when developing partnerships with the broader community. These steps include exploring, identifying, thinking, and contacting. First, schools should explore areas within a one-mile radius of the school that include potential partners such as community groups, service agencies, or businesses. Schools can extend their net a bit further if the exploration

Book cover: *Helping Your Child Learn Science*

comes up short. Second, identify the names and addresses of businesses, agencies, and organizations that may have resources and educational partnership potential and create a list. Third, consider the major goals of your school and consider which organizations could assist you in achieving those goals. Finally, contact the partner or partners that you would like to develop a reciprocal partnership with. You may want to send an e-mail or make a phone call when you initially contact the individual, organization, or other group. However, you should set up a meeting and make face-to-face contact after the initial communication. During this face-to-face meeting, discuss your ideas and goals for the partnership and how it will benefit *both* parties. It might be beneficial to seek community partners who have personal connections to families, students, or teachers at the school first, before "cold calling" businesses or other groups in the area.

The National Parent Teacher Association (2000) published a book, *Building Successful Partnerships: A Guide for Developing Parent and Family Involvement Programs,* for schools to plan for partnerships. The guide provides an organizer that helps schools match their goals and needs with community organizations and families. Table 9.2 includes an example of a planning sheet that schools can use that is adapted from the National PTA guidelines. The Planning for Community Partnerships Organizer provides a quick way to determine potential partners that meet the needs of your school, families, teachers, and students.

Inviting Partnerships With Families

Some schools have family resource centers at the school site. Coffee, tea, and water are provided, as is information in various languages on colorful bulletin boards. Some area donut shops or bakeries may donate day-old items to serve in the room each weekday. This is also a room that parents can use when they volunteer at school and need to bring younger siblings. There should be puzzles, books, games, and blocks that can entice children while their parents communicate with other parents, help teachers cut out objects for a bulletin board, or access community and school information.

Ron Clark was a teacher in a rural area of North Carolina and in the inner city of Harlem, New York. He made it a priority to get to know his students and their

Table 9.2 Planning for Community Partnerships Organizer

Community or Professional Resources	Name of the Company or Organization	Contact Person(s)	Partnership Possibilities	Barriers
Faith-based organizations				
Museums and other cultural institutions				
Social services organizations				
Public health organizations				
Universities				
Corporations				
Sports organizations				

families. He has highlighted many of his experiences connecting with students, their families, and the community through books and media appearances. He recently took 15 of his former students from New York and North Carolina to South Africa to deliver school supplies to 12 different schools and orphanages. His students were able to learn about other cultures and participate in service-learning activities in another country. In 2007, the Ron Clark Academy for low-income families was established in Atlanta, Georgia, with the help of corporate sponsors such as Delta Airlines. This type of school is quite different from traditional public and private schools. Teachers are required to form partnerships with families in the school as their students in grades 5–8 study and prepare for visits to different countries of the world. Although this type of school is rare, it demonstrates how partnerships and service learning around the globe can be included as part of the overall school curriculum.

Creating Questionnaires for Families

Glenda, a third-grade teacher, created a series of questionnaires to seek input from teachers, students, and families about the potential for a lunch club at her K–5 elementary school. The club would encourage senior citizens and other adults to become "buddies" during lunchtime with students struggling with school-related issues such as socialization, academic development, and other issues. Glenda did not ask personal questions, and she kept her focus on the information that would help in the implementation of a Lunch Club. The data she collected from the questionnaires would serve as a needs assessment to gain multiple perspectives from teachers, students, and parents. Sample questions from her questionnaires are outlined below.

Questionnaire for Teachers

I am planning a "Lunch Club" for "at-risk" students. The purpose of the club is to have students who might benefit spend one-on-one time with an adult volunteer. They would eat lunch with the volunteer and then spend time with him or her on an activity. I'd like to get some input from you to see what type of program might be valuable and which students should be included.

1. Do you have "at-risk" students who might benefit from special one-on-one time with an adult volunteer over lunch? If so, how many?

2. If your student(s) participated, what type of activities do you think would be most valuable? Would you prefer he/she/they do homework, practice a particular skill (math facts, for instance), read to an adult, be read to, play a learning game, or do another activity?

3. How does your student(s) respond to adult volunteers (easy to work with, needs someone extra patient, etc.)?

4. Do you think listening to a volunteer read aloud while eating lunch is a good idea? Why or why not?

5. Would missing playtime after lunch be a problem?

6. How many days a week do you think would be beneficial?

7. Are there any particular parent volunteers you would like to be contacted for a program to work with children at lunchtime?

8. Any other suggestions or ideas?

Questionnaire for Students

We are planning a new program at lunchtime for kids who would like some help with their homework or schoolwork or would like to spend some time with an adult reading or playing a learning game. Students who participate would eat lunch in the classroom with the adult volunteers. Then, each student would work with his or her volunteer. Help us make a plan for Lunch Club by answering these questions.

1. Would you like to be included in Lunch Club? Why or why not?

2. What type of program would help you the most?

_____ help with homework
_____ practicing reading
_____ practicing math facts
_____ listening to a book be read aloud
_____ playing a learning game
_____ other ideas

3. What kind of adult volunteer do you think would be good at working with kids who want to participate in Lunch Club?

4. If you would like to try out Lunch Club, how many days a week would you like to participate?

5. What are some things that you would like your adult volunteer to do with you?

Questionnaire for Parents

We are planning a new program at lunchtime for kids who would like some help with their homework or schoolwork or would like to spend some time with an adult reading or playing a learning game. Students who participate would eat lunch in the classroom with the adult volunteers. Then, each student would get help from his or her volunteer to complete homework or class work or would simply enjoy time playing an educational game or reading with the volunteer. Our primary purpose is to provide some extra emotional and academic support in an attractive environment.

1. In what ways do you feel a school volunteer might provide support for your child?

2. What kind of homework or schoolwork help, if any, might your child need?

3. What other thoughts, ideas, or suggestions do you have that would help us make Lunch Club a place that would offer some academic and emotional support for children?

Notice that Glenda asked for feedback from teachers, students, and parents before implementing the program. This feedback served as a needs assessment and a powerful way to gain feedback from multiple individuals before the program ever began. She empowered students to determine whether or not they wanted to participate in Lunch Club and asked them to divulge the types of activities they wanted to engage in, the number of days each week, and the type of adult they would like to work with. She empowered the students' parents to make decisions about whether the Lunch Club program would be helpful and the types of activities that they thought their child would benefit from most. The data from all three questionnaires provided Glenda with baseline information to begin Lunch Club. After implementation of Lunch Club, the partners continued to provide insight and make additional decisions related to the structure of the program.

Writing Grants That Support Teaching and Learning

A **grant** is a written agreement by two parties that is usually attached to some type of funding award. Granting agencies such as state or federal governments, private foundations, or corporations usually target a specific area and will offer funding for programs or research that aligns with their specific goals and expectations. **Requests for proposals**, also known as RFPs, are usually generated by these agencies for the purpose of seeking individuals or groups who would like to write a proposal; receive an award in the form of funds, materials, or equipment; and then implement an innovative program. Contributions are considered gifts, and these differ from grants. Many grants are very competitive because a large number of people are applying for limited funding or awards.

Usually, schools and districts seek out funding sources for specific programs they are interested in. These funding sources vary and can offer educators or organizations various sums of money ranging from a $50 grant to buy books for the classroom to a $2 million grant to implement a social studies civic involvement program for teachers and students. When a $50 grant is awarded, it usually has minimal stipulations but high expectations nonetheless. Grants totaling more than $10,000 and multimillion-dollar grants, on the other hand, usually require specific plans of action, a description of systematic changes, and support from various educational administrative units. There are various categories of these grants provided for different purposes. Some grants fund classroom materials and projects, other grants support districtwide initiatives, and other grants support professional development opportunities. In most cases, the action plan that you will create in Chapter 10 can serve as a rough draft or a stepping-stone for writing a grant proposal. Most granting agencies request similar information such as a rationale, goals and objectives, a description of the project, a timeline, and some type of evaluation measure.

Some people claim that successful grant proposal writing is an art form. If this is true, then educators should carefully sculpt their proposal to demonstrate innovation, desire, and the ability to execute the project proposed. There are many guidelines that one can follow to write a grant proposal. Many government- and corporate-sponsored publications and Web sites provide strategies and examples to assist educators in writing grant proposals. My colleague Dr. Loretta Donovan and I created a series of guidelines that we have used with our students at California State University, Fullerton. These are basic steps to jump-start your proposal. The specific steps are outlined in the next part of the chapter. However, it will be up to you to craft your proposal and show how and why your idea or project is innovative and should be funded.

Notes From the Classroom: Seeking Grants to Assist in Working With Families

One kindergarten teacher discussed the language barrier that she experienced when working with families:

I have a personal connection to the language barrier. Many of my parents speak Spanish, and I do not. This was quite intimidating my first year of teaching, and I did not communicate much with my Spanish-speaking parents. This created a barrier between my parents and me. I was intimidated and did not involve the parents in my class. This did a disservice to my students especially since they were kindergarteners where parent involvement is essential. I am looking for grants that are available to provide funding to support more family-teacher-student events at my school.

Before You Begin

The very first thing that you should do before you begin writing a grant proposal is to read the fine print! Actually, it is not usually fine, but it is lengthy. All grants provide a list of requirements and procedures that relate to who can apply for the grant, what the grant should focus on, and what the grant funds may be used for. This information will relate to whether funding is available only to elementary teachers, teachers in rural areas, or teachers who work with low socioeconomic populations. In addition, the requirements within the RFP will state the goals of the grant and what the activity or project should relate to—a particular subject area, a particular type of project such as service learning, or a collaboration of various organizations or individuals. Once you have read the requirements, determine to what extent you meet them. If you do not meet the minimum requirements, then move on and locate a different grant funding opportunity. If you decide to proceed with the grant proposal, you may want to determine if it is worth your time and effort depending on the amount of money being offered and the deadline to apply. Once you have met all the requirements and decide that you want to pursue a grant within a specific organization or corporation, your next step will be to recruit partners (if necessary) and begin writing.

Writing the Proposal

When writing the draft of your grant proposal, you should reread the components or requirements of the grant carefully and address every area. It is helpful to use a highlighter to mark what is required, who is required, and the overall format of the proposal or application. Usually, the granting agency will require that you reveal your goals, your objective, a summary of the project, a timeline of events, responsible parties, and a budget. Take a look at the differences between objectives and goals presented in Chapter 10 to assist you. Goals are overarching long-range outcomes, and objectives are short-term outcomes to meet your goals. The chart you will create for your action plan includes what you are doing, when you are doing it, and who will be responsible for implementing it. You will need to make sure that your outcomes stated in your goals and your objectives align with the activities within your timeline and plan. In addition, telling how you will evaluate your project (even if the granting agency does not specifically ask for this information) may be helpful to the reader and the funding decision makers.

When writing, it is helpful to use an active voice to show your enthusiasm for your project. Spell out the names of all policies such as No Child Left Behind or the Individuals with Disabilities Education Act. Be specific about your plans when describing your idea and provide as many examples as possible. It is often helpful to the reader if you include charts or bullet points to highlight important information or project tasks.

It is important to write a draft of your grant at least one week before it is due to the funding organization. Circulate your draft around to your colleagues and have them read it and determine if they understand what you are proposing. Ask them to provide suggestions and proof the proposal for grammatical errors. Many grant proposals are accepted online by a certain due date. Although technology is helpful, it is not perfect. Therefore, consider submitting your grant proposal at least one day before it is due to bypass any last-minute problems that may arise. Table 9.3 shows an example of a chart that was created to show the objectives of a project, activities, and responsible partners. This was a large-scale grant proposal that targeted four different community partners: a local school district, a university, an engineering firm, and a museum.

Seeking Grants to Support and Acknowledge Teachers

A variety of information is outlined in this section related to resources, Web sites, and other information that will assist you in planning for grant proposal development. The grants information is organized into four different groups including grants for instructional purposes, grants that encourage partnerships, general grant information sites, and grants that recognize teachers and/or provide professional development. Take a look at the variety of grant and award programs available, and consider finding out more about them. In addition, search for additional grant and award information that is not presented in this section.

Grants for Instructional Purposes

- **Mathematics Education Trust: Using Music to Teach Mathematics Grants for Grades Pre-K–2 Teachers**

http://www.nctm.org/resources/content.aspx?id=1318

The National Council of Teachers of Mathematics created this grant to incorporate music with teaching mathematics. It can be given to either a single classroom teacher or groups of teachers who collaborate in one grade level or across grade levels.

Table 9.3 Action Plan and Timeline for a *Research Experiences for Children* Grant Proposal

Project Goals	Related Objectives	Task Plan	Responsible Party	Timeline
Recruit and expose at least 100 students in grades 4–6 to a summer science research camp, targeting girls and historically underrepresented groups	**Objective 1** Host in-school and evening information sessions	Arrange sessions Plan activities Plan schedule	XX School District XX University	January 2007
	Objective 2 Inform the public and teachers from the school district about the summer science camp	Pass out flyers and encourage students and families to participate in summer camp activities	XX School District XX University	January 2007– May 2007
	Objective 3 Present innovative, interactive activities at the summer camp	Join forces with partners to create curriculum aligned with state standards	XX University XX School District XX Engineering Firm Science Center Staff	Summer 2007
	Objective 4 Continue mentoring students in an after-school science academy	Recruit university students to serve as role models and facilitate after-school activities	XX University professors and students XX School District teachers	September 2007– May 2008

- **Mathematics Education Trust: Improving Students' Understanding of Geometry Grants for Grades Pre-K–8 Teachers**

http://www.nctm.org/resources/content.aspx?id=1324

The purpose of this grant is to develop activities and projects that would inspire students to understand and appreciate the concepts of geometry and its many applications to art, literature, music, architecture, and nature. The grant also encourages the integration of technology with teaching geometry.

- **Mockingbird Foundation**

http://www.mockingbirdfoundation.org/funding/guidelines.html

This foundation offers competitive grants toward music education. It encourages funding projects that encourage instruction in any type of musical form with applications to a variety of musical styles, genres, forms, and philosophies.

- **P. Buckley Moss Foundation for Children's Education**

http://www.teacherscount.org/teacher/grants.shtml

This grant is designed to award five teachers each year to help further their arts program goals. With emphasis in teaching children with learning disabilities and other needs, this grant aids teachers' effective art learning tools.

- **Teacher Leader Grant for Teachers of Grades 3–5**

http://www.grantwrangler.com/

This grant is specifically geared toward teachers with an interest to advance reading and writing. The grant includes the usage of the In2Books program, which includes curriculum materials in addition to books and mentor activities. It also stresses building a relationship between students and adult mentors to enhance reading and writing.

- **American Institute of Aeronautics and Astronautics (AIAA) Classroom Grant**

http://www.aiaa.org/content.cfm?pageid=216

This grant is allocated to teachers who develop or apply science, mathematics, and technology in the curriculum. The AIAA supports and suggests supplements to learning programs, such as classroom demonstration kits, science supplies, math and science software, graphing supplies, and other materials to assist in integrating science, math, and technology in the classroom.

Grants That Support Educational Partnerships

Home visits are gaining in popularity so that teachers and schools can connect better with students and their families. There are many grants that teachers can apply for to supplement the time to visit students and their families in their homes. One grant, the Nell Soto Parent/Teacher Involvement Program in California, states on its Web site that its goal is to "strengthen communication between schools and parents as a means of improving pupil academic achievement." This grant and other educational grants for teachers are listed here.

- **Dominion Educational Partnership**

http://www.dom.com/about/education/grants/index.jsp

This partnership fund encourages the development of new programs, primarily to enhance education in math and science. The Dominion Foundation as a whole supports a variety of developments from environmental to educational to cultural to community.

- **Nell Soto Parent/Teacher Involvement Program**

http://www.cde.ca.gov/sp/sw/t1/nellsoto.asp

Schools can apply for funding to coordinate student home visits or community meetings if at least 50% of the teachers at the school voluntarily agree to participate. The grant will assist schools in teacher education and home and community involvement and may supplement costs associated with implementing the program.

- **Partners in Learning Grants Initiative**

http://www.microsoft.com/emea/education/partnersInLearning/pilGrant.mspx

This grant encourages schools to participate and stay updated on technological uses in educational life. Microsoft has partnered with local government and education leaders who extend grants and provide ICT (information and communications technology) skills and training to teachers and students.

- **Rhode Island Higher Education Partnership Grants**

http://www.ribghe.org/itq.htm

These grants support professional development activities in all academic areas. Included is a range of grants from curriculum development to hands-on activities.

- **Starbucks Foundation Grants**

http://www.starbucksfoundation.com/index.cfm?objectid=998E83C8-1D09-317F-BB5BE9229D58A739

The Starbucks Foundation accepts applications for grants to empower students to make changes to make the world a better place. Grants are awarded for projects that encourage students to take actions that result in positive solutions within their community.

General Grant Information Sites

- **American Association of University Women Educational Foundation**

http://www.aauw.org/ef/

This foundation is an enormous source of funding exclusively for graduate women. It supports an array of scholars, teachers, activists, and those who wish to advance their careers. The foundation offers a variety of grants and fellowships.

- **Career Development Grants**

http://www.aauw.org/fga/fellowships_grants/career_development.cfm

This grant supports women who are in the process of either advancing their careers, changing careers, or reentering the workforce. It emphasizes the importance of professional development and supports women who have a bachelor's degree.

- **Grants Alert**

http://www.grantsalert.com/gsft.cfm

Information related to current RFPs for educators and "Fast Fundraising Ideas" are available here. The site is designed to provide teachers with easy access to quick funding opportunities.

- **The Jordan Fundamentals Grant Program**

http://www.nike.com/jumpman23/features/fundamentals/about.html

This grant program seeks opportunities to contribute to teachers and schools from the elementary level to the high school level. It is geared toward helping develop or contribute resources to improve student results.

- **Lowe's Toolbox for Education Grant Program**

http://www.toolboxforeducation.com/

Lowe's Charitable and Educational Foundation (LCEF) is a strong advocate of parent-teacher groups to encourage more involvement with their children's schools. This grant program provides money for public school improvement projects.

- **Merrill Lynch Foundation**

http://philanthropy.ml.com/index.asp?id=66319_67031_67433

This foundation contains grants in a variety of areas, such as arts and culture, education, health and hospitals, and human services. Merrill Lynch's principal philanthropic focus involves assisting in the education of underserved children and youth in areas ranging from financial literacy to leadership development.

- **Teachers Network: Teacher Grants**

http://www.teachersnetwork.org/grants

This site provides lesson plans and unit plans and lists a variety of granting agencies and information. The grant information is organized by subject area such as science, social studies, or mathematics. The site also provides a list of steps for writing grant proposals.

Grants That Recognize Teachers and/or Provide Professional Development

- **Earthwatch Teacher Fellowships**

http://www.earthwatch.org/aboutus/education

Grants are made available to teachers who want to participate in one of the many Earthwatch expeditions with top researchers at sites around the world and engage in the actual scientific research process. Some expeditions include a study of Australia's forest marsupials, dolphins of Greece, Easter Island cultures, and Alaskan glaciers. Teachers who are awarded fellowships receive funding that covers their participation in one of the research expeditions, food, accommodations, and onsite travel. Some fellowships also cover travel reimbursement.

- **Foundation Educator Achievement Award**

http://www.aiaa.org/content.cfm?pageid=217

The American Institute of Aeronautics and Astronautics pays tribute to seven teachers every 2 years for their accomplishments with K–12 students. This award goes to teachers who inspire and excite students about math and science and prepare them to use and contribute to future technology. The organization also offers classroom grants to teachers.

- **The Freida J. Riley Teacher Award**

http://nmoe.org/riley/index.htm

This is an annual award that recognizes a teacher who effectively and positively impacts students. In addition to impacting students, this teacher gets recognition for overcoming some type of adversity or making a considerable sacrifice.

- **National Teachers Hall of Fame Teacher Recognition**

http://www.nthf.org/teacher.htm

This national teacher recognition honors five teachers annually. Candidates include those who have demonstrated commitment and dedication to teaching. Awards also include a scholarship for a student pursuing an education career and a monetary award for classroom materials.

- **International Reading Association**

http://www.reading.org/Resources/AwardsandGrants.aspx

This organization offers more than 40 awards and grants to honor teachers, authors, and other people involved in literacy education. The Eleanor M. Johnson award recognizes an elementary classroom teacher of the specific subject area of reading/language arts. The IRA Award for Technology and Reading recognizes K–12 teachers who integrate technology and reading.

- **Presidential Awards for Excellence in Mathematics and Science Teaching**

http://www.paemst.org/

Receiving a Presidential Award is one of the highest honors for teachers in grades K–12 throughout the United States. These awards are administered by the White House and the National Science Foundation. Teachers must demonstrate their exemplary contributions within their classroom and within their professional community. Winners in each state receive a $10,000 classroom award, a trip to Washington, DC, to attend congratulatory events, and additional gifts from sponsors.

- **Time Warner Cable's National Teacher Awards**

http://www.timewarnercable.com/Corporate/about/community/nationalteachers/default.html

Numerous awards recognize projects for creative educational use of cable resources. Winners will be granted two monetary amounts, one of cash and the other for further school technology advancement.

Communicating With Families About Resources

Teachers, as educators, have responsibilities and obligations to know about the wide array of community resources available to families. Teachers can provide a list of resources through consistent communication via e-mail or class newsletters or post information on the school Web site. These resources can include information about social services, the local library, and community events connected to the formal curriculum. The following "Notes From the Classroom" section features a newsletter created by a teacher, Cathy, to inform parents of community resources related to the study of dinosaurs—the focus of a summer camp for young children. Cathy provides background about herself and her family before introducing the content and activities that children will be learning about. In addition, she incorporates specific questions that parents can ask their children about their learning experiences, and she provides links to other dinosaur sites so that children can continue learning after the camp is over.

Notes From the Classroom: Sample Teacher Newsletter to Families

Dino-Mite Summer Camp, June 19 to 29, 2009

Welcome to summer camp! My name is Cathy Aiken. I am a Messiah Preschool Staff alumnus. I taught preschool for 11 years, 5 at Hephatha Lutheran Preschool in Anaheim Hills and 6 years here at Messiah. I currently teach kindergarten in the Anaheim City School District. My free time is spent working on my master's in education in curriculum and instruction at Cal State Fullerton. My housemates include Jake the Dog, a 4-year-old flat-coated retriever, and his best friend, Murphy, a year-old tuxedo cat.

I have two grown children. My daughter, Casey, is a fourth-grade teacher in the Walnut Unified School District. She will be celebrating her second wedding anniversary in July to Charlie Weinkauf, a history teacher at Canyon High School and a professional bass fisherman. My son, Brian, is a full-time student finishing up his degree in philosophy at the University of California, San Diego. He works part-time as a teacher in the school outreach

(Continued)

(Continued)

program at the San Diego Natural History Museum, on the Midway aircraft carrier, and as a chemistry tutor. At the age of 4, Brian decided he wanted to become a paleontologist. He even wrote a song about dinosaurs (which your children will learn). Over the years, he became an expert on dinosaurs and shared his love of these extinct beasts with his family. I hope to share my love of learning and dinosaurs with your children during camp.

As you know, at Messiah, children are allowed to choose which activities they wish to engage in. These are just some of the activities that will be offered.

Math	Language Arts	Science
1-to-1 correspondence	Retelling stories	Observing
Counting	Writing stories	Questioning
Ordinal numbers	Drawing and labeling	Classifying
Sorting	Discussions	Communicating
Matching	Predicting	
Graphing	Inferring	

All of the above activities will have dinosaurs incorporated in them. In addition, we will have open-ended art experiences, music, and daily digging for dinosaurs.

Parent Link

- Ask your child daily:

  What was the best thing that happened today?

  What was the worst thing that happened today?

- At the end of the first week, ask your child:

  What is your favorite dinosaur? Why?

  Can you sing the Dinosaur Song for me?

- At the end of the second week, ask your child:

  How many horns does a triceratops have?

  What dinosaur is known as the "Terrible Lizard"?

  Name a dinosaur with plates on its back.

  What dinosaur can fly? Does it have feathers like our birds?

  What does *extinct* mean?

  Do any animals living today remind you of a dinosaur? Why?

For Further Investigation

To add to your child's dinosaur experience, here are some great places to go where children can interact with dinosaurs:

San Diego Natural History Museum, "Dinosaurs: Reel and Robotic": http://www.sdnhm.org

- The first Tuesday of every month is free for local residents, as is admission to the San Diego Model Railroad Museum and the Reuben H. Fleet Science Center. If you go to the Natural History Museum's "Fossil Mysteries" Web page, you will see how the animated dinosaur exhibit was made.
- The Orange County Discovery Science Center: http://www.discoverycube.org/exhibits/dinosaurs.htm
- Life-size dinosaurs will be on exhibit such as the *T. rex* and *Argentinosaurus*.
- Cabazon, California: If you are ever on your way to Palm Springs, stop in at the EAT sign in Cabazon (just past the outlet mall) where there are two life-size dinosaurs you can visit up close.
- Other fun places to visit with your child on your computer include http://www.enchantedlearning.com/subjects/dinosaurs/allabout (to look at and read about different dinosaurs) and http://enchantedlearning.com/categories/preschool/shtml (scroll down until you see dinosaurs—a dinosaur alphabet book, dinosaur jokes, scrambled dinosaurs, dinosaur coloring sheets to print out, and dinosaur coloring to do online).

If you have any questions or concerns, please do not hesitate to contact me. I am looking forward to a dino-mite time at summer camp. I hope you and your child are too!

—Ms. Aiken

SOURCE: Used with permission of Cathy Aiken.

Interagency Collaboration

In education, **interagency collaboration** includes groups or individuals collaborating to address issues such as health education, special education, and safety. Different agencies or groups work together and integrate their services for the purpose of early intervention and support for families, schools, and communities. They exchange information, link information, share resources, and work together to accomplish goals. Specific benefits of this collaboration include (a) better use of resources with limited capital, (b) less fragmentation among different services, (c) higher-quality outcomes, (d) the integration of diverse perspectives, (e) improved communication among agencies, (f) increased trust, (g) potential for organization and individual learning, and (h) likelihood of achieving important outcomes (National Association of County and City Health Officials, 2007). A K–8 school in

Arkansas embraces interagency collaboration and has provided school nurses, social workers, counselors, and adult education experts to work together at the school site to provide integrated services for students and their families. Once a month a medical doctor visits the site and follows up on recommendations from the nurses, social workers, and counselors.

Interagency collaboration has become more popular over the past 20 years due to the increase in poverty, unemployment, inadequate health insurance, poor health and nutrition, teen pregnancy, and other social issues. Therefore, these partnerships provide a more comprehensive approach to servicing children and families. The *Communities in Schools* program collaborates with local government, corporations, and volunteer organizations to reposition support staff from human services and volunteer agencies to work at school sites. They become a part of interdisciplinary teams that focus on small groups of at-risk students. This program brings support from social service organizations, businesses, and volunteers directly to schools. Physical fitness, nutrition, safety, drug awareness, and other services are integrated as part of the total school program. This program provides access to services and empowers families, schools, and the community to make decisions together. A Web site and additional information are provided in the "Additional Reading and Information" section at the end of this chapter.

The Australian Health Promoting Schools Association program, *Healthpact*, promotes collaboration among students, families, and the community. This Australian collaboration encourages decision making, input, and responsibility from families, students, teachers, and government and nongovernment organizations. Families are encouraged and empowered to change some of their own health and nutrition behaviors; students are educated and asked to take responsibility for their personal and community health; and teachers enact a curriculum that is grounded in everyday health issues, and they address real concerns and issues related to families. The government and community organizations work together to promote good health. Health-promoting schools are defined and described as those that take action and demonstrate commitment to enhancing the emotional, social, physical, and moral well-being of all members of their community. The criteria for a school to classify as a health-promoting school include the following:

- An organization culture that promotes a safe, healthy, and stimulating learning environment for students and teachers
- Identification of the school community's specific needs
- Priorities established and focused on relevant health issues
- Collaboration with parents and students on decision making, problem solving, and action related to school health issues
- Implementation of a holistic, coordinated health education plan
- Development of effective partnerships with health services to develop, implement, and monitor health programs

Communities offer a variety of services. Schools and educators should make it a priority to become aware of these resources and services and provide lists for parents. Some examples of community services are outlined below.

- Adult protective services hotlines
- AIDS information
- Anger management counseling
- Bereavement
- Caregiver support groups
- Child abuse hotlines
- Community counseling centers
- Crime victims
- Cross-cultural services for diverse families
- Domestic violence help lines
- Domestic violence shelters, youth shelters, and adult shelters
- Eating disorders
- Emergency assistance for food, clothing, and utilities
- Family counseling
- Gay and lesbian services
- Health care referrals
- Legal aid
- Mental illness resources
- Psychiatric services and emergency psychiatric services
- Psychiatrist referral sources
- Senior citizens
- Substance abuse
- Suicide prevention

Even if schools do not have formal partnerships with outside health and welfare organizations, teachers can be proactive in creating an ongoing list of community resources that will benefit families. Often, children do not have adequate health care, and they need counseling or other community services. When this happens, schools should be able to provide information promptly about free or low-cost services within the local community.

Chapter Summary

Community resources are only resources if accessed by schools, families, and community members. This chapter provided a plethora of information and step-by-step procedures needed to seek out partnerships and educational resources. Teachers

Musicians work with parents, teachers, and administrators to help children develop an appreciation and a love for the power of music in their lives.

and schools should make it a priority to inform families of community resources available to them. Many of the partnerships involving community resources can be externally funded by a variety of grants from government and private organizations.

CASE STUDIES

The first case study will be presented to show a regional partnership where multiple groups work together to enhance the music curriculum for students in Southern California. The partnership is called *Class Act* and includes partners from the Pacific Symphony, public and private school administrators, teachers, students, and families. The second case study describes a fit lifestyle program where schools, families, and students work together to promote better overall wellness.

❖ Case Study 9.1: Class Act and the Pacific Symphony Orchestra

The Pacific Symphony initiated the Class Act program in 1994 to connect the symphony and its music to schools, children, and their families. The program was founded and created by a group of parents who were interested in increasing music education opportunities at their children's schools. Pacific Symphony musicians work closely with parents, teachers, and administrators to help children develop an appreciation and a love for the power of music in their lives. About 40 schools that apply to the program participate each year. Music is integrated throughout the regular school curriculum throughout the entire school year.

The Pacific Symphony and schools form a partnership to produce the following outcomes: (a) form close relationships between school communities, (b) enrich the quality of music education and encourage interactions with professional musicians, (c) develop a foundation for lifelong learning through the arts, and (d) facilitate the teaching of and exposure to the arts. The Class Act program includes a prelude assembly where a storyteller, assisted by the school's music teacher, presents the life and times of a particular composer. Second, the Pacific Symphony musician introduces his or her instrument to groups of students, and musical elements employed by the same composer are featured during the storytelling. Third, there is a family night where a concert is presented at the school site for the community featuring the school's music teacher and a small ensemble from the Pacific Symphony. Fourth, there is a youth concert where the students at the school attend a performance at the Segerstrom Concert Hall, featuring the same composer they have been learning about in school. The year ends with a Bravo Assembly or series of assemblies where the entire student body presents what it has learned and enjoyed as a result of all elements within the *Class Act* program. Voices from a musician, a parent, and students are featured below. For additional information, visit www.pacificsymphony.org.

Voice of the Community Partner: Cynthia Ellis, Flutist, Pacific Symphony, and Class Act Teaching Artist

I've been a part of the Class Act program as a teaching artist since the beginning, when we started with only 3 schools, and we have come a long way since then, serving 40 schools. The program gives the general student access to musical experiences beyond that of public school music programs. I think the students receive a real boost for their imagination: They are able to meet with a professional musician "up close and personal." I can relate this to an experience of my own in elementary school. The Marine band came and played for us, and it was the first time I realized one could be a career musician: What a powerful spark that was for me! I can only hope that Class Act provides this same boost for 21st-century students. This program draws in the whole school, involving the parents as volunteers, all teachers, and administration (principals are highly involved too), with materials, teaching support, and training included as part of the package. It's a very special opportunity to share the gift of music with the community.

Voice of a Parent, Susan Kinsey

The introduction of *Peter and the Wolf* has changed my 6-year-old son from a passive music listener to an involved music enthusiast. The exposure of instrumentation and orchestration took his musical interest to a higher level of awareness where he can now pick out a French horn, a flute, an oboe, a clarinet, a bassoon, and strings in nearly any piece of music. Prior to Class Act's children's series, my son was limited to the typical child music that involves rhythm, rhyme, patterns, and elementary instruments. However, the Class Act music series, with its hands-on approach, gave him the opportunity to handle instruments such as the French horn and oboe and allowed him to explore how they're played and the reasons why one wind instrument makes a different sound than another. Further, the orchestration of *Peter and the Wolf* was presented in such a lively way with costumed musicians that making the connection of the instruments to the characters turned into a game. When my son heard the French horn, he screamed with fear in anticipation of the wolf, and when he heard the strings, he sighed with relief knowing that Peter was nearby to help.

His interest in Sergei Prokofiev was so intent that he began listening to *Peter and the Wolf* at home. I was astonished to learn that in addition to being able to identify the instruments and their corresponding character, my son could also follow the story line based on the orchestra; he was able to describe what was happening in the scene and could predict the next scene—beginning with the introduction, moving into the drama of the wolf eating the duck and stalking the bird and cat, to knowing when Peter was preparing to catch the wolf, and, ultimately, identifying the culmination of the story with the procession to the zoo.

Voice of a Kindergarten Student, Grant

My favorite part was the concert because the whole school was there. Each instrument was played by different characters. I laughed when I saw their costumes.

Voice of a Sixth-Grade Student, Kallin

I liked hearing the music the most because I could really imagine it. You learn a lot from the music itself. I liked learning about the artist, Sergei Prokofiev.

SOURCE: Used with permission of Cynthia Ellis and Susan Kinsey.

❖ Case Study 9.2: Promoting a Fit Lifestyle for Children

Voice of Elisa, First-Grade Teacher

Promoting a fit lifestyle for children encompasses a balanced diet, exercise, decision making, self-esteem, resilience, and problem solving. I find that many families and schools believe that they maintain or contribute to a healthy lifestyle; however, busy schedules and inadequate diets contribute to an ongoing predicament. What are our children eating? Are they exercising? Who is responsible for teaching a fit lifestyle philosophy? As I look at the partnership among schools, community, and the home, I ask, "Do schools and families contribute to a fit lifestyle, or are they contributing to childhood obesity?"

Instilling a fit lifestyle mentality is crucial in the early childhood years. Teaching children about making the right choices with food and exercise at a young age would ideally reduce the statistics on obesity. In my school, 38 first-grade parents were asked about their beliefs on a Fit for Life lifestyle. I sent home a 10-question Fit for Life Parent Survey, with some background information on the study. Questions inquired about eating habits for breakfast, lunch, and dinner, as well as school-time and after-school snacks. Also, parents were asked about their own exercise regimens as well as those of their children. Finally, the survey posed questions regarding the frequency of television viewing. The parents involved in the survey come from a variety of cultural and socioeconomic backgrounds. The school is predominantly upper-middle-class and demonstrates strong values regarding nutrition and education.

Additionally, the first-grade students of these same parents were given an open-ended survey question that asked, "What does it mean to live a healthy life, and why is it important?" The students varied in ages, from 6 to 8 years old, and were representative of a variety of cultural backgrounds. A first-grade teacher and the mother of two young children were also interviewed. I asked questions about integrating health and physical education into the curriculum and about what would make up a fit lifestyle for children. Finally, the principal at the same school was asked about her philosophy and how her school embraces a fit lifestyle. I also asked her what improvements might be made in the current health and physical education programs at the school.

Data from the 10-item parent questionnaire was analyzed by tallying the responses. Several parents gave multiple answers to questions, so I included all information in the final data. For questions that asked about frequency, I categorized the responses by time periods (e.g., weekly, often, never) and then tallied parent responses. For questions that asked about opinion or food choices, I listed all the responses and looked for common answers to determine what the majority thought.

Based on parent responses, student beliefs, and teacher and principal interviews, I was able to make some generalizations about families and school and a fit lifestyle and was able to create a plan to encourage this in first grade and throughout the rest of the school.

SOURCE: Used with permission of Elisa Gornbein.

❖ Reflecting on the Cases

1. Explain how *Class Act* extends the traditional performing arts curriculum. Explain how the *Fit for Life* program extends the traditional physical education and health curriculum.

2. Describe the benefits of having *Class Act* work with teachers and students throughout the school year and in subsequent school years rather than having a one-shot event or a one-shot concert.

3. What elements make these projects successful? What is the role of the school? The families? The students? The teachers? The community?

Activities for Further Development

1. Take a walk and/or drive through the neighborhood connected to your school. Compose a description of the school's community and create a list of resources that can contribute and enhance the subject areas that you teach.

2. Create a list of specific services in your community so that you will have the information available (phone number, address, Web site, e-mail) for families in your school.

3. Explain how you could encourage an ongoing interagency collaboration at your school based on the information provided in this chapter.

4. Go online and look at one of the educational grants described in this chapter. Locate the amount of money available, application requirements, and procedures needed to submit the grant.

Additional Reading and Information

Browing, B. A. (2004). *Grant writing for educators: Practical strategies for teachers, administrators, and staff.* Bloomington, IN: Solution Tree. This book features information about seeking and applying for corporate, foundation, and government grants.

Glaister, A., & Glaister, B. (2005). *Inter-agency collaboration: Providing for children.* Edinburgh, Scotland: Dunedin Academic Press. This book provides information about how professional service organizations work across their traditionally defined boundaries.

Communities of Practice (part of the IDEA Partnership) provides information and partnership examples related to special education: http://www.ideapartnership.org/index.php?option=com_content&view=section&id=11&Itemid=45

The National Child Care Information and Technical Assistance Center is sponsored by the U.S. Department of Health and Human Services and provides resources, articles, and publications to promote collaborative early childhood education and partnerships: http://nccic.acf.hhs.gov

Ron Clark Academy and partnership projects: http://www.ronclarkacademy.com

The U.S. Department of Health and Human Services: Administration for Children and Families provides information about interagency collaboration and partnership examples, Webinars, and programs related to child abuse and neglect: http://www.acf.hhs.gov/programs/cb/fediawg/index.htm

10

Planning for Partnerships

After reading this chapter, you should have a better understanding of:

- characteristics of an action plan;
- the purpose of creating an action plan;
- locating potential partners to participate in your action plan project;
- conducting a front-end assessment;
- action plan examples, steps, procedures, and timelines;
- the purpose of creating goals and objectives to guide your action plan;
- distinguishing between formative assessments and summative evaluations; and
- tips from teachers for teachers to help you develop an action plan.

Table 10.1	Prior Knowledge and Beliefs Organizer

List characteristics of an effective partnership.	List barriers that pose challenges to the partnership.	List procedures to overcome these barriers.

Table 10.1 asks you to reflect on the content of the previous chapters and outline characteristics of effective partnerships, barriers, and ways to overcome the barriers. Use Table 10.1 as an organizer to help you plan for a partnership. This chapter will focus on the steps required to develop a partnership project or to improve a partnership project that is already in place.

Creating an Action Plan

Many researchers in the field of family and community partnerships refer to this process as creating a plan for action or an **action plan** (e.g., Epstein, 2001). In addition, practitioners in multiple fields including city planning, agriculture, marketing, and sales create action plans in order to carry out goals and objectives related to a particular product or project. Specific steps for creating an action plan and examples of plans will be presented to help you organize a rationale and strategy for developing a school-family partnership, a professional partnership, a school-community partnership, or a school-community-family partnership. Basic guidelines for creating an action plan are outlined below to provide an overview of the information that you will need to get started. An action plan is an explicit plan where partners create goals, strategies, and outcomes to enhance one or more areas of education. The partners publicize these goals for all to know.

1. *Describe the project or program that you want to develop.* Create a rationale statement based on current research.

2. *Describe which of Epstein's (2001) six types of involvement you will focus on most.* These are described in Chapter 5: parenting, communicating, volunteering, learning at home, decision making, and community collaborations. Although many of the six areas will be addressed, describe one or two areas that fit most closely with what you want to accomplish. The best partnerships usually start small and then move into other areas of the six types of involvement once the project is more established.

3. *Identify the partners who will be involved. Be very specific about who will be included.* Will there be 15 parents of English learners, 15 students, and 3 teachers? Will there be 64 fourth-grade students, 10 senior citizens, and an after-school coordinator? Describe their roles.

4. *Describe how you will assess the current involvement of the partners involved.*

5. *State the partnership goals (long-term outcomes) and objectives (short-term outcomes) related to your project.* These are important to help guide the partnership project and activities.

6. *Determine which barriers you will need to address and explain steps you will take to overcome them.* Because barriers can impede the progress of a partnership, they must be anticipated in advance.

7. *Provide a timeline of events.* Include dates and specific activities and/or benchmarks. In addition, provide the name of a person or group that will be responsible for each event or activity. It usually takes about 3 years for a partnership to overcome challenges and to become more sustainable. Therefore, you may want to consider a short timeline for the first year and include additional activities for years 2 and 3.

8. *Describe how you will evaluate the partnership.* Include formative and summative evaluation procedures. These two types of evaluation procedures are discussed later in this chapter.

Future Teachers: What the Research Says

The University of Texas at El Paso presented results of a school-university-community partnership program called Project *Podemos* ("We can do it"), which involved a partnership among the university, public schools, and the local community. This collaboration resulted in future teachers interacting with families within a diverse community. They reported that they could enhance the education of children in the community by respecting the larger context in which these students live. In addition, many of these future teachers developed a new appreciation and respect for their own family's values, beliefs, and customs (De la Piedra, Munter, & Giron, 2006).

Locating Potential Partners

Chapters 1 through 9 describe different types of partnerships, the barriers involved, and ways to seek successful partnerships. When creating an action plan, you may want to use information from your case study and other collaborative activities to create a new program with new partners or to enhance an existing educational partnership. Partnerships can be large or small and can involve educational partners, government partners, faith-based partners, high-profile partners, large foundations, or local businesses. Consider your overall goals related to what you would like to improve or enhance. This can align with teaching or learning or both. This will help you determine who an ideal partner will be.

One action plan was developed by elementary teachers who collaborated with a university professor to integrate the visual arts into subjects such as language arts, math, science, and social studies. Together, preservice teachers and practicing teachers collaborated on potential art projects that were aligned with the social studies and science curriculums. Projects included the art of ancient Egypt and ancient Greece to help students understand the context of the communities that people lived in long ago. After the social studies lessons were taught, the art projects were created. The teacher and university professor framed and displayed these projects throughout the six floors of the campus education building. One evening, students and their families joined the teacher, preservice teachers, and the university professor for a dessert reception to view the student art exhibition. An individual certificate of appreciation from the university was presented to each student for exhibiting his or her work. After the reception, families and students were given a tour of the education building by preservice teacher partners. Families were encouraged to explore the entire college campus after the event.

As you think about a partnership that you would like to improve or enhance, or one that you would like to develop, it is helpful to review some information from previous chapters related to partnership examples provided within the case studies, characteristics of effective partnerships described in each chapter, communication strategies, barriers, and culturally relevant considerations. A partnership is an agreement where two or more people or groups work together toward mutual goals. Partnerships can be formal, informal, or even unspoken as long as they include people or groups working together. Partnerships must benefit both sides in some way to be truly effective.

An action plan is an explicit plan where partners create goals, strategies, and outcomes to enhance one or more areas of education. The partners publicize these goals for all to know.

Stages of the Planning Process

The stages of the planning process and steps for creating an action plan are outlined and described below. You will want to use the key concepts and knowledge about what you learned from a variety of successful partnership examples to develop your plan. In addition, think about what makes a partnership successful and what procedures are most effective when addressing barriers. If you have not determined the topic of your action plan, you can begin by thinking about something in your community or your school environment that you are passionate about, something you would like to see improved, or something new that you would like to develop. Next, think about extending the walls of the school to seek assistance from families, other professionals, or the broader community. The action plan will focus on the planning process. The implementation process will take place when you actually follow the steps listed in your plan. Nevertheless, the action plan is just that, a plan—it can be revised and changed throughout the implementation process to meet partners' views and needs and any constraints. To illustrate the steps required when creating an action plan, a variety of examples created by Rohanna, a sixth-grade teacher who teaches students from diverse ethnic and language backgrounds, are provided (Ylagan, 2005).

Introduction and Rationale

Before beginning the actual planning process, take a look at research studies and other literature that relate to your topic. Next, provide an overview or description of the partnership as well as a rationale based on current literature and the unique needs of your school or classroom. In the following "Notes From the Classroom," you will see Rohanna's introduction and rationale based on the case study she conducted prior to creating an action plan. (See p. 254, "Notes From the Classroom: Rohanna's Action Plan—Sources Cited," for sources cited in this series.)

Notes From the Classroom: Rohanna's Action Plan—Rationale

Research shows that parental involvement with children and schooling definitely contributes to students' learning. The benefits of parental participation include increased student attendance, decreased student dropout rate, and improved student motivation (Buttery & Anderson, 1999; Epstein, 2001). Epstein (2001) states that "interactive homework activities also help families remain aware of their children's curriculum, monitor their children's work, show interest in what their children are learning, and motivate their children to work in school" (p. 495). This sense of interactive homework creates a network between children and their parents to ensure that they are completing homework and better prepared for the next day's class work. Parents can also show interest by discussing assignments and checking their accuracy as well (Finn, 1998).

Homework, student involvement, and parent engagement have always been an interest to me due to the fact that there are always some students with incomplete homework. Due to this incompletion of homework, I was wondering how homework was being accomplished at home.

Based on my current case study, I realized that a large number of parents do not even check to see if their children's homework is complete; therefore, the interactive homework is lacking at home. With the understanding that many parents work, have other children to look after, and basically have a busy schedule, sometimes the parental involvement with homework is hard to achieve. This very point brings me to the core of my project. I had the idea that students should and could have the opportunity for homework support through a partnership created with local high school students. This support program ("Learners Club") would definitely benefit those students who do not get the support needed at home. Sixth graders would be paired up with high school students a few days out of the week to work on homework and study skills. These high school students would be tutors as well as mentors to the sixth graders. In addition to this offered homework support during school, another advantage of such a program would be geared toward children actually having extra time for after-school outdoor activities.

SOURCE: Used with permission of Rohanna Ylagan.

Determining the Type of Involvement

The next step in developing an action plan is to determine which of Epstein's six types of involvement your partnership will focus on or address most (Epstein, 2001). As noted above, the types include parenting, communicating, volunteering, learning at home, decision making, and community collaboration. To review, here is a description of each type of involvement from Chapter 5:

1. *Parenting* involves establishing home environments that support children and youth's social, cognitive, emotional, and physical health. Teachers, as educators, have the responsibility to support families in their roles related to parenting. However, support must include respecting cultural differences and philosophies related to child rearing practices.

2. *Communicating* with families involves school-to-home and home-to-school interactions related to children's education and their overall well-being. Open communication between all parties in any partnership is essential to enhancing students' overall educational experience. Communication can be formal or informal. Both are necessary for optimum collaboration.

3. *Volunteering* can take place at the school site, at home, or within the community. Some companies have been identified as "family friendly" based on flexible hours, onsite child care, shared positions, and other characteristics to encourage families to become more involved in their child's education during school hours. However, volunteering can be encouraged after the school day ends when families are together at home.

4. *Learning at home* involves supplementing and extending the formal and informal educational experiences of children while not in school. Teachers should be proactive in collaborating with families and sharing information related to learning-based home activities. Teachers can communicate helpful learning activities, homework tips, and other educational opportunities through regular newsletters or e-mails in a variety of languages.

5. *Shared decision making* in schools encourages families, students, teachers, and members of the community to work together to improve teaching, learning, and the overall well-being of students. When looking at shared decision making, it does not have to happen within a formal structure such as a school-based management committee; it can include informal processes and small committee groups as well. True collaboration among students, colleagues, and families plays a key role in real decision-making opportunities.

6. *Community collaboration* includes ways to identify and integrate community resources and services within the school curriculum for the purpose of strengthening student achievement, student health and welfare, school programs, and family practices. Communication in this area includes home-to-community, school-to-community, and home-to-school-to-community. Businesses, cultural institutions, health and social service agencies, and other community groups possess resources and expertise to strengthen education and promote partnerships with educators.

When developing your action plan, you may find that the partnership is focused on more than one type of involvement. For example, a series of school-family literacy events might focus on parenting but also on learning at home when encouraging more reading on weekends. Or the school-family literacy events might focus more on just one area of involvement such as communicating where schools and families work together to communicate expectations, reading activities, and reading enrichment resources. It is important to identify one or two areas (not more) that you will focus on for your partnership. This will help you concentrate on specific areas rather than trying to focus on too many at one time.

In the following "Notes From the Classroom," Rohanna describes volunteering as the major type of involvement and specifies research related to best practices to inform her project.

Notes From the Classroom: Rohanna's Action Plan—Type of Involvement

Epstein's Types of Involvement: Type 3, Volunteering

According to Epstein (2001), volunteering no longer necessarily refers to obtaining parent help and support. The new definition of volunteering no longer limits itself to parents but includes anyone who supports the learning and development of children's school goals. There are no time restraints as well. Volunteering can occur anytime and any place. This new definition of volunteering helps solve the challenges of schedules and organization of volunteers. Some expected results due to this new volunteering definition include children's increased learning skills due to the fact that they receive support, attention, and tutoring from volunteers.

Communities in Schools (CIS) is an example of a program that not only helps students academically but provides a caring one-on-one relationship with a mentor. This mentor, usually an older adult, acts not only as a tutor but also as a role model for younger students. Different organizations throughout the United States provided by CIS serve the community with various services aside from tutoring (Lewis & Morris, 1998).

The importance of making every experience a learning experience supports the fact that children develop emotionally, socially, and academically through relationships. Utilizing and connecting with a community of volunteers, in this case high school students, can encourage younger students' learning, as did the successful Philadelphia community-supported parent tutoring program titled "Reading Together" (Neuman, 1995). Similarly, this proposed project could increase high school students' self-esteem and build their confidence as they would motivate and mentor younger students.

SOURCE: Used with permission of Rohanna Ylagan.

Identifying Partners

The next step in creating your action plan is to identify the partners involved in your project. A partner implies that there are at least two people, two groups, or two organizations working together. The partners could be a sixth-grade teacher and a family who has a child in his or her class who is struggling socially or academically. The partners could also be a local grocery store and a second-grade class of teachers and students. Be specific about who will be included and give a description of the roles and responsibilities of each partner. Rohanna describes the community, the students, and the families where she teaches in the following "Notes From the Classroom."

Notes From the Classroom: Rohanna's Action Plan—Description of Partners

The community of learners at Drumbury Elementary is very similar to the high school students at Danford Hills High School. The elementary school is a Title I school and is located one block away from the high school. Both schools are located in a middle- to lower-socioeconomic area of the county. The Hispanic or Latino ethnic group makes up the racial majority at the elementary school similarly to the high school (67%). The other races included are 3.8% African American, 0.4% American Indian or Alaska Native, 1.6% Asian, 1.9% Filipino, 0.4% Pacific Islander, and 25.4% White or Caucasian. The following table provides a breakdown of who would potentially be involved with this project.

Partners for "Learners Club"	
Amount	**Individuals**
1	(Danford) high school principal
1	(Drumbury) elementary school principal
All/referred	(Danford) high school 10th-grade English teachers
33	(Drumbury) 6th-grade students
33	(Danford) high school students

SOURCE: Used with permission of Rohanna Ylagan.

Front-End Assessment

The next step in creating an action plan is to determine how you will assess the current involvement of the partners. This front-end assessment, or needs assessment, can help you determine the state and history of the partnership at present, if it is an existing partnership. It can also help you identify needs, barriers, and critical partners. Common methods to determining front-end assessment data include written surveys, observations, past academic achievement test scores, interviews, demographic information, statistics related to attendance, socioeconomic status, and languages, in addition to other sources. Rohanna's description of her front-end assessment is included in the following "Notes From the Classroom." Rohanna's example originated from her case study related to the same topic, homework improvement.

Notes From the Classroom: Rohanna's Action Plan—Front-End Assessment

Since the front-end assessment of this action plan assesses the current involvement of the partners throughout, two main assessments would include data collection in the form of surveys and a collection and analysis of existing homework logs.

Surveys were given to high school and sixth-grade students: (a) an interest survey to assess if and how many students (high school and elementary) would be interested in participating in the program and (b) an interest survey to assess general interests, hobbies, and future careers. Another survey was given to parents of sixth-grade students that included (a) questions related to everyday schedules, including work, and after-school availability and (b) questions related to their interest in having their child participate in the homework partnership program. A third type of data included homework collection and analysis of sixth-grade students. A review of homework logs and homework grades was used to assess which students would benefit most from the program.

SOURCE: Used with permission of Rohanna Ylagan.

Stating Goals and Objectives

For this next step, determine the overall goals of the partnership (long-term outcomes) and specific objectives (short-term outcomes). Each of these should be specifically stated in your action plan to keep you focused as you prepare activities, determine responsibilities, and create a timeline of events. Having specific goals and objectives also allows you to revisit them at various points to determine how they can be met. **Objectives** should be attainable and measurable during a short period of time. **Goals** are more long term in nature and should take place over time. Objectives and goals both describe the outcomes, but they differ based on their specificity (objectives) and generality (goals). Each of them, however, relates to what students or teachers or schools or families or communities will *do* as a result of the project. Objectives are important because they guide the activities related to the project. The activities include the process and procedures. Objectives and goals also relate to the actual product. There are multiple reasons to include goals and objectives, but for the most part it keeps partners focused and allows each partner to understand the mutual objectives and goals that will be accomplished through partnership activities.

To give you an example, there is a partnership among families, students, and teachers related to literacy called "Pajama Nights" with an organized set of objectives and goals to guide the partnership activities related to literacy. Together, a K–8 elementary school and faculty from a local university planned a series of family literacy nights where students, their parents, and their siblings are invited to participate in activities on several evenings at the school site. They are asked to wear their pajamas or other comfortable clothing. These literacy nights are held four times during the school year so that families can come together with teachers and university faculty to read, share stories, and gather sets of literacy activities that can be replicated in students' homes. If parents cannot attend the event with their child, a grandparent or neighbor can attend with the child instead. The goals and objectives of the project are outlined as follows.

Pajama Nights

Goals:

1. Students and families will develop an appreciation for reading.
2. Students and families will engage in a variety of literacy practices at home.
3. Students will gain emotional and academic support from multiple caring adults.
4. Teachers will develop positive, collaborative relationships with families.
5. Students' reading achievement will increase at school and on standardized tests.

Objectives:

1. Families, teachers, and university faculty will attend at least two literacy nights each year.
2. Families will demonstrate literacy practices with their children such as picture walks, using context clues, and asking questions.
3. Families will engage in a variety of literacy practices at home.
4. Students will create home literacy plans.
5. Teachers and families will talk to each other and discover at least one interesting thing about each other each time they participate in Pajama Nights.

Notice that the goals and objectives relate to families, students, and teachers. If you would like to plan a similar program at your school, ensure that all students have access to pajamas. If some students do not own pajamas, you can ask children and families to come in comfortable clothing, or you could ask a local clothing manufacturer to donate pajamas to each student for the event. In addition, you might seek donations so that each family can select a book to take home at the end of each family night. This type of activity helps build community, encourage respect for other families, and promote literacy activities for the entire family.

Rohanna's list of short-term objectives and long-term goals is shown in Table 10.2. The objectives are measurable within a somewhat short period of time. The project goals are farther reaching and will take time to accomplish—possibly over the course of the next year or two.

Table 10.2	Rohanna's Action Plan—Partnership Goals and Objectives

Short-term objectives	Sixth-grade students will interact with high school students to gain help in completing homework.
	Sixth-grade students will complete their homework each week.
Long-term goals	Students will build responsibility through completing homework now and in the future.
	Students will build relationships and strengthen interpersonal and intrapersonal skills.
	Students will improve academically, as well as complete homework.

SOURCE: Used with permission of Rohanna Ylagan.

Identifying Potential Barriers

When forming teacher-parent-community partnerships, barriers must be anticipated in order to optimize collaboration and the partnership potential. When I conducted an informal survey of my graduate students—all of whom are elementary or middle school teachers—they suggested specific barriers that they encounter when developing partnerships with families and the community. They said that first and foremost they are overwhelmed with responsibilities related to accountability requirements that involve standardized testing and other district-mandated procedures, which makes it difficult to find time to actually seek partnerships. Second, they said that there is often an "us versus them" mentality when dealing with families. Usually, teachers are on one side and families are on the other without ever truly coming together to share in the education of their students. Furthermore, these teachers indicated that many teachers in their schools do not always value families as partners because of the time and communication involved. Nevertheless, these teachers acknowledged that the "us versus them" view leads to both parties having different agendas, poor communication, and an overall disconnection. This perpetual cycle makes it challenging for families and teachers to be on the same page at the same time. This creates a large barrier before a partnership is ever created.

Therefore, it is critical that all partners anticipate barriers when planning collaborative educational projects. In addition, unanticipated barriers must be noted and addressed as they arise. Even partnerships that have existed over a long period of time still must address ongoing barriers and new barriers. The most prevalent barriers exist in the form of management, time, commitment, culture, language, power, and trust. These are considered critical barriers because they are the most difficult to address and overcome. Failure to take specific action related to these barriers may result in demise of a partnership. Other less critical barriers also exist and may be more specifically related to a particular project or group. Consider reviewing some of the different barriers discussed in Chapter 8 to guide you in determining potential barriers.

As part of your action plan, it is important to determine the barriers you will need to address and overcome when creating your action plan. These barriers should be specific to the partners and the project itself. For example, if you are partnering with families from diverse cultures and ethnic backgrounds, then you will have to address various cultural barriers. If you are partnering with a local corporation, then you will have to address the business needs and time associated with the project goals. Remember that barriers challenge the development and sustainability of educational partnerships. They must be acknowledged, addressed, and overcome in order for a partnership to be successful.

Rohanna's outline of barriers related to her Learners Club partnership action plan is given in the following "Notes From the Classroom."

Notes From the Classroom: Rohanna's Action Plan—Outline of Barriers

Time: Time may be an issue when schedules need to be taken into consideration. Working out a schedule that works with both the high school students and the elementary students, as well as principals and teachers, will take time to figure out since schedules in a regular school day are never set. There may be last-minute assemblies, meetings, IEPs [individual education plans], testing, grade-level activities, field trips, and so on. Time may also be a barrier when some students work at a different pace as well.

Inexperience: In this case, since this "Learners Club" is a very first-time proposal and program, inexperience can be a barrier merely because this would be a learning experience for every partner involved. Inexperience can be a barrier when there are no official rules, procedures, or knowledge of how things should be done. For this reason, it is important that all involved are well informed and communication is always open.

Communication: To ensure communication is open the tone has to be set from the start. All partners need to know and feel they can and ought to communicate any concerns or suggestions anytime. Showing appreciation and being welcoming can affect setting that tone. Keeping doors open and offering an e-mail address and school telephone number can help as well. To prevent any miscommunication and keep all parties informed, monthly newsletters can be made to inform what is and what will be occurring throughout the "Learners Club." Everything should be translated into Spanish as well, whether it is printed material going home or an orientation to the program for the parents.

Language: Because a Spanish-speaking community dominates the target population of this program, there may be a language barrier for non-English-speaking parents. For this reason, it is very important to ensure all printed materials and meetings be translated and conducted in their primary language. Assuring parents that there are Spanish-speaking personnel available to translate for phone calls is important as well.

SOURCE: Used with permission of Rohanna Ylagan.

Timeline for Implementation

It is important to provide a timeline of events within your action plan. Include dates and specific activities and/or benchmarks. **Benchmarks** are pivotal events or activities that take place throughout the project. Rohanna's detailed list of activities within the Learners Club project is provided in Table 10.3. In this case, Rohanna is responsible for the implementation of all of the events and activities described. However, when you are writing your plan, you may want to include a third column where you can write the name of the person or persons who are responsible for a particular task.

Epstein et al. (2002) suggest that schools create action teams to create or provide feedback related to the action plan. This action team would also participate in activities such as assessing present practices, making suggestions for improvements, implementing specific activities, conducting assessments and evaluations, and coordinating events. Epstein et al. suggest that the action team include at least three teachers from different grade levels, three parents who have children in different grades, at least one administrator, and one member of the community. The leader of the group might be a parent, a community member, or a teacher.

Table 10.3	Rohanna's Action Plan—Timeline of Events

Month	Events and Activities
1. September	Contact and propose program to principal of Danford Hills High School.
	Collaborate with high school principal to create rules, procedures, guidelines, and handbook of program.
	Obtain list of recommended high school teachers willing to participate in program.
	Send out surveys to high school students, elementary students, and parents.
2. October	Collect and analyze data from surveys.
	Create lists of (a) students in need of program's services and (b) students not in need of program's services.
	Match high school students with elementary students according to interest surveys and needs.
	Match students not in need of program with other high school students.
3. November	Speak to high school students and present program (go over rules, guidelines, and procedures).
	Model examples of sessions.
	Give each participating high school student handbook of guidelines.
	Conduct presentation night to participating parents and elementary students to explain and present program.
	Give each participating elementary student and parents handbook of guidelines for program.

Month	Events and Activities
4. December	"Get to Know You" session to introduce high school students to elementary students.
	Go over rules and expectations with high school students and elementary students.
	Show students locations of homework sessions.
	Go over schedules for homework sessions.
5. January	Start program (meeting twice a week each month).
	Hand each student schedules and map of where to report.
	Distribute a question-and-answer survey with a Likert scale at the end of the month to elementary and high school students. The survey will address concerns, such as whether the students have been matched well, whether or not they are being provided with beneficial help, why or why not, and so on.
	Collect and analyze data from surveys.
	Make any new adjustments to switching partners.
	Assign a New Year's resolution writing project for students to work on together.
6. February	Students will continue working on homework, as well as a valentine-making project.
	Monitor, observe, and conduct informal interviews with partners together to assess how everything is going and, if not, what can be done to change or meet needs.
7. March	Assign pairs to work on a research project for ancient civilizations utilizing a variety of resources (school library, encyclopedias, books, computer lab, etc.).
	Conduct informal interview midmonth to assess if more time is needed for project.
8. April	Partners work on oral presentation for ancient civilization project and focus on effective presentation and communication skills.
	Conduct a question-and-answer survey of elementary school students midmonth to assess if they need more help on the oral presentation project and what skills they need help on that they aren't getting from their high school partner.
	Elementary school students give oral presentations at the end of the month.
9. May	Create memory books together.
	Provide end-of-program party with food, fun, and games.
	Give an open-ended question survey to high school students and elementary school students.

SOURCE: Ylagan (2005, pp. 10–11). Used with permission of Rohanna Ylagan.

Evaluation of the Partnership

The final step when creating an action plan is to describe how you will assess and evaluate the partnership. Using assessment and evaluation tools can assist schools and partners in collecting evidence to support and improve the partnership over time. Assessments should take place during the course of the partnership activities (**formative assessment**), and an evaluation can take place after the project or part of the project is complete (**summative evaluation**).

Evaluation often means different things to different people. Note the difference between assessment and evaluation. Many educators use assessment and evaluation to describe the same process even though the two terms differ in meaning. **Assessment** is an ongoing process that influences planning and implementing educational practices. **Evaluation** refers to a benchmark or a cumulative event at which decisions are made in relation to a particular project. Thus, it is important that you assess your partnership project at different times to revise areas in need. It is also important that you conduct a summative evaluation at the end of an academic year or at some other time to make decisions about issues such as the success of the project, whether the project should continue, or how the project should continue. A formative assessment takes place while the project is being implemented. A summative evaluation takes place at the conclusion of the project or at some other integral point. Making sure that both the formative assessment and the summative evaluation are linked back to your project goals and objectives should be a priority to determine to what extent the partnership is meeting the expectations of all parties. When determining formative assessments and summative evaluation plans, consider how the evidence will be gathered, what evidence will be gathered, and when it will be collected. Rohanna's formative assessment and summative evaluation is included in the following "Notes From the Classroom."

Notes From the Classroom: Rohanna's Action Plan—Formative Assessment and Summative Evaluation Plans

Formative Assessment

Different types of formative assessment will occur throughout the 9-month program after the "Learners Club" sessions start. One of the first types of formative assessment is a survey with a Likert scale that includes five choices for each question asked. This Likert scale will be distributed to the high school and elementary students individually at the end of the first month. This assessment will address concerns, such as if students feel they were matched appropriately and whether or not they are being sufficiently helped. Toward the end of the second month, all students will be monitored, observed, and informally interviewed as partners. The informal interview will assess whether everything is going smoothly and, if there are any concerns, what could be done to meet needs. About midmonth after the partner informal interview, another informal interview of all the partners will be conducted to assess how their project is going and whether or not more time is needed. Toward the middle of the following month, elementary students will be individually interviewed to assess whether or not they need more assistance with preparation of their current project, which is delivering an oral presentation. The last assessment that will be given to the elementary school students in the following month is an open-ended question survey. This will assess the benefits and experiences of the students, as well as any suggestions for an improved program next year.

Summative Evaluation

The summative evaluation that will occur at the end of the program will assess whether or not the program's objectives have been met and will determine if the project should be continued. The first part will focus on whether homework was being accomplished and will include an analysis of homework logs. In order to learn if any meaningful relationships were built with high school partners, data will be collected and analyzed in the form of a survey with open-ended questions given to the elementary students at the end of the program. Simple observations, as well as checklists for desired behaviors, can be created to assess students' behaviors in small- and large-group settings with classmates as well. This assessment can demonstrate students' strengthened intrapersonal and social skills, which may have been affected by the social benefits gained from their relationships with high school students.

SOURCE: Used with permission of Rohanna Ylagan.

Cite Your References

Any references related to the literature that you reviewed or provided to support your rationale should be included on the final page of your action plan. It is essential that your partnership project be informed by educational research and best practices. Past and current literature informs you of the challenges and what has been most successful within specific curriculum areas or partnership areas. The following "Notes From the Classroom" shows a listing of articles that informed Rohanna's development of her action plan and the Learners Club partnership project. These articles are cited in the "Notes From the Classroom" sections earlier in this chapter.

> ### Notes From the Classroom:
> ### Rohanna's Action Plan—Sources Cited
>
> Buttery, T. J., & Anderson, P. (1999). Community, school, and parent dynamics: A synthesis of literature and activities. *Teacher Education Quarterly, 26*(4), 111–120.
> Epstein, J. L. (2001). *School, family, and community partnerships.* Boulder, CO: Westview Press, a Member of the Perseus Books Group.
> Finn, J. D. (1998). Parental engagement that makes a difference. *Education Leadership, 55,* 20–24.
> Lewis, R., & Morris, J. (1998). Communities for children. *Educational Leadership, 55,* 34–36.
> Neuman, S. B. (1995). Reading together: A community-supported parent tutoring program. *The Reading Teacher, 49,* 120–129.
>
> **SOURCE:** Used with permission from Rohanna Ylagan.

Appendix

Any materials or other information that may be relevant to implementation of the proposed partnership should be included in an appendix. For example, you may want to include a copy of a survey that you intend to distribute to families or a copy of the interview questions that you will ask during a community focus group.

Tips for Teachers From Teachers for Creating an Action Plan

Specific tips are listed to help you begin thinking about creating an action plan. Teachers in my university graduate classes over the past 11 years helped create these tips. These teachers always suggest that you begin with a topic or project that you are committed to and that you are passionate about.

1. Start with a topic or issue that you are passionate about and create an action plan that relates to it.

2. Use your findings from your case study to serve as a front-end assessment or needs assessment to develop your plan.

3. Create a specific timeline of events and partners who are responsible for each task.

4. Discuss how you are going to recruit and motivate participants to be an integral part of the project.

5. Your turn: Can you think of additional tips?

Implementing Your Action Plan

The action plan is the first and most important step when developing and planning for a partnership project. The real challenge, however, is implementing an idea and putting it into action. In order to implement your project successfully, you should not try to do it alone. This is why it is referred to as a partnership project. Certainly you will have some individuals who work with you as real decision makers and other people who work within the project itself as partial decision makers and participants. Nevertheless, you *must* have a variety of people who are committed to seeing the partnership work, based on the goals, objectives, and proposed activities. Issues related to connecting with additional resources and sustaining the partnerships will be discussed in Chapter 11.

Peer tutoring is an effective way to enhance academic achievement and encourage better social and emotional development. Peer tutoring is effective with all students, including students with special learning needs or disabilities.

Enhancing Learning for Students With Special Needs: Peer Tutoring

Peer tutoring usually involves two students working together where one student who has mastered certain skills or knowledge works together with another student who is less developed in this area. Peer tutoring can promote academic achievement in all students, particularly those with special needs.

Fuchs et al. (1997) inquired into a classroom peer tutoring program in reading with low achievers with special needs, low achievers without special needs, and average achievers. Twelve schools participated and were assigned to random experimental or control groups. Data indicate that students in peer tutoring classrooms performed better in reading regardless of the type of learner. This study shows that students can also work together as partners to enhance learning.

(Continued)

(Continued)

You may want to consider a student-student-teacher partnership for your action plan that involves peer tutoring. Here are a few steps to get you started:

1. Create a survey and ask students what they are good at and what they would like help with. In addition, ask such questions as "What is your favorite book?" and "What is your favorite thing to do?" This will help teachers have a better understanding of students' self-concepts of their abilities.

2. Once teachers have a better understanding of students' view of themselves, it is then easier to pair students to work together based on their responses to the survey.

3. For younger students, have them draw pictures or make smiling or frowning faces related to their favorite things and perceived abilities.

Chapter Summary

This chapter provided information about why an action plan is important when developing and implementing any type of partnership—small or large. It provided you with information related to locating potential partners to participate in your plan. Steps and procedures were featured to help guide the process. These steps include (a) fully describing the partnership program that you would like to develop; (b) incorporating one or more of Epstein's six types of involvement (i.e., parenting, communicating, volunteering, learning at home, decision making, and community collaborations) into the plan; (c) identifying specific partners who will be involved and their roles; (d) developing overarching goals and specific objectives that will guide your plan; (e) determining potential barriers and ways to address them; (f) creating a timeline of events, activities, and responsibilities; and (g) describing formative assessment and summative evaluation procedures.

CASE STUDIES

These two case studies describe action plans that were completed by two different teachers. The first case study is adapted from an action plan written by Jeanie Lee (2005) in which she describes her rationale for creating a Family Art Night, gives a description of the project, and explains how she will assess and evaluate the project. The second case study was developed by Caroline Ngo (2008), who created a plan to inquire into family views and promote more parent involvement at her school.

❖ **Case Study 10.1: Creating a Family Art Night**

Rationale for Developing the Family Art Night

"Daisy Drive" Elementary School has a diverse student body that includes about 47% White students, 16% Hispanic students, 35% Asian students, and a combined 2% Filipino, African American, Pacific Islander, and American Indian students. Many students in the school are from non-English language backgrounds. Despite its high levels of parent participation, Daisy Drive Elementary has witnessed very few ethnic minority parents who are involved in school events. Lee (2005) believes that more parents would participate in school activities if their participation did not require the use of English, so she "decided that hosting Family Art Nights would be a useful and exciting way to bring together families of all backgrounds, allow students all the benefits of art education, and target other desirable goals of Daisy Drive Elementary School" (p. 3).

A Description and Plan

Lee (2005) plans to hold a total of six Family Art Nights during the school year. Each event will be presented through the eyes of a famous artist such as Vincent van Gogh or Georgia O'Keeffe. The event will include a pizza dinner and hands-on art projects related to the celebrated artist. Local artists, art instructors, and classroom teachers will be invited to participate and speak about what the artist and his or her art means to them. The Family Art Nights will include multimedia slides, posters, prints, and videos featuring each artist. At the end of the evening, families will be encouraged to create their own work of art. Local art stores in the community will donate many of the art supplies. Books and posters will be obtained from the public library and school library.

Formative Assessment and Summative Evaluation

Students and their parents will be asked to complete a brief questionnaire at the conclusion of each Family Art Night. Children can assist their parents in completing the questions in English or in their native language. Teachers and parents will analyze the questionnaire responses to determine if changes need to be made before the next art event. The final summative evaluation will include a larger questionnaire that will have families provide their ideas about the effectiveness of the program and what they gained from the experience given a list of outcomes (with space on the questionnaire for their own ideas): learning art with their child, gaining knowledge about famous artists, increased family-school relations, and other similar prompts. A group of teachers and parents will determine themes related to the questionnaire responses and use them to plan future Family Art Nights.

SOURCE: Used with permission of Jeanie Lee.

❖ **Case Study 10.2: Promoting More Family Involvement**

Voice of Caroline Ngo, Third-Grade Teacher

I am a third-grade teacher at a school that has been known to have low parental involvement. Most of the parents whose students attend the school speak Spanish and understand a limited amount of English.

Recently, the school has been making an effort to reach out to the parents with educational programs and parental involvement opportunities such as the Parent Institute for Quality Education, also known as PIQE, and the Parent Teacher Association (PTA). I have heard that parental involvement can improve student motivation, self-esteem, and academics. Here are some responsibilities that I am planning to promote at my school:

I will be including my third-grade team, the school principal, the assistant principal, families, and students as partners. The following is an outline of the roles and responsibilities of the partners involved:

1. Teacher Responsibilities

   - Communicate parenting information and suggestions in a newsletter every month.
   - Distribute flyers and pamphlets on parenting classes or health care offered in the local community.
   - Complete at least two home visits.

2. Family Responsibilities

   - Read all information sent home in the parenting newsletter.
   - Attend two parenting workshops or discussion groups.
   - Agree to participate in a home visit by a teacher, if chosen.
   - Provide a home environment that offers a quiet area for the child to study and includes adequate school materials when needed.

3. Student Responsibilities

   - Give parents any communication newsletters that are sent home.
   - Inform parents about what they have learned in school that day.
   - Complete homework and ask parents for help when needed.
   - Respect and comply with teachers and parents.

4. Principal Responsibilities

   - Support and encourage the partnership established among families, teachers, and students.
   - Assist teachers in organizing and planning activities for this partnership.
   - Give advice that could be helpful in this partnership.

5. Office Staff (and Teacher) Responsibility

   - Assist in translating information for Spanish-speaking parents.

Front-End Assessment

I sent home questionnaire surveys to parents, in both Spanish and English. The survey consisted of about seven questions. One of the questions required parents to check the type of activities from a list of eight types of parent involvement activities they had participated in. Another type of question required parents to rate four statements, according to their importance, relating to why they enjoyed being involved at the school.

I interviewed the school principal and a community office liaison. The interview questions were prepared ahead of time and were open-ended. Results from the study supported the need for parenting resources and better parent communication. Parents expressed motivation to help their child do well in school but lacked the "know-how" to effectively help their child. Parents were interested in attending parenting classes. They did express that attending classes on a regular basis would be difficult because they had to take care of children and other responsibilities at home. Parents were also interested in receiving literature sent home about parenting.

Short-Term Objectives and Long-Term Goals

Short-term goals	• Parents and families will provide a home environment that supports student learning. • Parents will participate in more school events based on their responses to surveys. • Teachers and the principal will promote parent communication and parenting resources on a regular basis.
Long-term goals	• Parents will experience an increase in their self-confidence to help their child at home and at school. • Parents will obtain knowledge to seek resources dealing with child care, health care, or parenting. • Students will experience increased academic success. • Teachers will have better communication and relationships with families.

SOURCE: Ngo (2008, pp. 8–9).

Formative Assessment

In order to effectively and accurately evaluate this partnership, a variety of formative assessments will occur throughout the 9-month program. The first type of assessment will be an interest survey with open-ended questions where parents must rank the importance of certain responses and volunteer activities. This survey will be sent home with the students' Welcome Back to School packet. This feedback will be used to guide the research and development of future parental involvement activities inside and outside of the classrooms. Informal, open-ended interviews will be conducted during parent conferences to inquire about volunteer interests at the school. This information will be used to plan and develop future partnerships with families that focus on parental involvement.

Summative Evaluation

The summative evaluation will occur at the end of the program and will be in the form of another open-ended question survey. The goal is to assess whether or not the program's objectives have been met and to determine the future needs of the project. The survey will focus on whether parents feel they have adequately met the needs of their involvement interests. Parents are also encouraged to provide comments and suggestions on how parental involvement can improve next year. These assessments will be informative in deciding whether parental involvement was effective in encouraging parents to play a bigger role in their children's education.

SOURCE: Used with permission of Caroline Ngo.

❖ Reflecting on the Cases

1. Discuss the culturally relevant elements of the Family Art Night and Ms. Ngo's family involvement plan. Describe ways that you can make both projects more accessible and more culturally relevant to all families who attend the school.

2. Describe how you would recruit families to participate more fully in school events such as the Family Art Night and parent involvement activities.

3. Think of additional ways to collect information (besides questionnaires/surveys) to enhance a formative assessment and a summative evaluation related to these two projects.

Activities for Further Development

1. Describe ways that you can determine or measure the success of a family or community partnership within a K–8 school.

2. Describe what a traditional 20th-century partnership looked like and what a 21st-century partnership should look like in regard to inclusive practices, culturally relevant activities, and joint decision making.

3. Create a set of goals and objectives for a partnership plan that you would like to develop that involves a local museum, a university, families, or students. Discuss how you will assess and evaluate whether or not your objectives have been met during the project and at the end of the project.

4. Create a list of ways that teachers can promote more family involvement while considering barriers such as time, language, comfort level, and other factors.

Additional Reading and Information

Epstein, J. L., Sanders, M. G., Simon, B. S., Salinas, K. C., Jansorn, N. R., & Van Voorhis, F. L. (2002). *School, family and community partnerships: Your handbook for action* (2nd ed.). Thousand Oaks, CA: Corwin. This book provides redefinitions of Epstein's six types of involvement, provides strategies for developing action plans, and provides sample surveys and worksheets.

Mundry, S. E., Britton, E., Raizen, S. A., & Loucks-Horsley, S. (2000). *Designing successful professional meetings and conferences in education: Planning, implementation, and evaluation.* Thousand Oaks, CA: Corwin. This book provides principles and strategies related to designing effective meetings. The information will be helpful if you are planning a partnership that includes professional meetings and other formal events.

Stringer, E. T. (2007). *Action research* (3rd ed.). Thousand Oaks, CA: Sage. This book provides information about community-based research practices, tools to help teachers engage in the action research process, and information about conducting literature reviews.

Stufflebeam, D. L., Madaus, G. F., & Kellaghan, T. (2000). *Evaluation models: Viewpoints on educational and human services evaluation* (2nd ed.). New York: Springer. This book provides information and strategies related to educational evaluation. It also includes formative assessment and summative evaluation techniques and examples.

The *Developing Industry/Education Partnerships* Web site provides a planning guide that encourages students to gain career awareness and academic enrichment skills. The site provides examples and strategies related to creating partnerships between schools and different industries: http://www.buildingcareers.org/planning

The *Learning Partnerships Planning Workbook* is an online workbook to help educators and organizations plan for partnership meetings and other events from the University of Massachusetts: http://www-unix.oit.umass.edu/~aes1/LPPlanWorkbook.pdf

11

Implementing and Sustaining Successful Partnerships

After reading this chapter, you should have a better understanding of:

- a review of characteristics of successful partnerships;
- misconceptions related to families and schools as partners;
- characteristics of professional learning communities and curriculum mapping;
- the benefits of professional peer mentoring and coaching;
- teachers as reflective practitioners;
- steps for implementing and sustaining partnerships over time;
- long-running partnership examples;
- local library resources and activities; and
- implementing and sustaining partnerships with families.

Table 11.1	Prior Knowledge and Beliefs Organizer

Long-Running Partnership Examples	Why They Have Sustained Over Time

Table 11.1 asks you to create a list of long-running educational partnerships you know of or have experience with and list reasons why you believe the partnership has stood the test of time.

Characteristics of Successful Partnerships Revisited

Throughout this text, we have discussed that an educational partnership involves two or more parties who come together for the common good to enhance teaching and learning. Partners can include anyone who is interested in or committed to common goals and who will work collaboratively to make decisions. Educational partnerships can include families, schools, professionals, and the broader educational community. Partnerships are established to provide the best education possible for all children. The following characteristics are at the forefront of partnerships that have proven successful over time:

- Collegial relations
- Support (e.g., financial, emotional, buy-in)
- Shared responsibility for implementing the partnership
- Respect for all partners
- Appreciation and acknowledgement of cultural and linguistic differences
- Shared common goals for the purpose of the partnership
- Accountability and positive outcomes
- High returns for all parties
- Commitment to the goals of the partnership
- Leadership to plan, enact, and assess the partnership

True partnerships are mutually created and involve ongoing trust, communication, and respect from all parties. In addition, all groups and individuals must feel that they benefit in some way while making sure that activities and events are culturally relevant, feasible, and a high priority. Prior to this chapter, basic steps were provided to assist you when building community-school-family collaborative projects. The first step is to identify the type of partnership that will enhance the curriculum most and that will fit with the needs of the school, families, and students. Second, explore partnership possibilities in the community from a list of potential businesses, museums, libraries, clubs, senior citizens, or other groups. Third, contact potential partners and meet face-to-face with them to discuss a possible partnership. Fourth, work with partners and other stakeholders to develop a plan of action. Finally, seek funding, if appropriate, from a variety of government and private grants to provide resources, staffing, and supplies to implement small- and large-scale partnership projects. Once you have the basic planning steps completed, you will need to implement and sustain the partnership project. This chapter will discuss ways to accomplish that. Long-running educational partnerships will be featured as a way to show which partnerships are sustained over time and why.

Parents, News, and Misconceptions

Previously, we discussed the *Time* magazine cover headline "What Teachers Hate About Parents." This is not exactly the kind of press that educators are looking for when they are trying to improve relationships with students and their families. One article within this issue was titled "Parents Behaving Badly" and created a bit of outrage in some

SOURCE: Used with permission of Tom Baker.

Teachers and parents work together to organize an art community event for families and the community.

communities (Gibbs, 2005). The article discusses how parents argue with teachers because they do not agree with their discipline strategies, teaching methods, content, or other issues. The article also discusses how parents are looking for the perfect teacher while at the same time teachers are looking for the perfect parents. Teachers in the article claim that the thing they like most about their job is working with children but the thing they like least about their job is communicating with parents. This article was written from the perspective of teachers who proclaim that parent involvement can be negative, particularly with overbearing parents. In contrast, there are also families who never come to school, never communicate with their child's teacher, and would never think of second-guessing the teacher's decision about content or instructional method. Therefore, we have a continuum where at one end of the spectrum we have parents who feel so comfortable that they virtually pester the teacher and make his or her job more difficult, and then at the other end of the spectrum we have other parents who believe that they should give all of the educational responsibility to the teacher without providing much feedback or making any contributions. We have heard stories of parents who bring their lawyers to parent-teacher conferences, and we have also heard stories of parents who cannot attend parent-teacher conferences because they work three jobs and have no transportation or child care. It is important for teachers to take a look at all families and treat them with respect—without exception. Yes, there are going to be times when parents on both sides of the continuum make teachers feel so frustrated that they have a difficult time doing their job. In this chapter we will investigate the process of assessing the needs to obtain multiple perspectives and perceptions of families, teachers, students, and the broader community to promote a more collaborative working relationship for all.

Although the magnitude and frequency of parent involvement have been linked to a family's educational experiences and cultural beliefs, we know that all parents want their child to succeed. However, many parents feel uncomfortable talking with the teacher or even taking a step into the school building. The same *Time* magazine news article that describes the disconnect between teachers and parents also reports that 90% of new teachers thought that involving families in the education of their children was a top priority even though 73% of new teachers in this group thought of families and teachers as adversaries (Gibbs, 2005). Therefore, it is entirely up to the school and district to set a positive or negative precedence related to relationships with families. Administrators and teachers can have a tremendous impact on how much or how little positive family involvement happens in a school and how the school is set up to welcome parents or keep them away.

Professional Education Partnerships

Professional partnerships exist among teachers throughout a school district, throughout a school, or in collaboration with universities. Teachers can build professional education partnerships through peer mentoring, collaborating on class projects, creating teacher networks, and developing school-university partnership activities. Some examples related to professional partnerships among educators are described more fully in the next section.

Professional Learning Communities

Creating a community among teachers contributes to the overall educational achievement and the social/emotional development of students. Collaborative work between teachers is not limited to the classroom. It may involve a series of activities and ongoing relationships within the school, the school district, and beyond. School staff, administration, and teachers work together as colleagues within a mini community each day. Louis, Marks, and Kruse (1996) reported that how teachers interact with each other outside the classroom impacts their overall development as professionals. **Professional learning communities** is a term popularized by Peter Senge's (1990) *The Fifth Discipline: The Art and Practice of the Learning Organization.* Senge visualized a group of teachers who would collaborate and share their knowledge and skills to enhance student learning. The overall goal of professional learning communities is to restructure schools and their interactions—also called "reculturing." Eaker, Dufour, and Dufour (2002) outlined characteristics of professional learning communities and provided a list of steps and procedures for teachers to follow to encourage reculturization of schools. This reculturization moves away from a culture where teachers work in the solitude of their own classrooms and moves toward their working together as learners and collaborators. Eaker et al. outlined the following characteristics of professional learning communities:

1. A shared vision and common goals

2. Collaborative educator teams that focus on learning

3. Collaborative inquiry into the best teaching and learning practices

4. Implementation of action research and experimentation

5. Commitment by all to focus on improvement

6. Outcomes-based initiatives

Based on this view, teaching is viewed as a dynamic process that includes continuous learning and collaboration among educators. All educators and staff within the school share the responsibility for ensuring student learning and development. Shared decision making about student learning and achievement is at the heart of the *professional learning communities* philosophy. The overarching goal is for teachers to inquire into what students are actually learning versus what teachers are teaching. Together, groups of teachers revise lesson plans and assessment strategies. The entire process is collaborative and focuses on the students, their strengths, their needs, and their learning.

Teaming for the Learning of All Children (TLC) is a program that uses the *professional learning communities* approach to differentiate instruction for students (Bento, Brooks, Cunningham, & Robbins, 2007). A TLC team is organized in grades K–5 to service all students, particularly students needing extra instructional support. The TLC team consists of a resource teacher, a regular classroom teacher, and two teacher assistants. During the "supplementary skills" portion of the day, students are grouped according to their instructional level for reading and mathematics. The groups are "fluid," and students can move in and out of groups according to their needs and individualized pace. This approach differs from the traditional blue bird–red bird model where students are assigned to a group and stay in that group during the school year. Teachers meet weekly to collaborate and discuss **scaffolding** strategies that are most effective and challenges that they face within the groups. Scaffolding involves supporting students as they acquire new skills and strategies. The teacher provides assistance to help students acquire greater skills as they become more sophisticated in their learning and development. Teachers are proud of the success that the program has brought to students and families, but they have indicated a few challenges: (a) taking time to organize, educate, and create a sense of professional learning community within the school; (b) communicating with families about the changes occurring within the structure of traditional classrooms to improve student learning; and (c) the rigid schedules that all teachers must follow at the same time to keep instruction flowing within different groups. This TLC model, like all restructuring efforts and changes, takes time to create buy-in from teachers, students, and families.

Peer Mentoring and Coaching

Peer mentoring or coaching involves two or more teachers who support each other during the teaching and learning process. This is a professional development strategy that takes place in the teachers' own classroom. According to Joyce and Showers (1988), peer coaching is designed to implement innovations and build a community of teachers who continuously study their craft, develop shared language, and develop a common understanding of new knowledge. Peer coaching is continuous and can be experimental in nature. Teachers should feel free to explore new teaching strategies while gaining valuable feedback and support from their colleagues. This process is very different from supervision, evaluation, or mentors who tell teachers what they should and should not be doing. By engaging in peer coaching strategies, teachers are considered equal as they develop relationships to enhance their teaching and students' learning.

Lemlech (1995) provides additional nontraditional models of professional development for teachers such as dialog journal writing and professional reading groups. With dialog journals, two or more individuals communicate professionally via journals. This can involve principals and teachers or teachers and other teachers. With professional reading groups, a teacher or principal can select a book or a series of articles related to a mutually negotiated topic. These articles are read and discussed in study groups. It is important that these readings be not mandatory but voluntary to provide empowerment and choice.

Curriculum Mapping

Curriculum maps are tools that educators use to record data related to content, skills, assessment, resources, and state content standards. Curriculum mapping is a dynamic collaborative process where teachers organize information and provide authentic evidence related to what is happening in the classroom (Jacobs, 1997). Curriculum mapping focuses on (a) communication, (b) curricular dialog, and (c) coherence. Communication involves Internet-based mapping structures that allow teachers access to planned and actual activities. These activities serve as an impetus to spark collaborative conversations about teaching and learning. These conversations are referred to as curricular dialog where teachers work within a collegial environment to make decisions about curriculum and instructional practices. Coherence involves inquiry into what was planned and what was actually taught. It involves reflective practice as teachers examine the horizontal curriculum (over the course of a year) and the vertical curriculum (over the course of students' academic experience). Curriculum mapping activities require that teachers utilize technology as they take on collaborative roles as learners and decision makers.

National Board Certification and Collaboration

Applying for National Board Certification as a teacher has many rewards. Many teachers decide to engage in the intensive reflective process with a colleague. Although the entries must be written separately, having someone who is experiencing the same intensive reflection and writing process can be helpful. The next "Notes From the Classroom" section features the voice of a third-grade teacher, Kristine, who was supported and motivated by a colleague when working on certification. She discusses why she enjoyed working with a colleague and how the National Board Certification process helped her identify partnership possibilities with families and the community.

Notes From the Classroom: Seeking National Board Certification

Voice of Kristine, Third-Grade Teacher

Participating and completing the National Board for Professional Teaching Standards assessment and portfolio changed my teaching and my outlook regarding family and community outreach. Working with a teacher colleague throughout the entire process helped me when I needed support and needed to discuss the challenges I faced as I reflected on my teaching activities. As a teacher in an upper-income community with high parent and community involvement, it seemed an easy task to accomplish. In my entry I wrote about my involvement in the Public Science Day that was sponsored by the American Association for the Advancement of Science (AAAS) in collaboration with KCET Public Television. I was given the opportunity to make the connection through a university professor. My principal enthusiastically agreed to a school-wide plan that involved all grade levels, parents, and community members. The event included participation of 40 selected students to attend the AAAS conference and present their projects to professional scientists. Parents not only helped prepare presentation materials but also attended with their children. The public television station provided a school-wide science assembly. The community was involved through gardening projects and an open house held at the school. The events were very successful, and although they took a lot of work, multiple groups benefited from the collaboration.

The challenges that I did not face that are continuous obstacles to many teachers are lack of parent support and lack of administrative support. It is easy to be successful with help, but those teachers who work in communities without parent involvement, for whatever reason, have a much larger battle to fight. The process of National Board Certification helped me appreciate how families and communities can come together to bring enriching and meaningful experiences to children, but the larger question is how to involve families and communities across the board, in all neighborhoods.

SOURCE: Used with permission of Kristine Quinn.

Teachers as Reflective Practitioners

Before beginning any educational partnership, it is important for teachers to critically reflect about challenges, questions, and concerns related to teaching and learning. Reflection is a professional development strategy throughout all disciplines. In fact, Schon (1987) encourages the use of reflection in varied professions to analyze, discuss, evaluate, and change practice. When teachers reflect about their practice and needs, they can delineate their thinking and anticipate decisions needed to reach students and their families more effectively. Calderhead and Gates (1993) recommend reflection as part of teacher education to encourage

- analyzing, discussing, and evaluating instructional practice;
- fostering an appreciation of social and political contexts;

- evaluating moral and ethical issues;
- taking responsibility for professional growth;
- facilitating the development of each teacher's personal philosophy; and
- empowering teachers to influence future directions related to education.

Reflection can take place in the form of teacher journals, self-narratives, biographies, and life histories. Reflection in the form of journals or other instruments about day-to-day practices and concerns can lead to specific questions that direct the course of an educational case study. Reflections can include learning theories that impact your educational views, educational values that you hold, how this work will inform who you are as a teacher, and the historical contexts of your experiences with schools and partnership programs (Mills, 2003).

Implementing and Sustaining Educational Partnerships

Once a partnership is developed, it must be implemented. The true test of any partnership is its sustainability over time. Some experts have argued that the process of implementing the partnership is as important as the outcome and goals. The process is critical because of the interrelationships and tasks necessary to actually implement a project. Through time, partnerships change because of a variety of reasons including changes in leadership, goals, or priorities. The process and interrelationships must be strong to overcome inevitable changes. The first step in implementation, therefore, is to take a look at the plan of action (discussed in Chapter 10) and actually make it all happen. When implementing an action plan, there are a few steps that will help make it more successful: (a) creating an action team, (b) "selling" the partnership to others, (c) promoting empowered participation, and (d) encouraging ongoing communication.

Creating an Action Team

Epstein (2001) advocates the need for building an action team after an action plan is developed or when planning for a potential partnership. The action team participates in front-end assessment or needs assessments related to what is already happening educationally in the school, the community, and families. The team can work together to create an action plan or enact a current plan that has already been developed. The team should consist of people from a variety of perspectives such as teachers, students, administrators, and family and community members. A leader should be selected who can work effectively with all members of the team to implement the action plan and instill a sense of community for all. The team may consider creating charts, such as the following, to organize tasks and timelines to move the action plan forward.

What needs to be done?	Who will accomplish this?	By what date?

"Selling" the Partnership

Many people who were involved in developing the project will be motivated to promote the partnership and want it to succeed. Nevertheless, other people involved in the project, either directly or indirectly, will need to be "sold" on the value of the project for the purpose of encouraging broad participation and buy-in. Word of mouth remains one of the best ways to promote interest in any educational project. But it may take specific strategies to advertise the project and recruit participants. Once a project is established, it is easier to promote the value of the project based on past participants' testimonials and outcomes. The biggest challenge in promoting a new partnership is that there is no record of previous accomplishment. Nevertheless, a partnership program must adapt to the culture of the community, school, and context in which it exists. The success of the partnership will depend on how well it is accepted and how much it is valued by participants and stakeholders.

Once a partnership program is up and running, it is often advantageous to promote partnership accomplishments and activities in school e-mails, school newsletters, or community newspapers and during community events. Publicizing the activities allows all participants to demonstrate what they have gained as a result of the project, allows them to share their experiences, and instills in them a sense of pride for all the merit and accomplishments. In addition, partners can receive public recognition for their contributions, whether they are local businesses, teachers, students, or family members. Promoting the partnership in a variety of ways provides a link between the school and the broader community. Pictures of partnership activities and outcomes can be beneficial in all types of print and media. Better yet, have students take the photographs and write articles for their local newspaper.

Empowering Participation From Multiple Partners

When enacting an action plan, it is important to define specific roles of groups and individuals who will participate in overall project organization and activities. Part of this process includes formalizing roles and responsibilities of all involved including the organizers, the partners, and participants. Identify one or two liaisons within the community, particularly someone who lives within a diverse community, who can work among the school, the community, and families to promote and encourage broader participation in a project. At times compromises will have to be made within the action team, but the core goals and inclusion of multiple partners should remain a high priority. In addition, all individuals and organizational representatives should play a critical role in the decision-making processes. Diverse partners with real power will bring unique perspectives, skills, and knowledge to the project. Respect among all groups will lend itself to better communication, positive interactions, and worthwhile outcomes.

The environment where the partnership takes place should be welcoming and inviting for all who are involved so that each partner feels valued. William Foster (1986) redefines leadership and the importance of joint decision making and empowerment. He provides a framework for enhancing democratic decision making in schools, maintaining that schools should promote fluid participation where at times members of the school community may be leaders and at other times they may be followers. He describes leadership as an act that opens up conversations to all groups so that they may provide their own insights, ideas, and arguments. The notion is to create a power shift, while making sure that all perspectives are acknowledged and roles and responsibilities are equitably distributed.

Promoting Ongoing Communication

Successful partnerships seek feedback from all parties on a regular basis. This encourages ongoing collegial relationships and ensures that partnership activities are progressing according to everyone's expectations and satisfaction. When this happens, any needs and concerns can be addressed quickly and appropriately. Communication can take place in the form of weekly or monthly e-mail updates, monthly face-to-face meetings, or even video conferences. It is advantageous to organize regular meetings or e-mail updates in advance so that the expectations are known. In addition, questions such as the following should be asked of all stakeholders periodically to assess the partnership and lead the way for improvements:

- How are we doing?
- Do we see an improvement in children's emotional, social, or academic well-being (depending on the goals of the partnership)?
- How well are we connected with any community or family partners?
- What are the current concerns or barriers?
- What political, social, and cultural factors are acknowledged to enhance the partnership?

The partners involved in a project will likely have very busy schedules, whether it is a father who is working full-time or teachers and community members with an array of responsibilities. Therefore, meetings are most meaningful when tasks and discussions are focused and include consistent feedback.

Long-Running Partnership Examples

There is no magical formula for why some partnership programs progress and sustain themselves over time. However, we do know that adhering to characteristics such as respect, commitment, accountability, and shared goals contributes to a successful project. We also know that barriers can inhibit partnerships, even those developed with the best intentions. Some of the reasons that partnerships do not succeed or continue over time include a lack or loss of commitment, power struggles, or different cultural or personal priorities. Three well-known partnership programs that have stood the test of time will be discussed below. These programs include Junior Achievement, Drug Abuse Resistance Education (DARE), and Book It!

Junior Achievement

The Junior Achievement program is one of the oldest continuous partnership programs in the United States. The American Telephone and Telegraph Company, Strathmore Paper Company, and a senator from Massachusetts created the program in 1919. The first project started as an after-school program for high school students, and *Project Business* was integrated into middle schools in 1975. Cumulatively, the program initiates activities to help children in grades K–12 learn more about business and economics. The K–6 program includes seven sequential themes with five hands-on activities and two capstone projects. It is designed to teach students about their roles as individuals, consumers, and workers in a diverse cultural environment. About 112,000 volunteers work with students and teachers in the classroom by facilitating activities and sharing personal experiences. It has been estimated that Junior Achievement works with about 4 million children and youth each year throughout the world. So, why has this program succeeded for almost 100 years while other programs cease to exist after a few years? I am not sure we can truly know the answer to this question. We do know that the program operates through volunteers and relies on both corporate and individual funding to implement all activities. In theory, this would be a hardship because funding ebbs and flows through many education programs. However, the curriculum seems to be popular with schools because it provides real-world connections and has a name that many educators are familiar with. The partnership is more of an arms-length example but has been sustained over time because the activities and resources assist teachers with their curriculum needs rather than add more work to their busy day.

Drug Abuse Resistance Education (DARE)

DARE, the Drug Abuse Resistance Education program, is another long-standing program that allows students to interact with community police officers who share real experiences and the challenges and addictions people face when using drugs. The program was founded in Los Angeles in 1983 and now serves 75% of schools in the United States and in over 40 other countries. The primary mission of DARE is to provide children and families with information and skills needed to live drug and violence free. In addition, children are taught how to resist peer pressure and make good personal decisions. Local police officers visit classrooms and present the DARE curriculum. They offer personal stories and answer students' questions. The Monitoring the Future survey released by the National Institute on Drug Abuse in 2004 found that 600,000 fewer teenagers used drugs than in 2001. Rosenbaum (1998) conducted a 6-year study and found that students who participated in the DARE program demonstrated statistically significant improvements in social skills, attitudes toward police, attitudes toward drugs, and self-esteem.

The DARE program has been successful for a variety of reasons. One reason is that the police officers receive training in the areas of child development, instructional strategies, classroom management, and presentation techniques. In addition, many government leaders and teachers continue to support and acknowledge DARE as a worthwhile partnership among students, teachers, and the community given the nature of the program. The DARE curriculum teaches skills to resist peer pressure, gang activities, and drug use. Moreover, the program provides a positive link between the local police officers and schools to promote collaborative educational efforts.

Book It!

The Pizza Hut *Book It!* Program is another long-running program that started in 1985. About 20 million students in grades K–6 participate. In 1998, the program extended its partnership to preschool students and families. This partnership is explicit but requires little collaboration time between the corporation and schools. It does, however, outline steps and procedures for teachers, students, and families to work together as partners to encourage reading at home. Teachers are required to have conferences with students and set up individual reading goals based on the students' reading level. Teachers then distribute reading logs to the families of the students. Once students, with encouragement from their families, reach their goal, they are rewarded with an individual pizza. Students are able to set new goals each month. The information related to the program is provided for families in Spanish and English. One of the reasons for the long-term sustainability of this program is the mutual benefit to families (free pizza and reading motivation) and teachers (reading motivation and increased achievement in reading). Another reason that the program has continued is that Pizza Hut and schools have maintained their mutual commitment to the program. Teachers have enrolled in the program, and Pizza Hut continues offering rewards.

Local Libraries and Activities

Libraries offer a wealth of information about educational, informational, recreational, and cultural resources within local communities. However, families and teachers are not always aware of the array of resources including hands-on learning activities, active storytelling, computer skill training, career sessions, senior citizen programs, and more. Most libraries within the United States offer summer reading programs that can encourage children to continue reading during the summer months and long holidays. Some libraries offer family story time sessions that often integrate art, science, social studies, and other content areas. Other libraries offer basic computer skills, an introduction to the Internet, and e-mail basic training as a free service to the community. These free workshops are offered throughout the year and often include hands-on instruction with librarians or other volunteers. Many libraries within the United States publish an electronic or paper-copy newsletter each month outlining their classes available to the community, sometimes in multiple languages. All of these programs promote literacy and a love of reading while promoting community involvement. Teachers who inquire into the activities and events at their local libraries on a regular basis can share the wealth of resources with students and their families. Even better, teachers and schools may wish to form an ongoing partnership with the local library to promote literacy, cultural awareness, or other topics.

Notes From the Classroom: Royal Readers Program

One elementary school features a monthly "Royal Readers" program where parents, grandparents, aunts, uncles, siblings, friends, or older school peers are involved in promoting a love of reading. This is a small-scale partnership project that requires no outside funding and minimal leadership and organization. Family members or other individuals volunteer to read one of their favorite books to a class of students. The "Reader" is kept secret until he or she enters the classroom wearing a crown that is provided in the office when he or she arrives. The program, organized by parents, is enacted during the early morning hours to allow more readers to participate, particularly working family members and friends. This type of partnership empowers everyone involved to value the reader, the content, and the excitement of multiple readers in the classroom (Morse, Nygart, & Parrish, 2008).

Implementing and Sustaining Partnerships With Families

Parent involvement and home-school connections are positive and effective when families and teachers work together to promote healthy communication, a sense of community, and education as a partnership. There are a number of programs and initiatives in every school district in the United States to encourage more family involvement in the education of students. However, this can only take place equitably when all families are included and their culture and beliefs are valued. Many times, parent involvement is more widespread in some cultures than others. Sheldon (2003) found that parental educational interactions are mostly associated with belief systems rather than family demographics. Abrams and Gibbs (2002) studied mothers at three different elementary schools and found that some ethnic groups were underrepresented in leadership and power roles. They found that White, middle-class mothers felt an entitlement to certain tasks, while Latina mothers were overtly excluded from parent-teacher association committee decisions and meetings because of their translation needs. Therefore, it is the responsibility of the school and teachers to welcome and encourage families as critical partners. The creation of an action plan with specific goals and objectives and strategies to meet the needs of all families is an effective way to get started.

> ## What Research Says About Family Educational Involvement
>
> Students from families with a high level of parental involvement in educational activities had academic success rates that were around 30% higher than those of students from families with a low level of parental involvement. Parent expectations had the strongest relationship to higher achievement, particularly in adolescents (Fan & Chen, 1999).

Another way to find out more about families' views is to have them assess teachers. Yes, that's right. Have families assess teachers and redefine the traditional view that teachers are the only assessors. A teacher assessment is useful because it provides an even playing field with all partners able to contribute their views and participate in decision making. One sample survey from the Anchorage (Alaska) School District (Rich, 1998) asks parents to rate teachers on a scale from A (*strongly agree*) to E (*don't know*) on 16 statements such as (a) understands how my child learns and tries to meet known needs; (b) treats my child fairly, treats my child with respect, and understands that all children are special; and (c) has regular contact with me about my child's conduct and performance. Parents are also encouraged to respond to an open-ended question that asks them to describe what they like best and least about their child's teacher. Asking families to complete an anonymous needs assessment allows the teacher to gather information about students' families and their perceptions, priorities, and viewpoints. This type of needs assessment should be looked at as a positive venture where teachers and families can work toward a better understanding of each other and shared goals.

Another way for teachers to gain information about encouraging more family involvement is to complete a self-assessment about their current practice and beliefs. This assessment can be in the form of short-answer responses or open-ended reflective journal entries. Self-assessments are meant to be private and inform the teacher of beliefs and practices that he or she may not necessarily be aware of. Below is a list of questions that teachers might ask themselves:

Do I enjoy working with parents? When?

Do I feel threatened by parents? When?

How can families offer their strengths and provide resources to support their children's learning and overall development?

How can I learn more about my students' special interests or talents?

How can I communicate more effectively and more frequently with families?

How can I create a more welcoming environment for students and families?

How can families be my educational partners?

Once teachers engage in self-reflection and self-assessment, a new window of possibilities will open for partnership opportunities with all families.

Tips for Implementing and Sustaining Partnerships

Reflect on the topics, information, research, and partnership examples featured within this book. Create a "Top 10" list of ideas that you believe will be beneficial to you and other teachers when implementing and sustaining educational partnerships. Table 11.2 provides a chart to help you organize your ideas.

Table 11.2	Creating a "Top 10" List for Implementing and Sustaining Partnerships

[Your name]'s "Top 10" list for implementing and sustaining [a partnership that you are interested in improving or developing]

1.	
2.	
3.	
4.	
5.	
6.	
7.	
8.	
9.	
10.	

Final Comments

Community and family partnerships are only effective if there is a common vision, respect for all parties, and a plan in place to implement and sustain. Research has shown a variety of factors promote effective partnerships, particularly when they are built on trust, respect, and appreciation for various views and beliefs. It is my hope that you will view teaching and learning as more than a set of formal lesson plans that take place within the traditional four walls of the classroom. Instead, I would like you to consider assessing and embracing the resources around you such as other teachers, families, students, and the community to enhance learning for all students, particularly those students from diverse linguistic, cultural, or socioeconomic backgrounds. And then after you have noted valuable partners, consider research practices and effective partnerships featured in this book to create a plan of action to provide a more inclusive and dynamic education for your students. When we work together as educational partners, the educational potential for our students and their future is endless!

Activities for Further Development

1. Partnerships often are modeled after a top-down approach where teachers tell the parents what they should be doing (or sometimes vice versa). How can teachers create more of a shared vision of education and overcome this traditional view?

2. Describe how partnerships with families and the community can actually make the job of a teacher more manageable, successful, and interesting.

3. Describe how you would measure the success of an educational partnership over a long period of time such as 3 to 5 years.

4. Think about an educational partnership project that has lasted more than 10 years. Who is involved? Why has it succeeded over time? Why do you think it may or may not continue?

5. Create a list of six to eight guidelines to encourage teachers to involve families in greater decision making based on a culturally relevant perspective.

Additional Reading and Information

Eisler, R. (2000). *Tomorrow's children: A blueprint for partnership education in the 21st century.* New York: HarperCollins. This book discusses school reform and strategies to help children achieve their best. Eisler discusses partnerships, democratic education, and promotion of healthy children.

Hiatt-Michael, D. B. (2001). *Promising practices in family involvement in schools.* Greenwich, CT: Information Age Publishing. This book provides information, resources, and strategies to promote more successful family-school partnerships.

The DARE Web site provides information for students, teachers, and families: http://www.dare.com/home/default.asp

The Junior Achievement program is a partnership that includes industry representatives and local schools: http://www.ja.org

The Pizza Hut *Book It!* Program Web site features a description of partners, enrollment information, strategies for teachers and families, and literacy events: http://www.bookitprogram.com

U.S. Department of Education Partnerships Information for Families provides information about the implementation of No Child Left Behind and how families can assist children in literacy activities and provides educational resources: http://www.ed.gov/parents/academic/help/partnership.html

Research Studies and Articles That Support School-Community-Family Partnerships

Anderson, K. J., & Minke, K. M. (2007). Parent involvement in education: Toward an understanding of parents' decision making. *The Journal of Educational Research, 100,* 311–323.

Darling, S., & Westberg, L. (2004). Parent involvement in children's acquisition of reading. *The Reading Teacher, 57,* 774–776.

Desimone, L. (2001). Linking parent involvement with student achievement: Do race and income matter? *Journal of Educational Research, 93*(1), 11–30.

Evans, M., Shaw, D., & Bell, M. (2000). Home literacy activities and their influence on early literacy skills. *Canadian Journal of Experimental Psychology, 54*(2), 65–75.

Invernizzi, M. R., Richards, C., Juel, C., & Richards, H. C. (1997). At risk readers and community volunteers: A three-year perspective. *Scientific Studies of Reading, 1,* 277–300.

Miedel, W. T., & Reynolds, A. J. (1999). Parent involvement in early intervention for disadvantaged children: Does it matter? *Journal of School Psychology, 37,* 379–402.

Osterling, J. P. (2001). Waking the sleeping giant: Engaging and capitalizing on the sociocultural strengths of the Latino community. *Bilingual Research Journal, 25*(1 & 2), 59–89.

Rich, D. (1998). What parents want from teachers. *Educational Leadership, 55*(8), 37–39.

Senechal, M., & LeFevre, J. (2002). Parental involvement in the development of children's reading skills: A five-year longitudinal study. *Child Development, 73,* 445–460.

Sheldon, S. B., & Epstein, J. L. (2002). Improving student behavior and school discipline with family and community involvement. *Education and Urban Society, 35*(1), 4–26.

Shymansky, J., Hand, B., & Yore, L. (2000). Empowering families in hands-on science programs. *School Science and Mathematics, 100,* 48–56.

Yore, L., Anderson, J., & Shymansky, J. (2005). Sensing the impact of elementary-school science reform: A study of stakeholder perceptions of implementation, constructivist strategies, and home-school collaboration. *Journal of Science Teacher Education, 16,* 65–88.

Glossary

Ableism asserts that children with disabilities should use tools and act in the same way as their peers without disabilities. Ableist assumptions can be harmful to students with disabilities and contribute to an uneven playing field.

Acculturation celebrates the backgrounds and cultural beliefs of students and their families. It encourages individuals to integrate their beliefs with formal instruction and content, rather than abandon their beliefs altogether.

An **action plan** is an explicit plan where partners create goals, strategies, and outcomes to enhance one or more areas of education.

After-school programs take place after school hours usually on the school campus or at a community center. These programs often enhance and enrich physical education as well as the arts and other subject areas related to the formal school curriculum.

Asperger syndrome is a developmental disorder that usually results in social interaction inadequacies.

Assessment is an ongoing process that influences planning and implementing educational practices.

Assimilation focuses on the idea that students and families should abandon their ethnic backgrounds and beliefs and adopt a different culture, usually one that is more mainstream. The assimilation view usually results in the loss of ethnic identification.

Barriers are obstacles that groups face when they try to accomplish a task or project. Schools should acknowledge and address these in order to provide more equitable education for all students.

Benchmarks are pivotal events or activities that take place throughout a project.

A **charter school** is part of the public school system. It differs from a public school because its purpose is to encourage the use of innovative teaching methods and provide families, students, teachers, and administrators with expanded decision-making abilities.

Child abuse is a broad term used to describe acts of power or control over children that result in some form of maltreatment. The Child Abuse Prevention and Treatment Act defines abuse as an act or a failure to act by a parent or caregiver that results in any physical or emotional harm, sexual abuse, exploitation, or death. In addition, the act includes *any* act that presents a risk of serious harm as one that is classified as abusive or neglectful.

The **Child Abuse Prevention and Treatment Act** (CAPTA) was enacted in 1974 and amended in 2003 as the Keeping Children and Families Safe Act. It provides federal money for initiatives aimed at preventing, assessing, prosecuting, and treating individuals in need.

Children with special needs are those who have learning disabilities, emotional disorders, physical disabilities, behavioral issues, or communication challenges and those who are exceptionally gifted or talented.

Civic involvement is a part of service learning and stewardship but is organized specifically to encourage active community members. Such activities include volunteering time or a service, joining a civic organization, or supporting fundraising efforts for a particular cause.

Cognitive information processing theories of learning involve brain-based educational ideas where students form networks within their memory. Students determine whether knowledge and skills will be placed in their short-term memory, working memory, or long-term memory.

Colormute is defined by Pollock (2007) as a way to describe how teachers and parents actively suppress race labels when talking about diverse families and students in their schools.

Communities of practice include the practices spoken or unspoken that bind individuals or groups together based on common interests or beliefs.

Community is a broad term used to describe a place such as a city, a neighborhood, or a classroom. A community can also be used to describe interactions and relationships among people or groups.

A **community partnership** is an agreement between one or more community members. The agreement can be formal or informal.

Conditioning theories have roots in behaviorism where learning is viewed as a change in behavior that is reinforced by outside stimuli in the students' environment (i.e., external factors).

Constructivist theories, based on the work of Vygotsky (1978), hold that knowledge is constructed within the context of social and language processes—with the teacher, other students, and the community.

A **contemporary view of education** values partnerships between the school, family, and community where all parties have added value to enhance the knowledge, skills, and values of children.

Cultural capital is the advantage gained by the majority group from understanding and living the lifestyle congruent with the dominant culture (e.g., educational system).

Culturally relevant pedagogy addresses inequities and recognizes systematic power relationships within the curriculum, instructional practices, policies, and assessment.

Culturally relevant teaching according to Ladson-Billings (1995) includes (a) assisting all students to achieve academic success, (b) focusing on cultural competence to help students maintain their own cultural integrity through classroom activities, and (c) ensuring that critical consciousness activities address cultural norms, values, and social inequities.

Culture refers to behaviors exhibited by people or groups of people. These behaviors can include (but are not limited to) communication, language, gender roles, dwelling, clothing, art, music, food, and ethics.

Curriculum maps are tools that educators use to record data related to content, skills, assessment, resources, and state content standards. Curriculum mapping is a collaborative process where teachers organize information and provide authentic evidence related to what is happening in the classroom.

The **deficit view** of education relates to historical inequity among students from underrepresented groups. It is based on the notion that one group is superior while other groups are inferior when it comes to academic potential. When you relate this view to families, the deficit view tends to marginalize the potential of families who are less educated, from diverse ethnicities, or from working-class low-income backgrounds.

Democratic equality educational goals are organized so that all students, regardless of economic, language, or ethnic background, have the same equal rights and responsibilities in order to become contributing members of the community.

Differentiated instruction involves providing equitable opportunities for all students. This includes modifying or altering the time allotted for instructional activities such as writing or test taking or finding other ways to meet the needs of students.

Educational partnerships take place when two parties come together for the common good of a school or to enhance student learning. Partners can include anyone who is interested in or committed to enriching educational experiences for students, families, schools, and the community.

Effective communication with families involves school-to-home and home-to-school interactions related to children's education and their overall well-being.

Effective educational partnerships include respect, understanding, appreciation of cultural and linguistic differences, shared common goals, accountability, high returns, meaningful goals to all parties, commitment, leadership, partner feedback, and "buy-in." Partnerships are not one-sided (i.e., "I know best; you do not"), judgmental, forced, or dictated.

English language learners are students who are learning English as a second language and whose native language is not English. English language learners are also described as students from non-English language backgrounds. These terms are preferred over terms used in the past such as *limited English proficiency* and *language deficient*.

Ethnic groups refer to people who may be of the same race and who share common cultural views and customs.

Ethnicity is used to describe someone's social identification and/or common cultural views and customs.

Evaluation refers to a benchmark or a cumulative event in which decisions are made in relation to a particular project.

The **exosystem** is smaller than the macrosystem, and children do not actively participate in it. This includes such places as parents' work environment, city council meetings, and community service agencies. Although children are not active participants, the exosystem may affect their microsystem and daily experiences.

Explicit partnerships include schools, families, and communities that create written goals, strategies, and outcomes related to enhancing the education of children. The partners usually publicize these goals for all to know.

Faith-based partners include organized religious groups and organizations such as Islamic, Christian, Jewish, Hindu, or Buddhist groups. Under No Child Left Behind legislation, diverse faith-based organizations can receive federal funds to offer tutoring or other academic services for low-income students. They can also apply for and receive funding as a supplemental service provider to support initiatives such as after-school programs, early literacy programs, and mentoring programs.

Family is a term used to describe a group of people who usually, but not always, live together at the same location. Family can include parents and guardians in addition to extended family members who play a significant role in children's lives such as grandparents, aunts, uncles, and close friends.

In a **family-school partnership,** teachers, administrators, and staff work together with families to enhance the education of students.

A **family tree** is a chart, a graph, or another representation that shows current family members and family members over time.

Formative assessment includes collecting information during a project or an activity. The results of the assessment provide valuable information for families, students, and teachers.

Gifted and talented students demonstrate above-average intellectual ability and/or exceptional ability in areas such as drama, art, music, or leadership.

Goals are long-term outcomes that usually take place over time.

A **grant** is a written agreement by two parties that is usually attached to some type of funding award. Granting agencies such as state or federal governments, private foundations, or corporations usually target a specific area and will offer funding for programs or research that aligns with their specific goals and expectations.

Hate can be a noun or a verb. It relates to disliking something so much that it often results in hostile or intense feelings.

Homeless families have no permanent residence or reside in a place not intended for home use.

The **home literacy model** includes early literacy activities such as reading stories and direct teaching about literacy.

Home schooling takes place in homes where families or other members of the community teach students and provide for all their educational needs.

Home visits are visits to students' homes by the teacher. They bring greater awareness, understanding, and respect for the student and his or her family.

Implicit partnerships include schools, families, and communities that often "talk" about common goals and ideals, but there is no specific goal, strategy, or outcome in place.

Inclusion is a positive educational strategy where students with disabilities are educated with their nondisabled peers but with special services available when necessary. Special education teachers and general education teachers work together to create the most appropriate instructional plan to ensure that these students are supported throughout their educational experiences.

Inclusive classrooms respect diversity of all students and often include families in planning, communication, and other activities.

Individual education plans, commonly referred to by educators and parents as IEPs, are required to comply with the Individuals with Disabilities Education Act. An IEP team usually consists of teachers, service providers, and families who meet and create a mutually determined plan to assist a student with special needs educationally, emotionally, and/or physically.

The **Individuals with Disabilities Education Act**, known as **IDEA**, was enacted in 1997 to ensure the education of all children from birth to age 21. It was created to provide a pathway for students who are academically diverse or in need of special education to get the best education possible. IDEA notes that special education includes specific instruction designed to meet the needs of students with disabilities.

Instructionally congruent practices, as advocated by Lee and Fradd (1998), align with students' cultures, beliefs, and values to promote better understanding of content.

Interagency collaboration includes groups or individuals collaborating to address issues such as health education, special education, and safety. Different agencies or groups work together and integrate their services for the purpose of early intervention and support for families, schools, and communities.

A **joint enterprise** pertains to the overall purpose of a community that is continuously negotiated and renegotiated by the members.

The **macrosystem** is the largest of three systems (the others are the exosystem and microsystem) that includes society and the larger subculture to which children and families belong (i.e., lifestyles, social patterns, beliefs). It also includes outside influences such as the national government, political views, social trends, and larger cultural values and practices.

A **magnet school** is a public school that operates within a school district that is open to all qualifying students. Magnet schools are organized around a specific theme or subject area such as the performing arts, professional development, or science. Magnet schools were created to promote equity for all students and enhance learning.

Mainstreaming involves placing special education students primarily in a special education classroom but having them interact with their peers in the general education classroom for a specific period of the day.

A **microsystem** is a system that includes the child's greatest influence and frame of reference including his or her peers, neighborhood, school, and family. This microsystem is often a child's most important system because of the relationships that develop.

Multiracial refers to people who describe themselves as belonging to two or more racial groups.

Mutual engagement is what brings everyone together for a common goal. Members work together to create a functioning and ongoing partnership.

National Board Certification is the highest symbol of professional excellence based on a lengthy portfolio that is judged by teaching at different grade levels and within specific subject areas.

Neglect includes the deprivation of a child's needs in a way that leads to harm or emotional instability.

A **nonpublic special education school** provides services for students with severe learning disabilities, multiple disabilities, or mental retardation. A nonpublic school is a more restrictive environment because special needs students are not mainstreamed with their peers.

Null partnerships include individuals or groups that occupy the same space, but there is usually no communication related to specific goals, strategies, or outcomes for a partnership.

Objectives are attainable and measurable outcomes during a short period of time.

Parent is a term to describe primary caregivers of children. Anyone taking the role of raising a child is considered a parent. This includes legal guardians or grandparents who are responsible for a child or children. This also includes individuals who have shared custody of children.

Parenting involves establishing home environments that support children and youth's social, cognitive, emotional, and physical health.

A **partnership** is a written, spoken, or informal agreement where two or more people or groups work together toward mutual goals.

Peer mentoring or coaching involves two or more teachers who support each other during the teaching and learning process. This is a professional development strategy that takes place in the teachers' own classroom.

A **peer tutor** is someone who is of similar age or status to the person being tutored, and peer tutoring involves two or more students working together where at least one of the students/peers has mastered certain skills or knowledge.

Policy is a direct result of priorities and goals that include a set of decisions or mandates that are created and implemented. Policies are usually created by local, state, or federal governments or within school districts with long-term implementation in mind, not a short-term event or action.

Post–field trip activities take place at school after a field trip to extend the experiences and learning.

Pre–field trip activities take place at school prior to a field trip to prepare students for what they will see and do.

Prejudices usually relate to prejudgments of a person or groups of people.

Private schools can be religious or nonreligious and are not supported by tax dollars. Therefore, these schools generally charge tuition for each child who attends.

Professional is a term used to describe people who possess expertise and knowledge in a particular area. Their job usually requires some type of licensure or specific degree. In this text, professionals (for the most part) refer to professional educators including teachers, university faculty, and administrators.

Professional education partnerships take place through peer mentoring, collaborating on class projects, creating teacher networks, and developing school-university partnership activities.

Professional learning communities is a term popularized by Peter Senge's (1990) *The Fifth Discipline: The Art and Practice of the Learning Organization.* Senge visualized a group of teachers who would collaborate and share their knowledge and skills to enhance student learning. The overall goal of professional learning communities is to restructure schools and their interactions—also called "reculturing."

Public schools are supported by tax dollars. Public schools throughout the United States are organized into districts. District sizes vary as do the grade levels and location.

Race traditionally refers to a group of people sharing similar hereditary features or those who are united by nationality. Today, this term is used broadly to describe historical ancestry because there is little evidence of a "pure" human race.

Racism involves the subordination of members of a specific racial group who have little power socially, culturally, or ethnically.

Requests for proposals, also known as RFPs, are usually generated by government or private agencies for the purpose of seeking individuals or groups who would like to write a proposal; receive an award in the form of funds, materials, or equipment; and then implement an innovative program.

Scaffolding strategies involve supporting students as they acquire new skills and strategies.

School-community partnerships take place when teachers, administrators, and staff at a school form partnerships with community members, businesses, or other institutions.

School-to-home notebooks are journals or notebooks that provide written ongoing communication among the teacher, students, and families.

Service learning involves a learning process where students contribute and provide a service to the community while the community in turn provides a service to students and schools. This type of project results in reciprocal learning and partnerships.

Shared decision making occurs when families, teachers, administrators, students, and community members work together to make real decisions that affect the education of children.

Shared repertoire involves the type of resources such as routines, artifacts, and style that members develop over time. The repertoire is not verbally established but established through behaviors and expectations.

Situated learning (legitimate peripheral participation) is viewed as a social activity that develops from multiple experiences and different types of participation. We all partake in activities based on our home, community, and school. However, we have varying roles within each of these areas.

Social capital within a community includes the diversity of interactions and relationships including participating in community activities, service, and volunteering. Sometimes differences in the cultural capital of families may reduce their ability to obtain social capital from the school even though they attend school regularly.

Social cognitive theories of learning claim that students learn by actively engaging in particular tasks and by observing others.

Social efficiency goals are organized as a public good. Students are educated to take a different role in society that will benefit the community.

Social mobility goals provide students with educational, competitive opportunities to distinguish themselves from others. Therefore, the educational system becomes stratified according to ability and academic achievement.

Stereotypes can be positive or negative. They include mental views, comments, or beliefs related to preconceived ideas about particular groups of people.

Stewardship is closely linked to service learning and includes the call for responsibility to ensure welfare of the world and in the world. This can include environmental conservation, human rights, economic welfare, education, health care, disaster relief, and animal welfare.

The **structure of the traditional family** is two parents and two children.

Student-led conferences are organized by students and teachers. These types of conferences differ from the traditional teacher-led conferences because students take a major role in informing their parents about their achievement, interests, and assignments. Students take the initiative to showcase their work and progress during this time.

Summative evaluation is information that leads to a decision or change in a particular program. It takes place after the project or part of the project is complete.

A **survey** is a method of collecting information via written or selected responses.

Tolerance education is needed when addressing issues such as sexual orientation, race, ethnic background, religion, socioeconomic level, special education needs, and even physical appearance.

Transracial is a term used most often in cases where parents and children of different races live together. Transracial adoptions are common where a family in the United States adopts a child from another country or adopts a child of a different race within the United States. Many racial issues must be negotiated within the family during the child's life.

Volunteering includes providing a service without pay. Educational volunteering can take place at the school site, at home, or within the community.

References

Chapter 1

Barbour, C., Barbour, N. H., & Scully, P. A. (2005). *Families, schools, and communities: Building partnerships for educating children.* Upper Saddle River, NJ: Pearson.

Barrios, A. C. (2006). *The implementation of learning action walks to promote home and school partnerships.* Unpublished master's project, California State University, Fullerton.

Berliner, D. C., & Biddle, B. J. (1995). *The manufactured crisis: Myths, fraud, and the attack on America's public schools.* New York: Addison-Wesley.

Education Commission of the States. (2006). *Helping state leaders shape educational policy: Closing the achievement gap.* Retrieved May 21, 2007, from http://www.ecs.org

Eisner, E. W. (1985). *The educational imagination: On the design and evaluation of school programs.* New York: Macmillan.

Epstein, J. L. (1999). *National network of partnership schools at Johns Hopkins University.* Retrieved June 10, 2007, from http://www.csos.jhu.edu/p2000/

Epstein, J. L. (2001). *School, family, and community partnerships: Preparing educators and improving schools.* Boulder, CO: Westview Press.

Gibbs, N. (2005, February 13). Parents behaving badly. *Time.* Retrieved October 4, 2009, from http://www.time.com/time/magazine/article/0,9171,1027485,00.html

Guerrero, O. M. (2006). *Enhancing parent involvement through action learning walks.* Unpublished master's project, California State University, Fullerton.

Harris, J. R. (1999). *The nurture assumption: Why children turn out the way they do.* New York: Free Press.

Haynes, R. (2007). *Team time: A professional partnership action plan.* Unpublished paper, California State University, Fullerton.

Ladson-Billings, G. (1995). But that's just good teaching! The case for culturally relevant pedagogy. *Theory Into Practice, 34,* 159–165.

Lave, J., & Wenger, E. (1991). *Situated learning: Legitimate peripheral participation.* Cambridge, UK: Cambridge University Press.

Lueder, D. C. (1998). *Creating partnerships with parents: An educator's guide.* Lancaster, PA: Technomic.

National Assessment of Educational Progress. (2004). *The nation's report card.* Retrieved June 6, 2007, from http://nces.ed.gov/nationsreportcard

National Board for Professional Teaching Standards. (2007). *The five core propositions.* Retrieved October 24, 2009, from http://www.nbpts.org/the_standards/the_five_core_propositio

National Council for Accreditation of Teacher Education. (2007). *Standards.* Retrieved October 24, 2009, from http://www.ncate.org/public/standards.asp

Regional Educational Laboratory at AEL. (2003). *Interactions: A summary of research on school-community relationships.* Charleston, WV: Author.

Rogoff, B. (1994). Developing understanding of the idea of communities of learners. *Mind, Culture, and Activity, 4,* 209–229.

Roth-Vinson, C. (2000). CyberSisters jumpstart girls' interest in math, science, and technology. *ENC Focus, 7*(4), 23–27.

Sisters in Science. (n.d.). *Sisters in science, brothers of science.* Retrieved July 19, 2009, from www.sistersinscience.org

Veigel, J. M. (2000). Collaborative strategies: Good science plus bad management equals bad science. In J. S. Hauger & C. McEnaney (Eds.), *Strategies for competitiveness in academic research* (pp. 115–149). Washington, DC: American Association for the Advancement of Science.

Wenger, E. (1998). *Communities of practice: A brief introduction.* Retrieved May 21, 2007, from http://www.ewenger.com/theory/

Chapter 2

Arts Education Partnership. (1999). *Improving learning in schools with arts partners in the community.* Washington, DC: Author.

Arts Education Partnership. (2009). *Improving learning in schools with arts partners in the community.* Retrieved October 27, 2009, http://www.aep-arts.org/files/publications/Learning Partnerships.pdf

Bourdieu, P. (1977). *Outline of a theory of practice.* New York: Cambridge University Press.

Bronfenbrenner, U. (2005). *Making human beings human: Bioecological perspectives on human development.* Thousand Oaks, CA: Sage.

Bruner, J. S. (1966). *Toward a theory of instruction.* Boston: Harvard University Press.

Carson, R. (1962). *Silent spring.* Boston: Houghton Mifflin.

Coleman, J. S. (1988). Social capital in the creation of human capital. *American Journal of Sociology, 94,* 95–120.

Commission on the Reorganization of Secondary Education. (1918). *Cardinal principles of secondary education.* Retrieved October 1, 2009, from http://www.nd.edu/~rbarger/www7/cardprin.html

Dewey, J. (1897, January). My pedagogic creed. *School Journal, 54,* 77–80.

Dewey, J. (1920). *The school and society.* Chicago: University of Chicago Press.

Dewey, J. (1938). *Experience and education.* New York: Macmillan.

Dewey, J. (1997). *Democracy and education.* Florence, MA: Free Press. (Original work published 1916)

Epstein, J. L. (2001). *School, family, and community partnerships: Preparing educators and improving schools.* Boulder, CO: Westview Press.

Freire, P. (1970). *Pedagogy of the oppressed.* New York: Herder & Herder.

Harris, M. M., Jacobson, A., & Hemmer, R. (2004, November). Preparing teachers to engage parents. *FINE Network Newsletter.* Retrieved October 30, 2009, from http://www.hfrp.org/publications-resources/browse-our-publications/preparing-teachers-to-engage-parents

Hirsch, E. D., Jr. (1988). *Cultural literacy: What every American needs to know.* New York: Vintage Books.

Hofer, B. K., & Pintrich, P. R. (1997). The development of epistemological theories: Beliefs about knowledge and knowing and their relation to learning. *Review of Educational Research, 67*(1), 88–140.

Katz, L., & Bauch, J. P. (1999). The Peabody family involvement initiative: Preparing preservice teachers for family/school collaboration. *School Community Journal, 9*(1), 49–69.

Labaree, D. F. (1997). Public goods, private goods: The American struggle over educational goals. *American Educational Research Journal, 34,* 39–81.

Lane, B., & Dorfman, D. (1997). *Strengthening community networks: The basis for sustainable community renewal.* NW Archives Regional Education Laboratory. Retrieved June 27, 2007, from http://www.nwrel.org/ruraled/Strengthening.html#d

Lawrence-Lightfoot, S. (2004). *The essential conversation: What parents and teachers can learn from each other.* New York: Random House.

Lee, J. S., & Bowen, N. K. (2006). Parent involvement, cultural capital, and the achievement gap among elementary school children. *American Educational Research Journal, 43,* 193–218.

Montessori, M. (1936). *The secret of childhood.* New York: Ballantine.

National Association of Elementary School Principals. (1993). *Standards for quality school-age child care.* Retrieved October 24, 2009, from http://www.eric.ed.gov:80/ERICWebPortal/custom/portlets/recordDetails/detailmini.jsp?_nfpb=true&_&ERICExtSearch_SearchValue_0=ED36 2336&ERICExtSearch_SearchType_0=no&accno=ED362336

A nation at risk. (1983). Retrieved October 24, 2009, from http://www.ed.gov/pubs/NatAtRisk/index.html

Piaget, J. (1929). *The child's conception of the world.* New York: Harcourt, Brace & Co.

Roosevelt, E. (1930). Good citizenship: The purpose of education. *Pictorial Review, 4,* 94–97.

Schunk, D. H. (2008). *Learning theories: An educational perspective.* Upper Saddle River, NJ: Pearson/Merrill Prentice Hall.

Sizer, T. (1984). *Horace's compromise: The dilemma of the American high school.* Boston: Houghton Mifflin.

Trumbull, E., Rothstein-Fisch, C., Greenfield, P. M., & Quiroz, B. (2001). *Bridging cultures between home and school: A guide for teachers.* Mahwah, NJ: Lawrence Erlbaum.

Tyler, R. W. (1949). *Basic principles of curriculum and instruction.* Chicago: University of Chicago Press.

University of Minnesota. (2008). College of Education & Human Development timeline. Retrieved October 27, 2009, from http://www.cehd.umn.edu/History/TimeLine/default.html

U.S. Department of Education. (n.d.). *A 25-year history of the IDEA.* Retrieved October 24, 2009, from http://www.ed.gov/policy/speced/leg/idea/history.html

U.S. National Archives and Records Administration. (n.d.). *Federal records pertaining to* Brown v. Board of Education of Topeka, Kansas *(1954).* Retrieved October 30, 2009, from http://www.archives.gov/publications/ref-info-papers/112/

Vygotsky, L. S. (1978). *Mind in society* (M. Cole, V. John-Steiner, S. Scribner, & E. Souberman, Eds.). Cambridge, MA: Harvard University Press.

Chapter 3

Alexander, D. (2000). *The learning that lies between play and academics in after-school programs.* Wellesley College, MA: National Institute on Out-of-School Time.

American Psychiatric Association. (2000). *Diagnostic and statistical manual of mental disorders* (4th ed., text rev.). Washington, DC: Author.

California Department of Health Services. (2007a). *Harvest of the Month.* Retrieved June 22, 2007, from http://www.harvestofthemonth.com

California Department of Health Services. (2007b). *Network for a Healthy California.* Retrieved June 21, 2007, from www.cachampionsforchange.net

David and Lucile Packard Foundation. (2002). Children and welfare reform: Analysis. *The Future of Children, 12*(1), 1.

Drewnowski, A., & Darmon, N. (2005). The economics of obesity: Dietary energy density and energy cost. *American Journal of Clinical Nutrition, 82,* 265–273.

Fuchs, D., & Fuchs, L. S. (1994). Inclusive school movement and radicalization of special education reform. *Exceptional Children, 60,* 294–309.

Iannelli, V. (2008). Child abuse statistics. *New York Times,* About.com. Retrieved January 9, 2008, from http://pediatrics.about.com/od/childabuse/a/05_abuse_stats.htm

Kelder, S., Perry, C., Klepp, K., & Lytle, L. L. (1994). Longitudinal tracking of adolescent smoking, physical activity, and food choice behaviors. *American Journal of Public Health, 84,* 1121–1126.

Lewis, R. B., & Doorlag, D. H. (1995). *Teaching special education students in the mainstream.* New York: Merrill.

Louv, R. (2005). *Last child in the woods: Saving our children from nature-deficit disorder.* Chapel Hill, NC: Algonquin Books.

Lumsden, L. (2003). After-school programs. *Research Roundup, 20,* 1–4.

Mainichi Daily News. (2006, February 15). *Japan battles rising obesity, frets disease may cut world-class longevity.* Retrieved June 3, 2007, from http://mdn.mainichi-msn.co.jp/features/archive/news/2006/02/20060215p2g00m0fe027000c.html

McComb, E. M., & Scott-Little, C. (2003). A review of research on participant outcomes in after-school programs: Implications for school counselors. *Eric Digests.* Retrieved February 10, 2007, from www.eric.ed.gov

Meyers, A. F., Sampson, A. E., Weitzman, M., Rogers, B. L., and Kayne H. (1989). School breakfast program and school performance. *American Journal of Diseases of Children, 143,* 1234–1239.

Moya, S. A., & Hampl, J. S. (2003, Fall). Project GLEAN: Implementing a school-based food distribution program. *Childhood Education,* 36–37.

National Association for Sport and Physical Education and the American Heart Association. (2006). *Shape of the nation report: Status of physical education in the USA.* Retrieved October 21, 2009, from http://www.heartland.org/policybot/results/21578/2006_Shape_of_The_Nation_Report_Status_of_Physical_Education_in_the_USA.html

Neumark-Sztainer, D. (2006). Eating among teens: Do family mealtimes make a difference for adolescents' nutrition? *New Directions for Child and Adolescent Development, 111,* 91–105.

Northwest Education Collaboration. (2007). *Developing and maintaining successful partnerships.* Retrieved October 30, 2009, from http://www.nwrel.org/cfc/frc/resrch.html

O'Shea, M. (2005, November 27). *Parade*'s guide to better fitness. *Parade,* p. 8.

Pellegrini, A. (2005). *Recess: Its role in education and development.* Florence, KY: Lawrence Erlbaum.

Rescuing Recess. (n.d.). Retrieved May 21, 2007, from http://www.cartoonnetwork.com/promos/getanimated/index.html

Robbins, V. (2007). *The effects of home visits on a child with selective mutism.* Unpublished paper, California State University, Fullerton.

Sears, W., Sears, M., Sears, J., & Sears, R. (2006). *The healthiest kid in the neighborhood.* Boston: Little, Brown.

Simmons, R. (2007). *Richard goes to Washington.* Retrieved April 7, 2007, from http://www.richardsimmons.com/pages/richardgoestowashington.php

Stelzer, J. (2005). Promoting healthy lifestyles: Prescriptions for physical educators. *Journal of Physical Education, Recreation and Dance, 76,* 26.

Tower, C. (1999). *Understanding child abuse and neglect* (4th ed.). Boston: Allyn & Bacon.

United Nations Children's Fund. (2007). An overview of child well-being in rich countries. *Innocenti Report Card 7.* Florence, Italy: Innocenti Research Centre. Retrieved December 17, 2007, from http://www.unicef.org/media/files/ChildPovertyReport.pdf

U.S. Department of Agriculture. (2009, June 4). *National School Lunch Program.* Retrieved October 24, 2009, from http://www.fns.usda.gov/cnd/Lunch/

U.S. Department of Agriculture, Center for Nutrition Policy and Promotion. (2006). *MyPyramid.* Retrieved October 24, 2009, from http://www.cnpp.usda.gov/MyPyramid-breakout.htm

U.S. Department of Education, Office of Communications and Outreach. (2005). *No Child Left Behind: What parents need to know.* Washington, DC: Author.

Vadeboncoeur, J. A. (2006). Engaging young people: Learning in informal contexts. *Review of Research in Education, 30,* 239–278.

Vaughn, S., Bos, C. S., & Schumm, J. S. (2007). *Teaching students who are exceptional, diverse, and at risk: In the general education classroom.* Boston: Allyn & Bacon.

Walsh, J. P. (1986). *The green book.* New York: Farrar, Straus & Giroux.

Ward, E. (2003). *Asia Pacific Health and Development.* Australia: Australian Department of Health and Aging. Retrieved June 24, 2007, from http://www.wpro.who.int/NR/rdonlyres/7A746D09-CADC-496A-B2CC-2E9DBEBEFF77/0/aus.pdf

Yee, L. (2007). *Partnership action plan: Harvest of the month.* Unpublished paper, California State University, Fullerton.

Zigmond, N. (2003). Where should students with disabilities receive special education services: Is one place better than another? *The Journal of Special Education, 37,* 193–199.

Chapter 4

Allen, J. (2007). *Creating welcoming schools: A practical guide to home-school partnerships with diverse families.* New York: Teachers College Press.

Bennett, S., & Kalish, N. (2006). *The case against homework.* New York: Crown.

Bower, L. (2007, February). *Looking for a few good teachers: Lesbian mothers' visions for their children's schools.* Paper presented at the Association of Teacher Education conference, San Diego, CA.

Bureau of Labor Statistics. (2004). *Current population survey, March 1960–2004.* Washington, DC: Author.

Cooper, H. (1994). *The battle over homework.* Newbury Park, CA: Corwin.

Cooper, H., Lindsay, J. J., Nye, B., & Greathouse, S. (1998). Relationships among attitudes about homework, amount of homework assigned and completed, and student achievement. *Journal of Educational Psychology, 90,* 70–83.

Delgado-Gaitan, C. (2004). *Involving Latino families in schools: Raising student achievement through home-school partnerships.* Thousand Oaks, CA: Corwin.

Desimone, L. (1999). Linking parent involvement with student achievement: Do race and income matter? *Journal of Educational Research, 93*(1), 11–30.

DeVore, A. K., & Ambrose, K. (2007). *Health and science sacks: Creating meaningful health and science partnerships between families and schools.* Unpublished manuscript, California State University, Fullerton.

Eberly, J., Joshi, A., & Konzal, J. (2005). Dialogue across cultures: Teachers' perceptions about communication with diverse families. *Multicultural Education, 13*(2), 11–15.

Hehir, T. (2007). Confronting ableism: Negative cultural attitudes toward disability can undermine opportunities for all students to participate fully in school and society. *Educational Leadership, 64*(5), 8–14.

Jianzhong, X. (2005). Purposes for doing homework reported by middle and high school students. *Journal of Educational Research, 99,* 46.

Kalan, R. (1989). *Jump, frog, jump!* New York: Greenwillow Books.

Kilman, M. (2006). Math out of school: Families' math game playing at home. *The School Community Journal, 16,* 69–90.

Kissen, R. M. (2002). *Getting ready for Benjamin: Preparing teachers for sexual diversity in the classroom.* Lanham, MD: Rowan & Littlefield.

Kohn, A. (2006). *The homework myth: Why our kids get too much of a bad thing.* Cambridge, MA: Da Capo Press.

Lau, J. Y., & McBride-Chang, C. (2005). Home literacy and Chinese reading in Hong Kong children. *Early Education and Development, 16,* 5–22.

Lave, J., & Wenger, E. (1991). *Situated learning: Legitimate peripheral participation.* Cambridge, UK: Cambridge University Press.

MacCallum, F., & Golombok, S. (2004). Children raised in fatherless families from infancy: A follow-up of children of lesbian and single heterosexual mothers at early adolescence. *Journal of Child Psychology & Psychiatry & Allied Disciplines, 45,* 1407–1419.

Maney, D. W., & Cain, R. E. (1997). Preservice elementary teachers' attitudes toward gay and lesbian parenting. *Journal of School Health, 67,* 236–241.

Marques, C. (2005). *Student-led conferences.* Unpublished manuscript, California State University, Fullerton.

McLure, P. (2002, September). *Parents' right to know about their child's and school's achievement.* Leadership Development Conference at Johns Hopkins University. Retrieved February 23, 2007, from http://www.csos.jhu.edu/p2000/pdf/nochild/NCLB_Parents_Rights.pdf

Moll, L. C., & Gonzalez, N. (1997). Teachers as social scientists: Learning about culture from household research. In P. M. Hall (Ed.), *Race, ethnicity, and multiculturalism: Policy and practice* (pp. 89–114). New York: Garland.

Moll, L. C., Vélez-Ibáñez, C., Greenberg, J., & Rivera, C. (1990). *Community knowledge and classroom practice: Combining resources for literacy instruction* (OBEMLA contract No. 300-87-0131). Tucson: University of Arizona, College of Education and Bureau of Applied Research in Anthropology.

Morrison, C. G. (2008). *Home visits and the school-home connection: A case study.* Unpublished manuscript, California State University, Fullerton.

Mraz, M., & Rasinski, T. V. (2007). Summer reading loss. *The Reading Teacher, 60,* 784–789.

Nunez, R., & Collignon, K. (1997). Creating a community of learning for homeless children. *Educational Leadership, 55*(2), 56–60.

Paschal, R., Weinstein, T., & Walberg, H. J. (1984). The effects of homework on learning: A quantitative synthesis. *Journal of Educational Research, 78,* 97–104.

Patchen, T., Cox-Petersen, A., Ambrose, K., DeVore, A., & Koenings, N. (2008). *Teachers engaging in informal learning experiences within students' homes.* Paper presented at the annual meeting of the American Educational Research Association, New York.

Tuinstra, C., & Hiatt-Michael, D. (2003). Student-led conferences. *Family, School, Community AERA SIG Newsletter, 8,* 14.

U.S. Department of Education. (n.d.). *Elementary and Secondary Education Act § 1118.* Retrieved October 30, 2009, from http://www.ed.gov/policy/elsec/leg/esea02/pg2.html#sec1118

Vadeboncoeur, J. A. (2006). Engaging young people: Learning in informal contexts. *Review of Research in Education, 30,* 239–278.

Wainright, J. L., Russell, S. T., & Patterson, C. J. (2004). Psychosocial adjustment, school outcomes, and romantic relations of adolescents with same-sex parents. *Child Development, 75,* 1886–1896.

Wallis, C. (2006, August 29). The myth about homework. *Time.* Retrieved October 30, 2009, from http://www.time.com/time/magazine/article/0,9171,1376208,00.html

Chapter 5

Akroyd, S. (1995). Forming a parent reading-writing class: Connecting cultures, one pen at a time. *The Reading Teacher, 48,* 580–584.

Ambrose, K. (2008). *Let's learn together!* Unpublished master's project, California State University, Fullerton.

Armour, S. (2003, October 19). More companies downsize family friendly programs. *USA Today.* Retrieved October 9, 2009, from http://www.usatoday.com/money/workplace/2003-10-19-company-family-_x.htm

Barton, A. C., Drake, C., Perez, J. G., St. Louis, K., & George, M. (2004). Ecologies of parental engagement in urban education. *Educational Researcher, 33,* 3–12.

Brakeman, K. H. (2007, January 8). Students projects can't be left to kids: Teachers should realize how much time and money they're costing parents. *The Orange County Register.* Retrieved October 30, 2009, from http://www.ocregister.com/articles/the-orange-grove-1536488-students-projects-cant-be-left-to-kids

Caspe, M. S. (2003). How teachers come to understand families. *The School Community Journal, 13*(1), 115–131.

Come, B., & Fredericks, A. D. (1995). Family literacy in urban schools: Meeting the needs of at-risk children. *The Reading Teacher, 48,* 566–570.

Desimone, L. (1999). Linking parent involvement with student achievement: Do race and income matter? *Journal of Educational Research, 93*(1), 11–30.

Dodici, B., Draper, C., & Peterson, C. (2003). Early parent-child interactions and early literacy development. *Topics in Early Childhood Special Education, 23,* 124–136.

Epstein, J. L. (1992). School and family partnerships. In M. Alkin (Ed.), *Encyclopedia of educational research* (6th ed., pp. 1139–1151). New York: Macmillan.

Epstein, J. L. (2001). *School, family, and community partnerships: Preparing educators and improving schools.* Boulder, CO: Westview Press.

Epstein, J. L., Sanders, M. G., Simon, B. S., Salinas, K. C., Jansorn, N. R., & Van Voorhis, F. L. (2002). *School, family, and community partnerships: Your handbook for action.* Thousand Oaks, CA: Corwin.

Gibbs, N. (2005, February 13). Parents behaving badly. *Time.* Retrieved October 4, 2009, from http://www.time.com/time/magazine/article/0,9171,1027485,00.html

Griffith, J. (1996). Relation of parent involvement, empowerment, and school traits to student academic performance. *Journal of Educational Research, 90*(1), 33–41.

Hara, S. R., & Burke, D. J. (1998). Parent involvement: The key to improved student achievement. *School Community Journal, 8*(2), 9–19.

Hoover-Dempsey, K. V., & Sandler, H. M. (1995). Parental involvement in children's education: Why does it make a difference? *Teachers College Record, 97,* 310–331.

Hoover-Dempsey, K. V., & Sandler, H. M. (2005, March 22). *The social context of parental involvement: A path to enhanced achievement* (Final Performance Report for OERI Grant #R305T010673). Presented to Project Monitor, Institute of Education Sciences, U.S. Department of Education.

Katsaros, S. (2003, January 30). Fathers are hitting the books. *Dateline.* Fullerton: California State University.

Keith, T. Z., Keith, P. B., Troutman, G. C., Bickley, P. G., Trivette, P. S., & Singh, K. (1993). Does parental involvement affect eighth-grade student achievement? Structural analysis of national data. *School Psychology Review, 22*(3), 474–496.

Lezotte, L. (1997). *Learning for all.* Okemos, MI: Effective School Products.

Lightfoot, S. L. (1978). *Worlds apart: Relationships between families and schools.* New York: Basic Books.

McWayne, C., Hampton, V., Fantuzzo, J., Cohen, H. L., & Sekino, Y. (2004). A multivariate examination of parent involvement and the social and academic competencies of urban kindergarten children. *Psychology in the Schools, 41,* 363–377.

Moles, O. C. (1993). Collaboration between schools and disadvantaged parents: Obstacles and openings. In N. Chavkin (Ed.), *Families and schools in a pluralistic society* (pp. 21–49). Albany: State University of New York Press.

Moll, L. C. (Ed.). (1990). *Vygotsky and education: Instructional implications and applications of sociohistorical psychology.* New York: Cambridge University Press.

Moll, L. C., & Gonzalez, N. (1994). Critical issues: Lessons from research with language-minority children. *Journal of Reading Behavior, 26,* 439–456.

National Parent Teacher Association. (2000). *Building successful partnerships: A guide for developing parent and family involvement programs.* Bloomington, IN: National Educational Service.

National Sleep Foundation. (n.d.). *Information about children's sleep for parents and teachers.* Available at http://www.sleepforkids.org/html/uskids.html

Nichols-Solomon, R. (2000). Conquering the fear of flying. *Phi Delta Kappan, 82,* 19–21.

Parent Teacher Education Connection. (n.d.). *The four P's.* Retrieved October 30, 2009, from http://www.tcet.unt.edu/pteconnect/?module=Communicating&section=introduction&page=fourPs

Project Appleseed. (n.d.). *The six slices of parental involvement.* Retrieved October 30, 2009, from http://www.projectappleseed.org

Redding, S. (2001). The community of the school. In S. Redding & L. G. Thomas (Eds.), *The community of the school* (pp. 319–333). Lincoln, IL: Academic Development Institute.

Rogers, C. (1967). *On becoming a person: A therapist's view of psychotherapy.* London: Constable.

Rogers, C. R. (1969). *Freedom to learn: A view of what education might become.* Columbus, OH: Charles Merrill.

Sears, W., Sears, M., Sears, J., & Sears, R. (2006). *The healthiest kid in the neighborhood.* Boston: Little, Brown.

Senechal, M. (2006). Testing the home literacy model: Parent involvement in kindergarten is differentially related to grade 4 reading comprehension, fluency, spelling, and reading for pleasure. *Scientific Studies of Reading, 10,* 59–87.

Senechal, M., & LeFevre, J. (2002). Parental involvement in the development of children's reading skill: A five-year longitudinal study. *Child Development, 73,* 445–460.

Sleep for Kids. (n.d.). *Information about children's sleep for parents and teachers.* National Sleep Foundation. Retrieved October 10, 2009, from http://www.sleepforkids.org/html/uskids.html

Thorkildsen, R., Thorkildsen, M. R., & Stein, S. (1998, December). Is parent involvement related to student achievement? Exploring the evidence. *Research Bulletin Phi Delta Kappa Center for Evaluation, 22,* 17–20.

Valdes, G. (1996). *Con respeto: Bridging the gap between culturally diverse families and schools.* New York: Teachers College Press.

Chapter 6

Anaheim Ducks Hockey Club, LLC, and the American Hockey Association. (2009). *Ducks in the community.* Retrieved October 30, 2009, from http://ducks.nhl.com/club/page.htm?id=44877

Buchanan, A. M., Baldwin, S. C., & Rudisill, M. E. (2002). Service learning as scholarship in teacher education. *Educational Researcher, 31*(5), 28–34.

Center for Civic Education. (2006). *Project citizen.* Calabasas, CA: Author.

DuPont. (2009). *Education commitment.* Retrieved December 22, 2008, from http://www2.dupont.com/Social_Commitment/en_US/educational/index.html

Edison Schools. (2008). *Contact us.* Retrieved October 27, 2009, from http://www.edison-schools.com/edison-schools/contact-us

Eisenhart, M., & Edwards, L. (2004). Red-eared sliders and neighborhood dogs: Creating third spaces to support ethnic girls' interests in technological and scientific expertise. *Children, Youth and Environments, 14*(2), 156–177. Retrieved June 28, 2007, from http://www.colorado.edu/journals/cye

Encarta World English Dictionary. (2009). *Community.* Retrieved October 27, 2009, from http://encarta.msn.com/dictionary_1861599034/community.html

Freed, A. B. (2008, January). *Environmental service learning: Clean air zone campaign.* Paper presented at the annual meeting of the Association for Science Teacher Education, St. Louis, MO.

Goldstein, A. (2006, September 19). Civic involvement tied to education. *Washington Post,* p. A19.

Harpo, Inc. (2009). *Building a dream: The Oprah Winfrey Leadership Academy.* Retrieved October 30, 2009, from http://www2.Oprah.com/ophilanthropy/ophilanthropy_landing.jhtml

Jacobs, H. H. (1997). *Mapping the big picture: Integrating curriculum and assessment K–12.* Alexandria, VA: Association for Supervision and Curriculum Development.

Kaye, C. B. (2004). *The complete guide to service learning: Proven, practical ways to engage students in civic responsibility, academic curriculum, and social action.* Minneapolis, MN: Free Spirit.

Keeter, S., Zukin, C., Andolina, M., & Jenkins, K. (2002). *The civic and political health of the nation: A generational portrait.* College Park, MD: Center for Information and Research on Civic Learning and Engagement.

Kielburger, M., & Kielburger, C. (2002). *Take action! A guide to active citizenship.* Hoboken, NJ: Wiley.

Llewellyn, D., & Wicks, E. (2001). Thirty years and counting. *ENC Focus, 8*(1), 37–38.

NBA Media Ventures, LLC. (2009). *League launches "NBA Cares" global outreach initiative.* Retrieved June 25, 2007, from http://www.nba.com/community/NBACARES_051018.html

Orange County's Pacific Symphony. (2009). *Class act.* Retrieved October 30, 2009, from http://www.pacificsymphony.org/main.taf?p=6,3

Orange-Ulster BOCES. (2009). *Programs and services.* Retrieved October 30, 2009, from http://www.ouboces.org/

Parravano, C. (2001). The school-business partnership: What can it offer? *ENC Focus, 8*(1), 14–17.

Ponder, J., & Cox-Petersen, A. M. (2008, January). *Service-learning, stewardship, and civic involvement: Taking action in science methods courses.* Paper presented at the annual meeting of the Association for Science Teacher Education, St. Louis, MO.

Pumpian, I., Fisher, D., & Wachowiak, S. (2006). *Challenging the classroom standard through museum-based education.* Mahwah, NJ: Lawrence Erlbaum.

Sanders, M. G., & Harvey, A. (2002). Beyond the school walls: A case study of principal leadership for school-community collaboration. *Teachers College Record, 104,* 1345–1368.

Sobel, D. (2004). *Place-based education: Connecting classrooms and communities* (Nature Literacy Series, No. 4). Barrington, MA: Orion Society.

Wade, R. (Ed.). (1997). *Community service-learning: A guide to including service in the public school curriculum.* Albany: State University of New York Press.

Westheimer, J., & Kahne, J. (2004). What kind of citizen? The politics of educating for democracy. *American Educational Research Journal, 41*(2), 237–269.

Chapter 7

American Association of Museums. (1992). *Excellence and equity: Education and the public dimensions of museums.* New York: Author.

American Association of Museums. (2008). *What is a museum?* Retrieved January 11, 2008, from http://www.aam-us.org/aboutmuseums/whatis.cfm

Cox-Petersen, A. M., Marsh, D. D., Kisiel, J., & Melber, L. M. (2003). Investigation of guided school tours, student learning, and science reform recommendations at a museum of natural history. *Journal of Research in Science Teaching, 40,* 200–218.

Cox-Petersen, A. M., & Melber, L. M. (1999). Creating a classroom museum. *Science Scope, 20,* 38–41.

Cox-Petersen, A. M., & Melber, L. M. (2001). Linking technology to prepare and extend field trips. *The Clearing House, 75*(1), 18–20.

Cox-Petersen, A. M., & Olson, J. K. (2000). Authentic science learning in the digital age. *Learning & Leading With Technology, 27*(6), 32–35.

Falk, J. H., & Dierking, L. D. (1997). School field trips: Assessing their long-term impact. *Curator, 40,* 211–218.

Falk, J. H., & Dierking, L. D. (2000). *Learning from museums: Visitors' experiences and their making of meaning.* Walnut Creek, CA: AltaMira Press.

Finson, K. D., & Enochs, L. G. (1987). Student attitudes toward science-technology-society resulting from a visit to a science technology museum. *Journal of Research in Science Teaching, 24,* 593–609.

Goldman, M., & Laserna, C. (1998). Building school community relationships. *Journal of Computing and Higher Education, 9*(2), 44–70.

Greenfield, P. M. (1984). A theory of the teacher in the learning activities of everyday life. In B. Rogoff & J. Lave (Eds.), *Everyday cognition: Its development in social context* (pp. 117–138). Cambridge, MA: Harvard University Press.

Griffin, J., & Symington, D. (1997). Moving from task-oriented to learning-oriented strategies on school excursions to museums. *Science Education, 81*(6), 763–780.

Kisiel, J. E. (2003). Teachers, museums and worksheets: A closer look at a learning experience. *Journal of Science Teacher Education, 14,* 3–21.

Louv, R. (2005). *Last child in the woods: Saving our children from nature-deficit disorder.* Chapel Hill, NC: Algonquin Books.

Martin, W. W., Falk, J. H., & Balling, J. D. (1981). Environmental effects on learning: The outdoor field trip. *Science Education, 65,* 301–309.

Melber, L. M., & Abraham, L. M. (2002). History of science education in U.S. natural history museums. *Science and Education, 11,* 45–54.

Melber, L. M., & Cox-Petersen, A. M. (2005). Teacher professional development and informal learning environments: Investigating partnerships and possibilities. *Journal of Science Teacher Education, 16,* 103–120.

Moles, O. C. (1993). Collaboration between schools and disadvantaged parents: Obstacles and openings. In N. Chavkin (Ed.), *Families and schools in a pluralistic society* (pp. 21–49). Albany: State University of New York Press.

Paulu, N. (1992). *Helping your child learn science.* Washington, DC: U.S. Department of Education Office of Educational Research and Improvement.

Ramey-Gassert, L., Walberg, H. J., III, & Walberg, H. J. (1994). Reexamining connections: Museums as science learning environments. *Science Education, 78,* 345–363.

Ross, D. (2006). The opportunity to learn science like scientists: Museums are a good idea. In I. Pumpian, D. Fisher, & S. Wachowiak (Eds.), *Challenging the classroom standard through museum-based education* (pp. 109–122). Mahwah, NJ: Lawrence Erlbaum.

Stevens, D. D. (1999). The ideal, real, and surreal in university-school partnerships. *Teaching and Teacher Education, 15,* 287–299.

Valdes, G. (1996). *Con respeto: Bridging the gap between culturally diverse families and schools.* New York: Teachers College Press.

Chapter 8

Bermudez, A. (1994). *Doing our homework: How schools can engage Hispanic communities* (Chapter 1). Retrieved November 1, 2009, from http://clas.uiuc.edu/fulltext/cl00136/chapter1.html

Bohon, S. A., Macpherson, H., and Atiles, J. H. (2005). Educational barriers for new Latinos in Georgia. *Journal of Latinos and Education, 4,* 43–58.

Buttery, T. J., & Anderson, P. J. (1999). Community, school, and parent dynamics: A synthesis of literature and activities. *Teacher Education Quarterly, 26,* 111–122.

Cerra, C., & Jacoby, R. (2005, September). Getting along with the grown-ups: Expert ideas for solving your toughest parent problems. *Instructor,* 45–48.

Diller, J. V., & Moule, J. (2005). *Cultural competence: A primer for educators.* Belmont, CA: Thomson Wadsworth.

Forum on Child and Family Statistics. (2006). *America's children in brief: Key national indicators of well-being.* Washington, DC: Federal Interagency on Child and Family Statistics.

Guerrero, O. M. (2006). *Enhancing parent involvement through action learning walks.* Unpublished master's project, California State University, Fullerton.

Human Rights Watch. (2008). Retrieved November 1, 2009, from http://www.hrw.org/

Huss-Keeler, R. L. (1997). Teacher perception of ethnic and linguistic minority parental involvement and its relationships to children's language and literacy learning: A case study. *Teaching and Teacher Education, 13,* 171–182.

Knowledge iTrust, Inc. (2002). *Peace diaries.* Retrieved October 30, 2009, from http://www.peacediaries.org

Ladson-Billings, G. (1995). But that's just good teaching! The case for culturally relevant pedagogy. *Theory Into Practice, 34,* 159–165.

Lee, O. (2005). Science education with English language learners: Synthesis and research agenda. *Review of Educational Research, 75,* 491–530.

Lee, O., & Fradd, S. H. (1998). Science for all, including students from non-English-language backgrounds. *Educational Researcher, 27,* 12–21.

Leuder, D. C. (1998). *Creating partnerships with parents: An educator's guide.* Lancaster, PA: Technomic.

Mattingly, D., Prislin, R., McKenzie, T., Rodriguez, J., & Kayzar, B. (2002). Evaluating evaluations: The case of parent involvement programs. *Review of Educational Research, 72,* 549–576.

Melber, L. M., & Abraham, L. M. (2000). *Pigeons, parents, and children: Understanding science together.* Paper presented at the annual meeting of the National Association for Research in Science Teaching, New Orleans, LA.

Milner, H. R. (2007). Race, culture, and researcher positionality: Working through dangers seen, unseen and unforeseen. *Educational Researcher, 36,* 388–400.

Moles, O. C. (1993). Collaboration between schools and disadvantaged parents: Obstacles and openings. In N. Chavkin (Ed.), *Families and schools in a pluralistic society* (pp. 21–49). Albany: State University of New York Press.

National Association of School Psychologists. (2007, July). *Vision, mission, and goals.* Retrieved November 1, 2009, from http://www.nasponline.org/about_nasp/strategicplan.pdf

National Center for Education Statistics. (2000). *Digest of educational statistics.* Washington, DC: Government Printing Office.

Nichols-Solomon, R. (2000). Conquering the fear of flying. *Phi Delta Kappan, 82*(1), 19–21.

Onikama, D. L., Hammond, O. W., & Koki, S. (1998). *Family involvement in education: A synthesis of research for Pacific educators.* Honolulu, HI: Pacific Resources for Educational Learning.

Pollock, M. (2007). *Colormute: Race talk dilemmas in an American school.* Princeton, NJ: Princeton University Press.

Robles, S. (2006). *Helping immigrant families and teachers participate in immigrant students' academic and social development.* Unpublished master's project, California State University, Fullerton.

Southern Poverty Law Center. (n.d.). *Teaching tolerance.* Retrieved October 30, 2009, from http://www.tolerance.org/index.jsp

Van Allsburg, C. (1992). *The widow's broom.* New York: Houghton Mifflin Books.

Williams, D. A. (2007). *Beyond the golden rule: A parent's guide to preventing and responding to prejudice.* Montgomery, AL: Teaching Tolerance.

Zuniga, C., & Alva, S. (1996). Parents as resources in schools: A community-of-learners perspective. *The Journal of Educational Issue of Language Minority Students, 16,* 207–224.

Chapter 9

Freedom Writers (with Gruwell, E.). (1999). *The freedom writers diary: How a teacher and 150 teens used writing to change themselves and the world around them.* New York: Broadway Books.

National Association of County and City Health Officials. (2007). Retrieved October 31, 2009, from http://www.naccho.org/about/

National Parent Teacher Association. (2000). *Building successful partnerships: A guide for developing parent and family involvement programs.* Bloomington, IN: National Educational Service.

Sanders, M. G. (2006). *Building school-community partnerships: Collaboration for student success.* Thousand Oaks, CA: Corwin.

U.S. Department of Education. (n.d.). *Helping your child series.* Retrieved October 30, 2009, from http://www.ed.gov/parents/academic/help/hyc.html

Chapter 10

De la Piedra, M. T., Munter, J. H., & Giron, H. (2006). Creating links, "Atando Cabitos": Connecting parents, communities, and future teachers on the U.S./Mexico border. *The School Community Journal, 16,* 57–80.

Epstein, J. L. (2001). *School, family, and community partnerships: Preparing educators and improving schools.* Boulder, CO: Westview Press.

Epstein, J. L., Sanders, M. G., Simon, B. S., Salinas, K. C., Jansorn, N. R., & Van Voorhis, F. L. (2002). *School, family and community partnerships: Your handbook for action* (2nd ed.). Thousand Oaks, CA: Corwin.

Fuchs, L. S., Fuchs, D., Hamlett, C. L., Phillips, N. B., Karns, K., & Dutka, S. (1997). Enhancing students' helping behavior during peer tutoring with conceptual mathematical explanations. *Elementary School Journal, 97*(3), 223–250.

Lee, J. Y. (2005). *Family art night: A partnership of parents, school, and community.* Unpublished manuscript, California State University, Fullerton.

Ngo, C. Z. (2008). *An action plan for family involvement.* Unpublished manuscript, California State University, Fullerton.

Ylagan, R. (2005). *An effective partnership: Learner's Club.* Unpublished manuscript, California State University, Fullerton.

Chapter 11

Abrams, L. S., & Gibbs, J. T. (2002). Disrupting the logic of home-school relations: Parent involvement strategies and practices of inclusion and exclusion. *Urban Education, 37,* 384–407.

Bento, K., Brooks, T., Cunningham, C., & Robbins, V. (2007). *Professional partnership project example: TLC.* Unpublished paper presentation, California State University, Fullerton.

Calderhead, J., & Gates, P. (1993). Introduction. In J. Calderhead & P. Gates (Eds.), *Conceptualizing reflection in teacher development* (pp. 1–10). Washington, DC: Falmer Press.

Eaker, R., Dufour, R., & Dufour, R. (2002). *Getting started: Reculturing schools to become professional learning communities.* Bloomington, IN: National Educational Service.

Epstein, J. L. (2001). *School, family, and community partnerships: Preparing educators and improving schools.* Boulder, CO: Westview Press.

Fan, X., & Chen, M. (1999). Parental involvement and students' academic achievement: A meta-analysis. *Center for Educational Statistics.* Arlington, VA: National Science Foundation.

Foster, W. (1986). *Paradigms and promises: New approaches to educational administration.* Buffalo, NY: Prometheus Books.

Gibbs, N. (2005, February 13). Parents behaving badly. *Time.* Retrieved October 4, 2009, from http://www.time.com/time/magazine/article/0,9171,1027485,00.html

Jacobs, H. H. (1997). *Mapping the big picture: Integrating curriculum and assessment K–12.* Alexandria, VA: Association for Supervision and Curriculum Development.

Joyce, B., & Showers, J. (1988). *Student achievement through staff development.* New York: Longman.

Lemlech, J. K. (1995). *Becoming a professional leader.* New York: Scholastic.

Louis, K. S., Marks, H. M., & Kruse, S. D. (1996). Teachers' professional community in restructuring schools. *American Educational Research Journal, 33,* 757–798.

Mills, G. E. (2003). *Action research: A guide for the teacher researcher* (2nd ed.). Upper Saddle River, NJ: Merrill/Prentice Hall.

Morse, A., Nygart, K., & Parrish, K. (2008). *Working with families: Royal Readers.* Unpublished paper, California State University, Fullerton.

National Institute on Drug Abuse. (2004). *D.A.R.E.* Retrieved November 1, 2009, from http://www.dare.com/home/Resources/NIDA.asp

Rich, D. (1998). What parents want from teachers. *Educational Leadership, 55*(8), 37–39.

Rosenbaum, D. P. (1998). *Assessing the effects of school-based drug education: A six-year multilevel analysis of project D.A.R.E.* Chicago: University of Illinois Department of Criminal Justice and Center for Research in Law and Justice. Retrieved September 13, 2008, from http://tfy.drugsense.org/uic.htm

Schon, D. A. (1987). *Educating the reflective practitioner: Toward a new design for teaching and learning in the professions.* San Francisco: Jossey-Bass.

Senge, P. (1990). *The fifth discipline: The art and practice of the learning organization.* New York: Doubleday/Currency.

Sheldon, S. B. (2003). Linking school-family-community partnerships in urban elementary schools to student achievement on state tests. *The Urban Review, 35,* 149–165.

Woods, P. (1985). Conversations with teachers: Some aspects of life history method. *British Educational Research Journal, 11,* 13–25.

Index

Ableism, 85, 281

Abraham, Linda, 204

Abrams, L. S., 276

Accreditation
  National Board for Professional Teaching
    Standards (NBPTS) and, 12–13, 41, 270
  National Council for Accreditation of
    Teacher Education (NCATE) and, 12

Acculturation, 16, 281
  assimilation *vs.*, 16–17

Achievement gap
  collaborative education of children to
    alleviate, 13–14
  parent and teacher disconnect and, 6
  partnerships effect on, 6
  socioeconomic factors and, 13

Action-based pedagogical strategies, K-8, 146
  barriers to partnerships eliminated by,
    184, 188
  citizenship participation, 150–154
  civic involvement, 148–149, 150
  service learning, 147, 149
  stewardship, 147–148, 149–150

Action Learning Walks case study, 24–26,
  194–195

Action plan, 239, 281
  creating an action plan and, 239–241
  development of, 186
  goals, strategies, and outcomes of, 239,
    241 (photo)
  implementation of, 254–255
  locating potential partners and, 240
  stages of: introduction and rationale, 242
  stages of: determining the type of
    involvement, 239, 243–244
  stages of: identifying partners, 239,
    244–245, 265
  stages of: front-end assessment, 239,
    245–246, 258–259

stages of: stating goals and objectives, 239,
  246–247, 248 (table), 259
stages of: identifying potential barriers, 239,
  248–249
stages of: timeline for implementation, 239,
  250, 251–252 (table)
stages of: evaluation of the partnership, 239,
  252–253, 259–260
stages of: cite your references, 253–254
stages of: appendix, 254
tips for teachers from teachers regarding, 254

Adoption, 85

After-school programs, 73–74, 281
  faith-based partnerships and, 140
  popularity of, 43
  YMCA and Stevenson Elementary School ,
    Long Beach, California partnership, 211

Aiken, Cathy, 227–229

Akroyd, Susan, 132–133

Allen, Debbie, 141

Allen, J., 87

Allen, Kim, 48–50

Alliance for Healthier Generation collaborative
  partnership, 68, 70

Alva, S., 190

Ambrose, Kari, 50–51, 95, 98

American Association of Museums, 166, 168

American Association of University Women
  Educational Foundation, 224

American Association of University Women
  Education Foundation, 224

American Institute of Aeronautics and
  Astronautics (AIAA) Classroom Grant, 223

American Museum of Natural History's Urban
  Advantage program, 179

Amrose, Kari, 134–135

A Nation At Risk (National Commission on
  Excellence in Education), 41, 42

Anderson, P. J., 192

Andolina, M., 148
Art Around the Corner program
    (National Gallery of Art), 167
Arts education, 173
    after-school programs and, 73, 74, 281
    Anna Simpson Artmobile program,
        Wyoming, 173
    Arts Education Partnership and, 46
    assessing resources and, 214
    case study: Class Act program, Pacific
        Symphony Orchestra, 232–233
    community partnership programs and,
        15–16
    grants for, 223, 225
    *Improving Learning in Schools With Arts
        Partners in the Community* report
        and, 46
    magnet schools and, 32, 39, 286
    See also Museums and cultural institutions
        partnerships
Asperger syndrome, 121, 281
Assessment, 251, 281
Assimilation, 16, 281
    acculturation *vs.*, 16–17
Assistive technology, 143
    Individual Education Plan (IEP) and, 61
    museum field trips and, 169
    online partnerships and, 143
    special needs student requirements and, 22
Association of Zoos and Aquariums, 179

Back-to-school night event, 88
Baker, Lisa Renee, 72
Baker, Tom, 145 (photo), 163 (photo)
Baldwin, S. C., 147
Barbour, C., 19
Barbour, N. H., 19
Barriers to partnerships, 185, 281
    acknowledging differences and showing
        respect and, 199
    action-based strategies and, 146–154,
        184, 188
    activist interaction and connections
        and, 183
    authority distribution within the classroom
        and, 184
    "being American" concept and, 189
    *Beyond the Golden Rule: A Parent's Guide to
        Preventing and Responding to Prejudice*
        (Williams) and, 187

books that promote partnerships and
    diversity and, 201
case study: Action Learning Walks, 24–26,
    194–195
case study: Pakistani families and teachers,
    202–204
case study: PIPE Pigeon project, 204
challenging intolerance and, 199
characteristics of effective partnerships
    and, 192
collaborating, role of families in school
    collaboration and, 193–194
collaborating, role of schools in family
    collaboration and, 193
collaborating, role of the school psychologist
    in family collaboration and, 194
collaborative planning and, 192–194,
    193 (table)
colormute concept and, 186–187
communication importance and, 192,
    193 (table), 194–195
community of learners program and, 190
culturally relevant pedagogy and,
    183–184, 283
culturally relevant teaching and learning
    and, 183–184
culture and language barriers, 186–188
diversity as "spice of the school" concept
    and, 186–187
emphasizing positive aspects of diversity
    and, 199–200
flexibility mechanisms to overcome and,
    183–184
Forum on Child and Family Statistics data
    and, 183
hate and, 195–196
Human Rights Watch report and, 198–199
instructionally congruent practices
    and, 184
language barrier, 190
management barriers, 185
modeling equity strategy and, 187–188, 199
music that promotes peace and tolerance
    and, 201–202
Peace Diaries online interactive global
    forum and, 200, 205
political conditions barriers, 191
power distribution inequities barriers, 140,
    190–191
prejudice and, 188

prior knowledge and beliefs
    organizer and, 182
proactive learning and, 184
racial and cultural differences,
    third grade, 189
resources limitations and, 248
stereotypes and, 198–199
stereotypes of special needs students
    and, 188
strategies to address barriers and, 192, 193
    (table), 200 (table)
summary regarding, 202
taking action and, 194–200
talking to parents and, 193 (table)
teachable moment emphasis and, 199
teachers' deficit views barriers, 191
teacher self-knowledge importance and, 184
Teaching Tolerance group and, 187, 199, 205
time and commitment barriers,
    185–186, 248
Title I: Improving America's School Act
    (1994) and, 185
tolerance education and, 195–197, 196
trust and respect to overcome, 192
trust barriers, 191
"us versus them" mentality and, 248
welcoming school environment
    importance and, 186
The Widow's Broom (Allsburg) and,
    198, 198 (table)
Barrios, Angelica Casas, 24–26
Barton, A. C., 129
Basic Principles of Curriculum and Instruction
    (Tyler), 36
Bauch, J. P., 45
Becerra, Sra., 93
Benchmarks, 250, 281
Bennett, S., 96
Berliner, D. C., 16
Beyond the Golden Rule: A Parent's Guide to
    Preventing and Responding to Prejudice
    (Williams), 187
Biddle, B. J., 16
Bilingual education
    Head Start legislation, bilingual and
        bicultural programs, 40
Blust, Lani Char, 189
Book It! Program of Pizza Hut, as successful
    partnership example, 274–275
Bos, C. S., 58

Bourdieu, P., 33
Bowen, N. K., 33
Bower, L., 83–84
Brendzel, Elisa, 234
Bronfenbrenner, Uri, 32–33
Brown v. Board of Education of Topeka,
    Kansas, 36
Buchanan, A. M., 147
Buddies of Petersburg (BOP) program,
    Virginia, 149
Building effective partnerships. See Building
    family-school partnerships;
    Community-school partnerships:
    respecting diversity; Family-school
    partnerships; Innovative partnership
    strategies; Partnering with community
    organizations and resources; Planning for
    partnerships; Seeking and sustaining
    successful partnerships
Building family-school partnerships
    academic achievement improved by, 111, 129
    Asperger syndrome and, 121
    best homework practices communication
        and, 127–128
    book exchange program and, 126
    case study: developing writers, elementary
        school, 132–133
    case study: "Kamp Kino" dinner, activities,
        and literacy event, elementary grades,
        134–135
    children with special needs and, 121
    common experiences components in,
        111–112
    communicating type of, 116–121
    community collaboration and, 128–129
    creating a literate environment at home and,
        124–126
    deficit view of family involvement and, 114
    Doughnuts for Dads program and, 124
    early literacy and family support and,
        130–131
    effective communication and, 116–117
    effective partnerships with families and, 111
    engaging parents in school events and, 129,
        130 (table)
    entrepreneurship, neighborhood businesses
        and, 126
    families today and, 129–131
    "family friendly" businesses, school
        volunteer time and, 121

family involvement redefinition and, 129
family literacy creation guidelines and, 125
Family-School Partnership Act (California)
 and, 122
family surveys tool and, 112
four Ps communication strategies and, 119
"funds of knowledge" concept and, 114
genuineness, respect, and empathy
 conditions of teacher communications
 and, 120–121
getting to know students and their families
 and, 112
"grow foods" concept and, 127
healthy nutrition habits and, 70, 126
home literacy model and, 131
home visits and, 121
Hoover-Dempsey Sandler Model of Parental
 Involvement and, 112, 113 (fig.)
how families are included and, 114
Illinois Fatherhood Initiative and, 124
learning at home type of, 124–128
open-door policies and, 118–119
outdoor activities importance and, 126
parental involvement types and, 114–129,
 130 (table)
parenting type of, 116
Parent Teacher Education Connection Web
 site and, 119
personalized information strategy and, 119
positive and inviting school environment
 element of, 111–112
positive parenting suggestions and, 116
prior knowledge and beliefs organizer
 and, 110 (table)
proactive communication and, 119–120
Project Appleseed and, 122, 124–125, 136
reflective practice shared decision making
 model and, 128
reporting positive information and, 119
The School Community Journal
 (Caspe) and, 118
school-to-home notebook sample and, 120
Searching for Lots of Volunteers
 questionnaire, K-5 grades and, 123
shared decision making and, 5, 128
site-based or school-based management
 and, 128
sleep recommendations and, 126,
 127 (table)
solving problems at home and, 126–129

summary regarding, 131
teacher information for visiting parents,
 kindergarten and, 117–118
teacher information visiting parents
 and, 117–118
tips for families and teachers and, 131
volunteering type of, 121–124
volunteerism levels and, 122–123
See also Families today; Family-school
 partnerships
*Building Successful Partnerships: A Guide for
 Developing Parent and Family Involvement
 Programs* (National Parent Teacher
 Association), 216, 216 (table)
Bureau of Labor Statistics Population Survey,
 83 (table)
Bush, George W. *See* No Child Left Behind
 (NCLB)
Buttery, T. J., 192

Calderhead, J., 270–271
California Department of Health Service,
 74–76
Cantu, Rochelle, 60–61
Cardinal Principles of Secondary Education
 (Commission on the Reorganization of
 Secondary Education), 35
Career Development Grants, 224
Case studies of partnerships, xiv
 Action Learning Walks, 24–26, 194–195
 Class Act program, Pacific Symphony
  Orchestra, 232–233
 clean air zone campaign, elementary and
  middle schools, 156–157
 creating a family art night, 257
 CyberSisters, 26–27
 developing writers, elementary school,
  132–133
 Harvest of the Month nutrition partnership
  program, 74–76
 home visit home-school connection, first
  grade, 103–105
 "Kamp Kino" dinner, activities, and literacy
  event, elementary grades, 134–135
 learning and motivation, first grade, 50–51
 learning styles, fourth-grade, 48–49
 Pakistani families and teachers, U.K.
  primary school, 202–204
 parent-teacher-child partnership, selective
  mutism, 76–77

pigeons, parents, and children, PIPE Pigeon project, 204
professional development program, Red Rock Canyon State Park, Mojave Desert, California, 178
promoting a fit lifestyle for children, first grade, 234
promoting more family involvement, third grade, 257–260
School in the Park, museums of Balboa Park, San Diego, California, 173, 176–178
Simply the Best! after-school science and technology program, middle and high school girls, 157–158
student-led conferences, fifth-grade, 90, 90 (table), 103
teacher-family partnership for success, second grade, 76–77
Caspe, M. S., 118
CATA. *See* Child Abuse Prevention and Treatment Act (CAPTA, 1974)
Center for Parent Education and Family Support, North Texas University, 136
Center on School, Family, and Community Partnerships, Johns Hopkins University, 5
Centers for Disease Control and Prevention, 67
Cerra, C., 192, 193 (table)
Champions for Change (California Department of Health Services), 70
Charter school, 32, 281
    as community of practice, 15
    Edison Project holistic educational experience and, 144–145
    first official charter school, Minnesota, 43
    popularity of, 42
    teacher, community, and family empowerment themes of, 45
Child abuse and neglect, 64, 282
    characteristics of abused and neglected children and, 65
    child abuse, 64
    Child Abuse Prevention and Treatment Act (CATA, 1974) and, 64
    Childhelp nonprofit organization and, 64–65, 78
    dos and don'ts of dealing with, 66 (table)
    emotional abuse, 64
    Keeping Children and Families Safe Act (2003) and, 63
    National Child Abuse Hotline and, 64
    national child abuse statistics and, 65 (table)
    neglect, 64
    physical abuse, 64
    sexual abuse, 64
Child Abuse Prevention and Treatment Act (CAPTA, 1974), 64, 282
Childhelp nonprofit organization, 64–65, 78
Childhood Hunger Relief Act (1975), 40
Child Nutrition Act (1968), 36, 37, 66
Child Nutrition and WIC Reauthorization Act (2004), 70
Children's needs in the 21st century. *See* After-school programs; Child abuse and neglect; Health and nutrition issues; No Child Left Behind (NCLB); Physical fitness and health; Special needs students
Children with special needs, 121, 282
    See also Special needs students
The Child's Conception of the World (Piaget), 35
Cisneros, Sandra, 201
Citizenship participation, 150–151, 150 (table)
Citizenship training, 31
    Corporation for National and Community Service and, 43
    National and Community Service Act (1990) and, 43
Civic involvement, 148, 282
    Buddies of Petersburg (BOP) program, Virginia and, 149
    core indicators of engagement and, 148
    samples of, 150
Civil Rights Act (1964)
    Coleman Report result of, 38
    desegregation of schools and, 37
Clark, Ron, 216–217, 235
Clinton, Bill, 43
Coalition of Essential Schools, 42
Cognitive information processing learning theories, 47, 282
Cognitive learning theories, 47
Cohen, H. L., 111
Coleman, J. S., 33
Coleman Report, 38
Collaborative descriptions
    arm-in-arm collaboration, 18
    arms-length collaboration, 18
    hand-in-hand collaboration, 18
    no-collaboration collaboration, 17
    one-time collaboration, 17

partnership types, examples, and
characteristics and, 18 (table)
process and task orientation of
collaboration and, 33
professional learning communities and,
267–268
social *vs.* cultural capital and, 33–34
See also Barriers to partnerships;
Community-school partnerships;
Family-school partnerships;
Interagency collaboration; Professional
education partnerships
Colormute, 186–187, 282
Come, B., 122, 125, 126
Comer, James P., 38
Comer School Development Program
teamwork education approach, 38
Communities in Schools program,
179, 230, 244
Communities of practice, 14–16, 235, 282
charter school example of, 15
"community of learners" model of, 15
components and examples of, 14–15
joint enterprise component of, 15
mutual engagement component of, 15
shared repertoire component of, 15
situated learning and, 14
See also Community-school partnerships;
Educational partnerships: importance of
Community, 22, 282
Community in Schools program, 230
Community partnership, 9, 282
Community-school partnerships, 9, 282
after-school programs, 73–74
arts education programs, 15–16
as beneficiaries of educational
partnerships, 9
case study: PIPE Pigeon science project, 204
case study: School in the Park museum field
trip program, San Diego California,
173, 176–178
Communities in Schools program,
179, 230, 244
"community of learners" model and, 15
as educational partnership example, 9
factors affecting, 212–213
family nutrition and, 70
The Freedom Writers Diary (Gruwell)
and, 211
Lunch Mentors senior citizens community
partnership program, 211

Mayan families, Guatemala and, 15
Parent Teacher Education Connection, 52
physical fitness and health education and,
71–72
public charter school, K-8 and, 15
reasons for creation of, third-grade, 10
research studies and articles on
school-community-family
partnerships and, 279
Sisters in Science community partnership, 9
teachers as members of learning
communities and, 12
YMCA and Stevenson Elementary School,
Long Beach, California partnership, 211
See also Communities of practice;
Community-school partnerships:
respecting diversity; Community-school
partnerships: respecting diversity
examples; Implementing and sustaining
successful partnerships; Partnering
with community organizations and
resources; Planning for partnerships;
Seeking and sustaining successful
partnerships
Community-school partnerships: respecting
diversity
academic achievement improvements
and, 139
action-based pedagogical strategies, K-8
and, 146–154, 184, 187–188
administrator support factor in, 139
case study: clean air zone campaign,
156–157
case study: *Simply the Best!* after-school
science and technology program,
middle and high school girls, 157–158
citizen participation types and, 150–151,
150 (table)
citizenship action and practice and, 152–154
"civic health gap" concept and, 148
civic involvement and, 148–150
commitment to learning factor in, 139
community definitions and, 139
community partnerships and, 140–146
community partnerships and, tips for
community members, 155
community partnerships and, tips for
schools, 154–155
corporate partnerships and, 143–144
expansion of, 139
faith-based partners and, 140–141

high-profile partners and, 141–142
innovative collaborative partnerships and,
    144–146
NCLB and, 140
online partnerships and, 142–143
power inequities as a barrier to, 140
prior knowledge and beliefs organizer and,
    138 (table)
school, community, and business
    partnerships and, 139–140
service learning and, 147, 149
service learning and, sixth grade, 151–152
shared decision making element in, 140
sports teams and, 141–142
stewardship and, 147–148, 149–150
students with special needs and, assistive
    technology and, 142–143
summary regarding, 155
supporting factors regarding, 139
two-way communication factor in, 139
welcoming school climate factor in, 139
See also Barriers to partnerships;
        Community-school partnerships;
        Community-school partnerships:
        respecting diversity examples;
        Partnering with community
        organizations and resources
Community-school partnerships: respecting
    diversity examples
    Buddies of Petersburg (BOP) program,
        Virginia, 149
    Cary Academy, Cary, North Carolina, 145
    case study: clean air zone campaign,
        156–157
    case study: Simply the Best! after-school
        science and technology program,
        middle and high school girls, 157–158
    Dupont Corporation, Dupont Office of
        Education, 144
    EcoJustice Education movement, 159
    Edison Project holistic educational
        experience, 144–145
    Europa Penpal Web site, 142, 159
    Global Gateway Project (U.K.), 142, 159
    Global SchoolNet Foundation, 142, 159
    GLOBE Program hands-on environmental
        science and education project, 142
    KIDS (Kids Involved Doing Service
        Learning) Consortium, 147
    Orange County Partnership for Young
        Children, New York, 140–141

Reach to Achieve NBA program, 141–142
Science Controversies on-line: Partnerships
        in Education (SCOPE) project, 142
Xerox Science Consultant Program (XSCP),
        143–144
Youth Stewardship Program, San Francisco,
        148, 159
Computers. See Internet; Technology
Conditioning learning theories, 47, 282
Conferences. See Parent-teacher conferences
Connections to the National Board
        Certification, xiv
Constructivist learning theories, 47, 283
Contemporary view of education, 87, 283
Cooper, H., 96
Corporate partnerships, 143–144
    Anaheim Ducks matching program, 141
    Delta Airlines, Ron Clark Academy, 217
    Dupont Corporation, Dupont Office of
        Education, 144
    Junior Achievement, 274
    Xerox Science Consultant Program (XSCP),
        143–144
Corporation for National and Community
        Service, 43
Cox-Petersen, Amy M., 95
    author's experiences and, xvii–xviii
    grant writing guidelines co-developed by,
        219–221
    museum visit recommendations of, 170
    professional development program case
        study, Red Rock Canyon State Park,
        Mojave Desert, California and, 178
Cultural capital, 33–34, 283
    teacher education about educational
        partnerships and, 46
    See also Family-school partnerships
Cultural institutions. See Museums and
        cultural institutions partnerships
Cultural Literacy: What Every American Needs
        to Know (Hirsch), 42
Culturally relevant pedagogy, xiv, 183, 283
Culturally relevant strategies of
        partnerships, xvi
    vs. deficit models, xvi
    homevisits, 94–95, 95 (table)
    incorporating multicultural and culturally
        relevant materials, 95–96
    See also Barriers to partnerships; Culturally
        relevant teaching; Family-school
        partnerships

Culturally relevant teaching, 22, 283
    See also Barriers to partnerships; Culturally
        relevant pedagogy; Family-school
        partnerships
Culture, 22, 283
Curriculum maps, 269, 283
CyberSisters case study, 26–27
Dafour, R., 267–268

DARE (Drug Abuse Resistance Education)
    program, as successful partnership
    example, 274, 278
David and Lucile Packard Foundation, 73
Davis, Cynthia, 232–233
Deficit view, xvi, 114, 283
Delgado-Gaitan, C., 87, 102
Democracy and Education (Dewey), 47
Democratic equality goal of education, 31, 283
    Democracy and Education (Dewey) and, 47
    Good Citizenship: The Purpose of Education
        (E. Roosevelt) and, 36
Desegregation of schools
    Brown v. Board of Education of Topeka,
        Kansas and, 36
Desimone, L., 96, 129
Developing Industry/Education Partnerships
    Web site, 261
DeVore, A., 95
DeVore, A. K., 99
Dewey, John, 35 (photo)
    active learning theory of, 47
    Democracy and Education written by, 47
    Experience and Education written by, 35
    experiential learning work of, 35
    "My Pedagogic Creed" written by, 34, 35
    The School and Society written by, 35
Dierking, L. D., 170
Differentiated instruction, 57, 283
Digital divide concept, 44
Disabled students. See Individuals with
    Disabilities Education Act (IDEA);
    Special needs students
Diversity
    acculturation vs. assimilation and, 16–17
    author experiences in, xvii–xviii
    "being American" concept and, 189
    See also Barriers to partnerships;
        Community-school partnerships:
        respecting diversity; Culturally relevant
        teaching; Family-school partnerships
Dominion Educational Leadership, 223

Donovan, Loretta, 219–220
Doorlag, D. H., 61
Dorfman, D., 33
Drake, C., 129
Drug Abuse Education Act (1970), 39
Drug Abuse Office and Treatment Act
    (1972), 39
Drug Abuse Resistance Education. See DARE
    (Drug Abuse Resistance Education)
    program, as successful partnership
    example
Dupont Corporation, Dupont Office of
    Education, 144
Dutka, S., 255

Eaker, R., 267–268
Earthwatch Teacher Fellowships, 225–226
EcoJustice Education movement, 159
Economic Opportunity Act (1964), 37
    amendments to, Head Start, 38
    amendments to, special needs children, 40
Edison Project holistic educational experience,
    144–145
Educational partnerships, 284
    book features and, xv–xvi
    research studies and articles on
        school-community-family
        partnerships and, 279
    See also Barriers to partnerships; Building
        family-school partnerships;
        Community-school partnerships;
        Community-school partnerships:
        respecting diversity; Culturally relevant
        strategies of partnerships; Educational
        partnerships: importance of; Families
        today; Family-school partnerships;
        History of educational partnerships;
        History of educational partnerships:
        specific subject; Implementing and
        sustaining successful partnerships;
        Partnering with community
        organizations and resources; Planning
        for partnerships; Seeking and
        sustaining successful partnerships
Educational partnerships: importance of, 5
    acculturation vs. assimilation and, 16–17
    administrators benefits of, 8
    benefits and justification of, 5–9, 15 (photo)
    collaborative decision-making and, 5, 128
    collaborative descriptions and, 17–18,
        18 (table)

collaborative view of educating children
and, 13–14
communities of practice and, 14–16
community benefits of, 9
community examples of, 9
community partnership, reasons for
creation of, third grade, 10
definitions regarding, 5
effective partnership characteristics
and, 11
equitable teaching and learning and, 16–17
examples of, 9–11
families benefits of, 7–8
family examples of, 9
influences on students' education and,
19–20, 19 (table)
"Island-Themed Day" example of,
7 (photo)
National Board for Professional Teaching
Standards (NBPTS) and, 12–13
partnership tree and, 21(fig.)
partnership types, examples, and
characteristics and, 5, 22–24
prior knowledge and beliefs organizer
and, 4 (table)
professional examples of, 10
reaching out to families and, 16
school benefits of, 7
shared, sequential, and separate
responsibilities and, 20–21,
20–21(table), 21(fig.)
situated learning and, 14
students benefits of, 8
students with special needs and, 22
summary regarding, 24
teachers benefits of, 8
types of educational partnerships and, 17
value of, 11–14
"What Teachers Hate About Parents"
(Time magazine) and, 6, 265–266
See also History of educational partnerships;
History of educational partnerships:
books/reports/organizations; History
of educational partnerships: legislation
Education for All Handicapped Children Act
(1975), 40
Edwards, L., 157–158
Effective communications, 116–117, 284
Effective educational partnerships, 284
characteristics of, 11
Eisenhart, M., 157–158

Elementary and Secondary Education Act
(1965), 37
See also No Child Left Behind (NCLB)
emTech Web site, 52
English language learners, 22, 284
Environmental education, 37
Environmental Education Act, 39
Epstein, Joyce
action plans, action teams and, 250, 271
Center on School, Family, and Community
Partnerships, Johns Hopkins University
developed by, 5
family partnership activities work of, 129,
130 (table)
interactive homework views of, 242
involvement types developed by, 46,
114–129, 130 (table), 131, 239, 243
National Network of Partnerships Schools,
Johns Hopkins University and, 44
shared, sequential, and separate
responsibilities concept of,
20–21 (fig.)
teacher and administrator role in
family-school partnerships and, 111
volunteerism levels and, 122–123, 244
Equal access education goal, 31
Equal treatment education goal, 31
The Essential Conversation: What Parents and
Teachers Can Learn from Each Other
(Lawrence-Lightfoot), 45
Ethnic groups, 23, 284
Ethnicity, 23, 284
Europa Penpal Web site, 142, 159
Evaluation, 251, 284
"Every child. One voice." National PTA
motto, 45
Exosystem, 33, 284
Experience and Education (Dewey), 35
Experiential learning, 35
Explicit partnerships, 17, 284

Faith-based partners, 140–141, 284
Falk, J. H., 170
Families today
adopted children and, 81, 84, 85
backpack homework assignment examples,
97–98
case study: student-led conferences, 90, 90
(table), 103
case study: teacher-family partnership for
success, second grade, 76–77

changes in traditional family structure and, 81–84
communicating with irate parents and, 89–90
contemporary family tree and, 84
contemporary view of education and, 87
cultural and linguistic education for families and teachers and, 87
culturally responsive home-school partnership and, 86–87
diverse family structures and, 81–82
family participation initiatives and, 86
family-school bonding events and, 100–101
homeless children and, 82
home visits and, 94–95, 95 (table), 103–105
homework assignments and, 96–100, 99–100 (table)
inclusive classrooms and, 84–86
listening to and communicating with families and, 87
multicultural and culturally relevant materials and, 95–96
multiple communication methods and, 92–93
NCLB and, 86
open house, back-to-school night, and conferences, 87–88
parent-child-teacher contract and, 90 (fig.)
parent-child-teacher contrast and, 90 (table)
parent-teacher conferences and, 88–89
parent-teacher conferences and, advance organizer, 88 (table)
parent-teacher conferences and, parent-child-teacher contract and, 89, 90
parent-teacher conferences and, tips for families, 101
parent-teacher conferences and, tips for teachers, 102
prior knowledge and beliefs organizer, 80 (table)
reflective journals tool and, 86–87
same-sex parents and, 83–84
science newsletter sample and, third grade, 92–93
sharing, connecting, and supporting families and, 87
special needs children and, 85–86
structure of the traditional family and, 81
summary regarding, 102
survey of students' families and, 86

weekly news brief example and, kindergarten, 93
working mothers increase and, 82–83, 83 (table)
See also Building family-school partnerships; Family-school partnerships
Family, 23, 285
See also Building family-school partnerships; Families today; Family-school partnerships
Family Education Rights and Privacy Act (FERPA, 1974), 40
Family Involvement Network of Educators (FINE), 28
Family Policy Compliance Office, 40
Family-School Partnership Act (California), 122
Family-school partnerships, 9, 23, 285
acculturation *vs.* assimilation and, 16–17
achievement gap reduction and, 6
beneficiaries of educational partnerships and, 7–8
Building Successful Partnerships: A Guide for Developing Parent and Family Involvement Programs (National Parent Teacher Association) and, 214–216
case study: Action Learning Walks, 24–26, 194–195
case study: creating a family art night, 257
case study: home visits, first grade, 103–105
case study: Pakistani families and teachers, 202–204
case study: promoting more family involvement, third grade, 257–260
case study: student-led conferences, fifth grade, 103
case study: teacher-family partnership for success, second grade, 76–77
collaboration, role of families and, 193–194
collaboration, role of school psychologist and, 194
collaboration, role of schools and, 193
communicating with families about resources and, 227–229
as educational partnership example, 9
Family Involvement Network of Educators (FINE) and, 28
family nutrition and, 70
home school associations (HAS) and, 39

implementing and sustaining partnerships
and, 276–277
Institute for Responsive Education and, 28
Literacy Mornings partnership
program and, 9
"Lunch Club" for at-risk" students and,
217–219
NCLB links and, 56–57
Nell Soto Parent/Teacher Involvement
Program and, 224
parental involvement types and, 46
parent communication councils
(PCC) and, 39
Parent Teacher Education Connection
and, 52
physical fitness and health education
and, 71–72
reaching out to families and, 16
research studies and articles on
school-community-family
partnerships and, 279
student-led conferences and, 90,
90 (table), 103
teacher assessments by families and, 276
teacher newsletter to families and, 227–228
"What Teachers Hate About Parents"
(*Time* magazine) and, 6, 265–266
See also Building family-school
partnerships; Culturally relevant
strategies of partnerships; Families
today; Implementing and sustaining
successful partnerships; Planning for
partnerships; Seeking and sustaining
successful partnerships
Family tree, 84, 285
Fantuzzo, J., 111
Federson, Yvonne, 64
Fick, Sarah, 59
Field trips. *See* Partnering with community
organizations and resources
*The Fifth Discipline: The Art and Practice of the
Learning Organization* (Senge), 267
FINE. *See* Family Involvement Network of
Educators (FINE)
Finson, K. D., 168
Flournoy, Valerie, 201
Forestry Institute for Teachers collaborative
project, 174
Formative assessment, 252–253, 257,
259, 285

Forum on Child and Family Statistics
data, 183
Foster, William, 272–273
Foster care families, 81, 84
Foundation Educator Achievement Award,
225–226
Fradd, S. H., 184
Fredericks, A. D., 122, 125, 126
Free Appropriate Public Education (FAPE)
Education for All Handicapped Children Act
(EAHCA) and, 40
IDEA and, 44
Freed, Andrea, 156–157
The Freedom Writers Diary (Gruwell), 211
Free schools, 39
development of, 39
popularity of, 39
Freida J. Riley Teacher Award, 226
Freire, Paulo
Pedagogy of the Oppressed written by, 37
Fuchs, D., 255
Fuchs, L. S., 255

Gates, P., 270–271
Gender gap
in math and science, CyberSisters case study
and, 26–27
Title IX, women's equality in sports and
education and, 39
George, M., 129
Gibbs, J. T., 276
Gifted and talented students, 61, 285
differentiated instruction and, 63
enhancing learning for, 63
gifted *vs.* talented and, 61
intelligence test assessments and, 61
National Association for Gifted Children
(NAGC) and, 61
NCLB elements and, 61–63
teaching of, 61–63
Global Gateway educational partnership
project (U.K.), 142, 159
Global SchoolNet Foundation, 142, 159
GLOBE Program hands-on environmental
science and education project, 142
Goals, 246, 285
Goals 2000: Educate America Act (1996), 43
Safe Schools Act and, 43
Goldstein, A., 148
Gonzalez, N., 94, 114

Good Citizenship: The Purpose of Education
(E. Roosevelt), 36
Good Luck Gold and Other Poems (Wong), 201
Grandparents as parents, 81
Grant, grants, 219, 285
action plans and, 219
action plans and, timeline example of,
222 (table)
to assist in working with families, 220
as funding sources, 219
general grant information sites and,
224–225
goals *vs.* objectives and, 221
grant writing guidelines and, 220–221
information sites regarding, 224–225
for instructional purposes, 221–223
to recognize teachers and/or provide
professional development, 225–227
requests for proposals (RFPs) and, 219
Research Experiences for Children, grant
proposal action plan and timeline
and, 222 (table)
to support and acknowledge teachers,
221–227
to support educational partnerships,
223–224
to support teaching and learning, 219–221
writing the proposal and, 220–221
See also Grant, grants: specific grants and
aids; Seeking and sustaining successful
partnerships
Grant, grants: specific grants and aids
American Association of University Women
Educational Foundation, 224
American Institute of Aeronautics and
Astronautics (AIAA) Classroom
Grant, 223
Career Development Grants, 224
Dominion Educational Leadership, 223
Earthwatch Teacher Fellowships, 225–226
Foundation Educator Achievement Award,
225–226
Freida J. Riley Teacher Award, 226
Grants Alert, 225
International Reading Association
grants, 226
The Jordan Fundamentals Grant
Program, 225
Lowe's Toolbox for Education Grant
Program, 225

Mathematics Education Trust: Improving
Students' Understanding of Geometry
Grants, 222
Mathematics Education Trust: Using Music
to Teach Mathematics, 221
Merrill Lunch Foundation, 225
Mockingbird Foundation, 223
National Teachers Hall of Fame Teacher
Recognition, 226
Nell Soto Parent/Teacher Involvement
Program, 223
P. Buckley Moss Foundation for Children's
Education, 223
Partners in Learning Grants Initiative, 224
Professional Awards for Excellence in
Mathematics and Science Teaching,
226–227
Rhode Island Higher Education Partnership
Grants, 224
Starbucks Foundation Grants, 224
Teacher Leader Grant for Teachers of Grades
3–5, 223
Teachers Network: Teacher Grants, 225
Time Warner Cable's National Teacher
Awards, 227
Grants Alert, 224, 225
Greathouse, S., 96
Greenfield, P. M., 46
Gruwell, Erin, 211
Guerrero, Olivia M., 24–26, 194

Hamlett, C. L., 255
Hampton, V., 111
Harris, Judith Rich, 19
Harris, M. M., 46
Harvest of the Month nutrition partnership
program, 74–76
Harvey, A., 139
Hate, 285
Head Start legislation, 38
bilingual and bicultural Head Start
programs and, 40
Economic Opportunity Act and, 40
Even Start literacy programs and, 41
family involvement in, 43
Sesame Street created by, 38
Health and nutrition issues
abused and neglected children
and, 64–66
after-school programs and, 73–74

Alliance for Healthier Generation
  collaborative partnership and, 68
  body-mass index (BMI) and, 67
  case study: Harvest of the Month nutrition
    partnership program, 74–76
  case study: parent-teacher-child partnership,
    selective mutism, 76–77
  case study: promoting a fit lifestyle for
    children, first grade, 234
  Champions for Change (California
    Department of Health Services)
    and, 70
  Child Nutrition Act (1968) and, 66
  Child Nutrition and WIC Reauthorization
    Act (2004) and, 70
  children's well-being and, 66–74
  Communities in Schools program and,
    179, 230, 244
  as community issue, 68
  family meals importance and, 70
  food pyramid and, 68, 69 (fig.)
  The Future of Children newsletter and, 73
  Healthpact, Australian Health Promoting
    Schools Association program and, 230
  healthy eating at home and, 70, 126
  history of nutrition in schools and, 66–67
  Last Child in the Woods (Louv) and, 71, 174
  learning in out-of-school programs and,
    73–74
  National Conference of State Legislatures
    and, 45
  National School Lunch Act (1946) and,
    36, 66
  "nature-deficit disorder" concept and,
    71, 174
  Nutrition Network, Network for a Healthy
    California and, 75
  obesity and nutrition and, 67–68
  physical education and, 71–72
  Project GLEAN (Gaining Leverage and
    Empowerment through Aequate
    Nutrition) and, 70
  recess and, 72, 78
  responsibility and nutrition and, 68–70
  school lunch program and, 36, 66–67
  United Nations Children's Fund and, 63
  value of partnerships to make healthy
    choices and, 73
  See also Child abuse and neglect; Physical
    fitness and health

Healthpact, Australian Health Promoting
  Schools Association program, 230
Healthy School Healthy Families program,
  Columbia University, 165
Heather Has Two Mommies (Newman), 201
Hehir, T., 85
Hemmer, R., 46
Hiatt-Michael, D., 91
Hirsch, Edward, 42
History of educational partnerships
  after-school programs, 43
  arts education, 46
  Alice McLellan Birney and, 34
  *Brown v. Board of Education of Topeka,
    Kansas,* 36
  case study: learning styles in fourth-grade
    classroom, 48–50
  case study: student learning and motivation,
    first grade, 50–51
  charter schools, 42, 43, 45
  community, family, and school partnership
    initiatives and, 44
  democratic equality goal of education
    and, 31
  digital divide concept, 44
  educational learning theories and, 46–47
  educational policy and, 45–46
  environmental education, 37
  "Every child. One voice." concept, 45
  health and nutrition issues, 45
  Phoebe Apperson Hearst and, 34
  magnet schools, open schools, and free
    schools, 39
  national education standards movement, 43
  prior knowledge and beliefs organizer and,
    30 (table)
  public good *vs.* private good and, 31–32
  school-based management, 43
  Schools, Students, and Tomorrow restructure
    education plan, 41–42
  school-to-work issues, 41
  Sesame Street creation, 38
  Skyline High School in Dallas, Texas, 39
  social efficiency goal of education and, 31
  social mobility goal of education and, 31–32
  social *vs.* cultural capital and, 33–34
  Sputnik launch, 36
  students and families as part of a system
    and, 32–33
  summary regarding, 47

summer youth employment programs, 41

teacher education about educational partnerships and, 45–46

teachers' colleges, 35

timeline of: 1900–1920, families determine the school curriculum, 34–35

timeline of: 1920–1940, change in responsibility, 35–36

timeline of: 1940–1960, desegregation of schools and national defense, 36

timeline of: 1960–1970, change in educational programs, 36–38

timeline of: 1970–1980, shared responsibilities and opportunities, 39–41

timeline of: 1980–1990, back to basics, 41–42

timeline of: 1990–2000, academic standards and shared decisions, 42–44

timeline of: 2000-present, educational accountability, 44–45

timeline of at University of Minnesota College of Education and Human Development, 52

types of schools and, 32

See also Educational partnerships: importance of; History of educational partnerships: books/reports/organizations; History of educational partnerships: legislation

History of educational partnerships: books/reports/organizations

Basic Principles of Curriculum and Instruction (Tyler), 36

Cardinal Principles of Secondary Education (Commission on the Reorganization of Secondary Education), 35

The Child's Conception of the World (Piaget), 35

Coalition of Essential Schools, 42

Coleman Report, 38

Comer School Development Program teamwork education approach, 38

Corporation for National and Community Service, 43

Cultural Literacy: What Every American Needs to Know (Hirsch), 42

The Essential Conversation: What Parents and Teachers Can Learn from Each Other (Lawrence-Lightfoot), 45

Experience and Education (Dewey), 35

Family Policy Compliance Office, 40

"Federal Programs for Education and Related Activities," 52

Good Citizenship: The Purpose of Education (E. Roosevelt), 36

Horace's Compromise (Sizer), 42

"I have a Dream" speech (King), 37, 38 (photo)

Learning Disabilities Association of America, 37

"My Pedagogic Creed" (Dewey), 34, 35

National Association of Elementary School Principals, 43

National Board for Professional Teaching Standards, 41

National Center for Education Statistics, 52

National Congress of Mothers, 34

National Council of Teachers of Mathematics (NCTM) standards, 43

National Institute on Drug Abuse, 39

National Network of Partnerships Schools, Johns Hopkins University, 44

National Organization for Women, 37

National Parent Teacher Association (PTA), 34, 45

National Science Education Standards, 43

A Nation At Risk (National Commission on Excellence in Education), 41, 42

Parent Teacher Education Connection/North Texas Partnership Program Modules, 52

Parent-teacher organizations and associations (PTO/PTA), 39

Pedagogy of the Oppressed (Freire), 37

The School and Society (Dewey), 35

The Secret of Childhood (M. Montessori), 36

Silent Spring (Carson), 37

Toward a Theory of Instruction (Bruner), 38

See also History of educational partnerships; History of educational partnerships: legislation

History of educational partnerships: legislation

Childhood Hunger Relief Act (1975), 40

Child Nutrition Act, 36, 37

Civil Rights Act (1964), 37, 38

Drug Abuse Education Act (1970), 39

Drug Abuse Office and Treatment Act (1972), 39

Economic Opportunity Act (1964), 37

Economic Opportunity Act amendments, Head Start, 38
Economic Opportunity Act amendments, special needs children, 40
Education for All Handicapped Children Act (1975), 40
Elementary and Secondary Education Act, 37
Environmental Education Act, 39
Even Start literacy programs, 41
Family Education Rights and Privacy Act (FERPA, 1974), 40
free breakfast programs, 40
Goals 2000: Educate America Act (1996), 43
government-sponsored grant programs, 44
Head Start legislation, 38
Head Start legislation, bilingual and bicultural programs, 40
Improving America's Schools Act (1994), 43
Individuals with Disabilities Education Act (IDEA), 40–41, 44
Javits Act (1988), 41
Job Training Partnership Act (1982), 41
National and Community Service Act (1990), 43
National School Lunch Act (1946), 36, 66
Native American employment programs, 41
No Child Left Behind (NCLB), 44
Personal Responsibility and Work Opportunity Reconciliation Act (1996), 44
Public Law 99–457, 42
School Milk Program, 36
Service Act (1990), 43
Standards for Quality School-Age Child Care, 43
Title IX, women's equality in sports and education, 39
See also History of educational partnerships; History of educational partnerships: books/reports/organizations
Homeless, homelessness, 82, 285
Home literacy model, 131, 285
Home schools, 32, 285
home school associations (HAS) and, 39
Home visits, 94–95, 285
case study: home visit, first grade, 103–105
children with special needs and, 121
common themes of teachers who conduct, 95, 95 (table)
family communication and, 121

Homework
backpack homework assignment examples and, 97–99
best homework practices communication and, 127–128
conducive environment for, 56, 126
interactive homework assignment samples and, 99–100 (table)
interactive homework "Learners Club" support program and, 242, 245, 249, 252–253, 254
ten minute rule of, 96
Hoover-Dempsey, K. V., 112, 113 (fig.)
Horace's Compromise (Sizer), 42
The House on Mango Street (Cisneros), 201
Howard, Glenda, 10
Human Rights Watch report, 198–199
Huntington Library, Art Collections, and Botanical Gardens, San Marino, California, 166, 179

Iannelli, V., 64
IDEA. See Individuals with Disabilities Education Act (IDEA)
IEPs. See Individual education plans (IEPs)
"I Have a Dream" speech (King), 37
Illinois Fatherhood Initiative, 124
Implementing and sustaining successful partnerships
characteristics of successful partnerships and, 265
community-school-family collaborative projects, steps in, 265
curriculum mapping and, 269
democratic decision making and leadership and, 272–273
environmental considerations and, 272
example of: Book It! Program of Pizza Hut, 274–275
example of: DARE (Drug Abuse Resistance Education) program, 274, 278
example of: Junior Achievement program, 273–274
example of: "Royal Readers" program, 275
family partnerships and, 276–277
local libraries and activities and, 275
Monitoring the Future survey (National Institute on Drug Abuse) and, 274
National Board Certification and collaboration and, 269–270

parents, news, and misconceptions and, 265–267, 266 (photo)
parent-teacher relationships and, 265–267
peer mentoring and coaching and, 268–269
prior knowledge and beliefs organizer and, 264 (table)
professional educational partnerships and, 267–270
professional learning communities and, 267–268
steps in: creating an action team, 271
steps in: "selling" the partnership, 272
steps in: empowering participation from multiple partners, 272–273
steps in: promoting ongoing communication, 273
summary regarding, 278
teachers as reflective practitioners and, 270–271
teacher self-assessments and, 276–277
tips for, 277–278, 277 (table)
trust, communication, and respect elements in, 265
"What Teachers Hate About Parents" (*Time* magazine) and, 6, 265–266
See also Planning for partnerships; Professional education partnerships; Seeking and sustaining successful partnerships
Implicit partnerships, 17, 285
Improving America's Schools Act (1994), 43, 185
Improving Learning in Schools With Arts Partners in the Community report, 46
Inclusion, 57, 58, 286
Inclusive classrooms, 84, 286
home visits and, 94
Individual education plans (IEPs) element, of IDEA, 23, 44, 58, 60–61, 286
Individuals with Disabilities Education Act (IDEA), 286
differentiated instruction and, 57
free appropriate pubic education provision of, 44
gifted and talented students component of, 61–63
inclusion and, 58
individual education plan (IEP) component of, 23, 44, 58, 60–61, 286
least restrictive environment provision of, 44

mainstreaming and, 58
parental rights in, 44
provisions of, 40–41, 44
qualifications regarding, 57
revision of, NCLB and, 57
student study team (SST) component of, 58–59
support and instructional plans of, 58 (table)
Innovative partnership strategies, xvi
Institute for Responsive Education, 28
Instructionally congruent practices, 184, 286
Interagency collaboration, 229, 230 (photo), 286
benefits of, 229
Community in Schools program and, 230
community resources and services list and, 231
Healthpact, Australian Health Promoting Schools Association program and, 230
International Reading Association, 226
Internet
Europa Penpal Web site and, 142, 159
Global Gateway Project (U.K.) and, 142, 159
Global SchoolNet Foundation and, 142, 159
GLOBE Program hands-on environmental science and education project and, 142
online educational partnerships and, 142–143
Science Controversies on-line: Partnerships in Education (SCOPE) project and, 142
Tomasito's Mother Comes to School (Mayer) online storybook and, 201
virtual museum tours and, 173–174
Island Explorers program, University of Southern California Sea Grant Office, 164

Jacobson, A., 46
Jacoby, R., 192, 193 (table)
Javits Act (1988), 41
Jenkins, K., 148
Jianzhong, X., 96
Job Training Partnership Act (1982), 41
Johnson, Lyndon B.
Economic Opportunity Act and, 37
Head Start legislation of, 38
"war on poverty" programs of, 37
Joint enterprise, 15, 286
Jooyan, Gino, 196–197
Jordan Fundamentals Grant Program, 224, 225
Joyce, B., 268–269
Junior Achievement program, as successful partnership example, 273–274

Kahne, J., 150 (table)
Kalish, N., 96
Karns, K., 255
Katz, L., 45
Kaye, C. B., 147
Kayzar, B., 191
Kecker, Kendra, 15–16
Keeler, Huss, 202–204
Keeping Children and Families Safe
    Act (2003), 63
Keeter, S., 148
KIDS (Kids Involved Doing Service Learning)
    Consortium, 147
Kilman, M., 96–97
King, Martin Luther, Jr., 37
Kinsey, Susan, 232–233
Koenings, N., 95
Kohn, A., 96
Kruse, S. D., 267

Labaree, D. F., 31, 48
Ladson-Billings, Gloria, 22, 183
La mamá de Tomasito visita la excuela
    (Mayer), 201
Lane, B., 33
Last Child in the Woods (Louv), 71, 174
Lave, J., 94
Lawrence-Lightfoot, Sara, 45
"Learners Club" interactive homework
    mentoring program, 242, 245, 249,
    252–253, 254
Learning definition, 46
Learning Disabilities Association of
    America, 37
Learning theories
    cognitive information processing theories, 47
    conditioning theories, 47
    constructivist theories, 47
    emTech Web site and, 52
    social cognitive theories, 47
Lee, J. S., 33
Lee, Jee, 257
Lee, O., 184
LeFevre, J., 131
Legitimate peripheral participation, 14
Lemlech, J. K., 269
Leuder, D. C., 191
Lewis, R. B., 61
Library activities, 56
Lin, Serena, 115 (photo)
Lindsay, J. J., 96

Literacy. *See* Reading, literacy
Literacy Mornings family-school partnership
    program, 9
Little, C., 73
Louis, K. S., 267
Louv, Richard, 71, 174
Lowe's Toolbox for Education Grant Program,
    224, 225
Lueder, D. C., 6
Lumsden, L., 73
Lunch Mentors senior citizens community
    partnership program, 211

Macrosystem, 32–33, 286
Magnet school(s), 32, 286
    development of, 39
    popularity of, 39
Mainstreaming, 57, 287
Marks, H. M., 267
Marquez, Carrie, 102–103
Math and science
    American Association for the Advancement
        of Science (AAASI) and, 270
    case study: clean air zone campaign,
        elementary and middle schools, 156–157
    case study: CyberSisters, 26–27
    case study: PIPE Pigeon science project, 204
    case study: professional development
        program, Red Rock Canyon State Park,
        Mojave Desert, California, 178
    case study: School in the Park, museums of
        Balboa Park, San Diego, California, 173,
        176–178
    Dino-Mite Summer Camp and, 227–229
    Dupont Corporation, Dupont Office of
        Education and, 144
    EcoJustice Education movement and, 159
    GLOBE Program hands-on environmental
        science and education project and, 142
    grants: American Institute of Aeronautics
        and Astronautics (AIAA) Classroom
        Grant, 223
    grants: Dominion Educational
        Leadership, 223
    grants: Earthwatch Teacher Fellowships,
        225–226
    grants: Foundation Educator Achievement
        Award, 225–226
    grants: Mathematics Education Trust:
        Improving Students' Understanding of
        Geometry Grants, 222

grants: Mathematics Education Trust: Using Music to Teach Mathematics, 221
homework findings regarding, 96–97
National Council of Teachers of Mathematics (NCTM) standards and, 43
National Science Education Standards and, 43
Professional Awards for Excellence in Mathematics and Science Teaching and, 226–227
Public Science Day and, 270
Science Controversies on-line: Partnerships in Education (SCOPE) project and, 142
science newsletter sample, third grade, 92–93
Simply the Best! after-school science and technology program, middle and high school girls and, 157–158
Sisters in Science community partnership and, 9
Team Time partnership program and, 10
Urban Advantage science field trip program, New York City, 173
Xerox Science Consultant Program (XSCP) and, 143–144
Mathematics Education Trust: Improving Students' Understanding of Geometry Grants, 222
Mathematics Education Trust: Using Music to Teach Mathematics, 221
Mattingly, D., 191
Mayer, Ellen, 201
McComb, E. M., 73
McKenzie, T., 191
McWayne, C., 111
Media influence
impact of, 56
on student education, 19–20, 19 (fig.)
Meeting the needs of all children in the 21st century. *See* After-school programs; Child abuse and neglect; Health and nutrition issues; No Child Left Behind (NCLB); Physical fitness and health; Special needs students
Melber, L. M., 178, 204
Mentoring programs
classroom teachers as student teaching mentors and, 164–165
faith-based partnerships and, 140
interactive homework "Learners Club" support program and, 242, 245, 249, 252–253, 254
Lunch Mentors senior citizens community partnership program and, 211
peer mentoring and coaching and, 268–269
"Reading Together" Philadelphia community-supported parent tutoring program and, 179
Merrill Lunch Foundation, 225
Microsystem, 33, 287
Milner, H. R., 184
Mockingbird Foundation, 223
Moll, Luis C., 94, 114
Monitoring the Future survey (National Institute on Drug Abuse), 274
Montessori, Maria, 36
Morrison, Gayle, 103–105
Multiracial, 23, 287
Museum Educational Social Network Web site, 179
Museums and cultural institutions partnerships
American Association of Museums and, 166, 168
Ann Simpson Artmobile outreach art program, Wyoming, 173
Around the Corner Program (National Gallery of Art), 167
contextual model of learning and, 170
Earthmobile, Natural History Museum (Native American history), Los Angeles County, 173
field trips to, 173–174
field trips to, pretrip activities, 168–169
field trips to, special needs students, museum access, 169
field trips to, during the field trip, 169–170
field trips to, posttrip activities, 171
field trips to, tips for families, 175
field trips to, tips for teachers, 175
field trips to, zoo visit, sixth grade, 171–172
Huntington Library, Art Collections, and Botanical Gardens, San Marino, California, 166
Mission San Juan Capistrano historical site, San Jan Capistrano, California, 167
Museum Educational Social Network Web site and, 179

National Gallery of Art, Washington, D.C., 166–167
"novelty effect" concept and, 169
purpose of museums and, 166
virtual online field trips and, 173
visitor characteristics, demographics and, 167–168
Music case study: Class Act program, Pacific Symphony Orchestra, 232–233
Mutual engagement, 15, 287
"My Pedagogic Creed" (Dewey), 34, 35

NAGC. *See* National Association for Gifted Children (NAGC)
NASPE. *See* National Association for Sport and Physical Education (NASPE)
National and Community Service Act (1990), 43
National Assessment of Education Progress, 13
National Association for Gifted Children (NAGC), 61
National Association for Sport and Physical Education (NASPE), 71, 78
National Association of Elementary School Principals, 43
National Association of School Psychologists, 192
National Board Certification, 12, 287
collaboration and, 269–370
connections sections of book and, xvi
teacher experience of, 12–13
teacher experience of, third grade, 269–270
National Board for Professional Teaching Standards (NBPTS)
core propositions of, 12–13, 41
teacher experience and, third grade, 270
National Center for Education Statistics, 52
National Center for Health Statistics, 67
National Child Care Information and Technical Assistance Center, 235
National Congress of Mothers, 34
National Council for Accreditation of Teacher Education (NCATE), 12
National Council of Teachers of Mathematics (NCTM) standards, 43
National Dissemination Center for Children with Disabilities (NICHCY), 214
National Education Association, 41–42
National education standards movement, 43
National Endowment for the Arts, 46

National Gallery of Art, Washington, D.C., 166–167
National Institute on Drug Abuse, 39
National Network of Partnership Schools, Johns Hopkins University, 28, 44
National Organization for Women, 37
National Parent Teacher Association (PTA)
Building Successful Partnerships: A Guide for Developing Parent and Family Involvement Programs publication of, 216, 216 (table)
"Every child. One voice." motto of, 45
National Congress of Mothers and, 34
National School Lunch Act (1946), 36, 66
National Science Education Standards, 43
National Science Foundation, 204
National Teachers Hall of Fame Teacher Recognition, 226
"Nature-deficit disorder" concept, 71, 174
NBPTS. *See* National Board for Professional Teaching Standards (NBPTS)
NCATE. *See* National Council for Accreditation of Teacher Education (NCATE)
NCLB. *See* No Child Left Behind (NCLB)
Neglect, 64, 287
Nell Soto Parent/Teacher Involvement Program, 223
Nettie's Trip South (Turner), 201
Newman, Lesléa, 201
New Songs for Peace Web site, 201
Ngo, Caroline, 257–260
NICHCY. *See* National Dissemination Center for Children with Disabilities (NICHCY)
Nichols-Solomon, R., 128, 184
No Child Left Behind (NCLB), 44
academic achievement and goals element of, 55
accountability element of, 55, 55 (table)
Elementary and Secondary Education Act (1965) revised by, 44
faith-based organizations, federal funding and, 140
family choice element of, 55, 56 (table)
family participation initiatives element of, 86
Helping Your Child series (U.S. Department of Education) and, 214, 215 (photo)
highly qualified teachers element of, 55, 56 (table)

implementation of, 55–57

initiatives and implications of, 55–56 (table)

parent involvement focus of, 44, 56–57

parent "right to know" provisions of, 86

resources distribution inadequacies criticism of, 55

safety, and drug-free environment elements of, 55

school report card element of, 55

standardized tests bias criticism of, 55

state education accountability element of, 44

Nonpublic special education school, 32, 287

Northwest Education Collaboration, Alaska, 63

Null partnership(s), 17, 287

The Nurture Assumption (Harris), 19

Nutrition. *See* Health and nutrition issues

Nye, B., 96

Objectives, 246, 287

Office of Special Education Programs (OSEP) of U.S. Department of Education, 214

Olmos, Edward James, 141

O'Meara, Sara, 64

One Dad, Two Dads, Brown Dad, Blue Dads (Valentine and Sarecky), 201

Open-door policies, 118–119

Open house events, 87–88

Open schools, 39

Orange County Partnership for Young Children, New York, 140–141

Outdoor education. *See* Partnering with community organizations and resources

P. Buckley Moss Foundation for Children's Education, 223

Pacific Symphony, 232–233

Parent, 23, 287

See also Building family-school partnerships; Families today; Family-school partnerships

Parenting, 116, 287

See also Building family-school partnerships; Families today; Family-school partnerships

Parent-school partnership

U.S. Department of Education's strategies regarding, 56–57

See also Building family-school partnerships; Families today; Family-school partnerships

Parent-teacher conferences, 88, 101–102

See also Families today

Parent Teacher Education Connection, 52, 119

Parent-teacher organizations and associations (PTO/PTA), 39

Parravano, C., 144

Partnering with community organizations and resources

camping activities and, 175

case study: professional development program, Red Rock Canyon State Park, Mojave Desert, California, 178

case study: School in the Park museum field trip program, San Diego California, 173, 176–178

field trips and, 163, 168–171, 173–174

field trips and, tips for families, 175

field trips and, tips for teachers, 175

field trips and, zoo visit, sixth grade, 171–172

Forestry Institute for Teachers collaborative project and, 174

Last Child in the Woods (Louv) and, 71, 174

museums and cultural institutions and, 166–174

national/local parks and outdoor education and, 174–175

"nature-deficit disorder" concept and, 71, 174

prior knowledge and beliefs organizer and, 162

summary regarding, 176

university-school partnerships and, 164–166

Urban Advantage science field trip program, New York City and, 173

U.S. National Park Service and, 180

virtual online field trips and, 173

See also Community-school partnerships; Museums and cultural institutions partnerships; University-school partnerships

Partnership, 5, 23, 287

Partners in Learning Grants Initiative, 224

Paschal, R., 96

Patchen, T., 95

The Patchwork Quilt (Flournoy), 201

Pavlov, Ivan, 47

Peace Diaries online interactive global forum, 200, 205

Pedagogical strategies sections of book, xvi

Pedagogy of the Oppressed (Freire), 37

Peer mentoring or coaching, 288

Peer tutor, peer tutoring, 255–256, 255 (photo), 288

Pellegrini, A., 72

Perez, J. G., 129

Personal Responsibility and Work Opportunity Reconciliation Act (1996), 44

Phillips, N. B., 255

Physical fitness and health
  Healthy School Healthy Families program, Columbia University and, 165
  National Association for Sport and Physical Education (NASPE) and, 71, 78
  physical education and, 71–72
  See also Health and nutrition issues

Piaget, Jean, 35

Place-based education, 148

Planning for partnerships
  action plan creation and, 239–241, 241 (photo)
  assessment *vs.* evaluation and, 252
  benchmarks and, 250
  case study: creating a family art night, 257
  case study: promoting family involvement, third grade, 257–260
  community-school-family collaborative projects, steps in, 265
  Developing Industry/Education Partnerships Web site and, 261
  formative assessment *vs.* summative evaluation and, 252–253, 257
  implementation of, 254–255
  Learning Partnerships Planning Workbook, online workbook and, 261
  "Pajama Nights" literacy partnership example and, 246–247
  parent participation rationale example of, 242
  peer tutoring and, 255–256, 255 (photo)
  prior knowledge and beliefs organizer and, 238 (table)
  Project *Podemos* ("We can do it"), University of Texas at El Paso and, 240
  "Reading Together" Philadelphia community-supported parent tutoring program and, 179
  time limitations and, 248, 249
  tips for teachers from teachers regarding, 254

"us *versus* them" mentality and, 248

volunteering involvement type and, 244

See also Action plan; Implementing and sustaining successful partnerships; Seeking and sustaining successful partnerships

Policy, 31, 288

Pollock, M., 186–187

Post-field trip activities, 168, 171, 173–174, 288

Power
  as barrier to partnerships, 140, 190–191
  empowering participation from multiple partners and, 272–273

Pre-field trip activities, 169–170, 288

Prejudices, 188, 288
  See also Diversity; Racism

Preservice teachers
  case study: clean air zone campaign, elementary and middle schools, 156–157
  teacher education about educational partnerships and, 46

Prislin, R., 191

Private good, 31–32

Private schools, 288

Professional Awards for Excellence in Mathematics and Science Teaching, 226–227

Professional, 288

Professional education partnerships, 23, 288
  curriculum mapping and, 269
  dialog journal writing and, 269
  as educational partnership example, 10
  The Fifth Discipline: The Art and Practice of the Learning Organization (Senge) and, 267
  National Board Certification, collaboration and, 41, 269–270
  National Board Certification experience, third-grade teacher, 12–13
  peer mentoring and coaching, 268–269
  professional learning communities, 267–268
  professional reading groups, 269
  "reculturing" schools concept and, 267–268
  scaffolding concept and, 268
  Teaming for the Learning of All Children (TLC) program, 267–268
  Team Time partnership program, 10

Professional learning communities, 267–268, 288

Project Appleseed, 122, 124–125, 136
Project GLEAN (Gaining Leverage and
    Empowerment through Adequate
    Nutrition), 70
Public good, 31–32
Public Law 99–457, 42
Public school(s), 32, 288

Quinn, Kristine, 269–270
Quiroz, B., 46

Rabi, Isidor I., 174–175
Race, 23, 288
    transracial term and, 23, 290
    See also Racism
Racism, 23, 289
    See also Barriers to partnerships;
        Community-school partnerships:
        respecting diversity; Culturally relevant
        pedagogy; Diversity
Reading, literacy
    Book It! Program of Pizza Hut, as successful
        partnership example, 274–275
    case study: developing writers, elementary
        school, 132–133
    case study: "Kamp Kino" literacy event,
        elementary grades, 134–135
    early literacy and family support and,
        130–131
    The Freedom Writers Diary (Gruwell)
        and, 211
    home literacy model and, 131
    International Reading Association grants
        and awards and, 226
    NBA Cares programs and, 141
    parent reading with children
        recommendation and, 56
    personal characteristics, social interactions,
        and environmental influences and,
        50–51
    phonemic awareness and, 50–51
    Reach to Achieve NBA program and,
        141–142
    "Reading Together" Philadelphia
        community-supported parent tutoring
        program and, 179
    "Royal Readers" program and, 275
    volunteer tutoring program and, 10
Recess importance, 72, 78
Redding, S., 111

Reflective practice shared decision making
    model, 128
Remick, Denise, 101 (photo)
Requests for proposals (RFPs), 219, 289
    See also Seeking and sustaining successful
        partnerships
Rescuing Recess Web site, 78
Rhode Island Higher Education Partnership
    Grants, 224
Robles, S., 191
Rodriguez, J., 191
Rogers, Carl, 120
Rogoff, B., 15
Roosevelt, Eleanor, 36
Ross, D., 176–177
Rothstein-Fisch, C., 46
Roth-Vinson, C., 26–27
Rudisill, M. E., 147

Same-sex parent families, 81, 83–84
Sanders, M. G., 139, 214
Sandler, H. M., 112, 113 (fig.)
Sarecky, Melody, 201
Scaffolding, 268, 289
Schon, D. A., 270
The School and Society (Dewey), 35
School-based management, 43
School-community partnerships, 140, 289
    See also Community-school partnerships;
        Community-school partnerships:
        respecting diversity
School psychologist, collaborative role
    of, 194
Schools, Students, and Tomorrow restructure
    education plan, 41–42
School-to-home notebooks, 120, 289
School-to-work, Job Training Partnership Act
    (1982), 41
School/University Partnership Team program,
    Western Michigan University, 165
Schumm, J. S., 58
Schunk, D. H., 47
Science. *See* Math and science
Science Controversies on-line: Partnerships in
    Education (SCOPE) project, 142
Scully, P. A., 19
Searching for Lots of Volunteers questionnaire,
    K-5 grades, 123
Sears, W., 127
The Secret of Childhood (M. Montessori), 36

Seeking and sustaining successful partnerships
assessing resources and, 213–216
*Building Successful Partnerships: A Guide for
Developing Parent and Family
Involvement Programs* (National Parent
Teacher Association) and, 216,
216 (table)
case study: Class Act program, Pacific
Symphony Orchestra, 232–233
case study: promoting a fit lifestyle for
children, first grade, 234
communicating with families about
resources and, 227–229
creating questionnaires for families and,
217–219
Dino-Mite Summer Camp, sample teacher
to families newsletter and, 227–229
exploring, identifying, thinking, and
contacting steps in, 214–216
factors affecting, 212–213
family partnerships and, 216–219
The Freedom Writers Diary (Gruwell)
and, 211
grants and, 219–227
Helping Your Child series (U.S. Department
of Education) and, 214, 215 (photo)
interagency collaboration and, 229–231,
232 (photo)
"Lunch Club" for at-risk" students and,
217–219
Lunch Mentors senior citizens community
partnership program and, 211
National Dissemination Center for Children
with Disabilities (NICHCY) and, 214
"neighborhood watch" accountability and
safety program, Tennessee and, 211
Office of Special Education Programs
(OSEP) of U.S. DOE and, 214
partnership examples and, 211–212
planning for community partnerships
organizer and, 216 (table)
prior knowledge and beliefs organizer and,
210 (table)
Ron Clark Academy and, 216–217, 235
students with special needs and, 214
summary regarding, 231–232
teacher newsletter to families
and, 227–229
U.S. Department of Education family
resources and, 214

YMCA and Stevenson Elementary School,
Long Beach, California partnership
and, 211
See also Grant, grants; Grant, grants: specific
grants and aids; Implementing and
sustaining successful partnerships;
Interagency collaboration; Planning for
partnerships
Sekino, Y., 111
Selective mutism case study, 76–77
Senechal, M., 131
Senge, Peter, 267
Service Act (1990), 43
Service learning, 147, 149, 289
Sesame Street, 38, 81
Shared decision making, 128, 289
Shared repertoire, 15, 289
Sheldon, S. B., 276
Showers, J., 268–269
Silent Spring (Carson), 37
Simmons, Richard, 71–72
Simply the Best! after-school science and
technology program, middle and high
school girls, 157–158
Single-parent families, 81
Sisters in Science community partnership, 9
Situated learning (legitimate peripheral
participation), 14, 289
Sizer, Theodore
Coalition of Essential Schools and, 42
Horace's Compromise written by, 42
Skinner, B. F., 47
Skyline High School in Dallas, Texas, 39
Social capital, 33, 289
after-school programs and, 73–74
teacher education about educational
partnerships and, 46
Social cognitive learning theories, 47, 289
Social efficiency, 31, 289
Social justice
Pedagogy of the Oppressed (Freire) and, 37
Social mobility, 31, 290
Songs for Teaching Web site, 202
Songs for World Peace Web site, 202
Songs of Tolerance Web site, 202
Special needs students, 121, 282
ableism and, 85, 281
addressing stereotypes and, 188
augmentative and alternative
communication (AAC) devices and, 86

Elementary and Secondary Education
   Act and, 37
enhancing learning for, 22
family communication, home visits and, 121
inclusive classrooms and, 84–86
Individuals with Disabilities Education Act
   (IDEA) and, 40, 57–63
Learning Disabilities Association of America
   and, 37
museum field trip access and, 169
National Dissemination Center for Children
   with Disabilities (NICHCY) and, 214
online partnerships and assistive technology
   and, 143
peer tutoring and, 255–256
Public Law 99–457 and, 42
See also Gifted and talented students;
      Individuals with Disabilities Education
      Act (IDEA)
Sports teams, high-profile partnerships, 141
Sputnik launch, 36
St. Louis, K., 129
Standards. See Teacher standards
Standards for Quality School-Age Child
   Care, 43
Starbucks Foundation Grants, 224
Stelzer, J., 39, 73
Step-parent families, 84
Stereotypes, 23, 290
   hate personal experience and, 196–197
   Human Rights Watch report and, 198–199
   prejudice and, 189
   students with special needs and, 188
   Teaching Tolerance group and, 187, 199, 205
   The Widow's Broom (Allsburg) and, 198,
      198 (table)
Stevenson Elementary School and YMCA,
   Long Beach, California partnership, 211
Stewardship, 147–148, 290
   samples of, 149–150
   Youth Stewardship Program, 159
Structure of the traditional family, 81, 290
Student-led conferences, 90–91, 91 (table), 290
   case study: fifth grade, 103
Students
   as beneficiaries of educational
      partnerships, 8
   case study: learning and motivation, 50–51
   case study: learning styles, fourth grade,
      48–50

self-advocacy of, 48–49
See also Student-led conferences
Student study team (SST), IDEA component,
   58–59
Students with disabilities. See Special needs
   students
Summative evaluation, 252–253, 257,
   259–260, 290
Summer youth employment programs, 41
Survey, 86, 290

Teacher Leader Grant for Teachers of Grades
   3–5, 223
Teachers
   backpack homework assignment examples
      and, 97–98
   back-to-school night event and, 88
   as beneficiaries of educational
      partnerships, 8
   best homework practices communication
      and, 127–128
   case study: home visit, first grade, 103–105
   case study: learning styles, fourth grade,
      48–50
   case study: Pakistani families and teachers,
      202–204
   case study: professional development
      program, Red Rock Canyon State Park,
      Mojave Desert, California, 178
   case study: student learning and motivation,
      first grade, 50–51
   case study: teacher-family partnership for
      success, second grade, 76–77
   child abuse reporting and, 64
   child abuse reporting and, dos and don'ts of,
      66 (table)
   collaboration, role of schools and, 193
   communicating with irate parents and,
      89–90
   community-school partnership, reasons for
      creation of, third-grade, 10
   factors affecting partnerships and, 212–213
   genuineness, respect, and empathy
      conditions of teacher communications
      and, 120–121
   grants, for instructional purposes,
      221–223
   grants, that recognize teachers and/or
      provide professional development and,
      225–227

grants, to support and acknowledge teachers, 221–227

home visits and, 94–95, 95 (table), 103–105, 121, 285

"Lunch Club" for at-risk" students and, 217–219

as members of learning communities and, 12

National Board Certification experience, third-grade teacher, 12–13

National Board for Professional Teaching Standards and, 12–13, 41, 270

open house events and, 87–88

parent-child-teacher contract and, 89, 90 (fig.)

parents viewed as deficit by, 191

parent-teacher conferences and, 88–89, 88 (table), 101–102

racial and cultural differences, third grade, 189

as reflective practitioners, 270–271

sample science newsletter, third grade, 92–93

self-assessments by, 276–277

self-knowledge of, 184

shared decision making and, 128

taking action against barriers to education partnerships and, 194–200

teacher assessments by families and, 276

teacher education about educational partnerships and, 45–46

teacher education partnership courses and, 191

teacher feedback and, 48–49

teachers' colleges and, 35

weekly news brief example, kindergarten, 93

"What Teachers Hate About Parents" (*Time* magazine) and, 6, 265–266

See also Barriers to partnerships; Families today; Implementing and sustaining successful partnerships; Planning for partnerships; Preservice teachers; Professional learning communities; Seeking and sustaining successful partnerships; Teacher standards

Teachers Network: Teacher Grants, 225

Teacher standards

competence in forming partnerships and, xv

National Board for Professional Teaching Standards and, 12–13, 41, 270

Teaching Tolerance group, 187, 199, 205

Teaming for the Learning of All Children (TLC) program, 267–268

Technology

academic improvement and success and, 57

digital divide concept and, 44

Partners in Learning Grants Initiative grant and, 224

See also Internet

Time Warner Cable's National Teacher Awards, 227

Title I: Improving America's School Act (1994), 185

Title IX, women's equality in sports and education, 39

Tolerance education, 196, 290

Tomasito's Mother Comes to School (Mayer), 201

Toward a Theory of Instruction (Bruner), 38

Tower, C., 64

Transracial, 23, 290

Truman, Harry

National School Lunch Act (1946) and, 36, 66

Trumbull, E., 46

Trust element in partnerships, 191, 192

Tuinstra, C., 91

Turner, Ann Warner, 201

21st century families. *See* Families today

Tyler, Ralph, 36

United Nations Children's Fund, 63

University-school partnerships

classroom teachers as student teaching mentors and, 164–165

Healthy School Healthy Families program, Columbia University, 165

Island Explorers program, University of Southern California Sea Grant Office, 164

School/University Partnership Team program, Western Michigan University, 165

steps to forming, 166

Urban teaching

author experiences in, 41

See also Community-school partnerships

Urban teaching, author experiences in, xvii–xviii

U.S. Census Bureau, 23

U.S. Department of Education
  charter schools and, 43
  Helping Your Child series of, 214, 215 (photo)
  *Improving Learning in Schools With Arts
    Partners in the Community* report
    and, 46
  Office of Special Education Programs
    (OSEP) of, 214
  parent involvement strategies of, 56–57
  partnership resources of, 28
U.S. Department of Health and Human
    Services, Administration for Children and
    Families of, 235
U.S. National Park Service, 180

Vadeboncoeur, J. A., 73–74, 94
Valentine, Johnny, 201
Vaughn, S., 58
Veigel, J. M., 17
Volunteering, 121–124, 244, 290
Vygotsky, L. S., 47

Walberg, H. J., 96
Wallis, C., 96
Weinkaut, Casey, 92–93
Weinstein, T., 96

Well-being. *See* Child abuse and neglect;
  Health and nutrition issues; Physical
  fitness and health
Wenger, Etienne, 14, 94
Wenger, Jean Lave, 14
Westheimer, J., 150 (table)
The Widow's Broom (Allsburg), 198, 198 (table)
Williams, D. A., 187
William's Doll (Zolotow), 201
Winfrey, Oprah, 141
Wong, Janet, 201
Working mothers, 82–83, 83 (table)

Xerox Science Consultant Program (XSCP),
  143–144

Yee, Lindsay, 74–76
Ylagan, Rohanna, 242, 244, 245, 246, 248, 249,
  250–251 (table), 252–253, 254
YMCA and Stevenson Elementary School,
  Long Beach, California partnership, 211
Youth Stewardship Program, 159

Zolotow, Charlotte, 201
Zukin, C., 148
Zuniga, C., 190

About the Author

Amy Cox-Petersen (PhD, Curriculum and Instruction, Science Education Specialization, University of Southern California) is a professor in the Department of Elementary and Bilingual Education at California State University, Fullerton. Cox-Petersen received the Robert and Louise Lee Collaborative Teaching Award at Cal State Fullerton for her work with science professors across campus. She has written and received several grants related to service learning and collaborative partnerships with local schools and museums. Cox-Petersen has partnered with various organizations, schools, and interdisciplinary departments at Cal State Fullerton. As science education specialist at the Natural History Museum of Los Angeles County, she helped create partnerships within the educational community, with K–12 students and teachers, and with museum curators. As a public school teacher for 10 years, she collaborated with area businesses, universities, and parents. Cox-Petersen has published widely in leading education journals.

Supporting researchers for more than 40 years

Research methods have always been at the core of SAGE's publishing program. Founder Sara Miller McCune published SAGE's first methods book, *Public Policy Evaluation*, in 1970. Soon after, she launched the *Quantitative Applications in the Social Sciences* series—affectionately known as the "little green books."

Always at the forefront of developing and supporting new approaches in methods, SAGE published early groundbreaking texts and journals in the fields of qualitative methods and evaluation.

Today, more than 40 years and two million little green books later, SAGE continues to push the boundaries with a growing list of more than 1,200 research methods books, journals, and reference works across the social, behavioral, and health sciences. Its imprints—Pine Forge Press, home of innovative textbooks in sociology, and Corwin, publisher of PreK–12 resources for teachers and administrators—broaden SAGE's range of offerings in methods. SAGE further extended its impact in 2008 when it acquired CQ Press and its best-selling and highly respected political science research methods list.

From qualitative, quantitative, and mixed methods to evaluation, SAGE is the essential resource for academics and practitioners looking for the latest methods by leading scholars.

For more information, visit **www.sagepub.com**.